# HARUKI MURAKAMI

## UNDERGROUND

• • •

Haruki Murakami was born in Kyoto in 1949 and now lives near Tokyo. His work has been translated into more than fifty languages, and the most recent of his many international honors is the Jerusalem Prize, whose previous recipients include J. M. Coetzee, Milan Kundera, and V. S. Naipaul.

www.harukimurakami.com

INTERNATIONAL

# UNDERGROUND

· · ·

# HARUKI MURAKAMI

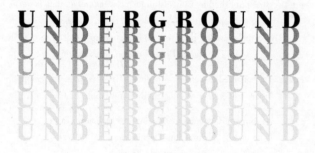

# UNDERGROUND

*Translated from the Japanese by*
ALFRED BIRNBAUM AND
PHILIP GABRIEL

VINTAGE INTERNATIONAL
VINTAGE BOOKS
A DIVISION OF PENGUIN RANDOM HOUSE LLC
NEW YORK

FIRST VINTAGE INTERNATIONAL EDITION, APRIL 2001

*English translation copyright © 2000 by Haruki Murakami*

All rights reserved. Published in the United States by Vintage Books, a
division of Penguin Random House LLC, New York, and in Canada by
Random House of Canada, a division of Penguin Random House
Canada Ltd., Toronto.
Part One first published by Kodansha Ltd. as *Andaguraundo* in 1997;
Part Two first published by Bungeishunjusha as *Yakusoku sareta basho de*
in 1998. Copyright © 1997, 1998 by Haruki Murakami.
This translation first published in hardcover in Great Britain
by The Harvill Press, London, in 2000.

Vintage is a registered trademark and Vintage International and colophon
are trademarks of Penguin Random House LLC.

Library of Congress Cataloging-in-Publication Data
Murakami, Haruki, 1949–
[Andaguraundo, English]
Underground : the Tokyo gas attack and the Japanese psyche /
Haruki Murakami ; translated from the Japanese by Alfred Birnbaum
and Philip Gabriel.
p.   cm.
1. Oumu Shinrikyo (Religious organization)  2. Terrorism—Japan.
I. Birnbaum, Alfred. II. Gabriel, J. Philip. III. Title.
BP605.O88 M8613 2001
364.15'23'0952—dc21          00-069310

Vintage Trade Paperback ISBN 978-0-375-72580-7
eBook ISBN 978-0-307-76275-7

*Book design by Cathryn S. Aison*

www.vintagebooks.com

Printed in the United States of America

22  21

# CONTENTS

• • •

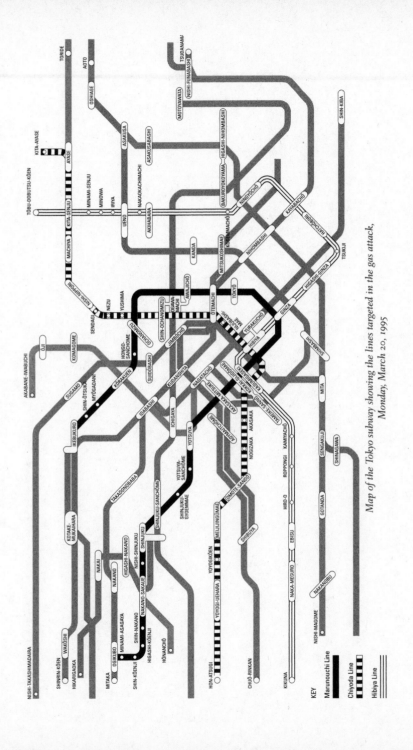

*Map of the Tokyo subway showing the lines targeted in the gas attack, Monday, March 20, 1995*

KEY

Marunouchi Line

Chiyoda Line

Hibiya Line

# PART ONE

# UNDERGROUND

• • •

# Preface*

• • •

Leafing through a magazine one afternoon, I found myself looking at the readers' letters page. I really don't remember why; I just probably had time on my hands. I rarely ever pick up *Ladies' Home Journal* or the like, much less read the letters page.

However, one of the letters caught my attention. It was from a woman whose husband had lost his job because of the Tokyo gas attack. A subway commuter, he had been unfortunate enough to be on his way to work in one of the cars in which the sarin gas was released.† He passed out and was taken to hospital. But even after several days' recuperation, the aftereffects lingered on, and he couldn't get himself back into the working routine. At first, he was tolerated, but as time went on his boss and colleagues began to make snide remarks. Unable to bear the icy atmosphere any longer, feeling almost forced out, he resigned.

The magazine has since disappeared, so I can't quote the letter exactly, but that was more or less what it said. As far as I can recall, there was nothing particularly plaintive about it, nor was it an angry rant. If anything, it was barely audible, a grumble under the breath.

*I would like to make clear that I borrowed useful ideas toward the composition of this book from the works of Studs Terkel and Bob Greene.

† Sarin is a nerve gas invented by German scientists in the 1930s as part of Adolf Hitler's preparations for World War II. During the 1980s it was used to lethal effect by Iraq, both in the war against Iran and against the Kurds. Twenty-six times as deadly as cyanide gas, a drop of sarin the size of a pinhead is sufficient to kill a person. [Tr.]

"How on earth did this happen to us . . . ?" she wonders, still unable to accept what had out of the blue befallen her family.

The letter shocked me. Here were people who still carried serious psychological scars. I felt sorry, truly sorry, although I knew that for the couple involved my sympathy was irrelevant. And yet, what else could I do?

Like most people, I'm sure, I simply turned the page with a sigh.

But sometime later I found myself thinking about the letter. That "How on earth . . . ?" stuck in my head like a big question mark. As if it weren't enough to be the victim of purely random violence, the man had suffered "secondary victimization" (everyday corporate violence of the most pervasive kind). Why could nobody do anything about it? That's when I began to piece together a very different picture.

Whatever the reason, his colleagues had singled out this young salaryman—"Hey, there's the guy from that weird attack"—it couldn't have made any sense to him. He was probably quite unaware of their "them-and-us" attitude. Appearances were deceptive. He would have considered himself a dyed-in-the-wool Japanese like everyone else.

I grew curious to learn more about the woman who wrote in about her husband. Personally, I wanted to probe deeper into how Japanese society could perpetrate such a double violence.

Soon after that I decided to interview the survivors of the attack.

The interviews were conducted over nearly a year between the beginning of January and the end of December 1996. Most sessions took one or two hours, but some lasted for as long as four hours. I recorded everything.

The tapes were then transcribed, which naturally generated a huge volume of text, much of which digressed this way and that, lost the thread completely, then pulled back into focus. Just like everyday speech. This was edited, reordered, or rephrased where necessary to make it more readable, and generally worked up into a manageable book-length manuscript. Occasionally, when the transcript seemed to lack something, I had to go back and listen to the original tape.

Only once did anyone refuse to be recorded. Although I had mentioned over the phone that I'd be recording the interview, when

I pulled a tape recorder out of my bag the interviewee claimed not to have been told. I spent the next two hours jotting down names and figures in longhand, then another few hours writing up the interview the moment I got home. (I was actually rather impressed that my own all-too-human powers of recall could reproduce an entire conversation from a handful of notes—no doubt daily fare to professional interviewers, but new to me.) Still, in the end I wasn't granted permission to include this interview in the book, so all my labors came to nothing.

Two assistants, Setsuo Oshikawa and Hidemi Takahashi, helped me track down the interviewees. We used one of two methods: scanning all previous media sources for listings of "Tokyo gas attack victims"; or asking around by word-of-mouth if anyone knew someone who'd been gassed. Quite frankly, this proved more difficult than I expected. So many passengers were on the Tokyo subway that day, I told myself, getting statements would be easy; after all, there was no formal legal ban on "external testimonies" during the trial, except as concerned the court or police investigations. They had a duty to protect people's privacy, and the same went for the hospitals. All we had to go on were newspaper listings of the hospitalized from the day of the gas attack itself. Names only; no addresses or telephone numbers.

Somehow we came up with a list of 700 names, of whom only 20 percent were identifiable. How does one go about tracing an "Ichiro Nakamura"—the Japanese equivalent of "John Smith"? Even when we did manage to contact the 140 or so positive identifications, they usually refused to be interviewed, saying "I'd rather forget the whole incident" or "I don't want to have anything to do with Aum" or "I don't trust the media." I can't tell you how often people slammed down the phone at the mere mention of publication. As a result, only about 40 percent of the 140 consented to be interviewed.

After the arrest of the principal members of the Aum cult, fewer people feared retributions, but still the rejections persisted—"My symptoms aren't really serious, so it's not worth making a statement." Or, in more than one case, the survivors themselves were willing but their families were not—"Don't get all of us involved." Testimonies from public servants and the employees of financial institutions were likewise unforthcoming.

For practical reasons there are also relatively few female interviewees, because they proved harder to trace by name alone. Unmarried young women in Japan—and this is pure conjecture on my part—don't appreciate strangers asking too many questions. Nevertheless, some did respond "despite family opposition."

Thus, out of thousands of victims, we found only sixty willing respondents, and that took a huge amount of dedication.

In the process of shaping the written interviews, drafts were sent to the respective interviewees for fact-checking. I attached a note asking them to let me know if there was anything they "didn't wish to see in print" and how the contents should be altered or abridged. Almost everyone asked for some changes or cuts, and I complied. Often the forfeited material had illuminated details about the interviewees' lives, which I, as a writer, was sorry to lose. Occasionally I came back with a counterproposal for them to approve. Some interviews went back and forth as many as five times. Every effort was made to avoid any exploitative mass-media scenario that might leave disgruntled interviewees shaking their heads, saying, "It wasn't supposed to be like this" or "You betrayed my trust." Things took time.

After such delicate and laborious orchestrations, we had a total of sixty-two interviews. However, as stated previously, there were two last-minute withdrawals, both very incisive, telling testimonies. Discarding the finished texts so late in the game, I honestly felt as though I were cutting away parts of my own flesh, but "No" means "No," especially when we had made clear from the start our intention to respect each individual voice.

Put another way, every remark in this book is a completely voluntary contribution. And by way of final confirmation—I am very pleased and grateful to say—almost everyone agreed to use his or her real name, which adds incalculably greater impact to the words: *their* words, *their* anger, *their* accusations, *their* sufferings . . . (this is not to slight those few who adopted pseudonyms, for whatever personal reasons).

At the beginning of every interview I would ask the interviewees about their background—where they were born, their upbringing, their family, their job (especially their job)—in order to give each a "face," to bring them into focus. What I did not want was a collection of disembodied voices. Perhaps it's an occupational hazard of the novelist's profession, but I am less interested in the "big picture," as it were, than in the concrete, irreducible humanity of each individual. So perhaps I devoted an inordinate proportion of each two-hour interview to seemingly unrelated details, but I wanted to make sure readers had a firm grasp of the "character" speaking. Much of this extra dimension did not, of course, survive into print.

The Japanese media had bombarded us with so many in-depth profiles of the Aum cult perpetrators—the "attackers"—forming such a slick, seductive narrative that the average citizen—the "victim"—was almost an afterthought. "Bystander A" was glimpsed only in passing. Very rarely was any "lesser" narrative presented in a way that commanded attention. Those few stories that got through were contextualized into formulaic glosses. Our media probably wanted to create a collective image of the "innocent Japanese sufferer," which is much easier to do when you don't have to deal with real faces. Besides, the classic dichotomy of "ugly (visible) villains" versus the "healthy (faceless) populace" makes for a better story.

Which is why I wanted, if at all possible, to get away from any formula; to recognize that each person on the subway that morning had a face, a life, a family, hopes and fears, contradictions and dilemmas—and that all these factors had a place in the drama.

Once I'd discovered the real person, I could then shift my focus to the events themselves. "What was the day like for you?," "What did you see/experience/feel?," and, if it seemed appropriate, "In what way did you suffer (physically or mentally) because of the gas attack?" and "Did these problems persist?"

The degree of suffering inflicted by the Tokyo gas attack varied considerably from person to person. Some escaped with little actual harm; those less fortunate died or are still undergoing therapy for serious health problems. Many experienced no major symptoms at the time, but have since developed posttraumatic stress disorders.

I interviewed people even if they were virtually unaffected by the sarin gas. Naturally those who escaped with relatively slight injury had been able to return to everyday life more quickly, but they, too, had their own stories to tell. Their fears, their lessons. In this sense, I did not practice any sort of editorial "triage."*

*See page 222–223 [Tr.]

One cannot overlook someone simply because they exhibit only "minor symptoms." For everyone involved in the gas attack, March 20 was a heavy, grueling day.

Furthermore, I had a hunch that we needed to see a true picture of all the survivors, whether they were severely traumatized or not, in order to better grasp the whole incident. I leave it to you, the reader, to lend an ear, then judge. No, even before that, I'd like you to imagine.

The date is Monday March 20, 1995. It is a beautiful clear spring morning. There is still a brisk breeze and people are bundled up in coats. Yesterday was Sunday, tomorrow is the Spring Equinox, a national holiday. Sandwiched right in the middle of what should have been a long weekend, you're probably thinking, "I wish I didn't have to go to work today." No such luck. You get up at the normal time, wash, dress, breakfast, and head for the subway station. You board the train, crowded as usual. Nothing out of the ordinary. It promises to be a perfectly run-of-the-mill day. Until a man in disguise pokes at the floor of the car with the sharpened tip of his umbrella, puncturing some plastic bags filled with a strange liquid . . .

# TOKYO METROPOLITAN SUBWAY:

## CHIYODA LINE

• • •

Two men were assigned to drop sarin gas on the Chiyoda Line: Ikuo Hayashi and Tomomitsu Niimi. Hayashi was the principal criminal, Niimi the driver-accomplice.

Why Hayashi—a senior medical doctor with an active "front-line" track record at the Ministry of Science and Technology—was chosen to carry out this mission remains unclear, but Hayashi himself conjectures it was to seal his lips. Implication in the gas attack cut off any possibility of escape. By this point Hayashi already knew too much. He was devoted to the Aum cult leader Shoko Asahara, but apparently Asahara did not trust him. When Asahara first told him to go and release the sarin gas Hayashi admitted: "I could feel my heart pounding in my chest—though where else would my heart be?"

Boarding the front car of the southwestbound 7:48 A.M. Chiyoda Line, running from the northeast Tokyo suburb of Kita-senju to the western suburb of Yoyogi-uehara, Hayashi punctured his plastic bag of sarin at Shin-ochanomizu Station in the central business district, then left the train. Outside the station, Niimi was waiting with a car and the two of them drove back to the Shibuya *ajid*—Aum local headquarters—their mission accomplished. There was no way for Hayashi to refuse. "This is just a yoga of the Mahamudra," he kept telling himself, Mahamudra being a crucial discipline for attaining the stage of the True Enlightened Master.

When asked by Asahara's legal team whether he could have refused if he had wanted to, Hayashi replied: "If that had been possible, the Tokyo gas attack would never have happened."

Born in 1947, Hayashi was the second son of a Tokyo medical practitioner. Groomed from middle and secondary school for Keio University, one of Tokyo's two top private universities, upon graduating from medical school he took employment as a heart and artery specialist at Keio Hospital, after which he went on to become head of the Circulatory Medicine department at the National Sanatorium Hospital at Tokaimura, Ibaragi, north of Tokyo. He is a member of what the Japanese call the "superelite." Clean-cut, he exudes the self-confidence of a professional. Medicine obviously came naturally to him. His hair is starting to thin on top, but like most of the Aum leadership, he has good posture, his eyes focused firmly ahead, although his speech is monotonous and somehow forced. From his testimony in court, I gained the distinct impression that he was blocking some flow of emotion inside himself.

Somewhere along the line Hayashi seems to have had profound doubts about his career as a doctor and, while searching for answers beyond orthodox science, he became seduced by the charismatic teachings of Shoko Asahara and suddenly converted to Aum. In 1990 he resigned from his job and left with his family for a religious life. His two children were promised a special education within the cult. His colleagues at the hospital were loath to lose a man of Hayashi's caliber and tried to stop him, but his mind was made up. It was as if the medical profession no longer held anything for him. Once initiated into the cult, he soon found himself among Asahara's favorites and was appointed Minister of Healing.

Once he had been called upon to carry out the sarin plan, Hayashi was brought to Aum's general headquarters, Satyam No. 7, in Kamikuishiki Village near Mt. Fuji, at 3 A.M. on March 20, where, together with the four other principal players, he rehearsed the attack. Using umbrellas sharpened with a file, they pierced plastic bags filled with water rather than sarin. The rehearsal was supervised by Hideo Murai of the Aum leadership. While comments from the other four members indicate that they enjoyed this practice session, Hayashi observed it all with cool reserve. Nor did he actually pierce his bag. To the 48-year-old doctor, the whole exercise must have seemed like a game.

"I did not need to practice," says Hayashi. "I could see what to do, though my heart wasn't in it."

After the session, all five were returned by car to the Shibuya *ajid*, whereupon our physician Hayashi handed out hypodermic needles filled with atropine sulphate to the team, instructing them to inject it at the first sign of sarin poisoning.

On the way to the station, Hayashi purchased gloves, a knife, tape, and sandals at a convenience store. Niimi, the driver, bought some newspapers in which to wrap the bags of sarin. They were sectarian newspapers—the Japan Communist Party's *Akahata* (*Red Flag*) and the Soka Gakkai's *Seikyo Shimbun* (*Sacred Teaching News*)—"more interesting because they're not papers you can buy just anywhere." That was Niimi's little in-joke. Of the two papers, Hayashi chose *Akahata*: a rival sect's publication would have been too obvious and therefore counterproductive.

Before getting on the subway, Hayashi donned a gauze surgical mask, of the sort commonly worn by many commuters in winter to prevent cold germs from spreading. The train number was A725K. Glancing at a woman and child in the car, Hayashi wavered slightly. "If I unleash the sarin here and now," he thought, "the woman opposite me is dead for sure. Unless she gets off somewhere." But he'd come this far; there was no going back. This was a Holy War. The weak were losers.

As the subway approached Shin-ochanomizu Station, he dropped the bags of sarin by his right foot, steeled his nerves, and poked one of them with the end of his umbrella. It was resilient and gave a "springy gush." He poked it again a few times—exactly how many times he doesn't remember. In the end, only one of the two bags was found to have been punctured; the other was untouched.

Still, the sarin liquid in one of the bags completely evaporated and did a lot of damage. At Kasumigaseki two station attendants died in the line of duty trying to dispose of the bag. Train A725K was stopped at the next station, Kokkai-gijidomae—the stop for the Japanese National Assembly—all passengers were evacuated, and the cars were cleaned.

Two people were killed and 231 suffered serious injuries from Hayashi's sarin drop alone.*

---

*Ikuo Hayashi was sentenced to life imprisonment. At the time of going to press he was serving time in prison and Tomomitsu Niimi was still on trial. [Tr.]

## "Nobody was dealing with things calmly"

### Kiyoka Izumi (26)*

*Ms. Kiyoka Izumi was born in Kanazawa, on the north central coast of the Sea of Japan. She works in the PR department of a foreign airline company. After graduation she went to work for Japan Railways (JR), but after three years she decided to pursue her childhood dream of working in aviation. Even though job transfers to airline companies are extremely difficult in Japan—only one in a thousand "midcareer" applicants is accepted—she beat the odds, only to encounter the Tokyo gas attack not long after starting work.*

*Her job at JR was boring to say the least. Her colleagues objected to her leaving, but she was determined. It was good training, but the union-dominated atmosphere was too confining and specialized. She wanted to use English at work. Still, the emergency training she received at JR proved invaluable in unexpected circumstances . . .*

● ● ●

At the time I was living in Waseda [*northwest central Tokyo*]. My company was in Kamiyacho [*southeast central Tokyo*], so I always commuted by subway, taking the Tozai Line, changing at Otemachi for the Chiyoda Line to Kasumigaseki, then one stop on the Hibiya Line to Kamiyacho. Work started at 8:30, so I'd leave home around 7:45 or 7:50. That got me there a little before 8:30, but I was always one of the earliest to start. Everybody else showed up just in time. With Japanese companies, I'd always learned you were expected to arrive thirty minutes to an hour before starting, but with a foreign company the thinking is that everyone starts work at his or her own pace. You don't get any brownie points for arriving early.

*Numbers in parentheses refer to the age of the interviewee at the time of the Tokyo gas attack. [Tr.]

I'd get up around 6:15 or 6:20. I rarely eat breakfast, just a quick cup of coffee. The Tozai Line gets pretty crowded during rush hour, but if you avoid the peak, it's not too bad. I never had any problem with perverts copping a feel or anything.

I never get ill, but on the morning of March 20 I wasn't feeling well. I caught the train to work anyway; got off the Tozai Line at Otemachi and transferred to the Chiyoda Line, thinking, "Gosh, I'm really out of it today." I inhaled, then suddenly my breathing froze— just like that.

I was traveling in the first car on the Chiyoda Line. It wasn't too crowded. All the seats were pretty much taken, but there were only a few passengers standing here and there. You could still see all the way to the other end.

I stood at the front next to the driver's compartment, holding the handrail by the door. Then, like I said, when I took a deep breath, I got this sudden pain. No, it wasn't so much painful. Really it was like I'd been shot or something, all of a sudden my breathing completely stopped. Like, if I inhaled any more, all my guts would come spilling right out of my mouth! Everything became a vacuum, probably because I wasn't feeling well, I thought; but, I mean, I'd never felt so bad. It was that intense.

And then, when I think back on it now it seems kind of odd, but I thought, "Just maybe my grandad's died." He lived up north in Ishikawa Prefecture and was 94 years old at the time. I'd heard he'd been taken ill, so maybe this was a kind of sign. That was my first thought. Maybe he'd died or something.

After a while I was able to breathe again somehow. But by the time we passed Hibiya Station, one stop before Kasumigaseki, I got this really bad cough. By then everyone in the car was coughing away like mad. I knew there was something strange going on in the car. The other people were so excited and everything . . .

Anyway, when the train stopped at Kasumigaseki I got off without giving it much thought. A few other passengers called out to the station attendant, "Something's wrong! Come quick!" and brought him into the car. I didn't see what happened after that, but this attendant was the one who carried out the sarin packet and later died.

I left the Chiyoda Line platform and headed for the Hibiya Line as usual. When I reached the platform at the bottom of the stairs I heard the emergency alarm go off: *Bee-eee-eep!* I knew immediately from my time working for Japan Railways there'd been an accident. That's when an announcement came over the station PA. And just as I was thinking "I'd better get out of here" a Hibiya Line train arrived from the opposite direction.

I could see from the station attendants' confusion that this was no ordinary situation. And the Hibiya Line train was completely empty, not a passenger on board. I only found out later, but in fact that train had also been planted with sarin gas. They'd had a crisis at Kamiya-cho Station or somewhere, and dragged off all the passengers.

After the alarm there was an announcement: "Everyone evacuate the station." People were making for the exits, but I was beginning to feel really sick. So instead of going straight out, I thought I'd better go to the toilet first. I looked all over the station to find the stationmaster's office, and right next to that the toilets.

As I was passing the office, I saw maybe three station attendants just lying there. There must have been a fatal accident. Still, I carried on to the toilet and when I came out I went to an exit that emerged in front of the Ministry of Trade and Industry building. This all took about ten minutes, I suppose. Meanwhile they'd brought up the station attendants I'd seen in the office.

Once out of the exit I took a good look around, but what I saw was—how shall I put it?—"hell" describes it perfectly. Three men were laid on the ground, spoons stuck in their mouths as a precaution against them choking on their tongues. About six other station staff were there too, but they all just sat on the flower beds holding their heads and crying. The moment I came out of the exit, a girl was crying her eyes out. I was at a loss for words. I didn't have a clue what was happening.

I grabbed hold of one of the station attendants and told him: "I used to work for Japan Railways. I'm used to dealing with emergencies. Is there any way I can help?" But he just stared off into space. All he could say was: "Yes, help." I turned to the others sitting there. "This is no time to be crying," I said. "We're not crying," they answered, though it looked like they were crying. I thought they were grieving for their dead colleagues.

"Has anyone called an ambulance?" I asked, and they said they had. But when I heard the ambulance siren, it didn't seem to be coming our way. For some reason, we were the last to get help, so those in the most serious condition were last to be taken to the hospital. As a result, two people died.

TV Tokyo cameramen were filming the whole scene. They'd parked their van nearby. I ran after the film crew, saying: "Now's not the time for that! If you've got transport, take these people to the hospital!" The driver conferred with his crew and said, "All right, fine."

When I worked for JR, I was taught always to carry a red scarf. In an emergency you could wave it to stop trains. So there I was, thinking "scarf." Someone lent me a handkerchief, but it was so small I ended up giving it to the TV-crew driver and instructing him: "Get these people to the nearest hospital. It's an emergency, so honk your horn and drive through red lights if you have to! Just keep going!"

I forget the color of the handkerchief; it was just some print. I don't remember whether I told him to wave it or tie it to his side mirror. I was pretty excited at the time, so my memory's not that clear. Later when I met Mr. Toyoda, he reminded me, "I never returned your handkerchief," and gave me a new one. He'd been sick in the backseat and used mine.

We managed to lift Mr. Takahashi, the station attendant who died, into the back, along with another assistant. And still there was room, so one more station assistant got into the van. I think Mr. Takahashi was still alive at that point. But at first glance I thought, "He's a goner." Not that I'd ever witnessed death, I just knew. I could picture it; he was going to die this way. But still I had to try and help, somehow.

The driver pleaded with me, "Miss, you come along with us," but I said, "No, I'm not going." There were still lots of others being brought above ground and someone had to look after them, so I stayed behind. I don't know to which hospital the van went. I don't know what happened to them afterward either.

Then there was that girl nearby, crying and trembling all over. I stayed with her and tried to comfort her, saying, "There there, it's all right," until finally the ambulance came. All that time I looked after lots of different people, all of them white-faced, completely washed out. One man, fairly old by the look of him, was foaming at the mouth. I had no idea humans could foam like that. I unbuttoned his shirt, loosened his belt, and took his pulse. It was really fast. I tried to rouse him, but it was no use. He was completely unconscious.

This "old man" was in fact a station attendant. Only he'd removed his uniform jacket. He was pale and his hair was thin, so I mistook him for an elderly passenger. I later found out he was Mr. Toyoda, a colleague of the two staff members [*Mr. Takahashi and Mr. Hishinuma*] who died. He was the only one of the three injured station attendants who survived, and he was one of the longest in the hospital.

The ambulance arrived. "Is he conscious?" they asked. "No!" I yelled. "But he has a pulse!" The ambulance team put an oxygen mask over his mouth. Then they said, "There's one more [*i.e., a respirator unit*]. If there's anyone else in pain, we'll take them." So I inhaled a little oxygen, and the crying girl took a good long dose. By the time we had finished there was a media stampede. They surrounded the girl and the poor thing was seen on television all day.

While I was looking after everyone, I completely forgot my own pain. It was only at the mention of oxygen that it occurred to me, "Come to think of it, I'm breathing funny myself." Yet at that very moment, I didn't make a connection between the gas attack and my condition. I was all right, so I had to look after the people who had really suffered. Just what the incident was I didn't know, but whatever it was it was big. And like I said before, I'd been feeling under the weather since the morning, so I was convinced my feeling a little off was just me.

In the midst of all this, a colleague from work passed by. He helped me rescue the girl from the clutches of the media. Then he suggested we walk to the office together, so I thought, "Okay, we'll walk to work." It takes about thirty minutes on foot from Kasumigaseki to my office. As I was walking, I found it a bit hard to breathe, but not so bad that I had to sit down and rest. I was able to walk.

When we got to the office, my boss had seen me on TV, and everyone was asking, "Ms. Izumi, are you really okay?" It was already ten o'clock by the time I got to the office. My boss said, "How about resting a bit? You shouldn't tax yourself," but I still didn't really understand what had happened, so I just got on with my work. After a while a message came from Personnel: "Seems it was poison gas, so if you start to feel ill you're to report to the hospital immediately." And just about then my condition was getting worse. So they put me in an ambulance at the Kamiyacho intersection and took me to Azabu Hospital, a small place not far away. Twenty people had gone there already.

I had coldlike symptoms for a week after that. I had this asthmatic cough, and three days later a high fever, with a temperature of over 40°C [104°F]. I was sure the thermometer was broken. The mercury shot up all the way to the top of the scale. So actually my temperature might have been even higher. All I know is I was completely immobilized.

Even after the fever resided, the wheezing persisted for about a month; clearly the effects of sarin in my bronchial tubes. It was incredibly painful. I mean, I'd start coughing and never stop. It was so painful I couldn't breathe. I was coughing all the time. I'd be talking like this and suddenly it would start. In PR you have to meet people, so working under those conditions was really hard.

And I kept having these dreams. The image of those station attendants with spoons in their mouths stuck in my head. In my dreams, there were hundreds of bodies lying on the ground, row upon row far into the distance. I don't know how many times I woke in the middle of the night. Frightening.

As I said, there were people foaming at the mouth where we were, in front of the Ministry of Trade and Industry. That half of the roadway was absolute hell. But on the other side, people were walking to work as usual. I'd be tending to someone and look up to see passersby glance my way with a "what-on-earth's-happened-here?" expression, but not one came over. It was as if we were a world apart. Nobody stopped. They all thought: "Nothing to do with me."

Some guards were standing right before our eyes at the ministry gate. Here we had three people laid out on the ground, waiting desperately for an ambulance that didn't arrive for a long, long time. Yet nobody at the ministry called for help. They didn't even call us a taxi.

It was 8:10 when the sarin was planted, so that makes over an hour and a half before the ambulance arrived. All that time those people just left us there. Occasionally the television would show Mr. Takahashi lying dead with a spoon in his mouth, but that was it. I couldn't bear to watch it.

MURAKAMI: *Just supposing, what if you'd been one of those people across the road at the time, on your way to work. Do you think you'd have crossed over to help?*

Yes, I think so. I wouldn't have just ignored them, no matter how out of character it might have been. I'd have crossed over. The fact is, the whole situation made me want to cry, but I knew if I lost control that would have been the end of it. Nobody was dealing with things calmly. No one even caring for the sick. Everyone just abandoned us there the whole time and walked on by. It was absolutely terrible.

As to the criminals who actually planted the sarin, I honestly can't say I feel much anger or hatred. I suppose I just don't make the connection, and I can't seem to find those emotions in me. What I really think about are those families that have to bear the tragedy, their suffering is so much bigger to me than any anger or hatred I might feel toward the criminals. The fact that someone from Aum brought sarin onto the subway . . . that's not the point. I don't think about Aum's role in the gas attack.

I never watch television reports or anything on Aum. I don't want to. I have no intention of giving interviews. If it will help those who suffered or the families of the deceased, then yes, I'll come forward and talk, but only if they want to know what happened. I'd rather not be danced around by the media.

Of course society should severely punish this crime. Especially when you consider the families of the deceased, there should be no getting off easy. What are those families supposed to do . . . ? But even if those criminals get the death penalty, does that solve anything in the end? Perhaps I'm oversensitive when it comes to human mortality, but it seems to me that however heavy the sentence, there is nothing you can say to those families.

## "I've been here since I first joined"

## Masaru Yuasa (24)

*Mr. Yuasa is much younger than Mr. Toyoda (interviewed on page 28), or the late Mr. Takahashi. He is more their sons' age. He looks about 16 with his youthful, tousled hair. There is still something naive and boyish about him, which makes him look younger than he is.*

*He was born in Ichikawa, across Tokyo Bay in Chiba, where he spent his childhood. He became interested in trains and went to Iwakura High School in Ueno, Tokyo, which is the place to be for anyone who wants to work on the railroad. He initially wanted to be a driver, so he opted for studies in engine mechanics. He was employed by the Subway Authority in 1988 and has worked at Kasumigaseki Station ever since. Forthright and plain-talking, he approaches his daily duties with a clear sense of purpose. This made the gas attack all the more shocking for him.*

*Mr. Yuasa's boss ordered him to help carry Mr. Takahashi on a stretcher from where he'd fallen on the Chiyoda Line platform to ground level and to wait there at the appointed area for an ambulance—which didn't arrive. He saw Mr. Takahashi's condition worsen before his eyes, but was powerless to do anything. As a result Mr. Takahashi failed to receive treatment in time and died. Mr. Yuasa's frustration, confusion, and anger are unimaginable. It is probably for this reason that his memory of the scene is foggy in places. As he himself admits, some details have been completely blanked out.*

*This explains how parallel accounts of the same scene may diverge slightly, but this, after all, is how Mr. Yuasa experienced it.*

•　•　•

In high school we studied Mechanics or Transport. The ones who took Transport were mostly statistics nerds, kept train schedules in their desk drawers (*laughs*). Me, I liked trains, but not like that. They weren't an obsession.

Japan Railways [JR] was the big thing to aim for in terms of jobs. So many guys wanted to be Shinkansen [bullet-train] drivers. JR turned me down when I graduated, but Seibu and Odakyu and Tokyu and other private lines were generally popular, although the catch was that you had to live in areas served by those lines to get the job. Yeah, pretty tough. I'd always wanted to work on the subway and the Subway Authority was pretty popular. The pay's no worse than anywhere else.

Station work involves all sorts of jobs. Not just ticket booth and platform duty, but lost property and sorting out arguments between passengers. It was tough joining at 18 and having to do all that. That's why the first round-the-clock duty was the longest. I'd pull down the shutters after the last train and heave a sigh of relief: "Ah, that's it for the day!" Not anymore, but that's how it was at first.

The drunks were the worst thing. They either get all chummy when they're drunk, or fight, or throw up. Kasumigaseki's not an entertainment district, so we don't get that many of them, but sometimes we do.

No, I never sat for the driver qualification. I had the chance to several times, but I thought it over and didn't. At the end of my first year there was a conductor's test, but after one year I'd only just got the hang of station work so I let it pass. Sure there were drunks, like I said, stuff I didn't care for especially, but still I thought I'd better learn the ropes a bit more. I suppose my initial impulse to be a driver just changed over time while I was working around the station.

Kasumigaseki Station has three lines coming in: the Marunouchi, the Hibiya, and the Chiyoda. Each has its own staff. I was with the Marunouchi Line at the time. The Hibiya Line office is the biggest, but the Marunouchi and Chiyoda Line both have their own offices, their own staffrooms.

The Sunday before the gas attack I was on round-the-clock duty in the Chiyoda Line office. They were short-staffed and I was filling in. A certain number of personnel has to be there for overnight duty. The staff on the other lines help each other out, like one big family.

Around 12:30 we lower the shutters, lock up the ticket booths, shut off the ticket machines, then wash up and turn in just after 1:00. The early shift finish work around 11:30 and are asleep by around 12:00. The following morning the early shift rises at 4:30 and the late shift at 5:30. The first train leaves around 5:00.

Wake up and first thing it's clean up, raise the shutters, prepare the ticket booth. Then we take turns eating breakfast. We cook our own rice, make our own miso soup. Meal duty's posted up there with all the other duties. We all share.

I was on late shift that night, so I woke up at 5:30, changed into my uniform, and reported to the ticket booth at 5:55. I worked until 7:00, then went to have breakfast from 7:00 to 7:30. Then I went to another ticket booth and worked there until 8:15 or so, then called it a day.

I was walking back to the office after the handover to my replacement when the Chief Officer, Matsumoto, came out with a mop. "What's that for?" I asked, and he said he had to clean inside a car. I'd just gone off duty and had my hands free, so it was, "Fine, I'll go with you." We headed up the escalator to the platform.

There we found Toyoda, Takahashi, and Hishinuma with a bundle of wet newspapers on the platform. They're stuffing it all by hand into plastic bags, but there's liquid coming from them and spilling onto the platform. Matsumoto mopped up the liquid. I didn't have a mop, and most of the newspaper had been bagged, so I wasn't much help. I just stood to one side, watching.

"What's this all about?" I wondered. There was a very strong smell. Then Takahashi walked over to a trash can at the end of the platform, probably to fetch some more newspaper to wipe up where it was still wet. Suddenly he sinks down in front of the bin and keels over.

Everyone ran toward Takahashi, shouting, "What's wrong?" I thought maybe he was ill, but nothing too serious. "Can you walk?" they asked, but it's obvious he can't, so I called the office over the platform intercom: "Send up the stretcher!"

Takahashi's face looked awful. He couldn't talk. We laid him on his side, loosened his tie . . . he looked in really bad shape.

We carried him down to the office on the stretcher, then phoned for an ambulance. That's when I asked Toyoda, "Which exit is the ambulance supposed to come to?" There's protocol for situations like this, saying where ambulances are supposed to pull up and so on. But Toyoda's tongue-tied. Kind of odd, but all I could think at the time was he was probably too confused to speak.

Anyway, I dashed up Exit A11. Yes, before carrying Takahashi up, I got up there myself and waited to signal the ambulance when it came. So I'm out of the exit and waiting by the Ministry of Trade and Industry.

On the way to Exit A11 I ran into one of the Hibiya Line staff, who tells me there's been an explosion at Tsukiji Station. Nothing more was known. A suspicious object had been found in our station that month on the fifteenth, so I'm thinking as I wait for the ambulance: "This is turning into one weird day."

But I wait and I wait and no ambulance. Soon other office staff come up and it's, "No ambulance yet? What'll we do?" We decide we ought to bring Takahashi up above ground. I've been outside all this time, but these two or three people who came up from the office tell me they've all started feeling sick down there. So they don't want to go back. It turns out they kept whatever was in those plastic packets in the office, and that's what's to blame.

Well, Takahashi still has to be carried up, so we all head downstairs again. Back at the office, there was a woman passenger who felt ill, sitting on the sofa by the entrance. Takahashi's behind her on a stretcher on the floor. By then he wasn't moving, practically frozen stiff. A lot worse than he looked before, barely conscious. The other staff were trying to talk to him, but there was no response. The four of us carried him above ground on the stretcher.

But we wait and wait and still there's no sign of an ambulance. We were getting pretty frustrated. Why wasn't anything coming? Now I know that all the ambulances had rushed over to Tsukiji. You could hear sirens in the distance, but none coming this way. I couldn't help feeling anxious, thinking they'd got the wrong location. I almost felt like shouting out: "Hey, over here!" Actually, I did try running in that direction, but I felt dizzy myself . . . I put it down to not having had enough sleep.

When we carried Takahashi up, there were already newspeople at the exit. This woman with a camera was snapping away at Takahashi lying there. I shouted to her: "No photos!" Her male assistant came in between us, but I told him, too: "No more photos!"—but taking pictures was her job.

Then a TV Tokyo van came along. They were asking so many questions, like "What's the situation here?"—but I was in no mood to be interviewed. Not when the ambulance was taking forever to come.

Suddenly I realized the TV crew had a big van, so I struck a deal with them: "You've got wheels, you have to take Takahashi." I was probably kind of angry, the way I spoke. I don't remember in detail, but I was pretty worked up, after all. Nobody knew what was going on, so it took some negotiating. No one said straightaway, "Oh, I get it," and sprang into action. The discussions took a while. But once things were settled, they lowered the backseat and laid Takahashi on it along with another station attendant [*Mr. Ohori*] who was also feeling ill. He'd been with Takahashi all the time, but started vomiting when he came above ground. Another member of staff [*Mr. Sawaguchi*] also went with them.

"You know which hospital?" the driver asked, but nobody had a clue. So I got in the front seat next to the driver and went along too, directing them to Hibiya Hospital, which is where we always sent people whenever they got ill at the station. A woman said, "Wave a red cloth or something from the window so they know it's an emergency." We didn't have a red cloth, so she gave us her handkerchief. Not red, just an ordinary pattern. I sat in the front seat waving that handkerchief out the window all the way to the hospital.

This was around 9:00, so traffic was pretty heavy. I was already so out of it, after all that time waiting for an ambulance that never came. I can't even remember the driver's face or the woman who gave me the handkerchief. No recollection at all. I was just gone. There was no time to think about what was going on. I do remember Ohori throwing up in the backseat. That I do remember.

The hospital wasn't open when we arrived. We took Takahashi out of the van on the stretcher and I went to the reception desk. "We've got an emergency here," I said, then went back outside and waited by Takahashi. He wasn't moving at all. Ohori had crouched down, immobile. Still no one came out of the hospital. They must have decided it wasn't all that serious. After all, I must have looked confused and hadn't given them any details. We just waited and waited and nobody came out.

So I went to Reception again, and raised my voice: "Please! Somebody come! This is serious!" Then a few people came out, saw Takahashi and Ohori's condition, and rushed them inside. How long did it take? Two or three minutes.

Sawaguchi stayed at Reception while I went back to the station exit with the TV van driver. By then I'd calmed down a lot, or at least I was telling myself I had to calm down. I apologized to the driver for Ohori throwing up all over the seat, but he didn't seem to mind. It was only then that I could manage even a simple conversation like that.

By then, I think they'd carried up Toyoda and Hishinuma, neither of them moving. They were trying to resuscitate them with oxygen masks and massaging their chests. Around them other staff and passengers were sitting down outside the Ministry of Trade and Industry. Nobody knew what on earth was going on.

Finally an ambulance arrived. My memory fails me here, but I seem to recall Toyoda and Hishinuma were taken away separately. Only one patient to an ambulance, so one of them had to be taken by car. They were the only ones to leave at that time. None of the others were as critical. By then, so many people had gathered around Exit A11: news crews, police, firemen—I remember the size of the crowd. The media were in full swing, mikes out, interviewing passengers and subway staff. They probably couldn't get into the station anymore.

Once the scene was under control, I walked to the hospital. When I got to the lobby, the TV was on. It was the NHK [*Japan Broadcasting Corporation*] news. They were showing live reports from the gas attack. That's when I learned Takahashi had died, from a running subtitle on-screen. "Ah," I thought, "he didn't make it. We were too late . . ." I can't tell you how sad I was.

My own condition? Well, my pupils were contracted and everything looked dark. I was coughing a little, too. Nothing too serious. They put me on a drip, just in case. I got off lightly. Probably because I'd gone outside early on. Ohori was in the hospital for ages.

After the drip, I walked back to the station with a few of the staff. The Chiyoda Line trains weren't stopping at Kasumigaseki Station, so we went to the Marunouchi Line office. What with this and that, it was evening before I finally got home. It had been a long, long day. I took off the next day and returned for round-the-clock duty on the twenty-second.

To be honest, my memories of the gas attack jump around. This or that detail I remember with burning clarity, but the rest is very sketchy. I was pretty wound up. Takahashi's collapse and taking him to the hospital—those things I remember fairly well.

I wasn't especially close to Takahashi. He was the assistant stationmaster and I'm only one of the younger staff—our positions were totally different. His son works for the subway, at another station, about the same age as me. I suppose that made us like father and son, though I never felt much age difference talking to Takahashi. He was never one to pull rank. He was the quiet type, everybody liked him. He was always polite to passengers, too.

The gas attack didn't upset me to the point where I thought: "I can't take it, I have to change jobs." Not at all. I've been here since I first joined. Can't compare it with others, but I really like it here.

## "At that point Takahashi was still alive"

### Minoru Miyata (54)

*Mr. Miyata has been a chauffeur for TV Tokyo for six years. He waits long hours on standby at the TV station until a news item breaks, then rushes to the scene in a van full of outside-broadcast equipment. Sometimes he has to put his foot down, and he'll drive a thousand miles, all the way from Tokyo to Hokkaido, if he has to. A tough job.*

*A professional driver, he's been chauffeuring since the mid-1960s. He's had a thing for cars ever since he was a boy. His face lights up when he talks about them. He's almost never had an accident or a ticket; although when he was ferrying victims from the Tokyo gas attack to the hospital, he admits he couldn't avoid breaking the rules a little.*

*He speaks quickly, and never mulls over his words. He is a model of split-second timing. His decisiveness helped save the day at the scene of the attack.*

• • •

I had a Toyota Hi-Ace van with TV TOKYO in big letters on the side. The staff members who come with me change all the time, but the van's always the same, loaded and ready to go when a news item breaks. I generally work from 9:30 to 6:00, but sometimes do overtime and get called out in the middle of the night.

You need real skill. It's big trouble if the other stations beat you to the scene. A car will only go so fast, so it's a matter of choosing the clearest route to get there a little faster, and that takes thought. In my spare time I'm always studying maps, memorizing routes. Ask me to go almost anywhere in the entire Tokyo region and I'll know the way.

Some incident comes up every day. There's never a day when nothing happens. I never get a break (*laughs*).

On March 20 I was at the station from 8:30. There are three of us in the van: me; Ikida, the cameraman; and Maki, the video engineer. We were scheduled to shoot some stock footage of Ueda Hollow over in the Kabutocho financial district, but there was no hurry. I'd planned to drive to the Kamiyacho crossing, then out to Showa Avenue, but when we reached the intersection everything was in complete confusion. "What's going on here?" I thought. So I slowed down, keeping my eyes peeled. "They'll call us in on this one before we get over there," said Ikida.

Then just before the Shimbashi Tunnel, right on cue, the call came from the station telling us to make tracks for the Kasumigaseki crossing, the big open area near all the ministries: the Ministry of Foreign Affairs, Ministry of Finance, Ministry of Trade and Industry, Ministry of Agriculture and Fisheries . . . When we got there I could see three or four subway workers in green uniforms collapsed on the ground by the exit. Two or three were sprawled out, and some were crouching. This young station attendant's shouting at the top of his voice: "Quick! Somebody call an ambulance!"

We were the first media on the scene. They were carrying people out on stretchers. Next to them was a policeman barking into his radio: "Get some ambulances here *now!*" But by that time St. Luke's and other hospitals were already in a panic and no ambulances were coming that way. They were even using unmarked police cars to carry the victims, it was so bad. Everybody screaming their heads off. Ikeda was shooting the whole scene.

That's when somebody—maybe one of the injured—spoke up: "How about instead of filming us, you help take one or two people to the hospital?" But we're loaded with equipment and stuff. We can't just run off. So me and the crew talk it over. "What the hell are we going to do?" "It'll look bad if we don't take them." In the end, I said, "Okay, I'll go." I ran to the shouting station attendant and asked where it is I'm supposed to be going. "Take them to Hibiya Hospital," he says. Which is strange, I thought at the time, because Toranomon Hospital's the closest. But it turns out that Hibiya's the one affiliated with the Subway Authority.

We unloaded all the equipment, just in case something came up, but the van hasn't got a flashing red light, so the young station attendant sits in the front seat next to me, his hand out the window waving a red handkerchief, and we're off and heading for Hibiya Hospital. The red handkerchief was a loan from this young nurse at the scene. She told us to wave it to show we were an emergency vehicle. In the car we had Assistant Stationmaster Takahashi, who died, and another guy—don't know his name—also a station attendant, 30-something, wasn't as bad as Takahashi. He even managed to get in the van by himself. We laid them both flat out across the backseat. The young station attendant kept asking, "Takahashi, you all right?" That's how I knew his name. But Takahashi was hardly conscious, he could barely groan in response.

Hibiya Hospital was near Shimbashi Station. A pretty big place. It only took about three minutes to get there . . . All that time the young station attendant had his hand out the window waving the handkerchief. We ran all the red lights; went the wrong way down one-way streets. The police saw us, but it was just: "Go ahead, quick!" We were desperate; I knew it was life-or-death.

But you know, the hospital wouldn't let us in. This nurse comes running out, and even when we told her, "They've been gassed in Kasumigaseki Station," she just said something about there being no doctor available. Abandoned us there on the pavement. How she could do that, I'll never know.

The young station attendant went inside, practically in tears, to plead with the receptionist—"He's going to die, you have to do something." I went in with him. At that point Takahashi was still alive. His eyes were blinking. We lowered him out of the van and he lay on the pavement, the other guy crouching by the roadside. We were all just blown away, so angry the blood just rushed to our heads. There we were for ages—can't really say how long—kicking our heels.

Then a little later a doctor comes out and they carry the two of them in on stretchers. The point is, they didn't have the least grasp of the situation. There'd been no word to the hospital about any injured people heading their way, so they were in the dark. Couldn't cope. It was 9:30 by then, over an hour since the gas attack. And yet the hospital didn't know what had happened. We must have been the first there with victims from the attack. They didn't have a clue.

It was pitiful to see the young station attendant watching his colleague, his superior, not knowing if he was going to pull through or not. In desperation he kept repeating, "Examine him, hurry, hurry!" And me, I was so worried, I stood around in front of the hospital for an hour or more, but I heard nothing, so I returned to the scene. I never went back to Hibiya Hospital and never saw that young station attendant again. That night I learned Takahashi had died, which made me so sad. To think that someone you'd transported didn't make it.

Anger toward the Aum cult? No, it goes beyond anger. But who are they kidding? They say they just did what Asahara told them to, but they're the ones who did it, so they should stand trial fully prepared to die.

I've been to the Aum headquarters' Kamikuishiki Village lots of times on the job. Most of the cultists there, they look spaced out, like their souls have been sucked away. They don't even laugh or cry. Like Noh masks, expressionless. I suppose you'd call it mind control. But not the Central Command. They've got expressions, they're thinking. They haven't undergone any mind control. They gave the orders. They joined forces with Asahara in that Universal State of theirs. Whatever they plead, there's no excuse. Why not give them all the death penalty?

When you've worked as long as I have, you get to see all kinds of scenes. I even went to the Kobe earthquake. But the Tokyo gas attack was different. That was really and truly hell. Okay, so there were lots of problems with how it was reported, but the people interviewed knew what a nightmare it was.

## "I'm not a sarin victim, I'm a survivor"

### Toshiaki Toyoda (52)

*Born in Yamagata Prefecture in northeastern Japan, Mr. Toyoda joined the Subway Authority on March 20 in 1961—thirty-four years to the day before the gas attack. "After graduating I came to Tokyo with literally just a futon to sleep on," he recalls. He wasn't particularly interested in the subway, but a relative's introduction landed him the job. He has worked in Tokyo as a station attendant ever since, but he still has a slight Yamagata accent.*

*Talking to Mr. Toyoda is a lesson in professional ethics. Or perhaps that should be civic ethics. Thirty-four years on the job have done him proud and made him someone people can depend upon. Just to look at him is to see the very model of a good citizen.*

*From what Mr. Toyoda tells us I would venture a guess that, to a greater or lesser degree, his two colleagues—who unfortunately sacrificed their lives while trying to dispose of the sarin—both shared his ethical stance.*

*Even at his age he jogs twice a week so that he has no problem doing the more physical tasks around the station. He even takes part in interstation sports events. "It's good to forget about the job and work up a good sweat," he says.*

*We talked for at least four hours. Not once did he complain. "I want to conquer my own weak spirit," he says, "and put the gas attack behind me." Surely easier said than done.*

*Since interviewing Mr. Toyoda, every time I'm on the subway I look very carefully at all the station attendants. They really do have a tough job.*

●　　●　　●

I want to say first of all that I'd really rather not talk about this whole thing. I spent the night before the gas attack at the station along with

Takahashi, who died. I was on monitor duty that day for the Chiyoda Line, and two colleagues died while I was responsible. Two men who ate in the same canteen as me. If I must speak, that's what comes to mind. To tell the truth, I'd rather not remember it.

MURAKAMI: *Understood. I appreciate how difficult this must be, and I certainly don't mean to open up wounds that are only now beginning to heal. However, for my part, the more living testimonies I can bring together in writing, the more accurate the picture I can put across to everyone of just what happened to the people who found themselves in the Tokyo subway on March 20, 1995.*

Well, all right, then, I'll do my best . . .

That day I had round-the-clock duty, so I'd stayed overnight and was working on Platform 5 until 8:00 A.M. About 7:40 I handed over to Okazawa, the assistant stationmaster, saying, "Everything's in order." Then I went around to check the ticket barriers and other parts of the station before returning to the office. Takahashi was there. When I'm out on the platforms, Takahashi has to stay in the office; when Takahashi's out on the platforms, I'm in the office— that's how our shift alternated.

Before 8 A.M. Hishinuma also came out to see an out-of-service train. Hishinuma was from the Transport department, so he was supervising the drivers and conductors. It was good weather that day and he was joking as we drank our tea: "Train's never late when it's my duty." Everyone was in good spirits.

About the same time Takahashi went to the platform upstairs, while I stayed in the office relaying the day's messages to those just reporting for work. Pretty soon Okazawa came by again, picked up the intercom, and said: "There was an explosion or something at Tsukiji Station, so they've stopped the train." Stopping the Hibiya Line train meant that we were going to be rushed off our feet, because if something happens at Tsukiji, they send the train back to Kasumigaseki. Next came a phone call from Central Office: "Suspicious item sighted on board. Please verify." It was Okazawa who took the call, but I said, "I'll go and have a look, you wait here," and headed out to the platform.

But when I got to Train A725K, all the doors were closed. It seemed ready to depart. I noticed there were spots all over the platform, almost like paraffin or something. There are ten cars and each car has four doors. Up toward the front of the train, I could see where this paraffin stuff must have dripped out of the second door of one of the cars. And around the base of a pillar were seven or eight big wads of newspaper. Takahashi was on the platform—he'd been trying to mop up the stuff.

Hishinuma had boarded the cab and was talking with the driver, but there seemed to be no particular operational problems. Just then a train pulled in on the opposite platform and maybe the breeze dispersed the sarin.

It didn't look as if an ordinary dustpan could collect all the wads of newspaper, so I called out to Takahashi, "I'll go get plastic bags," and went back to the office. I told the station attendants: "Paraffin or something's spilled all over the platform, so get a mop. Any free hands come along for backup." Okazawa let someone else take over and followed me. Around this time they announced over the station PA that the Hibiya Line had been shut down.

I got covered in sarin, so my memory's a bit vague on the order of things, but on the way back to the platform someone must have handed me a mop. Now, a mop's something we use every day. If we don't mop up muck and standing water immediately, a passenger could fall and get hurt. If someone spills a drink on the platform, it's the mop straightaway. Sprinkle sawdust over it, wipe it clean. Just comes with the job.

As I said, there were these bundles wrapped in newspaper placed at the base of the pillar. I crouched down, picked them up, and put them in a plastic bag that Okazawa held open for me. I didn't know what was in them, but whatever it was they were sticky with some kind of oily substance. The draft from the train hadn't budged them, so they must have been on the heavy side. After that Hishinuma came along, and all three of us gathered up the newspaper into plastic bags. Initially I'd had it in my head that this was paraffin, but there wasn't any paraffin or petrol smell. Hmm, how would I describe the smell? Very difficult.

I only heard this later, but apparently the smell disgusted Okazawa, so he kept looking away. I also thought it was pretty horrible. I once witnessed a cremation in the country and the smell was a bit like that, or else like a dead rat. A real stink.

I can't remember if I was wearing gloves or not. I always carry gloves (*he pulls out gloves*) just in case, but you can't open plastic bags very well with gloves on. So I can't have been wearing them. Later on Okazawa told me: "Toyoda, your hands were bare. That stuff was dripping from your fingers." I didn't think much about it at the time. But as it turned out, no gloves was better. They would have soaked up the sarin and carried the poison around with you. Bare hands let it drip off.

We managed to bag up all the newspaper, but still there was the paraffin stuff on the platform. At the time I was scared it might explode. The staff at Tsukiji had mentioned explosives, and only a few days before, on March 15, they'd found a booby-trapped attaché case at our station, on the Marunouchi Line, which they say was probably Aum's doing as well. It had *boccilinus* bacteria in it or something. The assistant member of staff who carried the attaché case out of the trash can over to an exit said: "For a second there, I felt sure my number was up."

In my line of work, I always tell my wife: "Remember, I may not come back tonight." You never know what's going to happen on the job. Maybe they'll plant sarin, or maybe there'll be a fight and somebody'll have a knife. Or then again, there's no telling when some psycho might suddenly come up from behind and push an assistant onto the tracks. Or if there's explosives, I can't very well tell a subordinate, "You take care of it." Maybe it's my character, but I just can't; I have to do it myself.

The bags were clear plastic trash-can liners. We closed them as best we could, but then we were thinking about where to take the stuff, so we probably forgot to tie them. Me and Okazawa carried them back to the office staffroom. Takahashi stayed on the platform, cleaning.

Sugatani was at the office, ready to start his shift. I was trembling all over by then. I tried to check the train timetable, but couldn't read the numbers. He said, "It's okay, I'll put the call into Central for you." Then, for want of a better place, I put the plastic bags at the foot of a chair in the office staffroom.

Meanwhile, Train A725K had already gone. They'd removed the suspicious items, swept out the cars, and just let it carry on. That was Hishinuma's department, so he'd probably been in touch with Central Office and asked for the go-ahead to continue to the next station.

Takahashi always stood on the platform at the front of the train, so naturally when a passenger tells him, "There's something strange inside," he'll try to deal with it as quickly as possible. I didn't actually see it—this is just a guess—but I'll bet Takahashi took it upon himself to remove the stuff. He was the nearest, after all.

There was a trash can on the opposite platform, so that must be where Takahashi got the newspapers to swab the car floor. It was probably just him and Hishinuma. If there'd been mops handy they'd have used them, of course, but they had to use newspaper. They had to think fast. It was the middle of rush hour, after all, with about two and a half minutes, more or less, between trains.

After that I checked the office clock, thinking to jot down a memo. In my work, I make a habit of making memos straightaway. Later I have to enter everything in the record book, so reminders are a must. It was 8:10, I remember, I was trying to write an "8" but my pen was shaking too much. I was trembling all over, but I couldn't just sit idly by. That's when my eyesight went. I couldn't make out the numbers. My field of vision got smaller and smaller.

Just then word came in that Takahashi had collapsed on the platform. An attendant who was helping clean up went to get a stretcher, and together with another staff member they tried to give Takahashi first aid. I was in no shape to go and help. I was shaking too much. It was all I could do to touch-dial the subway phone. I tried to call in to Central Office—"Takahashi's collapsed. Send support."—but I was trembling uncontrollably and my voice wouldn't come.

I felt so bad it seemed doubtful I would make work the next day, so I started to check over my paperwork and things. I thought it best to tidy up while I could. They'd already called an ambulance to take us to the hospital and I didn't know when I'd be back. Tomorrow was out of the question. That's what I was thinking, shaking all over as I tried to pack up. All the time those bundles of sarin-soaked newspapers were right there at my feet.

Takahashi was unconscious when they took him away on the

34

stretcher, and I called out, "Hang in there, Issho!" But he didn't move. All I could see in my narrowed field of vision was a woman passenger. She was in the office. That's when I thought I'd better do something about the plastic bags. If the stuff blew up here, it'd endanger the passengers and staff, too.

Word came in that Takahashi's teeth were chattering, just like an epileptic. I lifted the plastic bags, hoping to get rid of them, but knew I had to do something about Takahashi first. I issued instructions: "Stuff a handkerchief in his mouth. Careful he doesn't bite your hand." I'd heard that's what you're supposed to do during epileptic seizures. By then my nose was running, my eyes were sore. I was in a terrible state, though I was completely unaware of this. I only learned that later.

I told an attendant who had just arrived: "Take these plastic bags over there," to a bunk room in the back where they'd be less danger-ous if they exploded. There they'd be sealed off behind a stainless steel door.

The woman, I learned later, was the one who'd spotted the sus-picious object on board and had come to inform us. She had begun to feel sick and got off one station before at Nijubashi, then caught the next train to Kasumigaseki.*

Hishinuma returned from the platform. "What the hell was that stuff we brought in here?" he said. "I've never had the shakes so bad. In all my years on the subway, I never saw anything like it." He had come off the platform along with Takahashi on a stretcher. Hishinuma had lost his eyesight too, but now he had to sig-nal the next train, because the station attendant was out of com-mission.

"Okay for now," I thought, "I've done my job. Cleaned away the unidentified stuff. Hishinuma and Takahashi are both back inside. I've done the immediate tasks at hand." And I'd instructed a member of the support staff to meet the ambulance at Exit A11, the Trade Ministry exit. That's the most convenient place for an ambulance pickup. "We've done our jobs, so it's just a matter of the ambulance getting here"—I was focused on that.

*This woman refused to be interviewed.

So I had them bring Takahashi on the stretcher into the office to wait.

I went to wash my face. Nose running, eyes watering, not a pretty sight. Have to make myself a bit more presentable, I thought. I stripped off my jacket and washed my face at the sink. I always take off my uniform when I wash so as not to get it wet. Sheer habit. Only later did I find out that taking my uniform off was a good thing, because it was soaked with sarin. Same goes for washing my face.

Just then I started to tremble really badly. Not like shivering from a chill or something, this was much worse. I wasn't cold, but my body wouldn't stop shaking. I tried to hold my stomach in tight, but it didn't help. I headed over to the lockers to grab a towel, was wiping my face as I walked back, when I just couldn't stand any more. I went faint and collapsed.

I felt like throwing up, couldn't breathe. Me and Hishinuma had dropped at the same time, more or less. We complained of pains almost simultaneously. I can still hear his voice in my ear: "Agh, it hurts!" I can also hear others around us saying, "Hang in there, they've called the ambulance" and "Hold on, it's on its way." After that I don't remember a thing.

I didn't think I was going to die. I'll bet even Takahashi didn't think he was going to die. After all, an ambulance was coming to take us to the hospital. I was more worried about my work, what I needed to do.

I was foaming at the mouth. My hands just wouldn't let go of the towel. That's when one of the staff members did a smart thing. There were respirators in the office, which Konno took out and put on me and Hishinuma. I couldn't even hold the mouthpiece in place. My eyes were wide open. Hishinuma somehow managed to hold his own mouthpiece, so my symptoms were worse at that point.

They'd used the only stretcher to carry Takahashi, so there was nothing left for us. Someone went to the Uchisawaicho office to fetch a stretcher from there, and as my symptoms were more serious, they carried me out first. They laid Hishinuma on some sheets and carried him out like that. Then we all waited at the exit for the ambulance.

I was taken to Jie Medical University Hospital, but it was 11:00

the next morning before I came around. I had two tubes shoved in my mouth for oxygen and to keep my lungs working. I couldn't talk. And I had drips in my neck, feeding something into both arteries. My family was all around.

After that, four of the Kasumigaseki staff came to visit. I still couldn't speak, so I borrowed a pen. I couldn't hold it properly, so I clutched it in my hand and somehow managed to write ISSHO, Takahashi's first name, two simple characters. One of the guys just crossed his hands in an "X." I knew it was bad news. "Takahashi didn't make it," he said. I wanted to ask about Hishinuma, but his name wouldn't come. I had a mental block. So I scrawled TRANS for "transport staff." Another two-handed "X." That's how I knew he'd lost his life too.

After that I wrote KASUMI. Had any other station attendants been hurt? But they said everyone was okay; I was the one in the most serious condition.

"So it's only me who survived," I realized. I still had no idea what on earth had happened, but here I'd been close to death and had survived. The more people worried over me and came to see me, the stronger the realization grew that I'd been saved. I felt happy to have survived and ashamed for what had happened to the others. This put me on edge and that night—the twenty-first, when I regained consciousness—I couldn't get to sleep. Kids get all excited and can't sleep the night before a school trip—well, it was like that. I'd been spared, thanks to everyone. They'd pitched in and come to the rescue quick, which saved my life.

I was hospitalized until March 31, after which I convalesced at home for a while, then returned to work on May 2. I gradually got my strength back, but it was a lot harder to get a grip on my mental state. First, I was hardly sleeping. Barely two or three hours, then—bang!—I'd wake up and not be able to get back to sleep. It went on like that for days. And that was the good part.

After that came the anger. I was irritable, irrational, got upset at everything. It was clearly some sort of hyperexcited condition. I didn't drink, obviously, so I was short of any psychological release. I couldn't concentrate, either. I feel a lot more relaxed now, but this rage sometimes flares up over nothing.

At first my wife was really careful with me, but it seems I was so demanding over every little thing it became aggravating for her. It was time to get back to work. I wanted to put on my uniform again and be back on the platform. Returning to the job was the first step.

I have no physical symptoms, but psychologically there's this burden. I've got to get rid of it somehow. Of course, when I first went back to work I was scared the same thing might happen again. It takes positive thinking to overcome fear, otherwise you'll carry around this victim mentality forever.

There were ordinary passengers who unfortunately lost their lives or suffered injuries just because they were traveling on the subway. People who are still suffering mentally or are in pain. When I consider their lot, I don't have the luxury to keep seeing myself as a victim. That's why I say: "I'm not a sarin victim, I'm a survivor." Frankly, there are some latent symptoms, but nothing to keep me bedridden. I'm just glad I survived.

The fear, the mental wounds are still with me, of course, but there's no way to flush them out of my system. I could never find words to explain it to the families of those who died or who sacrificed their lives on the job.

I try not to hate Aum. I leave them to the authorities. I've already gone beyond hatred. My hating them wouldn't help anyway. I don't follow the news reports on the Aum trial—what would be the point? I know what's what without looking. Going back over the circumstances won't solve anything. I've no interest in the verdict or the punishment. That's for the judge to decide.

MURAKAMI: *What exactly do you mean, you know "what's what without looking"?*

I already knew society had gotten to the point where something like Aum had to happen. Dealing with passengers day after day, you see what you see. It's a question of morals. At the station, you get a very clear picture of people at their most negative, their downsides. For instance, if we're sweeping up the station with a dustpan and brush, just when we've finished, someone will flick a cigarette butt or a piece of litter right on the spot where we've cleaned. There are too many self-assertive people out there.

There's an upside to passengers too. A guy around 50, always travels on the first train of the day, always used to greet me, he probably thought I'd died until I returned to the job. Yesterday morning when we met, he said: "Alive and well means you've still got things to do. Don't give up the fight!" It's such an encouragement just to get a cheerful greeting. Nothing comes of hatred.

## *"It's not even whether or not to take the subway, just to go out walking scares me now"*

## Tomoko Takatsuki (26)

*Ms. Takatsuki lives with her husband at her grand-mother's house in Shibuya Ward, west central Tokyo. But at the time she got caught up in the Tokyo gas attack, the newlyweds were living in the outlying suburbs of Kawasaki to the south.*

*Their present house in Shibuya is the old family home where her mother grew up. Her grandmother now leases out the upper floor as flats, one of which they occupy. "It's more convenient here to get into the center of town," says Ms. Takatsuki, "plus the rent's cheap." But her grandmother is quick to add, "My legs aren't so good any-more, so they moved here to look after me."*

*Ms. Takatsuki is a slim, young-looking 26-year-old who could still pass for a student. While she plays down her own trauma—"Why interview me when I escaped unharmed?"—listening to her story it becomes clear that the gas attack still affects her even today. A strong woman, she's nonetheless not the type to come forward and talk without being prompted. It takes time for her true feelings to come out.*

*Her tall, silent husband thoughtfully left the room for the interview. They met at a party to which she hadn't wanted to go, but was urged on by a friend.*

• • •

My office is in Kamiyacho, so it used to take almost an hour to com-mute from the house in Kawasaki. I never found it a long journey. An hour's about average for your typical salaryman.

I get up about 5:30. Eat breakfast, leave the house, get to the office at 7:30. Office hours begin at 9:00, so I have a full hour and a half at my desk to read the newspaper or have a bite to eat.

Well, the trains are crowded. So I leave the house early, around 6:30. I don't like traveling on crowded trains. And the Odakyu Line, as you'd expect, has plenty of weirdos (*laughs*). I've never had trouble getting up early or anything, I was just a bit late that day.

It'll be five years this year since I started with the company. I graduated in political economy, but since working here I've been assigned to the Systems Department. I had to train for three months . . . Now I develop in-house software. There are 150 people in our department alone—more men than women.

The day of the gas attack fell between holidays, so only about half the staff showed up for work, but I wasn't going anywhere so I went to the office just the same. I usually travel with my husband, but for some reason I was running late that day and left the house alone.

I got off at Kasumigaseki, where I always change to the Hibiya Line, but the trains were so crowded and there was still time before office hours started, so I thought I'd walk the rest of the way. It's about a fifteen-minute walk. Then what do I see but a station attendant lying on the platform, in real pain. But the other station attendants were just standing around doing nothing. It was so odd. I stood there off to one side, just watching. Usually I'd have bounded up the stairs to catch my train, but this one time I felt like, "Let's just give this a moment."

Soon a station attendant came down the stairs and I thought, "Ah, I'll bet he's gone to call the ambulance. Time for me to get going." Then suddenly I started to feel really bad myself. "Standing here looking at all this has made me ill," I thought. "It's affected me"—I mean, women are more susceptible, aren't they?—so I decide I'd better go straight outside.

I'm up the stairs, but my head's a total vacuum, my nose is streaming. I'm crying, too. So I think, "Oh no, I've caught a cold." I'm outside by now, but everything looks so dark. "I must be running a temperature," I thought. I mean, when you're running a fever, you just sort of space out, don't you? So I walked on for a bit, but it gradually became more and more painful. I told myself, "I knew I shouldn't have stood there watching that collapsed station attendant."

My eyes hurt long after I reached work. The tears and runny

nose just wouldn't stop, and I kept saying, "My eyes hurt! My eyes hurt!"—I raised quite a fuss at the office. It was *so* painful I just couldn't work. It was dark inside, too. I glanced over to make sure the lights weren't switched off. "Strange," I thought, "how can everything be so dark with the lights on?" It was darker than if I'd been wearing sunglasses. Everyone else said, "It's not dark at all," as if they thought I was mad.

Later on the general manager came around asking, "Anyone here feeling ill?" I told him my eyes hurt and they'd mentioned the same symptoms on TV, so he told me to go to the hospital. But they still didn't know at that point it was poison gas. Some sort of explosion on the subway, was all they could say . . . There was one other person in the company who suffered injuries a lot worse than mine—hospitalized for a week, apparently.

As it turns out, sarin hadn't been planted on the train I took, I'd inhaled it at the station. I couldn't tell at the time. It was in the train across the platform. I was at the rear of the train and the sarin was at the front of the train opposite me. So when I got off my train I was right there . . . Talk about bad luck. That station attendant died, you know.

But when I left the station at that point, there was no ambulance and everyone was walking around like normal. You'd never have guessed anything was wrong. There was only that station attendant who keeled over. I thought he'd had a heart attack or something. If the station attendant hadn't been lying there, I might have just walked on by without noticing a thing.

Anyway, my eyes hurt, so I knew I ought to see an eye doctor. I didn't know what to expect. I went to an ordinary local eye clinic, but the doctor took one look at my eyes and said: "Nothing to worry about. The pupils are just a little contracted, that's all." "But it hurts," I said. At which point the senior doctor came out and said: "Hmm. This is bad. Better get to a major hospital." So I took a taxi to Tora-nomon Hospital, because it's the nearest. But by then the hospital was swamped with hundreds of people, and they directed me to the Jie Med. School instead, but in the taxi I heard on the news that that was full up, too. Okay, what about St. Luke's? Full up as well . . . So what am I supposed to do?

About this time someone came along and said: "What about Teishin?" Teishin Hospital in Gotanda, affiliated with the Ministry of Communication. It probably wouldn't be so crowded. By then we knew from the news that the cause was sarin. But what did that mean? How was I supposed to be treated for it? Even the doctor said, "I really don't know how I can help you" (*laughs*). The eye clinic had washed my eyes, just in case, which seemed to help. So I told the doctor and he said, "Okay then, let's wash everyone's eyes" (*laughs*). The staff at the hospital said, "We don't know about this, but it's worth a try."

Another good thing was, as soon as I got to the office I changed my clothes. At our company we wear uniforms. This seemed to help. Later they ran blood tests and put me on a drip. They decided I should be hospitalized. I was feeling really nauseated, plus my insides never were the greatest in the first place. I thought they'd finally packed up. The nausea went away after a while, but my eyes still hurt and I had a fever.

I was only hospitalized for a day. My husband came to see me, all worried. I didn't have a clue what was going on. My eyes hurt, so I couldn't watch TV, couldn't leave my hospital room. I was out of touch. Still, I felt quite secure.

The twenty-first was a holiday, so I went to work on the twenty-second, but I couldn't sit ten minutes in front of a computer screen. "I'm off," I said, and just went home. They didn't know whether to believe me at the office or not. It was like, "Well, whatever you say." I told them that was hardly a nice attitude, but then it was, "Well, how are we supposed to know?" Okay, the symptoms weren't pronounced, but still . . .

For a whole week I was like that and couldn't do any work. I'd try to look at something and just couldn't focus. It was all a blur. When I tried to explain it to someone, all I'd get was, "But your eyes never were that good, were they?"

I went to the hospital several times, but my pupils just weren't returning to normal. It took about a month. Even now they still hurt a bit. Hmm, I wonder. Sometimes I still worry. No, it's not that my eyesight's ruined. My vision isn't especially bad. It does affect my work, though. Still, I'm glad it's just my eyes.

Afterward people who'd been injured were scared to go on the subway, or so I hear from reports, but that really wasn't the case with me. Maybe it's because the sarin wasn't on my train. Two days later when I took the subway to work in the morning I didn't feel especially wary. There were others with me in the car, and—how can I put it?—it lacked reality for me. Someone right in front of me on the platform had died, but it still wasn't real.

I get a lot of headaches. I suppose it's on account of the sarin, but then I always did get headaches, so who knows? Only the frequency of my headaches has increased . . . That and when my eyes get tired, I begin to feel nauseated. That's the most unsettling thing of all. There's just no end to it once you start thinking, then you have to tell yourself, "No, that has nothing to do with it." On TV this doctor said, "Once the symptoms go away, there's no fear of aftereffects," but who really knows yet? I just hope nothing shows up later.

Of course it irritates me. I don't see why the criminals should be pardoned. I'd just like to know what they thought they were doing. I'd demand a full explanation and an apology. I'd absolutely insist on it.

I might easily have died there, I do think about that. I'm still nervous going out alone. It's not even whether or not to take the subway, just to go out walking scares me now. So now whenever I go out, I try to go with my husband. Is this a psychological aftereffect? . . . But I do often wonder, maybe I will die. I was always the nervous type and thinking like this doesn't help, it gives me knots in my stomach.

My husband is really worried about me, maybe more concerned than I am. He says I was discharged from the hospital so quickly, perhaps I should have stayed longer. Whenever anything happens, he blames it on the sarin. I'm glad he's here for me. I wish we had more time to spend together, just the two of us. During our morning commute when we split up at the station, I think, "Oh, I don't want to go off alone." Since that day, we've never had a fight. We used to before, over anything. Lately I wonder, supposing we parted at the station after having a fight and something happened—what would I do?

44

## "The day after the gas attack, I asked my wife for a divorce"

### Mitsuteru Izutsu (38)

*Mr. Izutsu works as the shrimp import buyer for a major trading house, but originally he was a sailor. After graduating from Tokyo Merchant Marine University, he sailed foreign sea routes until a severe recession in the shipping industry persuaded him to cut short his seafaring career at 30 and take a desk job at a shrimp import company. After seven years, he changed jobs to his present company as its shrimp specialist.*

*Seafood imports command higher prices than meat, but market values fluctuate greatly, making it a risky, make-or-break business. It requires a fair amount of overseas experience. Mr. Izutsu was never particularly drawn to the shrimp business, but his interest in foreign-related work gave him an opening into the fisheries trade. Actually, two years ago, when he left his last job, he wanted to start his own company and went to his present firm in the hope of raising capital.* "Can't be too optimistic, now that Japan's Bubble has burst," *they told him.* "But perhaps you'd consider working with us for a while?" *And so he became a salaryman. It's not your typical résumé.*

*This means his outlook is subtly different from that of the usual company man. Talk to him and you sense his fiercely independent spirit. He speaks his mind, though is never overbearing. He simply has his own way of thinking and likes to think things through to the end.*

*He practiced judo at the university, and still keeps in shape. Youthful in appearance, he dresses neatly and has a penchant for smart ties. All in all a striking individual— who one morning just happened to be gassed on the way to work.*

• • •

I live in Shin-maruko now, but back then I lived right in Yokohama at Sakuragicho. My office is in Kokkai-gijidomae, right in the heart of Tokyo, so I take the Toyoko Line, which connects to the subway. Work starts at 9:15, but I generally try to get there good and early by 8:00. At that hour the trains aren't so crowded and there's no one at the office, so I can get some work done in peace. I wake at 6:00: my eyes just snap open automatically. I'm a morning person, so I'm not much of a night owl. Unless there's something going on, I'm asleep by ten in the evening. Although there aren't many nights when there's "nothing going on." There's overtime and business dinners, and I go out drinking with the guys from work too.

That day I was running a little later than usual. I took the Toyoko Line just before 7:00, reached Naka-meguro around 7:15, took the Hibiya Line to Kasumigaseki, and changed to the Chiyoda Line. I encountered the sarin gas in the one-station interval between Kasumigaseki and Kokkai-gijidomae.

I always take the front car when I change trains at Kasumi-gaseki. That puts me right by the exit closest to my office. The bell was ringing when I reached the Chiyoda Line platform, so I raced to get on, but the train just sat there. I saw two station attendants wiping the floor in front of me. Liquid had leaked from a box, spilling out like water . . . The train remained stationary while the attendants did their business mopping up the liquid. This delay meant I caught the train.

No, it wasn't with mops, they were wiping the floor with wads of newspaper. The train had to get going again as soon as possible, so they can't have had time to fetch mops. An attendant carried the leaking box out of the car and finally the train pulled away. I only found out later, but it turns out the station attendant who carried out the box died. The other one died the day after.

We were delayed about five minutes at the station. All that time, the station attendants were right in front of me cleaning up. The car wasn't especially crowded, but there was nowhere to sit, so I just stood and watched them clean up. Thinking back on it I suppose there was a smell, but at the time I didn't notice. It didn't seem at all unusual. All the passengers were coughing, though, as if someone had left something behind that had evaporated. Yet even so, not one of them got up to change seats. After the train departed, I saw the floor was still dirty and moved a few feet away.

46

I didn't notice anything else out of the ordinary until I got off the train at Kokkai-gijidomae. A lot of people coughing, but that was all. I didn't pay much attention, I just went to the office. The TV is always on at work so we can keep up with the exchange rates. I was half watching the news when something strange happened. There seemed to be some big furor going on. The screen showed mainly Tsukiji Station and thereabouts.

The day before, I'd just gotten back from a ten-day business trip to South America. The next day was the Spring Equinox holiday, so there was no pressing reason for me to come in, but I'd been away for a while, so I thought I'd just see what work had piled up. But the office was dark. What's happened? I wondered. Was the place always this dark? When I saw the TV report I didn't think for a moment it was the very same train I'd taken, but slowly I started to feel ill: contracted pupils were a symptom, apparently. Everyone said I ought to go to a hospital.

First I went to a nearby eye doctor and had my pupils examined. No amount of light applied or taken away stimulated any movement of the iris. Already some policemen had come in for tests and had been referred to nearby Akasaka Hospital. There were a few other sarin victims and they'd set up a production line to test blood pressure and the like. Akasaka Hospital still didn't have any antidote, but I was put on a drip for an hour and a half, then I was told, "Would those who feel all right now please go home and come back tomorrow." They didn't do a blood test or anything. Come to think of it now, Akasaka Hospital didn't run any proper tests on me at all.

By this time they'd pretty much established it was sarin poisoning. I knew that's what I had too. They were talking about it on TV and it had been the same train, the same car . . . They hardly looked at me at Akasaka Hospital, so I thought maybe I'd just go home and die (*laughs*). But I'd been standing in the train, then moved to the back of the car, so I was still on the safe side. Those who were sitting in the same car and didn't move away were hospitalized for a long time. I heard this from the detective who came around later to gather information.

The pupil contraction didn't improve for a while. I went to the eye doctor at Akasaka Hospital for about ten days. But they didn't really give me any treatment.

The fact is, the very day of the gas attack I worked straight through at the office until 5:30. I didn't feel well enough to eat lunch, of course; had no appetite. I came out in a cold sweat, had chills, and everyone said I looked pale. If I'd actually collapsed I'd have packed it in and gone home, but since I wasn't falling over or anything . . . Everyone was saying it's probably hay fever. I'd just returned from South America, so it could be some kind of allergic reaction, they said. But my eyes wouldn't focus, my head ached. Thank goodness my job is mainly dealing over the phone and I could leave the reading to one of the girls.

The next day was a holiday, so I just lay down and rested. Everything still seemed dark, and I had no get-up-and-go. Couldn't sleep much at night. I was groaning, apparently. I'd dream and wake up halfway. I was scared that if I went to sleep I might never wake up again.

I live alone now, but at the time I had a family. A wife and kids. Sorry to drag out the sordid details (*laughs*). But, well, at the time I was with my family, though I might just as well have been alone . . .

Well, I'd hung up the clothes I was wearing that day in the wardrobe, and the kids started complaining that their eyes tingled. I have two kids and it was the youngest whose eyes hurt. I didn't know what was going on, but I decided it couldn't hurt just to throw out the suit, so I trashed it and everything else, even threw out my shoes.

In the end, people died and others suffered terrible aftereffects, so of course you have to feel angry toward the criminals; but me, I probably feel a little different from everyone else who came to harm traveling in that car. Anger, yeah, but my symptoms were relatively minor, so mine is a more objective anger. It isn't personal.

Maybe it sounds strange, but it's not like I don't understand all this religious fanatic stuff. I've always had a feel for that side of things. I don't want to reject it straight out. I've always enjoyed the constellations and myths from the time I was small, which is why I wanted to be a sailor in the first place. But when you start organizing and forming groups, I don't go in for all that. I have no interest in religious groups, but I don't believe taking that sort of thing seriously is necessarily all bad. I can understand that much.

But it's strange, you know, while I was in South America I was invited out to karaoke by someone from the Japanese Embassy in Colombia, then almost went back the next day to the same place, but I said, "No, let's try somewhere new." And that very day, the place got bombed. I remember thinking when I got back home, "At least Japan's a safe place," and the next day I go to work and the gas attack happens (*laughs*). What a joke. But seriously, when I'm in South America or Southeast Asia, death is never far away. Accidents are commonplace to them, not like in Japan.

To be honest, the day after the gas attack, I asked my wife for a divorce. We weren't on the best of terms at the time, and I'd done my fair share of thinking while I was in South America. I had meant to come out and say my piece when I got home, then I walked straight into the gas attack. Still, even after all I'd been through, she would barely speak to me.

After being gassed I phoned home from the office to tell my wife what had happened and my symptoms and everything, but I got almost no reaction from her. Perhaps she couldn't really grasp the situation, exactly what had occurred. But even so, well, I knew then that we'd come to a turning point. Or else, the state I was in had gotten me all worked up, maybe that's what it was. Maybe that's why I came straight out with it and said I wanted a divorce. Perhaps if this sarin thing hadn't happened, I wouldn't have been talking about divorce so soon. I probably wouldn't have said anything. It was a shock to the system and at the same time a kind of trigger.

My family had been in such a mess for so long, by then I didn't consider myself very important. Not that the possibility of dying wasn't real, but, had I died, I probably could have accepted it in my own way as just a kind of accident.

## *"Luckily I was dozing off"*

### Aya Kazaguchi (23)

*Ms. Kazaguchi was born in Machiya, Arakawa Ward, northeast Tokyo, and has never lived anywhere else. She likes it in Machiya and has never thought of moving. She lives with her mother and father and a sister who is fourteen years younger than she. Though she's a working adult in her own right, and sometimes considers striking out on her own, she still "sponges" off her parents.*

*After graduating from high school, she went to business school and studied data processing and bookkeeping, then found work with a clothing manufacturer. She is in charge of one of the company's own brands. It is an exclusive line that targets the "cute" and "frilly" tastes of debutantes and young wives from good families. Her father works in the clothing industry, which is how she was introduced to her present employer. Ms. Kazaguchi has no great interest in the clothing business, but she is happy to be able to use her computer and word-processing skills on the job.*

*She likes reggae, and her favorite sports include snowboarding, skateboarding, and surfing. "I admit I'm shallow," she jokes. She enjoys going out with her friends, many of whom she met at grade school. Most of them have stayed in Machiya too.*

*Fit and strong-willed, she is making the most of her free-and-single years. With her straight, shoulder-length hair, I imagine she's popular with boys. And, for what it's worth, her mother's my age—so she's young enough to be my daughter.*

●　　●　　●

It takes about forty minutes to get from my house to the office. I take the Chiyoda Line from Machiya Station to Nijubashi-mae Station, walk to Yurakucho Station, then change to the Yurakucho Line for Shintomicho Station. I generally get to the office around 9:05. Office hours start at ten after, so I aim for ten to twenty-five minutes' leeway. I've never been late. I catch the same trains every day.

They're, like, supercrowded. The Chiyoda Line between Machiya and Otemachi is impossible. You can't even move your arms. When you get on they shove in—*oomph!*—from the back, then just pile in willy-nilly. You get "feelie" guys too, sometimes. No fun.

At Otemachi there are all these connections, but once past there it clears out a bit. Nijubashi-mae's only the next stop, so it's pretty much crowded the whole way for me. From Machiya to Nishi-nippori, Sendagi, Nezu, Yushima, Shin-ochanomizu, Otemachi . . . can't do a thing. You're just trapped there. Once I'm on, I stand by the door just leaning into this solid mass of people, maybe sleeping. Yeah, that's right, I can doze off standing up. Almost everyone does. I just close my eyes nice and quiet. Couldn't move if I wanted to, so it's easier that way. People's faces are so up-close, like this, right? . . . so I close my eyes and drift off . . .

March 20 was a Monday, wasn't it? Yeah. Mondays around then our section had meetings first thing at 8:30. So that day I had to go in earlier than usual, left the house about 7:50. Took a different train than usual. Earlier, so a bit emptier. I actually felt I had some room. So I get on, settle into my nook between the seat and the door, just the perfect setup for a nice little nap.

I always board the front car, second door down. I head for the corner, hide in there, and don't move. But at Nijubashi-mae Station the door opens on the opposite side from Machiya, and at Otemachi I have to move to the other door.

So that day I'm trying to do that, getting ready to open my eyes. I can't move without opening my eyes, right? (*laughs*) Only I notice it's hard to breathe. It's like, there's this tight pressure in my chest, and as much as I try to inhale, no breath comes in . . . "That's odd," I'm thinking, "must be because I got up early" (*laughs*). I thought I was just spaced out. I'm pretty bad at waking up anyway, but this was just a little too stuffy.

It was okay while the door was open and let in some fresh air, but once the door closed at Otemachi the stuffiness got worse. How can I describe it? It was as if the air itself had shut down, even time had shut down . . . no, that's a bit exaggerated.

"Strange," I'm thinking. That's when the people hanging on to the handstraps started coughing. The car was pretty empty by then, maybe three or four people still standing in front of the seats. But I was so short of breath, I just wanted to get out of there as soon as possible. All I could think was, "Can't this train go any faster?" It's two, maybe three minutes between Otemachi and Nijubashi-mae, and all that time I was desperate for air. When you fall down and you wham your chest, sometimes you can't breathe. You inhale all right, but can't push the air out again—it was kind of like that.

That's when I look, and by the door opposite me there's something wrapped in newspaper. I was standing right in front of it and hadn't even noticed. It was about the size of a lunch box and the newspaper it was wrapped in was dripping wet. Water or some kind of liquid seeping out all around. I took a closer look, and the thing was sloshing around to the rhythm of the train.

I'm a downtown girl, so I know when you go to the fish shop, they wrap it in newspaper. That's what I thought it was: someone had bought fish or something and left it behind. But who'd buy fish and be traveling on the train first thing in the morning? One middle-aged man also seemed to think it was odd and had gone over, just staring at it. He was forty-something, a salaryman. He didn't touch it, though, just peered at it like, "What's that?"

Meanwhile the train reaches Nijubashi-mae, so I get off and everyone else who gets off with me is coughing. I'm hacking away, too. About ten people got off and every one of them was coughing, so I knew there had to be something, it wasn't just me. I knew I had to rush if I was to be on time. My heart was pounding and I ran along the platform, went straight up the passageway, and suddenly was out of breath. I slowed down and felt much better, but now my nose was running like mad. My heartbeat was back to normal, though.

By the time I got to the office and we were in the meeting, I started to feel really sick, like I'm going to throw up. Then it came on the news that something had happened on the subway, and I think, "Aha, so that's it!" When I heard I felt faint . . . I'm a real coward. I went straight to St. Luke's Hospital.

They put me on a drip for two hours and ran blood tests, then told me, "Okay, you can go home now." The tests didn't show up anything out of the ordinary. I showed no sign of contracted pupils, I just felt sick. I was still wearing the same clothes. I was really suffering then, but I've gotten better over time. Luckily I was dozing off. That's what a detective told me. My eyes were shut, and my breathing was lighter and shallower (*laughs*). Just lucky, I guess.

## "Everyone loves a scandal"

### Hideki Sono (36)

*Mr. Sono works in the Aoyama fashion district, at the Tokyo branch of a haute couture clothing manufacturer. He's in sales. After the "Bubble" burst and Japan's 1980s affluence dried up, most fashion-related businesses fell on hard times, or as Mr. Sono puts it, "We came back to our senses." Tired of the excesses of the previous decade—old men cavorting around with young girls, spending a fortune on image, selling overpriced brand-name clothes—he seems somewhat relieved that the economy has bottomed out.* "Now we can finally get back to normal."

*Although he says he's "cut out for sales," Mr. Sono has nothing of the usual hard-sell salesman about him. He seems rather cool and introverted. He doesn't care much for drinking or group tours or golf, but golf is important in sales, so he can't very well not play. He goes to the golf course, opens his long-neglected golf bag, and asks his playing partners,* "Er, which club do I need now?"—*he's that level of golfer.*

"With society the way it is, everyone just chasing after money, I can sort of understand how young people might be attracted to something more spiritual like religion. Not that I am myself." *He has experienced some fairly severe aftereffects from the gas attack, but harbors no personal anger or spite toward the Aum perpetrators. He doesn't know why.*

"I work in clothing, but I have virtually no interest in clothes myself," *he says.* "I'll see something, say 'I'll take that one,' and buy it. I don't labor over it." *If so, though, how come he's such a sharp dresser?*

●　　●　　●

54

My wife and I live alone. We married at 24, so that makes thirteen years. We live in Chiba. I leave the house around 7:30 and catch the 8:15 Chiyoda Line from Matsudo. Needless to say, I can never get a seat on the Chiyoda Line. I'm standing for forty-five minutes throughout. I can sometimes get a seat at Otemachi. I'm still half asleep, so if I can get a seat, I'll sit. Getting a seat means a good fifteen minutes' rest.

On March 20, I left the house thirty minutes early. I had a bit of business I wanted to take care of before work. It was the show season and I had a lot of little things to do for that. Added to which we're in sales, and it was almost time to start cranking out the figures—how many units of what item sold for the whole month. We've got our quotas—this much we have to sell—based on budget projections. I had to get the figures in to Head Office during the course of that week, then put in an appearance at a meeting the following week.

Actually, March 20 was the day my wife left the company where she'd worked for six years. It was an editing job at an advertising magazine, really demanding work that was wearing her down so she wanted to leave. Now she freelances as a copywriter. And also that day was her birthday, too. Which is why I remember the events of March 20 so clearly.

I always take the first car at the front of the train. That puts me nearest the exit, which brings me out by the Hanae Mori boutique building at Omote-sando. That day I happened to get a seat all the way from Shin-ochanomizu. I'd gotten up early and was pretty beat, so I was thinking, "Ah, what a break!" As soon as I sat down I was fast asleep. I woke up at Kasumigaseki Station, four stops later. I felt like I was going to cough and that's what woke me. And there was this weird smell. A lot of people were moving to the next car down. They were opening and closing the doors between the cars.

When I opened my eyes, I saw a station attendant in a green uniform coming in and out. The floor was wet, too. The wet patch was maybe five meters away from me. The criminals had pricked their bags of sarin and got off at Shin-ochanomizu. But anyway I'd been fast asleep and hadn't seen a thing. The police questioned me over and over about it, but what I didn't see I didn't see. They thought that sounded suspicious. I was traveling to Aoyama and the Aum headquarters are in Aoyama.

The train continued on to the next stop, Kokkai-gijidomae, where we all had to get off. No explanation was given over the PA, just, "This train is going out of service—all passengers please disembark." But between Kasumigaseki and Kokkai-gijidomae I was really in pain. I was coughing, I couldn't breathe. When we reached Kokkai-gijidomae there were people near me who couldn't even move. One woman in her fifties had to be lifted off by the station attendants. There were maybe ten people in the car and some of them held handkerchiefs over their mouths, coughing.

"Hey, what's going on here?" I thought, but I had to get to work. I had a whole list of things to do. Stepping out onto the platform, who knows how many people were squatting there? The station attendants had rounded up all those who were feeling sick, there must have been fifty in all. Two or three were completely immobilized, one or two lay stretched out on the platform.

Oddly enough, though, the atmosphere wasn't tense at all. Even though I was feeling strange. I'd inhale and no breath would come. It was almost as if the air was running out. I could still walk, though, so I thought I was fine. Instead of joining the "sick" group, I just caught the next train. It came straightaway, but no sooner had I gotten on than my legs started to feel shaky. My eyes stopped working. Suddenly it was as if night had fallen. "Damn," I thought, "I should have stayed back there with the others."

When I got to Omote-sando Station, I asked the attendant, "I don't know why I'm feeling so out of sorts . . . did something happen in the subway?" And he said, "There seems to have been an explosion at Hatchobori." "There was something wrong with the train I was on just now, too," I said, but this was explained away as "gasoline or something has been spilled inside." Totally mixed-up information. Then I went to the stationmaster's office and I told them, "I feel awful. I can hardly see," but news had yet to reach Omote-sando Station. Their response was, "Why don't you just sit down for a bit? Would you like a cold drink?" Very kind, but they didn't have a clue.

"This is useless," I thought, so I gave up and I went out above ground. It was a wonderful clear day, but everything was dark. "Uh-oh, this looks bad." I went to a hospital, near the office, but when I got there I couldn't really explain what had happened. "This is probably an emergency: I just left the subway and . . ." You know, I spelled it out as clearly as possible, but they couldn't see me straightaway. I called the office: "I'm not feeling so good. I'll be a little late." In the end I waited there for three hours. Three hours and they didn't do a damn thing! My breath was getting shorter and shorter, my eyesight dimmer and dimmer . . . I was going out of my mind, so I telephoned the Subway Authority, just to get some kind of explanation. After all, they had rounded up on the platform those people who were feeling ill. I wondered what had happened to them. But I couldn't get through on the phone.

At 11:00 news came that it was sarin. Finally the doctors would have a look at me! They got the picture. Straightaway it was transfusions, hospitalization. I was their first sarin patient, so suddenly the doctors were fascinated. They gathered around, poking me all over the place for symptoms, chatting among themselves: "See, this is what it does." I was in there for three days.

I was so exhausted I slept really well, but the three months after that were tough. I was tired all the time. Try and do something and I'd be worn out. My eyes had gone, my focus was blurry and my field of vision was tiny. My job involves a lot of driving, but after dark I couldn't see a thing. My vision's normally okay, but I couldn't even make out street signs. And if I can't read a computer screen I can't do business.

I probably went a little funny in the head, too. Seriously. I went around telling people, "Something's out there. You'll see, something strange is going to happen." I was buying survival gear at camping stores (*laughs*). After I came back to normal, I thought, what a fool I'd been . . . but at the time I was deadly serious. Now, what am I going to do with a survival knife?

It's odd, but I didn't feel anything like anger. Of course, it makes me angry to think of those who died. It makes me especially sad to think of the dead station attendants who carried out the sarin. If they hadn't been there, I might have died too. But I don't feel any personal hatred or bitterness toward the criminals. It feels more like I had an accident. Maybe you were expecting another response?

Either way, I couldn't stand the media coverage of Aum. I don't even want to look at it. Yes, you could say it's reinforced my mistrust of the media. The long and the short of it is, everyone loves a scandal. They just enjoy saying, "Oh, what a shame." I've even stopped reading magazines.

# TOKYO METROPOLITAN SUBWAY:

## MARUNOUCHI LINE

### (Destination: Ogikubo)

#### TRAIN A777

•  •  •

The team of Ken'ichi Hirose and Koichi Kitamura planted sarin on a westbound Marunouchi Line train destined for Ogikubo.

Born in Tokyo in 1964, Hirose was 30 years old at the time. After graduating from Waseda High School, a preparatory school for the prestigious Waseda University, he enrolled at the university's Engineering department, from which he graduated in Applied Physics at the top of a class of one hundred. He's the very model of an honor student. In 1989 he completed his postgraduate studies, only to spurn offers of employment and take vows instead.

He became an important member of the Aum cult's Chemical Brigade in their Ministry of Science and Technology. Along with fellow perpetrator Masato Yokoyama, Hirose was a key figure in their secret Automatic Light Weapon Development Scheme. A tall, serious-looking youth, he seems rather more boyish than his 32 years. In court he chooses his words carefully and speaks quietly and to the point.

The morning of March 18, Hirose received orders from his Ministry of Science and Technology superior Hideo Murai to plant sarin on the subway. "I was extremely surprised," he said later in court. "I shuddered to think of all the victims this would sacrifice. On the other hand, I knew I couldn't be well-versed enough in the teachings to be thinking like that." In awe of the gravity of his mission, he felt a strong "instinctual resistance," but his adherence to Aum's teachings was even stronger. While he now admits his error, he claims he realistically had neither the liberty nor the will to disobey orders from above—that is, as he says himself, from Shoko Asahara.

Hirose was ordered to board the second car of an Ogikubo-bound Marunouchi Line train at Ikebukuro Station. At Ochanomizu Station, he would poke holes in two packets of sarin and be picked up by Kitamura's car waiting outside. The train number was A777. Detailed instructions were provided by Hirose's "Big Brother," Yasuo Hayashi. After twenty days of training at Kamikuishiki Village, Hirose finally poked so hard with his umbrella that he bent the tip.

Leaving the Aum *ajid* in Shibuya, west central Tokyo, at 6:00 on the morning of March 20, Hirose and Kitamura drove to Yotsuya Station. There Hirose boarded a westbound Marunouchi Line train for Shinjuku, then changed to the Saikyo Line northbound for Ikebukuro. He bought a copy of a sports tabloid at a station kiosk and wrapped the sarin packets in it. He waited around before boarding the appointed Marunouchi Line train, standing by the middle door of the second car. But when it was time to release the sarin, the newspaper wrapping made such a noise it drew the attention of a nearby schoolgirl—or at least Hirose thought it had.

Unable to bear the mounting tension, he got off the train at Myogadani or Korakuen Station and stood on the platform. Overwhelmed by the horror of what he had been commanded to do, he was filled with an intense desire to leave the station without going through with it. He confessed to feeling "envious of the people who could just walk out of there." In retrospect, that was the crucial moment when things might have been very different. Had he simply left the station, hundreds of people would have been spared a major derailment in their lives . . .

But Ken'ichi Hirose gritted his teeth and overcame his doubts. "This is nothing less than salvation," he told himself. The act of doing it is what matters, and besides, it's not just him, all the others are doing the same thing too. He couldn't let the others down. Hirose got back on the train, taking another car, the third, to avoid the inquisitive schoolgirl. As the train approached Ochanomizu Station, he pulled the packet of sarin out of his bag and dropped it unobtrusively on the floor. The newspaper wrapper fell off as he did so and the plastic packet was exposed, but by then he didn't care. He didn't have time to care. He repeated an Aum mantra under his breath in order to steel himself, then, just as the doors opened at Ochanomizu, he banished all thoughts and stabbed at the bag with the tip of his umbrella.

Before getting into Kitamura's waiting car, Hirose rinsed the umbrella tip with some bottled water and tossed it into the trunk. Despite being extremely careful in his movements, he soon showed the unique symptoms of sarin poisoning. He couldn't speak properly and breathing was difficult. His right thigh began to twitch uncontrollably.

Hirose hurriedly injected himself in the thigh with the atropine sulphate given him by Ikuo Hayashi. With his excellent scientific background, Hirose knew how deadly sarin could be, but it was far more toxic than he had expected. The thought crossed his mind: "What if I just die like this?" He remembered Ikuo Hayashi's advice: "At the first sign of any physical abnormalities, report to Aum Shinrikyo Hospital in Nakano for immediate medical treatment." Hirose had Kitamura drive the car to Nakano, but was completely caught off-guard to find the doctors there knew nothing about the secret sarin drop. They returned swiftly to the Shibuya *ajid*, where Ikuo Hayashi administered emergency care.

Back at Kamikuishiki Village, Hirose and Kitamura joined the other perpetrators to deliver to Asahara the message: "Mission accomplished." Whereupon Asahara commended them, saying, "Trust the Ministry of Science and Technology to get the job done." When Hirose confessed to having changed to another car because he thought he'd been noticed, Asahara seemed to accept his explanation: "I was following everyone's astral projections the whole time," he said, "and I thought Sanjaya's (Hirose's cult name) astral projection seemed dark, as though something had happened. So that's what it was."

"The teachings tell us that human feelings are the result of seeing things in the wrong way," said Hirose. "We must overcome our human feelings." He had succeeded in puncturing two plastic packets, releasing 900 milliliters of liquid sarin onto the floor. As well as the one passenger who died, 358 were seriously injured.

At Nakano-sakaue Station a passenger reported that someone had collapsed. Two severe casualties were carried out: one died; the other, "Shizuko Akashi,"* was temporarily reduced to a vegetative state (*see pages* 87–95). Meanwhile, a station attendant, Sumio Nishimura, scooped up the sarin on board and cleared it from the station (*see page* 78). But the train itself continued on its way, the car floor still soaked with liquid sarin.

At 8:38 the train reached Ogikubo, the end of the line. New passengers got on and the train headed back eastward in the opposite direction. Passengers in the eastbound train complained of feeling ill. Several station attendants that had boarded the train at Ogikubo also mopped the floor, but they too gradually became unwell and had to be rushed to the hospital. The train was taken out of service two stops later at Shin-koenji Station.†

*All pseudonyms appear in quotation marks. [Tr.]

†At the time of going to press, Ken'ichi Hirose is sentenced to death. Koichi Kitamura was sentenced to life imprisonment and is appealing the sentence. [Tr.]

# "I felt like I was watching a program on TV"

## Mitsuo Arima (41)

*Mr. Arima lives south of Tokyo in Yokohama. His clean-cut features, smart clothes, and bearing give him a youth-ful appearance. He defines himself as optimistic and fun-loving; eloquent, but never dogmatic. It's not until you sit and talk to him that you realize he has one foot in middle age. After all, 40 is a turning point, an age when people begin to ponder the meaning of it all.*

*Married with two children, Mr. Arima works for a cos-metics company. He and his colleagues play in a band for fun. He plays guitar. Due to commitments at work, Mr. Arima had the bad luck to catch the Marunouchi Line—which he doesn't usually take—and get gassed.*

• • •

Actually, the whole week before I'd been down with the flu. That was the first time in my adult life I'd ever taken to my bed. I'm never ill.

So there I was, going back to work that day after my absence, which is why I wanted to get to the office a little early, to make up for lost time (*laughs*). I left the house ten minutes earlier than usual.

I always sit down and have a leisurely read of the newspaper on the Yokohama Line going west to the Hachioji office, but that day it just so happens I was supposed to go to the downtown Shinjuku office for a special meeting of regional managers. I planned to spend the morning in Shinjuku, then put in an appearance at Hachioji.

The meeting began at 9:45. I left the house before 7:00, taking the Yokosuka Line up to Shimbashi, then the Ginza Line to Akasaka-mitsuke, then changed to the Marunouchi Line for Shinjuku-gyoemmae: travel time, an hour and a half. The Marunouchi Line clears out after Akasaka-mitsuke, so I'm assured of a seat. But that day, I sit down and straightaway I notice an acid smell. Okay, trains often smell funny, but this was no ordinary smell, let me tell you. I remember a lady sitting across from me covering her nose with a handkerchief, but otherwise there was nothing obviously wrong. I'm not even sure that smell was sarin. It's only later I thought back, "Ah, so that's what it was."

I got off at Shinjuku-gyoemmae, except it was incredibly dark, like somebody had switched off all the lights. It had been a bright day when I left home, but when I exited above ground everything was dim. I thought the weather had taken a turn for the worse, but I looked up and there wasn't a cloud in the sky. I was taking a hay-fever remedy at the time, so I thought it might be a reaction to the drug. It was different from my usual, so maybe this was a side effect.

But everything was still dark when I reached the office and I felt so lethargic I just sat in a daze at my desk, gazing out of the window. The morning meeting ended and everyone else went out for lunch. But everything was still dark and I had no appetite. I didn't feel up to talking to anyone. So I ate quietly alone and then I broke out in a sweat. The TV was on in the ramen noodle shop and it's round-the-clock news about the gas attack. The others tease me, saying, "Hey, maybe you have sarin poisoning," but I knew it was the hay-fever remedy, so I just laughed along.

The meeting started again in the afternoon, but I'm not at all better. I decided to get examined by a hay-fever specialist. I excused myself from the meeting at 2:00. At that point I was starting to think, "Hey, what if it is sarin?"

For peace of mind, I decided to go to the local doctor near my home, the one who prepared the new hay-fever remedy. It was still a toss-up between hay-fever remedy or sarin poisoning. So I went all the way back to Yokohama, but when he heard I'd been on the subway before I came down with the symptoms he tested my pupils and recommended immediate hospitalization.

He took me by ambulance to Yokohama City College Hospital. I was able to get out of the ambulance and walk by myself, so my symptoms were slight then. But at night the headaches started. Around midnight a huge dull thud of pain. I called over the nurse, and she gave me an injection. The headache wasn't a sharp shooting pain, it squeezed tight and hard like a vise for a good hour. Maybe this is it, I thought, but soon the pain subsided, and I was thinking, "Yeah, I'll pull through."

The eyedrops they'd given me to dilate my pupils worked a bit too well, though, and now my pupils were wide open. The next day when I woke up everything was so bright . . . so they put up paper all around my bed to block out the glare. Thanks to that it was another day in the hospital before my pupils were normal again.

In the morning my family visited. I was still in no condition to read the newspaper, but I found out how serious the attack was. People died. I might have been killed myself. Oddly enough I didn't feel any sense of crisis. My reaction was, "Well, I'm okay." I'd been right at the epicenter, but instead of shuddering at the death toll, I felt like I was watching a program on TV, as if it were somebody else's problem.

It was only much later that I began to wonder how I could have been so callous. I ought to have been furious, ready to explode. It wasn't until the autumn that it really sank in, little by little. For instance, if someone had fallen down right in front of me, I like to think I'd have helped. But what if they fell fifty yards away? Would I go out of my way to help? I wonder. I might have seen it as somebody else's business and walked on by. If I'd gotten involved I'd have been late for work . . .

Since the war ended, Japan's economy has grown rapidly to the point where we've lost any sense of crisis and material things are all that matters. The idea that it's wrong to harm others has gradually disappeared. It's been said before, I know, but this really brought it home to me. What happens if you raise a child with that mentality? Is there any excuse for this kind of thing?

It's strange, you know, back in the hospital with everyone around me in a blind panic, I didn't feel in the least horrified. I was so calm and collected. If someone had made a joke about sarin, I wouldn't have cared in the least. That's how little it meant to me. That summer I began to forget that there had even been a "Tokyo gas attack." I'd read something in the newspaper about a lawsuit for damages and I'd think, "Ah yes, that again," as though it had nothing to do with me.

I've worked in Tokyo for twelve years, I know all about its peculiarly settled ways. Ultimately, from now on I think the individual in Japanese society has to become a lot stronger. Even Aum, after bringing together such brilliant minds, what do they do but plunge straight into mass terrorism? That's just how weak the individual is.

## "Looking back, it all started because the bus was two minutes early"

### Kenji Ohashi (41)

*Mr. Ohashi is married with three children and has worked at a major car dealership for twenty-two years. He is presently Business Department head at their service center in Ohta Ward, southeast Tokyo.*

*At the time of the Tokyo gas attack, the service center was still unfinished and he was working from a temporary office to the west in Nakano Honancho, Suginami Ward. Mr. Ohashi was exposed to sarin on his commute to this office, while traveling on the Marunouchi Line.*

*An old hand at the car-repair business, Mr. Ohashi stands in front of the shop and deals directly with the customers. An experienced technician, he is a real workingman, with short hair and a solid build. He's not the talkative type, and speaks slowly and thoughtfully about the gas attack.*

*He still suffers from particularly severe aftereffects, but he has also joined a victims' support group and actively participates in its campaigns. He is trying to organize a self-help network to link all the individual sufferers. The hour and a half he spent talking to me must have given him an excruciating headache. I can only offer my apologies and my sincere thanks for his cooperation.*

•   •   •

When I used to commute to Nakano, I'd go from Koiwa via Japan Railways to Yotsuya Station. From home I'd catch the bus or cycle to Koiwa Station; well, probably more often it was the bus.

On the day of the gas attack I left the house as usual just after 7:00. But as luck would have it, the bus was about two minutes early. It was always late, but for once it was ahead of schedule. I ran for the stop but didn't make it in time, so I had to catch the next bus at 7:30 instead. By the time I reached Yotsuya I had already missed two trains on the subway. Looking back, it all started because the bus was two minutes early. My timing has never been so bad! Until then I'd traveled back and forth like clockwork.

I always went for the third car from the front on the Marunouchi Line. That way you get the best view from the Yotsuya Station platform. Looking out past the roofline you can see the Sophia University soccer field, it's like a breath of fresh air! That day, however, the third car was ridiculously empty. It's never like that. Yotsuya is so crowded, you can never get a seat. You just get on and hope for a seat later. So I knew then something was up.

As soon as I got on, I noticed two people in odd postures behind me. A man hunched over in his seat, nearly falling off, and a huddled woman, head down and sort of curled up. And then there was this really strange smell. At first I thought there must be some drunk making the place stink, like when a drunk throws up. It wasn't a sharp smell, it was a little sweet, like something rotten. Not like paint thinner, either. We do paint jobs, too, so I know what thinner smells like. It didn't make your nose sting like that.

Well, I got a seat, so I was prepared to put up with a little smell; and once I'd sat down I soon closed my eyes and fell asleep. I usually read a book on the train, but it was Monday and I was sleepy. Still, I didn't fall asleep, really, just closed my eyes and half-dozed. Sounds still reached me, so when I suddenly heard the announcement, "This station is Nakano-sakaue," I snapped awake, like a reflex action, jumped up, and left the train.

Everything was dim. The lights on the platform were faint. My throat was parched and I was coughing; a really bad, chesty cough. There's a water cooler by a bench at the end of the station, so I thought I'd better go and rinse my mouth. That's when I heard the shouting: "Someone's fainted!" It was this tall young salaryman. When I looked back inside, I saw the man in the car had fallen right over, parallel to the seats.

But I didn't feel too good myself. I went to the water cooler and gargled. My nose was running and my legs were shaky. It was hard to breathe. I just plunked myself down on a bench. Then, maybe five minutes later, they carried out on a stretcher the man who'd fainted, and the train started off again.

I didn't have the foggiest idea what had hit me. Only everything had gone dark before my eyes. My lungs were wheezing like I was running a marathon and the whole lower half of my body was cold and trembling.

Altogether maybe five or six passengers were brought up to the station office. Two of them on stretchers. But the station attendants hadn't a clue either. They were asking us what had happened. The police arrived about half an hour later, and predictably started questioning us. It was really painful, but I made the effort to spell things out as best I could. Someone had fainted and I was afraid if I lost consciousness I'd be done for. That's why they were trying to keep us talking, I thought, so I forced myself to speak.

Meanwhile, during all this, the station attendants themselves began to feel sick. Their sight was going. We'd been in that office for at least forty minutes, everyone breathing the same air. We probably should have gone above ground earlier.

So we went upstairs. The fire department had set up a temporary relief shelter in an alleyway. "Just sit here for now," they told us. But it was so, so cold, I couldn't stay sitting there, just a thin plastic sheet on the ground. Lie down and you'd freeze. It was still March, after all. There was a bicycle parked there, so I propped myself against that. "Mustn't pass out," was all I could think. Two people did lie down, but the rest did like me. I tell you, it was damn cold. We were forty minutes in the station office and twenty minutes out there. A whole hour had gone by and none of us had received any treatment.

We couldn't all go in the ambulance, so I was taken by police van to Nakano General Hospital. There they laid me out on a bench while they examined me. The results weren't good, so they put me on intravenous straightaway. I'd heard reports in the police van over the radio about the effects of poisoning and so on. That's when I realized I'd been poisoned.

At this point, apparently, they knew it was sarin at Nakano General, but there we were still wearing our sarin-saturated clothes. Soon the hospital staff were complaining of eye trouble too. All through the morning my body was like ice. Even with an electric blanket, I was shivering. My blood pressure was up to 180. Ordinarily I run in the 150s tops. Still, I wasn't worried, just puzzled.

I was in the hospital for twelve days: vicious headaches the whole time. No painkiller worked. I was in agony. The headaches would come in waves all day, receding then getting stronger. I also ran a high fever for two days; as high as 40° C [104° F].

I had cramps in my legs and trouble breathing for the first three or four days. It was like there was something stuck in my throat. Excruciating. My eyes were so bad I'd look outside and see no light at all. Everything was a blur.

They kept me on intravenous for five days. On the fifth day, my cholinesterase level had returned to near normal, so they detached the drip.* My pupils slowly recovered, but whenever I focused on anything I felt a sharp shooting pain at the back of my eyes, like I was being stabbed with a pick.

They finally discharged me on March 3 and I took a month off work to recuperate at home. I still suffered from splitting headaches. And with my legs so wobbly, I was bound to fall and hurt myself while commuting—what they call "secondary injury."

First thing in the morning my head would hurt. It was like a killer hangover. My head throbbed with each pulse, every heartbeat, and it kept up relentlessly. Still, I didn't take any medicine. I simply buckled down and took the pain. Having absorbed sarin, the risk of taking the wrong medicine was worse than taking nothing, so I avoided all headache remedies.

I took off all of April, then put in an appearance at our newly constructed Showajima Center after the early May holidays, and started back on the job. We were arranging desks, connecting computers, straight through every day until late at night. I know I overdid it. My head still hurt. It got worse when the June rains set in. Every day it felt like I had some massive weight crushing my skull. And I still got shooting pains when I tried to look at anything.

I was afraid to commute again. I'd board the train and see the

*Like other poisonous organophosphorus compounds, sarin inhibits cholinesterase, an enzyme produced in the liver. For a brief explanation of cholinesterase see pages 218–19. [Tr.]

door slide shut before my eyes, and in that very instant my head would seethe with pain. I'd get off and go through the ticket barrier, thinking, "I'm okay," and the weight would still be there in my head, bearing down. I couldn't concentrate on anything. If I talked for more than an hour my head would be killing me. It's still that way now. In mid-April when I filed a police report, the effort wore me out.

Then, after a week's vacation in August, I felt a noticeable change. I was fine on the train. My headaches weren't so bad. Maybe the time away from work eased the tension. The first few days back at work were great, but a week later I was back to square one. Headaches again.

One day in August it took me three hours to get to work. I had to stop off all along the route and rest until the pain subsided; but the moment I was back on board a train it would flare up again, so I'd have to rest—over and over again. It was 10:30 by the time I reached the office!

I went to see a psychologist, Dr. Nakano, at St. Luke's Hospital. I related my case history and symptoms up to that point, and he said, "Absolutely hopeless! It's suicidal the way you're working!" He didn't mince his words. After that I went to him twice a week for counseling. I took tranquilizers, sleeping pills—finally I could sleep at night.

I ended up taking another three months off work, all the time keeping up the counseling and the medicine. You see, I had what's called posttraumatic stress disorder [PTSD]. Examples range from returning Vietnam War veterans to victims of the Kobe earthquake. It comes from severe shock. In my case, for four months after the gas attack, I'd pressured myself into working all hours, overtaxing my body, which piled on the stress even more. It was only thanks to my summer vacation that the tension snapped.

A complete cure of PTSD is apparently very rare. Unless you clear away all those memories, the psychological scars remain. But memories aren't so easily erased. All you can do is try to reduce stress and not overwork.

Commuting is still hard. One hour on the train from Koiwa, then change at Hamamatsucho to the monorail, gradually my head gets weighed down. Okay, I'm sure I look all right, but then no one understands this pain, which makes it doubly hard for me at work. My boss is decent enough, though, he sympathizes: "If I'd caught a different train," he says, "it could've been me."

For a while after the gas attack, when I was sleeping at the hospital, I had terrible nightmares. The one I remember best was a dream in which someone pulled me out of my bed next to the window and dragged me around the room. Or I turned and suddenly saw someone standing there who's supposed to be dead. Yeah, I often met dead people in my dreams.

I used to have dreams in which I was a bird flying in the sky, but then I'd get shot down. An arrow or a bullet, I don't know. I'm lying there wounded on the ground and I get trampled to death—dreams like that. Happy at first, flying through the sky, then a nightmare.

About the criminals themselves, what I feel goes beyond hatred or anger. Anger is too easy. I just want them dealt with as soon as possible—that's all I have to say.

*I interviewed Mr. Ohashi in early January 1996, but met him again at the end of October. I was curious what progress he'd made. He was still plagued by headaches and a feeling of lethargy.*

*At the same time, his most immediate problem is that he has been relieved of most of the work he used to do at his company. The week before this second interview, his boss had called him into his office and said, "For the time being, why don't you take it a little easier and do work that doesn't require such intense detail, so that you can get better?" After discussions, it was decided that the senior department head should take over Mr. Ohashi's duties as Business Department line director.*

*Nevertheless, Mr. Ohashi's complexion looked much healthier. He now travels from his house in Edogawa Ward to Dr. Nakano's clinic in central Tokyo by motorcycle (trains still give him headaches). He came to the interview by bike. He seemed more youthful and full of life than before. He was even smiling. But as he himself says, pain is invisible, and known only to the sufferer.*

Since February I've been getting into the office by 8:30, coming home around 3:00. I have headaches all day. They come in waves, mounting and receding. It hurts right now and will no doubt last a long time. It feels like a heavy weight bearing down, covering my head, like a mild hangover, all day, every day.

For a week or two in late August to early September, the pain was especially bad. I just got by with headache tablets and ice packs. My boss told me to just work mornings and go home, but the headaches haven't gotten any better. It's chronic, but I'm used to it. It's over here on the left now, but other days it comes on the right or all over . . .

This year I've been getting a processing system up and running for making car-repair estimates based on my twenty years' experience. If only the computer screen were monochrome green—I find that three or four colors make my eyes hurt. Focusing is also difficult. If I'm looking one way and someone calls me and I turn around suddenly, it hits me like a sledgehammer. This happens all the time—a shooting pain in the back of my eyes. As if I were being skewered. When it's very bad there have been times I've contemplated suicide. I almost think I'd be better off dead.

I've been to eye specialists, but they can't find anything wrong. Only one doctor told me, "Farmers sometimes get this, too." Apparently mixing up organic fertilizers damages their nerves, causing the same symptoms.

But here it is the end of summer, and my head is still killing me. The company still lets me go into work, but I've been relieved of my managerial responsibilities. My boss says that a high-stress workplace would be bad for me physically, but the result of this special treatment is that it's extremely hard for me to perform like a businessman in his prime. I'm grateful they want me to take it easy, and after the gas attack I did work harder than usual. Not wanting to inconvenience the company, I kept my headaches a secret and, well, overworked, but I'm not the type of person who can just sit idly by.

To be honest, my present position leaves me twiddling my thumbs. They even moved my desk. I go to the office and there's nothing much for me to do. I'll sit by myself and tally up slips, work that anyone could do. But having gained all this experience up to now, I can't very well not work.

Sometimes I think up different proposals on my own, regardless of whether they'll work or not. Realistically, though, not knowing if this pain will ever go away completely, or how long I'll have to keep living like this, I can't see any future. I'm working now from morning until noon and then I'm exhausted.

Because of my accident benefits, they've had to cut my bonus to 2.5 million yen a year, which is quite a squeeze financially. Bonuses are really important to a salaryman. They barely make up for the month-to-month shortcomings. I just had a new house built and there's a thirty-year loan to pay back. I'll be 70 then.

I know I don't appear to be in constant pain, but imagine wearing a heavy stone helmet, day in, day out . . . I doubt it makes much sense to anyone else. I feel very isolated. If I'd lost an arm, or was reduced to a vegetable, people could probably sympathize more. If only I'd died then, how much easier it would have been. None of this nonsense. But when I think of my family, I have to go on . . .

## "That day and that day only
## I took the first door"

### Soichi Inagawa (64)

*Mr. Inagawa's gray hair is thinning slightly, but combed neatly in place. His cheeks are red, though he's not especially plump. More than ten years ago he became diabetic and has been watching his diet ever since. Yet he still has his drinking companions and is especially fond of sake.*

*He wears a well-pressed charcoal gray three-piece suit and speaks clearly and succinctly. You can tell he prides himself on his working life up to now, having worked throughout Japan's postwar decades.*

*He was born in Kofu, a provincial city in the mountains, two hours west of Tokyo. After graduating from a vocational high school for electricians, he joined a Tokyo construction company in 1949. In time he moved from the construction site to an office and, at 60, he retired as Business Division director. He had other job offers, but "all of a sudden I got fed up with bosses." He and two friends his age decided to set up their own business dealing in lighting equipment. The office is located directly above Shin-nakano Station.*

*Business is steady though not especially busy, "But it still feels great not having to answer to anyone else." He and his wife live in Ichikawa, across Tokyo Bay to the east in Chiba Prefecture. Their two children have left home and they have three grandchildren, the youngest born a month after the gas attack.*

*He always carries two lucky charms his wife gave him—not that he really believes in that sort of thing . . .*

•   •   •

I leave the house at 7:25 and get to work by 8:40. Office hours are supposed to start at 9:00, but since it is my company I'm not so strict about it.

On March 20 I got a seat from Ochanomizu. I changed at Shinjuku to the Marunouchi Line, and again I managed to get a seat. I always travel in the third car from the front.

That day I sat in the first seat of the third car. Then I saw a puddle in the area between the rows of seats. This big pool was spreading, as if a liquid had leaked out. It was the color of beer and smelled funny. In fact it stank, which is why I noticed it.

That day the train was surprisingly empty. Not a soul standing, and only a few people sitting. Thinking back on it now, that strange smell had probably kept them away.

One thing bothered me: a man sitting alone right next to the puddle. I thought he was sleeping when I got on, but gradually his posture was slipping in a very odd way. "Strange, is he ill or what?" Then, just before Nakano-sakaue, I heard a thud. I was reading my book, but I looked up and saw the man had fallen right out of his seat and was lying on the floor faceup.

"This is terrible," I thought, trying to size up the situation. The train was almost at the station. As soon as the door opened a crack, I jumped out. I wanted to fetch help, when a young man ran past me to the front of the platform and summoned a station attendant.

There was a woman sitting across from the man who fell over and she was apparently flat out too. She was somewhere around 40 or 50. I'm really bad with women's ages. Anyway, a middle-aged woman. The man was fairly elderly. The station attendant managed to drag the man off the train, then another came running, lifted up the woman, and carried her out, saying, "Are you all right?" I just stood watching on the platform.

While all this was happening, a station attendant had picked up a bag of liquid and brought it out onto the platform. No one had any idea it was sarin, it was just something suspicious to be disposed of. Then I got back on the train and it moved off again. I moved to the next car down, as I didn't want to be where the strange smell was. I got off at the next station, Shin-nakano.

But then as I was walking along the underground passageway, I started sniffling. "Odd," I thought, "am I coming down with a cold?" The next thing I knew I was sneezing and coughing, then things started to go dim in front of my eyes. It happened almost simultaneously. "This is most odd," I thought, because I still felt perfectly all right. I was bright and aware. I could still walk.

I went straight to my office, which is right above the station, but my eyes were still dim, nose running and coughing like crazy. I told them, "I'm not feeling so well. Think I'll lie down for a bit," and stretched out on the sofa, cold towel over my eyes. A colleague of mine said a hot towel would be better, so next I tried a hot towel, and lay there for an hour, warming my eyes. And what do you know? My eyes were as good as new. I could see the blue sky again. Up until then it had been as black as night, nothing had any color.

I worked as though nothing had happened, then around 10:00 a call came from my wife saying, "There's been big trouble in the subway, are you all right?" Not wanting to worry her, I said, "Fine. Couldn't be better." Well, at least my eyes were fine.

At lunch I happened to see the TV at a soba noodle shop. What a commotion! I'd heard sirens nearby that morning, but I hadn't paid them any attention. The TV mentioned that the victim's vision goes dark, and that struck a note, but I still didn't connect my dimmed vision with those strange-smelling packets.

I went to Nakano General Hospital to have my eyes tested. As soon as they saw my contracted pupils they shot me up with an antidote and put me on an IV. Blood tests showed my cholinesterase level was way down. They hospitalized me straightaway, and I wasn't to be released until my cholinesterase was back to normal.

I phoned the office to tell them: "It's like this and I have to be hospitalized for I don't know how many days. Sorry to trouble you, but could you tidy up my desk?" I called home too, and my wife lays into me, saying, "What was all that about being perfectly fine?" (laughs)

I was in the hospital six days and felt hardly any pain all that time. The sarin had been right there next to me, yet my symptoms were miraculously light. I must have been upwind of it. Air flows through a train car from front to back, so I'd have been in a real fix if I'd sat at the back, even if only for a few stops. I suppose that's what you call Fate.

Afterward I wasn't scared to travel on the subway. No bad dreams either. Maybe I'm just dull-witted and thick-skinned. But I do feel it was Fate. Usually I don't go in through the first door nearest the front. I always use the second, which would have put me downwind of the sarin. But that day and that day only I took the first door, for no special reason. Pure chance. In my life up to now I never once felt blessed by the hand of Fate—nor cursed either, just nothing at all. I've had a pretty dull, ordinary sort of life . . . then something like this comes along.

## "If I hadn't been there, somebody else would have picked up the packets"

## Sumio Nishimura (46)

*Mr. Nishimura is a Subway Authority employee working at Nakano-sakaue Station. His title is Transport Assistant. On the day of the gas attack, he removed the packets of sarin from the Marunouchi Line train.*

*Mr. Nishimura lives in Saitama Prefecture. He got his job with the subway through the intervention of a friend. Railroad jobs were said to be "solid" work, much respected in the countryside, so he was overjoyed when he passed his employment exam in 1967.*

*Of average height, he's a little on the skinny side. Yet his complexion is good, his eyes steady and attentive. If I found myself sitting next to him at a bar, I probably wouldn't guess his profession. Not an office job—that much is apparent—he's worked his way up on-site, a self-made man. A closer look at his face would reveal that his job involved a fair amount of daily stress. So a bottle of sake with his friends after work is a real pleasure to him.*

*Mr. Nishimura kindly agreed to tell his story, even though it was obvious he didn't really want to talk about the gas attack. Or, as he said, he'd "rather not touch it." It was a terrible event for him, of course, a nightmare he'd rather forget.*

*This was true not only for Mr. Nishimura, but probably for all the subway staff. Keeping Tokyo's underground train system running on time without hitches or accidents is their prime objective every minute of the day. They don't want to recall the day when it all went horribly wrong. This made it all the more difficult to get any kind of statement from the subway staff. At the same time they don't want the gas attack to be forgotten or their colleagues to have died in vain. My deepest thanks go to him for his cooperation in contributing this invaluable testimony.*

• • •

At the subway we have a three-way rotation: day shift, round-the-clock duty, and days off. Round-the-clock is a twenty-four-hour shift from 8:00 in the morning to 8:00 the following morning. Naturally no one is expected to stay up all the way through. We have rest intervals in the bunk room. After that we get a day off, then go back to day-shift duty. Each week has two round-the-clocks and two days off.

With round-the-clock duty we can't just leave in the morning. The rush hour peaks between 8:00 and 9:30, so we do overtime. That March 20 was the morning after my round-the-clock duty and I was on "rush-hour standby." That's when the gas attack happened.

The day fell between holidays, a Monday; the same number of passengers as usual. Ogikubo-bound Marunouchi Line trains all suddenly empty out after passing Kasumigaseki. From Ikebukuro to Kasumigsaseki passengers keep boarding thick and fast, but after that it's just people getting off and no one getting on.

Rush-hour standby involves overseeing the train crew's operations, checking that there are no irregularities, seeing that the crew change goes smoothly, that the train isn't late; supervising, really.

Train A777 arrived on time at Nakano-sakaue at 8:26. When it pulled in, a passenger called over a station attendant, who then shouted across to an attendant over on the Ikebukuro platform, "Get over here quick, there's something wrong!"

I was about fifty yards away on the same platform and couldn't quite catch what he said, but it seemed something was up, so I hurried on over. Even if an irregularity's reported, the other attendant has the tracks in between and can't just hop over. That's why I went. I entered the third car from the front through the farthest back of the three doors and saw a sixty-five-year-old man sprawled on the floor. Opposite him, a fifty-year-old woman had slid off her seat. They were panting, gasping, bloodstained pink foam coming out of their mouths. The man seemed totally unconscious at first glance. The thought flashed through my mind: "Ah, a double love suicide." But of course they weren't; it was just a fleeting impression. The man died later. The woman, I hear, is still in a coma.

There were only those two in the car. No one else. The man on the floor, the woman on the seat opposite, and two packets in front of the nearest door. I spotted them the minute I got inside. Plastic pouches about thirty centimeters square, with liquid inside. One was puffed up, the other had collapsed. And this sticky-looking liquid had flowed out.

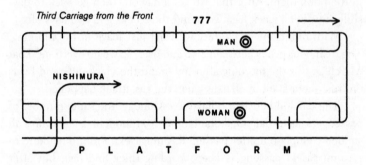

There was a smell, but I really can't begin to describe it. At first I told everyone it was like paint thinner, but actually it was more like a burnt smell. Oh, well, no matter how many times they ask me, I never know what to say. It just stank.

Soon other station attendants came running and we carried out the fallen passengers. We have only one stretcher, so we carried the man out first, then locked hands under the woman and set her down on the platform. Neither the driver nor the conductor on the train had any idea this situation had arisen.

So we helped the two passengers off and signaled that the train was ready to leave. "Take her out," just to move it on. You can't let a train sit still for long. There was no time to wipe the floor. But there's that strange smell, the floor's wet, so we had to get them to clean it up in Ogikubo at the end of the line. I rang Ogikubo Station, saying, "777 car number 3's floor needs cleaning, can you take care of it?" But gradually everyone is starting to feel ill, both attendants and passengers. This was about 8:40.

It's five stops from Nakano-sakaue to Ogikubo. The train takes twelve minutes. Train 777 was a switchback, numbered 877 on the return. But the passengers who boarded the 877 at Ogikubo were feeling funny too. They were mopping the car floor at Ogikubo—I think they were still cleaning it while the train was heading back this way—and what happens? Everyone who is cleaning starts to feel sick too. Likewise the passengers riding from Ogikubo to Shin-koenji. Word came down, "There's something wrong with that train."

Let's see, this time I think quite a lot of passengers got on at Ogikubo. The seats are generally all taken, some people standing. We knew we had to check the train this time, so we were waiting for 877 to reach Nakano-sakaue, scheduled for 8:53. But they took it out of service at Shin-koenji.

Well, after we carried out the two passengers, I picked up the plastic sarin packets with my fingers and put them on the platform. They were the sort of square, plastic packs they use for intravenous drips. I was wearing white nylon gloves, like we always wear on patrol duty. I tried to avoid touching the wet parts.

I assumed the man and woman had used these to commit suicide, so I thought, "These are dangerous objects, better report them to the police." I saw a newspaper tucked up on a shelf above the seats, so I grabbed that and placed the sarin packets on top, then lifted the whole thing out onto the platform. Set it down by a column on the platform. Then an attendant came out with a white plastic bag like you get at the supermarket. We dumped the sarin packets in that and tied up the bag. The attendant carried it to the station office and left it there. I didn't realize, but he apparently put it in a bucket near the door.

Soon passengers were complaining of feeling poorly, so we took them to the office; and not only them, but now many of the station staff were ill. The police and fire department showed up to ask about the circumstances, and they soon realized something strange was going on. At that point we took the bag outside. The police disposed of it somewhere, if memory serves.

When I went to the office to phone, I didn't actually realize it yet, but my nose was running and my eyes were acting funny. They didn't hurt, they were just blurred and tingled. I couldn't see very well. If I tried to focus, then they hurt like mad. It felt fine looking around in a fog, but focus on anything and it hurt. After a while the fluorescent lights and everything began to flare.

Around 8:55 I began to feel dizzy from the glare and it was about 9:00 when I went to the bathroom to wash my face, then lay down in a bunk room for a while. Because the outbreak on the Hibiya Line was earlier, it was about this time that we learned of other problems elsewhere, as well. By now everyone was panicking. It was getting full coverage on TV.

I was feeling ill, so I left the station. Ambulances were racing around the Nakano-sakaue intersection, having a devil of time rounding up all the patients to ferry them away. It was difficult finding an ambulance to take me. They were even using Special Mobile Task Force police vans for ambulances. You know, the ones with the wire screens. They took me in one of those. It was around 9:30 when I reached the hospital. Six of the Nakano-sakaue staff were taken to the hospital and two hospitalized, myself included.

At Nakano General Hospital they already knew that sarin was probably the cause, and they treated me for that: washed my eyes, gave me an immediate transfusion. I had to write my name and address in the register, but I couldn't see to write, so I scribbled as best I could out of focus.

I ended up six days in the hospital. March 20 was pretty grueling. I was tired out, with only the clothes I was wearing, and all the tests for this and that. My blood cholinesterase was abnormally low. It took three to four months of continual blood transfusions to bring it back to normal, and until then my irises wouldn't open properly. Contracted pupils, a lot worse in my case than others. My pupils remained contracted until my discharge. I'd look at a light and wince at the glare.

My wife came racing over to the hospital, but to be frank, I wasn't in any real life-or-death condition. No very severe symptoms or anything. I hadn't passed out. Only my eyes hurt and my nose ran.

Rough nights at the hospital, though. Lying there, my whole body felt cold as ice. I have no idea whether it was a dream or reality, but anyway it was vivid enough. It occured to me to push the call button for the nurse, but I just couldn't press the thing. I was in pain, groaning. That happened twice. Waking up with a start, trying to press the button, and failing.

Considering I lifted the packets of sarin by hand, I'm lucky to get away with such minor symptoms. Or perhaps it had something to do with the direction of the wind in the tunnel. Probably it was all to do with the way I picked them up so that I didn't inhale the fumes directly, because there were others who picked up the stuff the same way at other stations and died. I'm a heavy drinker, and some of the guys at the office say that's what saved me. That it was harder for me to become intoxicated. Well, maybe.

It never really hit me that I might have died there and then. I slept days, couldn't watch TV. Nights I was bored silly with nothing to do, but luckily the physical pain went away early on, so I wasn't depressed or anything. On March 25 I was discharged, then I rested at home until April 1; after that I went back on the job. I got bored hanging around at home, so I thought it was about time to get out and work.

To tell the truth, I didn't feel any anger toward the Aum perpetrators at first. When you're on the receiving end it doesn't much matter who did it. If someone hits you, you know how to respond. But, of course, as more things have come to light I've been outraged. To launch an indiscriminate attack on defenseless people, it's unforgivable. Because of them, two of my colleagues lost their lives. If the criminals were brought in front of me, I don't know if I could stop myself beating them to a pulp. I think the criminals should get the death penalty, sure. There are those who argue for the abolition of the death penalty, but after all they did, well, how can they go pardoned?

As for picking up the sarin packets, I just happened to be there at the time. If I hadn't been there, somebody else would have picked up the packets. Work means you fulfill your duties. You can't look the other way.

## "I was in pain, yet I still bought
## my milk as usual"

### Koichi Sakata (50)

*Mr. Sakata was born in Shinkyo (present-day Changchun)
in Japanese-occupied Manchuria, but now lives in Futamatagawa, southwest of Tokyo. He, his wife, and his
mother live in a bright, tastefully renovated house.*

*A full-time accountant, Mr. Sakata is exceedingly
meticulous about filing his papers. Any question I asked
would summon a related clipping, receipt, or memo from
a folder without the least searching or shuffling. If he kept
his home so orderly, I could just imagine his desk at work.*

*He enjoys a game of go, and he's a keen golfer—though
he's so busy at work he makes it to the course maybe only
five times a year. He's in good shape and has never once
been ill—until he was hospitalized with sarin poisoning.*

●　　●　　●

I've worked eleven years for —— Oil. We're tarmac specialists. In
my last company we had problems with the management. They
rubbed everyone the wrong way, so we all bailed out together:
"One—two—three—jump!" And we built up this company from
scratch.

Am I busy? Not as much as before during the "Bubble." Now,
the property market's in a downturn. Then there was the deregula-
tion of the petroleum industry. Our suppliers can now access
cheaper oil coming in from overseas and we have to start thinking
about restructuring.

I leave the house at 7:00 and dash to the station about a mile
away in twenty minutes. For exercise, you understand. My blood
sugar's been high lately, so I thought the walk would do me good.
From Futamatagawa it's the Sotetsu Line to Yokohama, then the
Yokosuka Line to Tokyo, and from there I take the Marunouchi Line

to Shinjuku-sanchome. The commute takes about an hour and a half. I always find a seat from Ginza or Kasumigaseki, so it's no strain.

On the day of the gas attack my wife had gone back to her family's house. Her father had died. I think it was the hundredth-day observances over his ashes. So she wasn't home. I left as usual and changed to the Marunouchi Line at Tokyo Station. I boarded the third car from the front, the one I always travel in when I have to buy milk.

That's right, when I buy milk I always get off at Shinjuku-gyoemmae. I drink milk at lunch, and every other day I buy two days' worth on my way in in the morning at a nearby store. If I don't buy any, I get off at Shinjuku-sanchome. My office is located between Shinjuku-gyoemmae and Shinjuku-sanchome. That day was my milk day, thanks to which, I got caught up in this sarin business. Just my luck.

That day I got a seat at Tokyo Station. If you read the written summary, the perpetrator, Hirose, first boarded the second car, then got off halfway and switched to the third car. He punctured the sarin packets at Ochanomizu, so they were right where I was sitting, by the middle door of the third car. I was too wrapped up in reading *Diamond Weekly* to notice anything. The detective grilled me later: How could I not notice? But, well, I didn't. I felt like I was a suspect or something—not nice, let me tell you.

Soon though, I began to feel funny. It was around Yotsuya Station I first felt sick. My nose ran all of a sudden. I thought I'd caught a cold, because I started to feel empty-headed, too, and everything before my eyes grew dark, like I had sunglasses on.

At the time I was scared it was some kind of brain hemorrhage. I'd never experienced anything like it before, so I naturally thought the worst. This wasn't just a cold; it was a lot more serious. I felt as though I might keel over any minute.

I don't remember much about the others in the car. I was too concerned about myself. Anyway, somehow I made it to Shinjuku-gyoemmae and got off. I was dizzy; everything was black. "I'm done for," I thought. Walking was a terrific struggle. I had to grope my way up the steps to the exit. Outside it might as well have been night-time. I was in pain, yet I still bought my milk as usual. Strange, isn't it? I went into the AM/PM store and bought some milk. It didn't even occur to me not to. Thinking back on it now, it's a mystery to me why I'd buy milk like that when I was in such agony.

I went to the office and stretched out on the sofa in the reception area. But I didn't feel the least bit better, and one of the women employees said I ought to go to the hospital, so around 9:00 I went to Shinjuku Hospital close by. While I was waiting, a salaryman came in saying, "I started feeling out of sorts on the subway," and I thought, "I must have the same thing too." A brain hemorrhage.

I was in the hospital for five days. I thought I was well enough to leave earlier, but my cholinesterase level still wasn't up to it. "Get good and well," the doctor told me. Even so I left early. I pleaded with them, I had a wedding to go to on Saturday. It still took me two weeks for my vision to improve. Even now my eyesight's bad. I drive, but at night the characters on the signs are hard to read. I had new glasses made, stronger ones. Recently I went to a meeting of victims and this lawyer said, "Everyone whose eyesight is worse, raise your hands," and there were plenty of people. So it must be the sarin.

Also, my memory's a lot worse. People's names just don't come. I deal with bank employees, right? I always carry a memo in my pocket: who's the director of which branch . . . Used to be that sort of thing would simply pop into my mind. Also I'm a go enthusiast, and used to play a game in the office at lunchtime. But now I can barely concentrate. It's worrying, I tell you. And this is only the first year—what's going to happen after two or three years? Is it going to stay like this, or is it going to get progressively worse?

I don't feel especially angry toward the individual culprits. It seems to me they were used by their organization. I see Asahara's face on television and for some reason I'm not filled with animosity. Instead I wish they'd do more to help the really badly affected victims.

86

## "The night before the gas attack, the family was saying over dinner, 'My, how lucky we are'"

### "Tatsuo Akashi" (now 37)
#### elder brother of critically injured "Shizuko Akashi"

*Ms. Shizuko Akashi suffered serious injuries traveling on the Marunouchi Line. She was temporarily reduced to a vegetative condition and at present remains in hospital care. Her brother, Tatsuo, works at a car dealership in Itabashi, north Tokyo. He is married with two children.*

*After his sister's collapse, he and his elderly parents took it in turn to visit Shizuko in the hospital. He saw to Shizuko's every need, with admirable devotion. As head of the family, his outrage toward this senseless crime is beyond words. You can sense it in your skin just talking to him. Behind his peaceful smile and softly spoken voice there is a reserve of bitterness and stubborn determination.*

*What had his earnest, gentle, devoted sister—who asked nothing more than a little corner of happiness—ever done to be struck down by those people? Until the day that Shizuko can walk out of the hospital on her own feet, Tatsuo will no doubt keep asking himself this difficult question.*

• • •

We're the only two siblings, born four years apart. My own two kids are also four years apart and my mother says they act just like we did. Which I suppose means we fought a lot (*laughs*), though I don't remember fighting much. Maybe over little things—what TV channel to watch, who got the last piece of cake . . . But my mother says whenever Shizuko got candy or something to eat, she would always be sure to say, "Give some to big brother, too." But then, come to mention it, so does my little girl.

Shizuko was always a helpful soul. At kindergarten or school, if some other kid was crying, she'd always go and ask, "What's the matter?" And she was painstaking by nature. She kept a diary up until junior high school. Never missed a day's entry. She filled three whole notebooks.

When she finished junior high, she decided not to go to high school and went to a dressmaking academy instead. Our parents were getting old, she said, so rather than studying any longer, she wanted to find work quickly and lighten their load. When I heard that I remember thinking, "You've got more moral strength than me." She was a serious child. Or rather, she always seemed to think things through to the end. She could never just rush something through and be done with it.

So she went to a dressmaking academy, then got a job sewing, but unfortunately the company was mismanaged and went under. That was after three or four years. She looked around for another job where she could continue to use her seamstress skills, but nothing came up. So she went to work at a supermarket. She was kind of disappointed, but she wasn't the sort to take off on her own and leave her parents in the lurch, and that was the only job she could find nearby.

She worked there for ten years. She took the bus to the supermarket and worked checkout mostly. Ten years on the job, she became a kind of veteran. Even now, after two years in the hospital, she's still officially listed as a full employee. And the supermarket's been a great help since the attack too.

Actually, on that day, she was supposed to attend an employee-training seminar over in Suginami [*west Tokyo*]. In April, the new trainees would be coming and Shizuko was down to help instruct them. She'd gone to the seminar the previous year, too, and apparently her boss had asked her to go again.

The day before the gas attack—Sunday, March 19—we'd gone to buy a backpack for my son, who was going to be entering grade school. My wife and I, my parents, and the kids all went out shopping together. Just after noon we all dropped by the supermarket to take Shizuko out to lunch at a nearby noodle shop. Supermarkets are always busy on Sundays and she can't usually take time off, but somehow that day she got free and we all ate out together.

That's when she mentioned, "Tomorrow there's this thing in Suginami I have to go to." So I said, "Okay, I'll drop you off at the station." I had to take the kids to nursery school, then drive my wife to the station anyway. After that I'd park the car and take the train. All I had to do was give her a lift together with my wife. But she said, "It's too much trouble for you. I'll just take the local line to the Saikyo Line, then change to the Marunouchi Line." And I said, "That'll take forever. You'd be better off going straight to Kasumigaseki, then change to the Marunouchi Line." Looking back on it now, if I hadn't suggested that to Shizuko, she would probably never have suffered like this.

Shizuko liked going places. She had one really close friend from school, and the two of them would go on vacation together. But a supermarket's not like a normal company; you don't get three or four days off in a row. So she had to pick a quiet time and get someone to fill in for her before she could get away.

Another thing, she loved going to Tokyo Disneyland. She went there a few times with her best friend, and whenever she managed to get a Sunday off she would invite us all: "C'mon, let's go!" We still have our snapshots of those times. Shizuko only liked the thrill rides: roller coasters and that sort of thing. My wife and our eldest, that's what they like, too. Not me, though. So while the three of them went on one of those scary rides, I'd sit with my younger daughter on the merry-go-round and wait for them. Like, "You all just go have fun. I'll wait right here." Yeah, come to think of it, the place we went to most often as a family was Disneyland.

Whenever there was a special occasion, Shizuko would always buy some kind of present. Like our parents' birthdays or the kids', our wedding anniversary. She kept all those dates in her head. She remembered everyone's favorite things. She never touched a drop of alcohol, but since our parents drink, she'd study which brands were supposed to be good and come by with a bottle. She was always so exacting, so attentive to those around her. For instance, if she went on vacation somewhere, she'd be sure to bring home souvenirs or buy cookies for her colleagues at work.

She'd fret so much over personal relationships at work. She's such an earnest soul; the least little problem she'd take so much to heart. Some throwaway remark would niggle at her, things like that.

Shizuko never married, in part because she felt so responsible toward our parents. There'd been matchmaking attempts, but either the man lived too far away or she didn't want to leave our parents behind, so in the end nothing came of it. I'd gotten married and left home, so I suppose she had a duty to look after our parents. By then Mother's knees had given out and she had to walk with a stick . . . which is what gave Shizuko such a strong sense of duty. Much stronger than mine.

Yeah, and Father's business had folded, which left him without work, so I suppose she decided to take up the extra financial burden. Shizuko was a hard worker. She'd say, "I don't need time off," and force herself to go to work.

On March 20 I passed by the old house and picked up Shizuko, then dropped her and my wife off at the station. That must have been around 7:15. Then I took the kids to nursery school just before 7:30, and walked to the station.

If Shizuko and my wife caught the 7:20, that would put her into Kasumigaseki just before 8:00, and it's a long walk between the Chiyoda Line and the Marunouchi Line, so that meant she got on the train with the sarin. And to make matters worse, she probably boarded the very car where the sarin packet was. Just once a year she took the Marunouchi Line to go to a training seminar.

She collapsed at Nakano-sakaue Station and was taken to the hospital. I heard that the station assistant who tried to give her mouth-to-mouth inhaled sarin himself and collapsed in the process. I didn't meet him, though, so I don't really know.

I learned about the gas attack through Head Office. It's on the Hibiya Line and several employees had been affected, so they called to ask if everything was all right at our end. I turned on the TV to find out what was going on and I've never seen such an uproar.

I phoned my wife straightaway, but she was okay. Then I called my mother, because if there'd been any trouble Shizuko would have called her. But there'd been no message. "She must be all right, then," I thought. "She's probably sitting in that seminar right now." Still, it made me uncomfortable not being able to get in touch with her. The timing was just right for her train to have hit the worst of it. I tried to stay calm; I knew it did no good to worry. I had taken the company car to see a client, when a call came in from the office. I was to contact my mother urgently. This was between 10:30 and 11:00. "We had a call from the police," she said. "Shizuko was injured in the subway and taken to the hospital. Go quickly!"

I rushed back to the office, took the train to Shinjuku, and reached the hospital around 12:00. I'd called from the office, but couldn't find out much about her condition over the phone: "We are not to tell members of the family anything unless they come here."

The hospital reception was filled with victims. All of them were on drips or getting examined. That's when I realized it was really serious, but I still didn't know much. The television had said something about poison gas, but nothing in detail. The doctors weren't much help either. All they told me that day was, "She inhaled a virulent chemical similar to a pesticide."

They wouldn't even let me see her straightaway. There I was hoping to see with my own eyes what state she was in, and they wouldn't tell me anything or let me into the ward. The hospital was crowded and confused, and Shizuko was in Emergency Care. I could only visit her between 12:30 and 1:00 in the afternoon, and 7:00 and 8:00 at night.

I waited for two hours—two grueling hours—and then just briefly I got to see her. She was dressed in a hospital gown and lying in bed getting dialysis. Her liver was quite weak and needed help to filter out all the toxins from her blood. She was on several intravenous drips too. Her eyes were closed. According to the nurse she was in a "sleeping state." I reached out to touch her but the doctor held me back; I wasn't wearing gloves.

I whispered in her ear, "Shizuko, it's your brother!" She twitched in response, or so I thought, but the doctor said her responding to my voice was practically unthinkable; she must have had a spasm in her sleep. She'd been having convulsions since they brought her in.

Her face, to be crude, looked more dead than asleep. She had an oxygen mask over her mouth, and her face had no expression whatsoever. No sign of pain or suffering or anything. The device that measured her heartbeat hardly flickered, just an occasional blip. She was that bad. I could hardly bear to look at her.

"To be perfectly frank," the doctor told me, "tonight is very critical. She's under complete care. Please limit your visit to this." I spent the night in the hospital waiting room in case something happened. At dawn when I asked, "How is she?" all they would say was, "She's stabilized for now."

That evening [*March* 20] our parents, my wife and kids all came to the hospital. I didn't know what to expect, so I had the kids come too, just to be safe. Of course they were too small to understand the situation, but seeing them eased my tension, or rather let me get some feelings out. "Something horrible's happened to Auntie Shizuko . . ." I started crying. My kids were upset; they knew it was serious; they'd never seen me cry before. They tried to comfort me, "Daddy, Daddy, don't cry!"—and then we were all crying. My parents are from an older generation: the stiff upper lip. They held back all the time they were at the hospital, but when they got home that evening they cried the whole night through.

I took a week off work. My wife did the same. Finally, on Wednesday, March 22, the doctor gave us a rundown on things. Her blood pressure and respiration had improved slightly and stabilized to some extent, but they were still testing her brain functions. She could still get worse.

There was no explanation about the effects of sarin. We were shown an X ray of her head and were told, "The brain's swollen." It seemed really puffed up, but whether this was due to the sarin or to prolonged oxygen starvation there was no telling as yet.

She couldn't breathe on her own, so she was hooked up to an artificial respirator. But that couldn't go on indefinitely, so on March 29 they opened a breathing valve in her throat. That's how she is now.

I visited every day while Shizuko was in the hospital in Nishi-shinjuku. Every day without fail after work, for the 7:00 visiting hours, unless I was really under the weather. My boss always had someone drive me there. I lost a lot of weight, but I kept it up for five months, until August 23 when she was moved to another hospital.

In my date book, I noted that her eyes moved on March 24. They didn't snap wide open, but rolled around slow, behind half-lifted lids. This was when I spoke to her. Again the doctor said that she wasn't looking around recognizing things. It was just another coincidence. I was warned not to raise my expectations too high. And in fact on

April 1 they said: "Judging from the pattern of brain damage due to contusions and hemorrhages in ordinary traffic accidents, there is virtually no chance of further recovery." In other words, while she wasn't a "vegetable," she would probably remain bedridden for the rest of her life. Unable to sit up, unable to speak, barely aware of anything.

It was hard to accept. My mother burst out saying, "Shizuko should have died. She'd have posed no more trouble to herself or to any of you." Those words really cut deep; I understood my mother completely, yet how could I answer her? In the end, all I could say was, "If Shizuko was of no further use, then God would have surely let her die. But that didn't happen. Shizuko is alive here and now. And there's the chance she'll get well, isn't there? If we don't believe that, Shizuko's beyond hope. We have to force ourselves to believe."

That was the hardest part for me. When my own father and mother could say such things—that Shizuko would have been better off dead—what was I supposed to say? That was about ten days after she collapsed.

Not long after that, my father had an attack. On May 6 they diagnosed cancer and he was admitted to the Kashiwa National Cancer Center for an operation. Every day I was rushing back and forth between Shizuko and my father. My mother was in no condition to move around.

In August, Shizuko was transferred to a hospital where there was a young doctor keen on therapy. And now she's progressed to the point where she can move her right hand. Little by little, she's able to move. Ask her, "Where's your mouth?" and she'll raise her right hand to her mouth.

It's still not easy for her to speak, but she seems to understand most of what we're saying. Only the doctor says he's not convinced she exactly understands the relationships between the family members. I always tell her, "It's your brother come to visit," but whether or not she knows what a "brother" is is another matter. Most of her memory has disappeared.

If I ask her, "Where were you living before?" she can only answer, "Don't know." At first our parents' names, her own age, how many brothers and sisters she had, her place of birth were all "Don't know." All she knew was her own name. But little by little she's recovering her faculties. Presently she's on two main therapy programs: physical recovery and speech recovery. She practices sitting in a wheelchair, standing on her right leg, moving her right hand, straightening her crooked leg, the vowel sounds—*a, i, u, e, o.*

She can still hardly move her mouth to eat, so they feed her through her nose straight to the stomach. The muscles in her throat are stiff. There's nothing actually wrong with her vocal cords, but the muscles that control them don't move much.

According to the doctor, the ultimate goal of therapy is for her to be able to walk out of the hospital on her own, but whether or not she'll ever make it that far he won't say. Still, I trust the hospital and the doctor, and I'm leaving everything in their hands.

Now I go the hospital every other day. It's 11:00 by the time I get home, which has me shifting between two schedules. I've put on weight, probably because I eat and drink late at night, just before bed.

Three times a week I go alone after work. Sundays the whole family goes: my mother, too. Father's back from the Cancer Center, but after long outings he gets a temperature, so he doesn't come along.

It's all on my shoulders, but it's my family, after all. My wife's the one I feel sorry for: if she hadn't married me, she wouldn't have to put up with all this. And the kids, too. If my sister was well we'd be taking vacations, going places.

But, you know, the first time Shizuko spoke, I was beside myself with joy. At first it was only a groan—*uuh*—but I cried when I heard it. The nurse cried too. And strangely enough, then Shizuko started crying and saying *uuh aah.* I have no real notion what her tears meant. According to the doctor the emotions in the brain take the unstable form of "crying out" when first expressed. So that was a first step.

On July 23 she spoke her first words in front of our parents. Shizuko cried out, "Mama." That was the first thing they'd heard her say in four months. They both cried.

This year she's been able to laugh. Her face can smile. She laughs at simple jokes, at me making farting noises with my mouth or anything like that. I'll say, "Who farted?" and she'll answer, "Brother."

She's recovered to that extent. She still can't speak too well; it's difficult to tell what she's saying, but at least she's talking.

"What do you want to do?" I ask, and she answers "Go for walk." She's developed her own self-will. She can't see much, though, only a little with her right eye.

The night before the gas attack, the family was saying over dinner, "My, how lucky we are. All together, having a good time" . . . a modest share of happiness. Destroyed the very next day by those idiots. Those criminals stole what little joy we had.

Right after the attack, I was insane with anger. I was pacing the hospital corridors pounding on the columns and walls. At that point I still didn't know it was Aum, but whoever it was I was ready to beat them up. I didn't even notice, but several days later my fist was sore. I asked my wife, "Odd, why does my hand hurt so much?" and she said, "You've been punching things, dear." I was so incensed.

But now, after nearly two years, things are a lot better thanks to everyone at my sister's company, my colleagues and my boss, the doctors and nurses. They've all been a great help.

## "Ii-yu-nii-an [Disneyland]"

## "Shizuko Akashi" (31)

*I talked to Shizuko Akashi's elder brother, Tatsuo, on December 2, 1996, and the plan was to visit her at a hospital in a Tokyo suburb the following evening.*

*I was uncertain whether or not Tatsuo would allow me to visit her until the very last moment. Finally he consented, though only after what must have been a considerable amount of anguished deliberation—not that he ever admitted as much. It's not hard to imagine how indelicate it must have seemed for him to allow a total stranger to see his sister's cruel disability. Or even if it was permissible for me as an individual to see her, the very idea of reporting her condition in a book for all the world to read would surely not go down well with the rest of the family. In this sense, I felt a great responsibility as a writer, not only toward the family but to Shizuko herself.*

*Yet whatever the consequences, I knew I had to meet Shizuko in order to include her story. Even though I had gotten most of the details from her brother, I felt it only fair that I meet her personally. Then, even if she responded to my questions with complete silence, at least I would have tried to interview her . . .*

*In all honestly, though, I wasn't at all certain that I would be able to write about her without hurting someone's feelings.*

*Even as I write, here at my desk the afternoon after seeing her, I lack confidence. I can only write what I saw, praying that no one takes offense. If I can set it all down well enough in words, just maybe . . .*

• • •

A wintry December. Autumn has slowly slipped past out of sight. I began preparations for this book last December, so that makes one

96

year already. And Shizuko Akashi makes my sixtieth interviewee—though unlike all the others, she can't speak her own mind.

By sheer coincidence, the very day I was to visit Shizuko the police arrested Yasuo Hayashi on faraway Ishigaki Island. The last of the perpetrators to be caught, Hayashi, the so-called Murder Machine, had released three packets of sarin at Akihabara Station on the Hibiya Line, claiming the lives of 8 people and injuring 250. I read the news in the early evening paper, then caught the 5:30 train for Shizuko's hospital. A police officer had been quoted as saying: "Hayashi had tired of living on the run so long."

Of course, Hayashi's capture would do nothing to reverse the damage he'd already done, the lives he had so radically changed. What was lost on March 20, 1995, will never be recovered. Even so, someone had to tie up the loose ends and apprehend him.

I cannot divulge the name or location of Shizuko's hospital. Shizuko and Tatsuo Akashi are pseudonyms, in keeping with the family's wishes. Actually, reporters once tried to force their way into the hospital to see Shizuko. The shock would surely have set back whatever progress she'd made in her therapy program, not to mention throwing the hospital into chaos. Tatsuo was particularly concerned about that.

Shizuko was moved to the Recuperation Therapy floor of the hospital in August 1995. Until then (for the five months after the gas attack) she had been in the Emergency Care Center of another hospital, where the principal mandate was to "maintain the life of the patient"—a far cry from recuperation. The doctor there had declared it "virtually impossible for Shizuko to wheel herself to the stairs." She'd been confined to bed, her mind in a blur. Her eyes refused to open, her muscles barely moved. Once she was removed to Recuperation, however, her progress exceeded all expectations. She now sits in a wheelchair and moves around the ward with a friendly push from the nurses; she can even manage simple conversations. "Miraculous" is the word.

Nevertheless, her memory has almost totally gone. Sadly, she remembers nothing before the attack. The doctor in charge says she's mentally "about grade-school level," but just what that means Tatsuo doesn't honestly know. Nor do I. Is that the overall level of her thought processes? Is it her synapses, the actual "hardware" of her thinking circuitry? Or is it a question of "software," the knowledge and information she has lost? At this point only a few things can be said with any certainty:

(1) Some mental faculties have been lost.

(2) It is as yet unknown whether they will ever be recovered.

She remembers most of what's happened to her since the attack, but not everything. Tatsuo can never predict what she'll remember and what she'll forget.

Her left arm and left leg are almost completely paralyzed, especially the leg. Having parts of the body immobilized entails various problems: last summer she had to have a painful operation to cut the tendon behind her left knee in order to straighten her crooked left leg.

She cannot eat or drink through her mouth. She cannot yet move her tongue or jaws. Ordinarily we never notice how our tongue and jaws perform complicated maneuvers whenever we eat or drink, wholly unconsciously. Only when we lose these functions do we become acutely aware of their importance. That is Shizuko's situation right now.

She can swallow soft foods like yogurt and ice cream. It has taken long months of patient practice to reach this stage. Shizuko likes strawberry yogurt, sour and sweet, but unfortunately most of her nutrition is still squeezed in by tube through her nose. The air valve that was implanted in her throat while she was hooked up to an artificial respirator still remains. It's now covered with a round metal plate—a blank souvenir of her struggle with death.

Her brother slowly pushes Shizuko's wheelchair out into the lounge area. She's petite, with hair cut short at the fringe. She resembles her brother. Her complexion is good, her eyes slightly glazed as if she has only just woken up. If it wasn't for the plastic tube coming from her nose, she probably wouldn't look handicapped.

Neither eye is fully open, but there is a glint to them—deep in the pupils; a gleam that led me beyond her external appearance to see an inner something that was not in pain.

"Hello," I say.

"Hello," says Shizuko, though it sounds more like *ehh-uoh*.

I introduce myself briefly, with some help from her brother. Shizuko nods. She has been told in advance I was coming.

"Ask her anything you want," says Tatsuo.

I'm at a loss. What on earth can I say?

"Who cuts your hair for you?" is my first question.

"Nurse," comes the answer, or more accurately, *uh-errff*, though in context the word is easy enough to guess. She responds quickly, without hesitation. Her mind is there, turning over at high speed in her head, only her tongue and jaws can't keep pace.

For a while at first Shizuko is nervous, a little shy in front of me. Not that I could tell, but to Tatsuo the difference is obvious.

"What's with you today? Why so shy?" he kids her, but really, when I think about it, what young woman wouldn't be shy about meeting someone for the first time and not looking her healthy best? And if the truth be known, I'm a little nervous myself.

Prior to the interview, Tatsuo had talked to Shizuko about me. "Mr. Murakami, the novelist, says he wants to write about you, Shizuko, in a book. What do you think about that? Is it all right with you? Is it okay if your brother tells him about you? Can he come here to meet you?"

Shizuko answered straightaway, "Yes."

Talking with her, the first thing I notice is her decisive "Yes" and "No," the speed with which she judges things. She readily made up her mind about most things, hardly ever hesitating.

I brought her yellow flowers in a small yellow vase. A color full of life. Sadly, however, Shizuko can't see them. She can make things out only in very bright sunlight. She made a small motion with her head and said, "*Uann-eyhh* [Can't tell]." I just hope that some of the warmth they brought to the room—to my eyes, at least—rubs off atmospherically on her.

She wore a pink cotton gown buttoned to the neck, a light throw over her lap from under which a stiff right hand protruded. Tatsuo, by her side, took up that hand from time to time and patted it lovingly. The hand is always there when words fail.

"Up to now, Shizuko, you've spoken in short words only," says her brother with a smile, "so from our point of view, it's been easier to understand. Recently, though, you seem to want to speak in longer sentences, so it's a bit harder for us to follow. I suppose that means you're making progress, but your mouth still can't keep up."

I can scarcely make out half of what she says. Tatsuo, of course, can discern lots more. The nurses even more still. "The nurses here

are all young and earnest and sincere. We owe them a show of gratitude," says Tatsuo. "They're nice people, isn't that right?"

"*Aayiih-ee-uh* [Nice people]," agrees Shizuko.

"But sometimes," Tatsuo continues, "when I don't understand
what Shizuko's saying, she gets really angry. You don't want me to
leave before I get what you're saying, do you? Like the last time. Isn't
that right, Shizuko?"

Silence. Embarrassed silence.

"Hey, what are you so shy about?" Tatsuo teases her. "You said so
yourself, didn't you? You wouldn't let Brother go before he understood."

At that Shizuko finally breaks into a smile. And when she smiles
she really lights up. She smiles a lot more than most people, though
perhaps she simply has less control over her facial muscles. I'd like to
imagine that Shizuko always smiled that way, it blends in so naturally
with her face. It strikes me that she and her brother probably carried
on this way as children.

"Not long ago," says Tatsuo, "Shizuko would cry and complain—
'No, don't go!'—when it was time for me to leave. Each time I
repeated the same thing until she gradually stopped fussing: 'Brother
has to go home or else the kids will be lonely from waiting. It's not
just you, you know, ——— and ——— get lonely too.' Eventually
Shizuko got what I was saying, which is great progress, isn't it?
Though it must get awfully lonely being left here, I admit."

Silence.

"Which is why I'd like to visit the hospital more often and spend
longer talking to my sister," says Tatsuo. In actual fact, however, it's
hard enough for Tatsuo to visit the hospital every other day. He has
to travel fifty minutes each way back and forth from work.

After work Tatsuo sits with his sister for an hour and talks. He
holds her hand, spoon-feeds her strawberry yogurt, coaches her in
conversation, fills up the blank spaces in her memory little by little:
"We all went there and this is what we did . . ."

"When the memories we share as a family get cut off and lost
like this," he says, "that's the hardest thing to accept. It's as if it has
been cut away with a knife. . . . Sometimes when I'm going back over
the past with her, my voice starts to quaver, then Shizuko asks me,
'Brother, you okay?'"

Hospital visiting hours officially end at 8 P.M., but they're less strict with Tatsuo. After the visit, he collects Shizuko's laundry, drives the car back to the office, walks five minutes to the subway, and travels another hour, changing three times before he gets back home. By the time he gets there the kids are asleep. He's kept up this regimen for a year and eight months now. He'd be lying if he said he wasn't exhausted; and no one can honestly say how much longer he'll have to continue.

Hands on the steering wheel on the way back, Tatsuo says: "If this had been caused by an accident or something, I could just about accept it. There'd have been a cause or some kind of reason. But with this totally senseless, idiotic criminal act . . . I'm at my wits' end. I can't take it!" He barely shakes his head, silencing any further comment from me.

"Can you move your right hand a little for me?" I ask Shizuko. And she lifts the fingers of her right hand. I'm sure she's trying, but the fingers move very slowly, patiently grasping, patiently extending. "If you don't mind, would you try holding my hand?"

"*O-eh* [Okay]," she says.

I place four fingers in the palm of her tiny hand—practically the hand of a child in size—and her fingers slowly enfold them, as gently as the petals of a flower going to sleep. Soft, cushioning, girlish fingers, yet far stronger than I had anticipated. Soon they clamp tight over my hand in the way that a child sent on an errand grips that "important item" she's not supposed to lose. There's a strong will at work here, clearly seeking some objective. Focused, but very likely not on me; she's after some "other" beyond me. Yet that "other" goes on a long journey and seems to find its way back to me. Please excuse this nebulous explanation, it's merely a fleeting impression.

*Something* in her must be trying to break out. I can feel it. A precious something. But it just can't find an outlet. If only temporarily, she's lost the power and means to enable to it to come to the surface. And yet that *something* exists unharmed and intact within the walls of her inner space. When she holds someone's hand, it's all she can do to communicate that "this thing is here."

She keeps holding my hand for a very long time, until I say, "Thank you," and slowly, little by little, her fingers unfold.

"Shizuko never says 'hurt' or 'tired,'" Tatsuo tells me driving back later. "She does therapy every day: arm-and-leg training, speech-training, various other programs with specialists—none of it easy, it's tough going—but when the doctor or nurses ask her if she's tired, only three times has she ever said 'Yes.' Three times.

"That's why—as everyone involved agrees—Shizuko has recovered as much as she has. From being unconscious on an artificial respirator to actually talking, it's like something out of a dream."

"What do you want to do when you get well?" I think to ask her.

"*Aeh-ehh,*" she says. I don't understand.

"'Travel,' maybe?" suggests Tatsuo after a moment's thought.

"*Ehf* [Yes]," concurs Shizuko with a nod.

"And where do you want to go?" I ask.

"*Ii-yu-nii-an.*" This no one understands, but with a bit of trial and error it becomes clear she means "Disneyland."

"*Ehf,*" says Shizuko with an emphatic nod.

It's not easy to associate "travel" with "Disneyland." Anyone who lives in Tokyo would not generally consider an outing to Tokyo Disneyland "travel." But in her mind, lacking an awareness of distance, going to Disneyland must be like some great adventure. It's no different, conceptually, than if we were to set out, say, for Greenland. For a fact, going to Disneyland would be a more difficult undertaking for her in practice than for us to travel to the ends of the earth.

Tatsuo's two children—eight and four—remember going to Tokyo Disneyland with their auntie and tell her about it each time they visit the hospital: "It was really fun," they say. So Disneyland as a place has become fixed in her mind as something like a symbol of freedom and health. Nobody knows if Shizuko can actually remember having been there herself. It may only be a later implanted memory. After all, she doesn't even remember her own room where she lived for so long.

Real or imaginary, however, Disneyland is a distinct place in her mind. We can get close to that image, but we can't see the view she sees.

"You want to go to Disneyland with the whole family?" I ask her.

"*Ehf,*" says Shizuko perkily.

"With your brother and sister-in-law and the kids?"

She nods.

Tatsuo looks at me and says, "When she can eat and drink normally with her mouth instead of that tube through her nose, then maybe we can all drive together to Disneyland again." He gives Shizuko's hand a little squeeze.

"I hope that's very very soon," I tell Shizuko.

Shizuko gives another nod. Her eyes are turned in my direction, but she's seeing "something else" beyond me.

"Well, when you get to Disneyland, what ride will you go on?" Tatsuo prompts.

"'Roller coaster'?" I interpret.

"Space Mountain!" Tatsuo chimes in. "Yeah, you always did like that one."

That evening when I visited the hospital, I'd wanted somehow to encourage her—but how? I'd thought it was up to me, but it wasn't that way at all; no need even to think about giving her encouragement. In the end, it was she who gave *me* encouragement.

In the course of writing this book, I've given a lot of serious thought to the Big Question: what does it mean to be alive? If I were in Shizuko's place, would I have the willpower to live as fully as she? Would I have the courage, or the persistence and determination? Could I hold someone's hand with such warmth and strength? Would the love of others save me? I don't know. To be honest, I'm not so sure.

People the world over turn to religion for salvation. But when religion hurts and maims, where are they to go for salvation? As I talked to Shizuko I tried to look into her eyes now and then. Just what did she see? What lit up those eyes? If ever she gets well enough to speak unhindered, that's something I'd want to ask: "That day I came to visit, what did you see?"

But that day is still far off. Before that comes Disneyland.

# TOKYO METROPOLITAN SUBWAY:

## MARUNOUCHI LINE

### (Destination: Ikebukuro)

#### TRAIN B801/A801/B901

• • •

Two men were assigned to drop sarin gas on the Ikebukuro-bound Marunouchi Line: Masato Yokoyama and Kiyotaka Tonozaki.

Yokoyama was born in 1963 in Kanagawa Prefecture, south of Tokyo. He was 31 at the time of the attack. A graduate in Applied Physics from Tokai University Engineering Department, he took employment with an electronics firm, only to leave after three years and take vows. Of the five perpetrators, he somehow makes the least lasting impression. There are no revealing details about his character; his name hardly even comes up in other cult members' testimonies. Quiet by nature, he probably never spoke much. He was an undersecretary at Aum's Ministry of Science and Technology. Along with Hirose, he was one of the key figures behind their clandestine Automatic Light Weapon Manufacturing Scheme. It was they who devotedly "offered" Asahara their finished rifle on New Year's Day 1995. (Yokoyama has up to now—January 1997—refused to testify in court concerning the gas attack.)

Tonozaki is an equally nondescript fellow. He was born in 1964 in Aomori Prefecture in the far north. After graduating from high school he had a series of odd jobs, then took vows in 1987. He belonged to Aum's Ministry of Construction.

En route to Shinjuku Station, in a car driven by Tonozaki, Yokoyama stopped to buy a copy of *Nihon Keizai Shimbun* [a Nikkei newspaper] and wrapped two packets of sarin in it. Initially Tonozaki had bought a sports tabloid, but Yokoyama argued instead for a general-interest paper. Before getting out of the car, Yokoyama put on a wig and fake glasses.

Yokoyama boarded the 7:39 Ikebukuro-bound Marunouchi Line train departing from Shinjuku, taking the fifth car from the front. As the train slowed down approaching Yotsuya Station, he poked several times at the packet of sarin on the floor of the car with the sharpened tip of his umbrella. Yet only one packet was punctured, and then only once. The other packet remained intact. If both packets had split, the casualties on this train would have been even worse.

Yokoyama got off at Yotsuya and washed the sarin liquid from the umbrella tip in a rest room by the exit. Then he got into Tonozaki's waiting car.

At 8:30 A.M. the train reached the end of the line at Ikebukuro and started to head back in the opposite direction. Perhaps because the sarin packet was slow to release its contents there were few casualties at this point. At Ikebukuro Station all the passengers were evacuated and the empty train searched, but somehow the station attendants failed to dispose of any suspicious objects.

At 8:32 the train left Ikebukuro Station as the Shinjuku-bound A801. Almost immediately several passengers began to feel physically uncomfortable. A passenger who got off three stations later at Korakuen reported a suspicious object on board and at Hongo-sanchome, the next station, subway staff boarded the train, removed the sarin packets, and did a quick cleanup inside the car. By now Tsukiji Station on the Hibiya Line was in complete uproar.

While a large number of casualties were taken off, the sarin-contaminated car nonetheless continued as normal to Shinjuku Station, where it arrived at 9:09. Then—and this is hard to believe—the train was sent back again in the other direction as the 9:13 Ikebukuro-bound B901. It was 9:27 before they finally stopped the train at Kokkai-gijidomae Station, whereupon all passengers were evacuated and the train was put out of service. It had kept running for a good hour and forty minutes after Yokoyama punctured the sarin packet.

This brief account may give some idea of the confusion at Subway Authority Central. Although they knew that a suspicious object had been sighted on board train B801, and knew that it had caused numerous casualties, not one person thought to take the train out of service at any point.

No deaths resulted, but two hundred people were left in serious condition.

March 21, 1995. Expecting a crackdown investigation, Yokoyama and Hirose attempted to escape. Hisako Ishii gave them 5 million yen "running capital" and provided them with a car. For a time, the two drifted through various hotels and sauna bathhouses around Tokyo before finally being arrested.*

*Masato Yokoyama was sentenced to death in September 1999. He is appealing the sentence. Kiyotaka Tonozaki was sentenced to life imprisonment and is appealing the sentence. [Tr.]

## "What can that be?" I thought

### Shintaro Komada (58)

*Mr. Komada had always worked at a major city bank when, aged 50, he was transferred to an affiliated real-estate firm. When he reached the retirement age of 53 he stayed on as an employee (not that Mr. Komada looks even close to retirement age). At present he runs one of their art-gallery businesses. With no prior experience, he has developed a taste for the gallery business in his six years on the job. He enjoys cars, and drives his wife to museums on holidays.*

*The very image of a banker, he strikes me as the serious type: the hardworking, clean-living family man. And he seems just as earnest about his "second career." As he himself says, he's "patient by nature." This unfortunately meant that he patiently sat near the packets of sarin even after he began to feel ill—"Only a little farther to my station," he thought—thereby incurring serious injuries. What saved him, he says, was that he was sitting "upwind" from the sarin packets. Otherwise he'd have been a lot worse.*

•   •   •

I commute from Tokorozawa by the Seibu Line to Ikebukuro, then on the Marunouchi Line to Ginza, and from there on the Hibiya Line to Higashi-ginza. It takes an hour and twenty minutes. The trains are always crowded. The Seibu Line is particularly bad. It's an exhausting haul from Ikebukuro to Ginza, so I wait a couple of trains for an empty one. I hate fighting for a seat, so I make sure I'm at the head of the line. I usually get on at the frontmost door of the second car.

Ikebukuro is the end of the line, so when a train arrives all the passengers get off. The morning of the gas attack very few passengers got off. Some days are like that, though, so I didn't pay it any attention.

Once all the passengers are off, the station attendants check around inside. Just to make sure no one's forgotten anything. If there's nothing, then it's "All aboard."

It's such a terrible, terrible shame that the person who did the check that day where I got on was a part-timer, not a fully fledged station attendant: a young kid wearing a vest. There are lots of those student part-timers in the mornings. They wear Subway Authority vests instead of the usual green uniform. There was a parcel wrapped in newspaper by the corner of the right-hand seat, directly in front of me. I saw it with my own eyes. "What can that be?" I thought, but the station attendant just let the passengers on without doing a thing. He must have seen it too, though he'd never admit that. If only he'd removed the thing there and then, there would have been far fewer injuries. It's a real shame.

Be that as it may, the train left with the packets still on board. I just consider myself lucky that I didn't head straight to where the sarin was, but took a seat to the left instead, so I wasn't sitting "down-wind." After two or three minutes, the train pulled out.

First of all someone vomited, and I thought, "It has to be that crumpled newspaper by the corner at the door." The newspaper and the space around it were sopping wet. Whichever way you look at it that station attendant not disposing of something he had obviously seen went against all common sense. Not long after we were under way, the smell came fuming up. I've heard sarin is supposed to be odorless, but not this. It was somehow syrupy sweet. I almost thought it was perfume, not unpleasant at all. If it had smelled really bad everyone would have been in a panic. Syrupy sweet—that's what it was.

The train carries on—Shin-otsuka, Myogadani, Korakuen—and around Myogadani lots of people are beginning to cough. Of course, I'm coughing too. Everyone has his handkerchief out over his mouth or nose. A very odd scene, with everyone hacking away at the same time. As I recall, passengers started getting off at Korakuen. As if on cue, everyone was opening the windows. Eyes itching, coughing, generally miserable . . . I didn't know what was wrong with me, it was all so strange, but anyway I went on reading my newspaper like always. It's a long-standing habit.

When the train stopped at Hongo-sanchome, five or six station attendants came on board. Like they'd received word and were standing ready, "Ah, yes, here it is." They picked up the parcel with their bare hands. By now the floor was soaked with sarin, but all they did was remove the parcel and maybe give the floor a quick wipe. The train was soon under way again. At Ochanomizu another five or six station attendants got on and gave the floor a once-over with rags.

From here on I'm really coughing, so bad that I can scarcely read the newspaper. "Only a little farther to Ginza," I tell myself, "just hold on for the rest of the journey." Already I can't keep my eyes open. By Awajicho, I'm thinking to myself, "Something dreadful's happened," but I still hang on until Ginza. Somehow I just about hold it together by shutting my eyes. I didn't have a violent headache or fits of vomiting or anything like that, but my head was in a fog.

It was around the time we reached Ginza that I noticed the car interior was pitch black when I opened my eyes, as if I was sitting in a cinema. I felt dizzy when I got off at Ginza, but somehow I managed to totter up the stairs, clinging to the handrail, aware that I might fall over any second.

Ordinarily I would have transferred to the Hibiya Line, but I heard an announcement: "Due to an accident, the Hibiya Line is temporarily delayed."

"It's happened there, too," I thought. "Whatever it is. It's not just me."

One thing I want you to understand: if the pain had been really bad or I'd been vomiting or I suddenly went blind, I'd have been off that train in a flash, but it wasn't like that. It spread through my body quite slowly, so that by the time we reached Ginza I was in a terrible state. I've never had any major illness or been hospitalized. I've always been healthy. Maybe that's why I put up with it for so long.

The train kept going, even after I got off. They should have stopped it at Hongo-sanchome or Ochanomizu. The passengers were so panic-stricken, how could they not have known something was desperately wrong? After all, half an hour before I caught that train, Kasumigaseki Station was already in complete chaos. They knew they had a crisis, they should have just stopped the train and taken off all the passengers. They could have reduced the injuries. It was a serious oversight. Complete communication breakdown.

Anyway, I crawled up the stairs. I knew I had to get myself out of there or I was dead. By then I was overcome by a sense of absolute dread. I finally managed to get above ground and I knew I had to get myself to a hospital quick. I thought I'd walk to my hospital in Ginza, but it was a good distance away. If I had gone by the main avenue I might have just fallen flat on my face, so I took the backstreets: slowly, slowly, weaving like a drunk. It's so dark and hazy outside, all the while I hear ambulances and fire engines, sirens and bells. People are scrambling about. I remember thinking: "I'm in serious trouble."

I went to the office and asked one of my coworkers to accompany me to the hospital. "Come with me," I said. "I can't see to walk." There were two or three people with similar symptoms at the hospital. I told the nurse at the reception desk, "I can't see," but all she said was, "Well, this isn't an eye clinic." No comprehension whatsoever. But others came in in the same condition and soon enough the television's blaring out details on the victims' symptoms. Slowly but surely the hospital realized it had a crisis on its hands. They made makeshift beds out of the reception area sofas and began administering blood transfusions. Pretty soon there were faxes coming in with medical information.

After that I was shifted to another hospital where I stayed four nights. Little by little my eyes got better, and by the second day I could see things fairly normally, only I had a tremendous pain in my forehead and temples. I could hardly sleep at all. I'd keep waking throughout the night, getting only two or three hours' rest. I resigned myself to thinking I might never return to work at this rate. All the news I was hearing was bad. Three or four people had died or had become vegetables.

Two days after being discharged I was commuting to work again, and I assure you, I was in no shape to be back at the office! I felt lethargic and tired easily. I couldn't remember anything. Even in the monotonous day-to-day routine, I'd think, "How'd that go again?" But strange and upsetting as it all was, I had no proof it was due to the sarin. I was still nervous about the whole thing. I was uneasy about going anywhere by car. Was it really all right to be driving?

For a while I was scared to travel on the subway, but I had no choice so I forced myself. Even now I don't like it, but I have to. After experiencing something like that, the fear of going underground in a metal box and something bad happening is overpowering, but what choice does a salaryman have? There isn't any other way to get to work.

It makes me angry, furious, when I hear what that Aum gang have to say for themselves. Why did they have to indiscriminately kill totally innocent people for the likes of him [*Asahara*]? What am I supposed to do with all this rage? I'd like to see the whole lot tried, sentenced, and done away with as quickly as possible.

# *"I knew it was sarin"*

## "Ikuko Nakayama" (in her 30s)

*She made it absolutely clear from the outset: no name, no address, no age. She wanted me to obscure any identifying details. She is still extremely wary of Aum followers, especially as she lives in close proximity to an Aum training center. There could be trouble if she were traceable, she says.*

*She's thirty-something and married, with no children. After university she worked at an ordinary office job for a while, then left to become a housewife. Recently, however, she became qualified to teach Japanese to foreigners. She enjoys the work and finds it challenging.*

*Among all the sarin victims I interviewed, she was one of the very few who, in the midst of the crisis, entertained the idea that it might be sarin. Whereas most people were dragged into confusion and nightmare not knowing what was happening, Ms. Nakayama was that rare individual who actually recognized the symptoms early on: "Contraction of the pupils! It must be sarin!" Talking to her, I was struck by her calm and rational manner, her cautious insights. Her powers of observation and memory are equally impressive, and no doubt make her an extremely competent language teacher.*

*She refuses to accept the world of Aum Shinrikyo, which differs so radically from her own. "It's not fear, exactly," she says, but whatever it is, it seems it will take a little more time for her to be free of it.*

●　　●　　●

Last March when the gas attack took place was very busy for me, with classes four or five days a week for about ten hours. In fact, that was the reason I was gassed by sarin.

My student that day worked in a company in Otemachi, which I get to on the Marunouchi Line. The class started at 9:00. Yes, rather early, but many of them want to get the lesson finished before office hours.

That morning I left home around 8:00, and took the 8:32 subway train from Ikebukuro Station. That way I'd be right on time for the 9:00 class. Get off at Otemachi, up the stairs, perfect.

Ikebukuro Station is the end of the Marunouchi Line, so empty trains sit waiting to depart on either side of the platform. That day the train was waiting on the left-hand side, with a lot of people on board already. People were lining up on the right-hand side, but that train still hadn't arrived. I decided I'd still be in time if I waited for the next train. They usually come in at two- or three-minute intervals. I felt a little run-down, so I wanted a seat.

The train pulled in, and I got on at the first door of the second car and sat on the right-hand side. The train started moving toward Shin-otsuka. Trains in Japan are quiet in the morning, right? The passengers hardly say a word. Quiet as it was, though, there were a lot of people coughing. "Uh-oh," I thought, "everyone's coming down with colds!"

Well, the Marunouchi Line gradually heads above ground after Shin-otsuka: Myogadani, Korakuen . . . at Myogadani Station, the exit's at the Ikebukuro end of the platform, so not many commuters get off at that station. Only that day, strangely enough, a lot of people got off. "That's odd," I thought, but I didn't pay much attention.

People were still coughing away like before, and the car interior looked awfully bright—or what I took at the time to be brightness, though thinking back on it later, it was yellow, or rather a light pearl tinged with yellow. I've fainted from anemia before, and it was like that. You'd have to have experienced it yourself.

Gradually it began to feel suffocating inside. It was a new car, so I thought the smell had something to do with the new materials or glue or something. So I turned around and opened the window. But no one else was opening their windows. I paused, then opened another.

I've always had a weak respiratory system, I get terrible sore throats and coughing when I catch a cold. Maybe that's also why I'm so sensitive to synthetics. It was still March and not warm outside, but I couldn't bear not to open the windows. I didn't see how the other passengers could put up with that strange smell. No, not strange . . .

It wasn't a pungent smell. How can I explain? It was more of a sensation, not a smell, a "suffocatingness." I opened the windows to get some ventilation. This must have been between Myogadani and Korakuen. When the train stopped at both those stations, lots of passengers got off, but there was no reaction whatsoever from anyone to my turning around to open the windows. No one said a thing, everyone was so quiet. No response, no communication. I lived in America for a year, and believe me, if the same thing had happened in America there would have been a real scene. With everyone shouting, "What's going on here?" and coming together to find the cause.

Later, when the police asked me, "Didn't people start to panic?" I thought back on it: "Everyone was so silent. No one uttered a word."

The people who got off the train were all coughing on the platform. I could see them through the train window.

After Korakuen it got more and more suffocating, the yellow tone more and more intense. I began to think, "I'll never make it to work today." Still, I thought, I should do my best to get there. So I stayed on the train, though I decided to switch to another car once we reached Hongo-sanchome Station. By then the car had really emptied out, vacant seats here and there. Which is truly unheard of! Usually the trains are packed at this hour of the morning.

I decided to exit by the middle or rear door. I couldn't stand it anymore. Suddenly I saw this man wearing a policeman's uniform and white gloves enter the car one door ahead of me, lift up a newspaper-wrapped object with both hands, like this, and carry it out. A station attendant on the platform brings out a plastic bin and in it goes. Two or three station attendants were rushing back and forth. This all took place just as I was stepping out of the car. The image of the policeman's white gloves and how he lifted up the newspaper bundle is etched on my mind even now.

The train was stationary for a long time. I moved two cars back. The car was practically empty, you could count the passengers on one hand. I felt absolutely awful. My eyes were twitching, like muscular convulsions, though they didn't hurt, but everything was yellow.

Only three people got off at Awajicho: a woman in her twenties, a man in his fifties, and me. Strange as it must seem, when I got off I thought, "This has to be sarin. My pupils are contracted, aren't they?" As part of my job, I read the newspaper thoroughly every day and watch the news without fail. I knew about the Matsumoto incident, which is when I first encountered the term "pupil contractions."*

Oddly enough, I was extremely calm. I knew it was sarin. Faced with a critical situation of unknown origin, I must have mobilized my entire stockpile of knowledge.

There were only three of us on the platform: me, the young woman, and the middle-aged man; which is unheard of for a Marunouchi Line platform at that hour! The woman sat down on a bench, her face in her hands, pressing a handkerchief to her mouth as if in pain. The man kept repeating, "Something's wrong, something's wrong," and wandering about the platform; then saying, "I can't see! I can't see!" (I heard later that he became completely paralyzed, but I don't know that for a fact.)

"This is insane," I said. "We have to get to a hospital." I somehow helped the woman up and, together with the man, we headed for the station office. The station attendant seemed flustered, but he did try to call an ambulance. The trouble was no one at the emergency number would pick up the phone. Now, that was scary. Only then did I feel real fear. Everything I'd believed up until then just crumbled.

From that moment on it was total chaos. Which is to say, the train we traveled on was later than the rest of the "sarin trains," so by then the other stations were already in a panic. Our Marunouchi Line train had already been to Ikebukuro and back with the sarin on board.

*On June 27, 1994, sarin gas was released in a neighborhood of Matsumoto, central Japan, killing seven people and injuring hundreds more. For months after the incident, the Matsumoto police singled out one of the victims, Yoshiyuki Kouno, as their prime suspect. The media dubbed him the Poison Gas Man and he received hate mail and threats against his life (while his wife lay in hospital in a vegetative state). Eventually the blame shifted to the Aum cult and Japanese officials, newspapers, and TV stations publicly apologized to Mr. Kouno. [Tr.]

One thing still bothers me, though. At Ikebukuro Station, when they clean the train and close the doors, they always inspect inside the cars. The station attendants check to see if anyone has left anything behind. Could they have accidentally missed it? If only they'd looked around more thoroughly.

There was no getting through to the emergency services over the phone, so the station attendant decided we'd better just walk. The hospital was only a two- or three-minute walk from the station. A young station attendant escorted us there. It was a good thing we got off the train when we did. If we'd gotten off at Hongo-sanchome, we'd have been with the sarin packets in a tightly enclosed space, which would have been disastrous.*

I took several months off work after the gas attack. I had trouble breathing. My job involves talking a lot, so that presented real problems. Of course, I was furious. As I said before, it was fairly obvious that Aum were the culprits . . . But to tell the truth, stronger than any anger now is the feeling that I just don't want to remember anymore. Between the time I was hospitalized and the time I was sent home I wanted to know everything that had happened; I was devouring the news on TV, but now I can't stand it. I'll change the channel. I don't ever want to see another image of the gas attack. Out of anger, out of consideration for those who were sacrificed and those who still suffer. Even now when a report touches on the gas attack, something tightens in my chest. I swear, I never want anything like this to happen ever again.

Hearing the reports on Aum, the more I learned about their background, I came to realize that there was no point in even giving them the time of day. At least now I've stopped yelling at the television screen. These people have a completely different ethic, they think differently from us, they totally believed in what they did; I just can't see there's any room for tolerance. They don't live in this world, they're from another dimension . . . once I realized that, I could contain my rage a little. Though of course, I still want to see them properly sentenced in court.

The question I hate being asked most of all is: "Do you have any

---

*Ms. Nakayama was hospitalized for five days in Emergency Care receiving specialized treatment.

aftereffects?" I'm getting on with my life in the belief that I'm fine, with no medical problems to speak of; though this is virtually a first in medical history, so that does leave uncertainties. I just can't bear anyone asking me that. Although my dislike of being asked if there are aftereffects might itself be a kind of aftereffect.

Somewhere in me there must be a wish that everything that happened could be banished to another dimension, to just hide it away somewhere. If it were possible, to banish it from the face of the earth . . .

If this were only half a year later, I'd probably have refused to be interviewed. But now being interviewed, thinking back on it, I realize I haven't traveled on that route since. Hongo-sanchome is one of my favorite places, but I haven't once been back. Not that I'm scared . . . it's just a problem for me.

# TOKYO METROPOLITAN SUBWAY:

# HIBIYA LINE

## (Departing: Naka-meguro)

### TRAIN B711T

• • •

The team of Toru Toyoda and Katsuya Takahashi planted sarin on a northeastbound Hibiya Line train leaving Naka-meguro for Tobu-dobutsu-koen (Tobu Animal Park). Toyoda was the perpetrator, Takahashi his driver-accomplice.

Toyoda was born in 1968 in Hyogo Prefecture, near Kobe, west central Japan, and was 27 at the time of the attack. One of the many science-trained "superelite" converts to Aum, he studied applied physics at Tokyo University Science Department and graduated with honors. Progressing to an elite postgraduate laboratory, he completed his master's and was about to go on to doctoral studies, when he threw it all away and took vows.

Within the cult hierarchy, Toyoda belonged to the Chemical Brigade under the Ministry of Science and Technology.

On the defendant's bench at his trial, his hair was close-cropped and he wore a white shirt and black jacket. He glowered at everyone, his sharp cheekbones accentuating his thin face. It was the severe scowl of a serious young student. There's a certain courage, a fiery "seeker-after-truth" streak about him. He's the type that never rests once he has set his mind on something—he likes to see things through to the end. Or perhaps he is more the type of person willing to martyr himself for a principle. He's sharp-witted, but is apparently interested only in direct, quantifiable objectives.

A longtime practitioner of Shaolin kick-boxing, he keeps his backbone amazingly straight. Chin down, face turned to the front, eyes closed ever so slightly (or politely) as if in meditation—throughout the entire trial proceedings, he maintained that posture and never let it slip. Once only, when there was some unusual movement in the courtroom, did he gently open his eyes, and even then his gaze never met anyone else's. His bearing seemed that of an ascetic undergoing the strictest discipline—or perhaps he actually was in training the whole time.

The contrast could not have been more marked between Toyoda and the spoiled, self-satisfied Ken'ichi Hirose seated next to him. There was just no knowing what Toyoda was thinking or feeling. It was as if he'd absolutely blocked out any wavering of emotion by sheer force of will.

On March 18 Toyoda received his gas attack orders from his superior at the Ministry of Science and Technology, Hideo Murai. Until then he had been involved with the cult's Automatic Light Weapons Development Scheme and had dirtied his hands in various illegal activities, but even he was shocked by the plan to release sarin on the subway. With his abundant knowledge of chemistry and having also participated in the secret manufacture of sarin at Satyam No. 7, he could easily imagine the tragic consequences of the plan. It was nothing short of random mass slaughter. And he was being asked to take part himself.

Naturally Toyoda anguished over the possibilities. To an ordinary person with normal human feelings, even entertaining the notion of such an outrageous act must seem inconceivable, but Toyoda could not criticize a command from his master. It was as if he'd climbed into a car that was about to plummet down a steep hill at breakneck speed. At this point he lacked both the courage and the judgment to bail out and avoid the coming destruction.

All Toyoda could do—and this is exactly what his colleague Hirose did as well—was adhere to the teachings ever more zealously, to crush all doubts; in short, to shut down his feelings. Rather than leaping out of a speeding car by his own will and judgment, then having to face the consequences, it was far easier just to obey. Toyoda steeled his nerves. Resolution, rather than faith, would see him through.

Toyoda left Aum's Shibuya *ajid* at 6:30 in the morning, and headed southwest in a car driven by Takahashi toward Naka-meguro Station on the Hibiya Line. On the way he purchased a copy of *Hochi Shimbun* and wrapped his two plastic packets of sarin in it.

His assigned train was B711T, departing at 7:59 for Tobu-dobutsu-koen. He boarded the first car, taking a seat near the door. As usual at this early hour, the train was crowded with commuters on their way to work. In all probability, for most of those who traveled with him, March 20, 1995, was just another ordinary day in their lives. Toyoda set down his bag by his feet, nonchalantly took out the newspaper-wrapped sarin parcels, and dropped them to the floor.

Toyoda was on the train a mere two minutes. When it stopped at the very next station, Ebisu, he unhesitatingly punctured the sarin packets several times with his umbrella, rose, and left. Then he rushed up the stairs to the exit and out to Takahashi's waiting car. Everything went according to schedule.

Driving back to the Shibuya *ajid*, Takahashi started to show symptoms of sarin poisoning—this was the only miscalculation in the operation. Liquid sarin from Toyoda's umbrella and clothes were taking effect. Luckily for him Shibuya is not far and there was no lasting damage.

The tip of Toyoda's umbrella went straight through the plastic packets, spilling all 900 milliliters of liquid sarin onto the floor. Around the time the train reached Roppongi two stops later, passengers in the first car began to "feel strange," breaking out in a panic just before the next station, Kamiyacho. They struggled to open the car windows, but even that was not enough to prevent the harmful effects. Many tumbled out onto the Kamiyacho Station platform and were taken by ambulance to hospital. Miraculously only one person died, though 532 were seriously injured.

Train B711T continued to Kasumigaseki with its first car empty, then all passengers were evacuated and the train taken out of service.*

---

*Toru Toyoda was sentenced to death. Katsuya Takahashi is still at large and is the subject of a special police investigation. [Tr.]

## "What if you never see your grandchild's face?"

### Hiroshige Sugazaki (58)

*Mr. Sugazaki is executive director of the Myojo Building Management Corporation, a subsidiary of Meiji Life Insurance. A typical Kyushu man, hailing from the westernmost main island of Japan whose native sons are known to be ambitious and forthright—not to say stubborn—Mr. Sugazaki has an innate dislike of anything "crooked." He has always been quick-tempered, which perhaps explains why he changed school five times. The son of a sake brewer, he for some reason hardly ever drinks.*

*He is small in stature, but tough and slim with an assertive posture, and you can hear the confidence in his voice. His powers of recall are frighteningly good. As the incredulous policeman taking down his account put it: "You have to suspect there's a screw loose when someone remembers everything in such vivid detail." At home he is the total master of the house and a strict father who has kept his three daughters so completely in line they have never once answered him back. They don't make them like him anymore.*

*I don't want to give the impression that he's totally inflexible; he also has a more laid-back side. "In the old days," he says, "I used to be very no-nonsense, but lately I've mellowed as a human being. At the office I try not to overextend myself, but rather underplay my role—like a lantern in broad daylight."*

*After the gas attack, Mr. Sugazaki was rushed to the hospital. His heart and lungs had stopped working. Both the doctors and his family had resigned themselves to the possibility that he was already gone, but after three days in a coma he miraculously came back to life. A true life-or-death struggle.*

•　•　•

I wake up at 6:30, eat a simple breakfast, and leave the house at around 7:05. I get the Toyoko Line to Naka-meguro, which takes thirty minutes. It's not too crowded, though I almost never find a seat. If an express comes along I'll always change. I'm a man in a hurry.

If I do get a seat, I read. Though I haven't done much reading since the gas attack . . . I like history books. At the time I was reading *Zero Fighter*. Long ago I used to dream of flying, and I still take an interest in airplanes. I was page-turning straight through on the Toyoko Line, a fascinating read. Which is why I didn't notice we'd reached Naka-meguro.

We line up in rows of three on the Hibiya Line platform. I usually line up around the third car from the front, but I was so preoccupied with my book I ended up farther back, about the sixth car down.

As soon as the door opened I turned right and got a seat. But then a woman came along and squeezed herself in, the fourth person in a seat meant for three, so that things were a little tight. "Well," I thought, "better get my book out now. People get the wrong idea if you start fumbling around later." I pulled out the book and carried on reading. I only had ten or twenty pages left and I wanted to finish it before I reached my station. But at Hiro-o, I looked up to see this man sitting directly to my left wearing a leather coat. I was still wrapped up in my book, but around Hiro-o it really began to get on my nerves. Leather coats often smell funny, don't they? A disinfectant or nail-polish-remover kind of smell. "This guy stinks," I thought, and I stared him right in the eye. He just stared back at me with this "You-got-a-problem, mister?" look.

But it really did stink, so I went on staring, only he doesn't seem to be looking at me. He's looking past me to something on my right. I turned around to look and saw something about the size of a notebook lying at the feet of the second person on my right. It's like a plastic pack. In the news, they said it was wrapped in newspaper, but what I saw was plastic, and something spilling out of it.

"Ah, so that's what's making the place smell," I thought, but I still just sat there. By that point, the third person to my right had gone. It must have been around Hiro-o or Roppongi I noticed that.

Soon everyone was saying, "Open the windows—it stinks." So they all open the windows. I remember thinking, "It's so cold, can't you just put up with the smell?" Then an old lady sat down next to me. It was all wet under her feet, so she stood up and moved to a seat opposite, walking straight through the pool of sarin.

There's nobody left at the back of the car. Everyone's moved to the front, saying, "It stinks! It stinks!" This was around the time we'd reached Roppongi. By then my head was spinning. I heard the announcement, "Next stop, Roppongi," and I thought to myself, "I really must be anemic today." The symptoms were pretty much the same: a little nauseous, can't see so well, breaking out in a sweat.

Still, I didn't connect it at all with the smell. I was utterly convinced it was anemia. Lots of my relatives are doctors, so I'm familiar with the smell of medicinal alcohol or cresol. I thought maybe some medical person had dropped a bag of something and it had leaked out. "But why can't someone pick it up?" I thought. I'm a little angry by now. Honestly, our morals have declined so far of late. If I'd been a bit more sound of body, I would have picked it up myself and tossed it out onto the platform.

But then after Roppongi, where the train slows, I knew something was wrong. My anemia was so bad I decided to get off at Kamiyacho and rest for a while, maybe let two or three trains go by. But when I tried to stand I couldn't get up. My legs had gone. I grabbed the handstrap and sort of dangled from it.

I moved from strap to strap until I reached the pole near the door. Finally I stepped off the train, my hand out ready to catch myself at the far wall of the Kamiyacho platform. I remember thinking: "If I don't make it to that wall and crouch down, I'm gonna fall and hit my head." Then I blanked out.

Actually, I hadn't left the train. I'd grabbed the stainless-steel pole and just slid down to the floor. What I thought was a wall was in fact the floor of the car, which felt chilly to my right hand. They ran a photo of me in the tabloids, so I could see later what happened.

They videoed me too. I was seen on television, lying like that on the car floor. I was flat out for at least half an hour. Nice and spread out (laughs). Then the station attendants carried me away. You can see it in the videos.

I came to in Toho University Omori Hospital, but I don't know when that was. Maybe that afternoon of March 20, when I had a moment of consciousness, then fell unconscious again.

When I finally came around for good, I was told I was well enough to move to the general hospital wing. It was March 23, though I was utterly convinced it was the day after the gas attack [March 21]. I had no awareness at all. But then, no awareness is paradise. True nothingness.

I didn't have any near-death experience or anything like that. Only, I swear I heard a faint roar of voices coming from far off on the wind, like kids cheering at a baseball game, something like that, but hushed and indistinct, cut off now and then by the wind . . .

Actually, around that time one of my daughters was pregnant—in her fourth month, was it? I'd been anxious about it. It would be my first grandchild. Well, apparently my sister-in-law came in and said to me: "What if you never see your grandchild's face?" Until then I'd shown absolutely no reaction to anything anyone had said, but this I heard and suddenly regained consciousness. My daughter had been at my side, saying, "Dad hold on! Don't die!" and all I had heard was a vague murmur. But "What if you never see your grandchild's face?"—those were the only words that reached me. My grandson was born in September, and thanks to him I came back to life.

I didn't regain consciousness for three days, and after that my memory didn't quite connect. Something somebody told me only half an hour before would go clean out of my head. That seems to be characteristic of sarin poisoning. The company president came to visit me several times, but I don't remember him being there, or what we talked about. I hope I didn't slight him. They say he dropped by ten times and I don't remember a thing.

It was only around the eighth day that my memory began to kick in again. It was about that long, too, before I could eat real food. I had no physical symptoms: no eye pain, no headaches, no other pains, no itching. I didn't notice that my vision was odd.

I probably shouldn't say this, but all the nurses were beautiful! I even said so to my wife: "Nurse So-and-so is *so* beautiful. They say beautiful women are cold, but she's so kind." For some time after I came around, I was convinced everyone in the world had turned beautiful on me (*laughs*).

I found nights at the hospital frightening, though. Lying in bed, I'd brush up against the bed frame and I'd feel like a cold, damp hand was about to drag me into the darkness. There was always someone around during the daytime so it was all right, but at night when I'd be trying to sleep, my hand or foot would touch the frame, and that cold hand would pull me under. The more conscious I became, the better my memories linked up and these frights got worse. I didn't recognize them as hallucinations; I was sure there was a dead person in the ward whispering, "Come with me! This way, this way . . ." It was scary, but I couldn't mention it to anyone. Ordinarily I'm the boss around the house, so I couldn't admit to being scared (*laughs*).

I knew I had to get out of that hospital as soon as possible. If I couldn't finish the hospital food, I'd get my wife to bag up what I had left and throw it out, to make it look as though I'd recovered. In that way, I was able to force the issue and get released in eleven days. I was supposed to have stayed in for at least fifteen days.

But back at home it was the same thing. Whenever I stepped onto a tatami mat, whenever I touched anything cold, those fears resurfaced. Even when I took a bath by myself. I couldn't do it alone, I was too scared. My wife had to scrub my back. "Stay with me until I get out," I told her. "I don't want to be the last to leave" (*laughs*).

Some of the victims are afraid to take the subway, even now. I was scared at first, too. The company thought I'd be reluctant to use the subway and told me to take the bullet train instead. They even offered to buy me a commuter pass, but I turned it down. I didn't want be coddled, and I didn't want to run away, either. I went back to work on May 10, and from that very first day I took the exact same 7:15 Hibiya Line train that had been targeted in the gas attack. I even made sure I sat in the same car—the same seat. Once the train passed Kamiyacho, I looked over my shoulder and said to myself, "That's where it happened." At that moment I felt a bit queasy, but having gotten it over and done with, my spirits lifted. That wiped the slate clean of any anxieties.

Those who died from inhaling sarin probably had no idea they were going to die. The last few minutes they were unconscious, after all. There was no time to see their wives, their children. No one could have foreseen something like this was going to happen—there has to be a better way to put it—what I want to say is: what on earth were those people sacrificed for?

I want anyone who could do such a thing given the maximum punishment. I say this on behalf of the people who died. I can say this because I came back to life—but what did they possibly have to gain from killing them? It wasn't this; it wasn't that; I don't know a thing about it; my disciples did it—all that is just crap. Killing people as if they were ants, all for purely selfish, egotistical reasons, or even just on a whim: It's unforgivable. I pray that those who were sacrificed may rest in peace.

# "I had some knowledge of sarin"

## Kozo Ishino (39)

*Mr. Ishino graduated from the Japan Self-Defense Forces
(JSDF) Academy and entered the Air Self-Defense Forces.
His present rank is air commander second class—roughly
lieutenant colonel in the old military ranking.*

*Nevertheless he originally had no strong desire to enter
the JSDF, Japan's equivalent of the Reserves. If anything,
he was the "nonpolitical type" as a youth, and could easily have gone to a good university, then found decent—if
undistinguished—employment almost anywhere. When
his elder brother entered the JSDF Academy, he went
along for the admissions ceremony and found the facilities
"not bad at all." Still, he never dreamed he'd be going
there himself. He sat the entrance exams merely as "a kind
of exercise."*

*He remembers thinking afterward,* "Won't it be great
to do something different with my life instead of the typical office grind?"—*and he decided to make a go of it,
despite the fact that he lacked any spirit to rally to the
nation's defense. According to Mr. Ishino (sotto voce):*
"There aren't actually that many in the Defense Academy with that kind of spirit."

*He's so retiring, you'd never know he was a military
man. He wears a suit to work, speaks ably and affably;
truly the competent young technocrat. His profession
notwithstanding, he is entirely sincere and straightforward in his worldview and values. He hasn't a biased bone
in his body. Heaven knows, we'd all have problems if he
did.*

*Many thanks to him for kindly granting me this inter-
view amid an impossible workload and chronic lack of
sleep.*

●　　●　　●

I've always liked airplanes a lot, though I never collected models or anything nerdy like that. It's just that, a human is so small and I wanted to see bigger things. So if I was to enter the JSDF I wanted to be a pilot. But you can't be a pilot with anything less than 20/20 vision, it's a rule, and for some reason during my four years in the academy, my eyesight got worse and worse. I wasn't even studying all that hard . . . I thought I'd slip by somehow, but, well, I got shot down during the in-flight exams. That only left ground duties, though my heart wasn't really in it.

Ever since, my career has been in Attack Intercept Command. There are twenty-eight radar sites around the country that maintain surveillance of Japanese airspace. Should any unidentified foreign aircraft approach, we scramble our intercept fighters and guide them to target. Watching the radar, we send our pilots. That's our job.

Knowing that I couldn't be a pilot, quite frankly, came as a bit of blow, but after thinking things over I realized there still had to be something here for me. My first posting was a radar site at Wajima, on the Noto Peninsula, Ishikawa Prefecture. A bit of a backwater. It's all right in summer when the tourists come. Young girls, too. But in winter there's absolutely nothing to do. It was lonely. Being single, the stress builds up. It was a struggle adjusting to that environment at first, but Wajima's a nice place. It's like my second home.

After six years of training there, suddenly I was sent to Tokyo. What a transfer, eh? (*laughs*) Ever since then I've been in Air Recruitment at the Roppongi JSDF headquarters.

I got married ten years ago. Not long after I transferred out of Wajima to Tokyo. A friend of a friend introduced us. We have two kids, a boy of eight and a girl of five. Bought a house six years ago in Saitama. Caught the "Bubble" right at its height . . .

I take the Yurakucho Line from ——— Station. If it's not raining, I get off at Sakuradamon and walk to Kasumigaseki. Then it's the Hibiya Line to Roppongi. It takes about an hour and fifteen minutes.

Our JSDF work doesn't really have office hours, each unit is on twenty-four-hour duty. There are shifts straight through the night to deal with anything that might come up. Technically we work in two shifts starting at 8:00 and 9:15. Meetings start around 9:00.

I come home late, generally about midnight. The kids are asleep by then, of course, but we've just got so much to do: upgrading our defense capabilities; furthering U.S.–Japan cooperation; contributing to UN peacekeeping operations—from the smallest projects to the biggest schemes, we've got to take care of them. Sometimes it might just be that the photocopier's broken.

March 20 falls at the end of the fiscal year, so the workload's lighter than usual. Quite a few of the men in my section took days off between the national holidays. I wanted to take the extended holiday weekend myself, maybe catch up on a little sleep, but we can't all take off at the same time, so I went to work.

The train was emptier than usual. I remember I got a seat all the way to Sakuradamon. There was no meeting that day, so I could take my time. I got to Sakuradamon about 8:20, then walked to Kasumi-gaseki, and went down to the station platform.

But when I tried to go through the ticket barrier there was a signboard saying something like: "Due to a bombing just now, all trains have been canceled." I went on down anyway and there were all these people waiting on the platform. "Well, if these people are waiting," I thought, "there's bound to be a train eventually." So I lined up with everyone else. But there was no sign of a train. I gave up and headed for the Chiyoda Line platform. I could just as easily walk from Nogizaka Station.

But the platform was so packed you couldn't move. Well, it so happened that the train on the opposite side of the platform was just waiting there with its doors wide open, so I decided to walk down through its cars. It was a Hibiya Line train from Naka-meguro, bound for Kita-senju. I must have walked through at least four or five cars. There wasn't a soul on board. A few others were doing the same, though. It didn't feel the least bit odd to be walking through the cars like that. There was nothing suspicious on the platform, either. It seemed like a perfectly ordinary train that had stopped due to an electrical fault or something.*

The Chiyoda Line was still running. There were a few delays, but I waited a while and got on a train. Then, just before Nogizaka Station I began to feel listless, lethargic. And when I got off, I was

---

*In fact, sarin packets had been discovered in the first car and the train had been taken out of service, though it remained in the station with all the doors open.

having heart palpitations. It was hard to climb the stairs, but my work is so hectic I'm chronically short on sleep and I often lose track of my health. I thought it was just fatigue from lack of sleep, but then every-thing was dark. It occurred to me they might be testing the lights in the station. It wasn't until I entered the JSDF building and couldn't turn my head properly that I thought: "Something's not right here."

At the office it wasn't long before reports came in on TV about the confusion at Kasumigaseki. The trains had been canceled and everything was in complete uproar. My superior told me, "Shouldn't you call home and tell your wife you made it here all right?," so I did. They still didn't know about any sarin at the time. I imagined it was an ordinary accident. Well, I started to work at my desk, but even typing was difficult—the computer screen was so dark. After a while the announcement came that it was sarin. I immediately thought, "Sarin? I must have inhaled some myself."

That's not to say all JSDF officers are briefed about sarin. But back when I was assigned to the Foreign Ministry we were closing negotiations on a ban on chemical weapons, so I had some knowl-edge of sarin. And of course I'd heard about the Matsumoto incident, although personally I wasn't very interested. To be honest, I didn't believe it was really sarin. I thought it was probably some other toxin. I just couldn't see anyone being able to produce chemical weapons in Japan. For one thing, they're not easy to manufacture.

I remembered that sarin causes contraction of the pupils, so I went to the bathroom and washed my eyes, then looked in the mir-ror. And what do I see but my pupils are like tiny dots. I went to see the medic and there were already several others there all with sarin injuries. There were a good number of sarin victims in the JSDF headquarters alone. Maybe more than in other places. We start work a little earlier than elsewhere, and lots of people commute on the Hibiya and Chiyoda lines. But to the best of my knowledge, no one here has suffered from any aftereffects.*

*Mr. Ishino was taken immediately to JSDF Central Hospital in Setagaya, southwest Tokyo. Luckily he had only minor symptoms, so he was discharged after one night, although his feelings of fatigue and lethargy persisted. His contracted pupils returned to normal after a month.

In Europe terrorism is more frequent, if not exactly common-place, but Japan up to now has had almost nothing like that. I studied overseas in France for a while and all the time I was there I remember thinking, "I'm so glad Japan's a safe place." Everyone said so: "We envy you Japan's safety record." And then to come home and straightaway this happens! Not only random terrorism, but with a chemical weapon like sarin—it was a double shock.

"Why?" was all I could think. Even with the IRA, I could at least see things from their side and maybe begin to understand what they hoped to achieve. But this gas attack was simply beyond all comprehension. I'm just lucky to get off with minor symptoms and no after-effects, though that's no consolation to those who lost their lives or still suffer from it. The dead are dead, of course, but there are surely more meaningful ways to die.

I hope they examine the gas attack from every conceivable angle. Okay, I personally feel that the people who did it are unforgivable. Japan, however, is a juridical state. I believe we must have a full debate to satisfy everyone, and use it as a test case of where responsibility lies with incidents of this sort. We must give serious thought to how we can make good such crimes and how any retribution is to be decided. Granted this case is unusual because it involves the unprecedented element of brainwashing, but still we must try to establish general standards. Furthermore, in order to prevent the recurrence of such a terrible incident, there needs to be a public debate about how we as a nation deal with such crises.

After this experience we must make every effort to ensure that this prosperous and peaceful nation, built on the labors of previous generations, is preserved and passed on for generations to come. The most important thing for Japan at this point is to pursue a new spiritual wholeness. I can't see any future for Japan if we blindly persist with today's materialistic pursuits.

There's another thing that has occurred to me since the gas attack: I've just turned 40 and up to now I've been living carelessly. It's about time I took control of myself, gave some deep thought to my own life. This is the first time I've ever had such fears. I've been concentrating on my career all these years, so I've never known real fear.

## "I kept shouting,
'Please, please, please!' in Japanese"

## Michael Kennedy (63)

*Mr. Kennedy is an Irish jockey. Having won countless major races, he is now retired. He was invited to Japan to coach young Japanese jockeys in professional equestrian skills at the Japan Racing Association (JRA) riding school in Chiba, east of Tokyo.*

*Born in Ireland, he still keeps a family house in the suburbs of Dublin. Healthy and active, he is outgoing by nature and loves meeting people. He really took to Japan, living here for four years with no complaints. The only thing he missed from his homeland was "conversation." Away from the big city, English speakers are few and far between—it gets lonely.*

*Nevertheless, Mr. Kennedy enjoyed passing on his experience to promising young jockeys at the riding school. He always smiled whenever the subject of his students came up.*

*No doubt the gas attack came as a big shock to him. I don't know if he's completely over it. While an attack of this nature makes no distinction between Japanese and foreigners, I sympathize with Mr. Kennedy, caught up in incomprehensible circumstances in a foreign country where he didn't even speak the language.*

*Several weeks after this interview, he completed his contract with the riding school and returned to Ireland.*

● ● ●

I've been in Japan four years now. That's a long time and I miss my family, but I go back to Dublin twice a year and my wife comes here once, so that's three honeymoons a year (*laughs*).

I've been a jockey for thirty years. I was an apprentice at fourteen and went professional at twenty. I've been lucky. I've had some injuries. I've broken my ribs seven or eight times, fractured a chest bone, had my shoulder knocked out, but nothing serious, thank God.

I retired in 1979, when I was 47, and I became the manager of a training ground in County Kildare. We had fifteen hundred horses in training. I was responsible for the facilities—the grounds, the tracks, the gallops. During my spare time, we had an apprentice training school, the RACE—Racing Apprentice Center of Education— where I'd go twice a week in the evening and go through racing videos with the kids. Then during the day I'd see them riding on the tracks. I was able to keep an eye on them and talk with them about their riding styles.

Now the JRA—the Japan Racing Association—had affiliations with the RACE, and I met many of these Japanese and gave them some insights into racing. I didn't know anything about Japanese racing, but the JRA were anxious to get a teacher.

So in March 1992, I came over to have a look at the school and went to racetracks in Miho and Mito. I went to Utsunomiya and Tokyo. I was really impressed by the facilities. Beautiful places. People were very nice to me. I went back to Ireland and told them I was leaving, I was going to take this job. Were they surprised! (*laughs*).

I live in a special dormitory at the school now. Very nice. I've become accustomed to living on my own; I've become a real bachelor. In the four years I've been in Japan, I've seen changes. The standard of riding is much better now. It was a little bit old-fashioned when I first arrived. The younger riders have got more imagination, more flair, but I still think they can improve their technique by becoming more communicative with the horses. Maybe it's the culture that regards horses as inferior?

I was in Tokyo on March 20. I'd been in town for St. Patrick's Day. The Emerald Ball was on Friday the seventeenth and I stayed with friends in Omote-sando. It's sort of a ritual every year. You'd be surprised how many Irish there are in Tokyo.

On Saturday, I stayed the night at a friend's house in Setagaya. On Sunday I went to a small Franciscan church in the morning, then there was the St. Patrick's Day Parade. At the parade I met the Irish ambassador, James Sharkey, and he invited me to dinner near his home in Roppongi. I was delighted. It was at the Hard Rock Cafe—very, very informal. We had some drinks—I can't drink too much, two glasses of beer is my limit—and the ambassador said to me, "You don't have to go back out to the school tonight. Why don't you stay at my place?" So I stayed in Roppongi that night.

I got up at 6:30 on Monday morning and said to his daughters, "Tell the ambassador I've left." But the girls insisted I stay for breakfast. Then I took my time and strolled down to Roppongi Station to get the subway. I was going to take the Hibiya Line as far as Kayabacho, then come out to Nishi-funabashi by the Tozai Line.

As I came down the steps at Roppongi, the first train was moving out and it was packed. This was around 7:30. The next train came and half the front carriage was empty. I couldn't believe it—half-empty—great! I entered at the rear door of the carriage and there was this big pool of some oily substance and a ball of newspaper—as if somebody had been mopping it up. I think actually it was still leaking out of the container that was wrapped in newspaper.

I moved right down the carriage looking at it, walked around it, and sat down, thinking, "What can that be?" Then I noticed that nobody came near it; there was only one other man next to me. Everyone else was at the front of the carriage. "Odd," I thought, then quickly decided to join them.

There was a girl starting to slump forward. She looked like she'd been crying. One man opened the window a bit because the train was moving now, and I said, "More, more." This particular gas is a heavy gas, so it sinks down. It wasn't so bad a stink, but then my sense of smell isn't so good. It stung my eyes and I began to feel a bit numb.

The next thing I knew, that girl had fallen over. She was very young, only about twenty-one, and she looked in a bad way. I don't know if she died or not.

When we got to Kamiyacho, we all piled out onto the platform and collapsed. Everyone panicked. We didn't know what to do; we were left sitting there. People told the driver, and he came and looked, then he went back and made a call on the radio. The station was getting polluted with the fumes, but we all just stayed there.

Now my eyes were beginning to weep too and I wasn't sure what was happening. Some people lay stretched out on the platform. I was sitting down. My eyes were streaming. I was trying to keep my hand on my shoulder bag, and my other hand held the hand of the unconscious girl. We had to get her out. We went one way, then stumbled back the other way, before we finally made it up the stairs. We got to the ticket barrier, but they were telling us to stay put: "Wait, wait, wait!" they said, and I kept shouting, "Please, please, please!" in Japanese. The girl was leaning on me and commuters were pushing past me.

We stayed huddled there at the top of the stairs, then suddenly a man with a briefcase came down, reached under the gate to open the barrier, grabbed the girl who was in my arms, and carried her up the stairs. Then someone was helping me.

We got out onto the street, and somebody told us to sit on the curb. I thought, "Fresh air, now we'll be okay," but then I began to feel really sick. I knew I was going to throw up all over myself, so I leaned to the left and was sick on the road. I think maybe it was lucky I vomited, because it attracted attention when the ambulances came ten minutes later. By then I'd reached the panic stage, thinking, "Why doesn't someone come and help us?"

I knew it was gas, obviously. And it affected me so badly; I felt so ill. I knew it was something serious, because it was getting progressively worse. The others were just sitting around, some with handkerchiefs over their mouths. They didn't know what was wrong.

When we got off the train, my first thought was to sit and wait for the next one. I really thought I'd be okay but no, it was deadly stuff. And then the train continued on from Kamiyacho. It probably had to, but that stuff was still on board.

By then there were about thirty or forty people on the street, sitting around, lying down. I often wonder about that girl who was unconscious. She was the most serious, maybe because she was small and she'd got on who knows how many stations before. I heard a girl of twenty-one had died and I always wondered if it was her. She looked like a secretary—a nice, decent, respectable sort of girl. There was one other foreigner, too. A big, tall man. I wonder what happened to him?

I was one of the first taken by ambulance. I don't remember the name of the hospital, but it wasn't too far from Kamiyacho. I was put on oxygen, intravenous drips. I had lots of needles in me. I was in the hospital for four days. JRA people were there the whole time, because Kamiyacho is the headquarters of the JRA. Once I'd been in the hospital a few hours I knew I was going to be all right. The shock of getting worse—you're out in the fresh air and you should be getting better, but you just feel worse—that was frightening. Once in the security of the hospital my attitude changed. I knew I was out of danger. My eyes were still sore, my head ached, and I was quite sick, but that gradually passed. Then the problem was my kidneys. They had to flush out my kidneys to get the chemicals out of my system.

When I checked out of the hospital, I went back to the ambassador's house and stayed another two or three days.

I slept very, very little for three weeks. I was afraid to go to sleep. I imagined someone was hitting me with a mallet. Always the same dream. As time went by the blows got softer, then it was only a pillow. Sarin has that effect: when you fall asleep you suddenly wake up again. I was afraid of the dark. I had to leave the lights on. Some nights I didn't sleep at all.

I was in a sort of trance. I continued to do my work, trying to get back on track. I would come to the office, but I wasn't really normal. It took a while, but I got better with time. My eyes were still sore, so I had to use drops. I went back to the hospital twice to be checked and I got a clean bill of health.

I watched TV in hospital and I saw myself falling down. I was afraid my wife would see it and be worried, so I called home to Ireland. "Everything's all right," I said. My daughter was staying over that night and my wife said: "That was your dad. He's been in an accident in the subway." And my daughter ran downstairs and saw me on television! So it's a good thing I called.

People were very nice. I got letters from people who could hardly write an English sentence, but I understood what they were saying, and it was lovely of them.

Of course, Tokyo is known as a safe city. The gas attack hasn't changed my opinion of Japan; there's no country in the world as safe as Japan. Wonderful! If all the world were like Japan, there'd be very little trouble.

I'm not easily frightened. There's not much I'm afraid of. Men like me grow old but never feel old—and that's often a danger (*laughs*). You think you can still do things. It was a frightening experience.

I'll tell you what's changed: I took a long, hard look at myself and I said, "Michael, what are you worrying about?" Everyone worries about the smallest things in life and then something like this happens . . .

No, I didn't think much about the possibility of dying. Riding horses all my life, I was always flirting with death.

# "That kind of fright is something you never forget"

## Yoko Iizuka (24)

*Born in Tokyo, Ms. Iizuka works at a major city bank. A keen sportswoman, many regard her as outgoing, but she thinks of herself as "laid back." She isn't really the type to forge ahead on her own initiative, she seems too polite.*

*Nevertheless, when you read her account you'll see that she is clearly not "laid back." She has a certain moral strength and gritty determination. Yet at the same time, she has her vulnerable, sensitive side.*

*I know it must have been hard for her to recount that day to a complete stranger. No doubt I made her remember things she would rather have forgotten. I can only hope that this interview helped her to "draw a line under it all," as she herself put it, after which she can move ahead in a positive direction.*

● ● ●

I had the flu on March 20. I'd been feverish for days, with a temperature of 39°C [102.2°F]; it just wouldn't go down. I took maybe one day off, I'm not sure. I made a real effort to go to work. If I take time off it leaves everyone else in the lurch.

That day I was running 37°C [98.6°F], which was only a slight temperature, less than it had been, but I was coughing like mad and my joints ached from the fever dragging on. Plus I was taking lots of medication, which made it hard to see the symptoms when I got hit with the sarin . . .

I still had an appetite, though. I always eat a good breakfast. Otherwise I'm in a daze and can't get my head in gear. I wake up around 5:00, which leaves plenty of time for doing things. I leave home at 8:00, so that's more than two hours. I can read, watch a video, things I can't do at night when I come home because I'm so run-down.

But that day I was still a little feverish and I knew that sleep was important, so I got up at 6:30, later than usual. March 20 was an important day for me. I was taking on a new responsibility at work, so that morning I was pretty nervous.

I ride the Hibiya Line from ———— Station, then change to the Marunouchi Line at Kasumigaseki. The first car is convenient for changing later, but it's awfully crowded, so I always take the second car, the rear door. But that day the train came as soon as I reached the platform, so I rushed to get on at the middle door. I moved back in the car and stood about halfway between the second and third doors.

I never hold the handstraps, they're dirty. I don't hold anything. When I was little my parents always told me: "You shouldn't touch the handstraps in trains because they're filthy." I'm quite steady on my feet. I play tennis; my legs are in shape, so I'm fine not holding anything. I wear high heels to work, so there's plenty of spring in my stride.

I always catch the 8:03 Tobu-dobutsu-koen-bound train, so I generally see the same faces. That day a lot of people were coughing, all the way to Roppongi. I thought there must be something going around. "Oh no, just what I needed to knock me flat on my back again," right? So I took out a handkerchief and covered my mouth.

But when the train reached Roppongi, about five people came running out of the first car and said something to the station attendant at the head of the train. The station attendant's always standing at the very front of the platform at Roppongi, but these passengers just flew out of the car as if they'd been dying for the doors to open. I saw them and thought, "That's odd, what's going on?" They seemed to be complaining about something. This meant the train left Roppongi a little behind schedule.

Just before Kamiyacho, the person next to me said, "I can't see." Then someone collapsed. To my left, people were just tottering then falling down. From that moment on the train there was complete chaos. A man was shouting, "Everyone open the windows! Open them or we'll die!" And he went around opening windows from one end of the car to the other.

When the train reached the station, people were shouting: "Everyone had better get out!" "Get off! Get off!" I didn't know what was happening, but decided to get off anyway just in case. The person who'd said "I can't see" got off too, but then collapsed on the platform. A man went to the driver's cabin and started pounding on the window. The station attendant was at the rear end of the Kamiyacho platform, so he let the driver know something was wrong.

Sarin had been left by the third door of the first car. The door where I usually get on. I saw it when everyone left and the car was empty. A square parcel. Liquid seeping out and forming a puddle. I remember thinking, "That must be the cause of it all." But until everyone got off the car was too crowded to know it was there.

I'm told the old man who sat right in front of the parcel died. He was foaming at the mouth by the time the train reached Kamiyacho. Completely unconscious apparently. People lifted him up and helped him off the train.

Several people collapsed on the platform. A few of them fell over flat on their faces. Lots more were crouching or propping themselves up against the wall. I asked the man who had said "I can't see" if he was all right.

I knew it was an emergency, but to be honest it didn't occur to me that it was anything really serious. I mean, what can happen? Japan's a supersafe country, isn't it? No guns, no terrorists, hardly anything like that. It never occurred to me I might be in danger or that I had to get myself out of there. I mean, just walking the streets there are people who fall ill, aren't there? Normally at times like that you ask, "Are you all right?" Just one passenger helping out another.

I knew something was a little "off" the moment I boarded the train. I could smell something like paint thinner or nail-polish remover. A smell that packed a punch, but I had no trouble breathing or queasiness or anything. Not at Roppongi and not at Kamiyacho. I'd had that handkerchief over my face the whole time, so maybe that kept me from breathing in so much sarin on the train. Still, I had gone over to people who had collapsed and spoken to them. I'd been rubbing up against them—maybe that's when my eyes were affected.

The train behind ours had already left the previous station, so our train quickly pulled out with the first car empty. An announcement said: "The train will proceed to Kasumigaseki. Please take any car other than the first. All the rest are still in service." My main thought was, "I can't be late for work." Of course, I felt bad about leaving people just lying there on the platform, but it was an important day for me so the pressure was on not to be late.

I wanted to be as far away as possible from that parcel, so I moved right to the end of the train and traveled in the fourth car to Kasumigaseki. But while I was changing to the Marunouchi Line, everything went dark. I felt weak, too. I thought maybe it was the cold remedy I was taking, so I didn't pay it much attention. The train went above ground for a while from ———— Station, and for some reason the sky was dark, as if it were black and white. Or sepia, just like an old photograph. "That's odd," I thought, "today was supposed to be sunny."

I arrived at the bank just at the last minute. I practically slid under the door, then rushed to change clothes and got right down to work. But something strange happened. Around 9:30, as I was getting started, I began to feel funny. First my eyes wouldn't focus. I couldn't read anything at all. Then I felt sick, like I was about to throw up. But it was an important day, and I knew I had to just bear with it— though everything went in one ear and out the other. I was "Yes, yes" all the time, pretending I was listening, but I felt sick, breaking out in a cold sweat. My nausea was terrible, but then I'd also felt the same with my flu, so I couldn't tell the difference. No, I take that back. I didn't feel like I was going to throw up, I only felt queasy.

After 11:00 everyone went out to lunch. I was in no condition to eat, so I declined and went instead to the company sickroom. That's when I finally found out I was suffering from sarin. Extremely serious, they told me. I rushed straight to the hospital.*

I never was much one for going out and about, but these days I spend all my Saturdays at home. When I do go out, I feel run-down straightaway. It's all I can handle just to go back and forth to the bank and do my job. I get back home and I'm a wreck. Even at work,

*Ms. Iizuka's recovery did not go altogether smoothly. For one week she could not see at all. Nausea and lethargy sapped her strength. Although she suffered from almost continual headaches, she didn't miss a day of work the whole time. She was in great pain, but continued to work out of a sense of duty. Even now, a year later, the fatigue persists. Since the gas attack, she's virtually given up tennis. Any physical activity, even climbing the stairs, leaves her short of breath. Her condition improves only very slightly.

3:00 comes around and I'm thinking, "I am *so* tired." Just worn out. It wasn't like this before. It's been this way the whole time since the gas attack.

Maybe it's partly psychological. I've tried to somehow put the whole incident behind me. But that kind of fright is something you never forget, no matter how hard you try. I don't think the memory will go away as long as I live. The more I try to forget, the more it comes out—that's what I'm starting to think. I can control it psychologically, depending on my mood, but it's difficult. There are times when I can see things objectively, and times when I go faint if I confront things head-on. It goes in waves. I see it very clearly. All of a sudden, something will set it off and the gas attack will cross my mind. And when that happens I close up inside.

I often have dreams about it too. Not so much right after the attack, but lately all the time. They're so vivid. Then I wake up with a start in the middle of the night. Now that's frightening.

Even when I'm not dreaming, sometimes I'll find myself in a confined space and I'll just stop, especially underground—in the subway or an underground entrance to a department store. I'll start to get on a train and my feet won't move. That's happened more and more since February. That's nearly a year after the event. Times like that, I feel that no one understands. Everyone at work is really considerate and everything. My family's been very kind too. But no one can really understand what it's like, this fear. Not that I'd really want them to . . .

Still, it makes a big difference, the way my boss at work and family and friends are so supportive. And then there are those with far more serious symptoms who are much worse off than me.

My parents were against me giving this interview. This isn't really the time for me to be remembering things I've been trying so hard to forget, but I made up my mind and accepted so that it would be a kind of cutoff point. I can't keep creeping around avoiding things forever.

# TOKYO METROPOLITAN SUBWAY:

## HIBIYA LINE

### (Departing: Kita-senju / Destination: Naka-meguro)

#### TRAIN A720S

• • •

The team of Yasuo Hayashi and Shigeo Sugimoto planted sarin on a southwestbound Hibiya Line train that departed from Kita-senju Station for Naka-meguro.

Yasuo Hayashi was born in Tokyo in 1957, and was 37 years old at the time of the gas attack. Apart from Ikuo Hayashi (no relation), Yasuo was the oldest person in Aum's Ministry of Science and Technology, a deputy leader under direct command of Hideo Murai. Yasuo came from a science background, but unlike the sheltered species of the "purebred" scientific elite represented by Ikuo Hayashi, Toyoda, and Hirose, he'd had his share of hard knocks and setbacks. His father had worked for the Japanese National Railways prior to privatization, but died twenty years ago. The youngest of three children, his mother spoiled him—as much as she could on such a low income.

After finishing high school on a part-time schedule, he entered Kogakuin University to study artificial intelligence. Without any prospects for steady employment after graduation, he was a temp in company after company, then went overseas. In India, he awoke to religion and began to frequent yoga ashrams, finally encountering the Aum cult, then becoming a follower of Shoko Asahara. In 1988, he took vows and rose to the number three position in Aum's Ministry of Science and Technology.

Said to have been one of the staunch defenders of the cult, he also had his kind and gentle side, and was looked up to as a sort of big brother by many of the younger converts.

The morning of March 20, when everyone else received two packets of sarin during the training session at Satyam No. 7, Yasuo Hayashi got three. The extra packet was a flawed leftover he himself asked for. It was all part of a ritual "character test" that Hideo Murai (and very likely Asahara himself) had set up. Who among the five gets the extra packet? When Hayashi came forward without hesitation, Murai smiled knowingly. Hirose, who was also there, recalled rather glumly that "it was as if Murai had just won a bet."

Asahara had once suspected Yasuo Hayashi of being an undercover spy, which had apparently affected him deeply and made him exaggerate his "go-getter" tough-guy tendencies. Unfortunately, his "go-getting" attitude on the Hibiya Line train to which he was assigned caused the most deaths and casualties of any of the five subway lines under siege. All three of the packets were punctured . . .

Yasuo Hayashi went to Ueno Station in a car driven by Shigeo Sugimoto. En route he wrapped his three packets securely in newspaper. He was scheduled to board the 7:43 A720S from Kita-senju. At Ueno, he boarded the third car, dropped his newspaper parcel onto the floor, and when the train reached Akihabara two stops later, he poked at it several times with the sharpened tip of his umbrella. He made the most number of holes of any of the five perpetrators. Alighting at Akihabara Station, he got into Sugimoto's waiting car and returned to the Shibuya *ajid* by 8:30. He'd fulfilled his duties without a hitch, not even a moment's hesitation.

The sarin began to leak out and smell shortly after the train left Akihabara. By the time it reached the next station, Kodemmacho, passengers traveling in the third car from the front began to feel physically ill. People spotted the newspaper parcel leaking liquid. There was already a puddle around it. Thinking it must be the problem, one passenger kicked the parcel out onto the Kodemmacho Station platform.

The ejected sarin quickly dispersed into the atmosphere of the tiny Kodemmacho platform area. Four people died here, including Japan Tobacco employee Eiji Wada.

Meanwhile, train A720S continued on its scheduled run with a puddle of sarin on the floor of the car, the number of casualties mounting with each subsequent stop—Ningyocho, Kayabacho, Hatchobori . . .—a real-life Hell Train.

At 8:10, soon after the train pulled out of Hatchobori Station, one passenger, unable to stand it anymore, pressed the emergency button in the third car. But according to regulations, a train cannot stop in the middle of a tunnel; so it proceeded to the next station, Tsukiji. When the doors opened, four or five passengers tumbled out and collapsed on the platform. A station attendant ran over. It took this long before any members of the Subway Authority realized something was wrong. The train was taken out of service immediately and medics called. The first communication to go out from Tsukiji Station to Subway Authority Central was the driver's report: "Something seems to have exploded with white smoke in the train, many people injured." As a result, for some time thereafter, the gas attack was known as the "explosion at Tsukiji Station," word of which traveled quickly to all stations on all lines.

The station attendants at Tsukiji recognized soon enough that it was not explosives. "Poison gas!" they shouted, trying to clear the station of passengers as quickly as possible. Subway Authority Central was slow to catch on: it was more than twenty minutes later—8:35—before it decided to completely shut down the Hibiya Line. Then the word came: "Evacuate all commuters, then evacuate all subway personnel."

At the five stations en route a total of 8 people died and 275 incurred serious injuries, a full-blown catastrophe.

Thereafter Yasuo Hayashi—the "Murder Machine"—went into hiding, living on the run until December 1996, nearly a year and nine months later. He was finally arrested on Ishigaki Island a thousand miles from Tokyo. Throughout his flight, he reputedly carried with him a small Buddhist altar to atone for the lives he'd taken.

What follows are comments from passengers who traveled on Hibiya Line train A720S, on which the sarin was planted.*

*At the time of going to press Yasuo Hayashi was sentenced to death and is appealing the sentence. Shigeo Sugimoto was sentenced to life imprisonment. [Tr.]

## "I'd borrowed the down payment, and my wife was expecting—it looked pretty bad"

### Noburu Terajima (35)

*Mr. Terajima is a maintenance technician for a major photocopier manufacturer. He commutes from Soka on the Hibiya Line to Higashi-ginza. He conducts regular spot checks on his company's machines and does repairs.*

*He lived alone in an apartment in Soka until he married six months before the gas attack. Then he obtained a loan and bought a new condominium in Soka. Not long after that his wife became pregnant. Just at the turning point between early adulthood and the responsibilities of middle age, he ran straight into the gas attack. The first things he thought of when he became ill from inhaling sarin at Kodemmacho Station were his unborn child and the huge loan he'd taken out to cover the down payment on his new condo.*

*We met upstairs at a coffee shop in Soka on a sunny Sunday afternoon. Outside the window, young couples and families with small children strolled down the avenue in front of Soka Station: a peaceful, suburban weekend scene.*

*Mr. Terajima answered questions slowly, with a great deal of thought, but was careful not to say too much.*

* * *

I always wanted to be a painter, but when my father died just after I graduated from high school, we needed money. My elder brother was in college, so we had to at least see him through to a degree. I failed my college entrance exams, but paid my way through vocational school, which meant I had to find work quickly.

At first I sold property. Not bad work, but really demanding, so I changed jobs after a year and settled into my present company. Actually, I wanted to work in planning or advertising props, but I lacked experience or I didn't have a driver's license. One thing or another. But, well, I ended up in a company with a solid reputation. In other words, I went for stability.

I was married the September before the gas attack and bought a condominium in Soka. Signed the contract in September for a full handover in April. Until then we continued living in my rental apartment in Soka. So we were getting ready to move in just around March 20 when the attack took place. We'd scoured the local stores for boxes and were packing up everything.

No, I never pictured myself buying a condominium. I didn't much care where I lived, but we went to a showroom and liked what we saw. When we discussed the interest, the broker convinced us, saying if we acted now it was 3.9 percent, but soon it was going up to 4.0. It was an impulse buy. A twenty-five-year loan. It's no joke, buying a home.

We have a little girl, noisy as hell. Up until two years ago I was living happily on my own, but now I'm married, a father, a loan on my back, and completely broke, just like that. All my money's gone (laughs).

If I wasn't married by 35, I wasn't going to get married at all. I decided it would be too much bother. But, well, I got married at 34. I met my wife windsurfing. I've been a keen windsurfer since I was 25. I can't be bothered now, but I was young and would drive all the way to the beaches at Shonan or Zaimokuza. Once a week I'd get up at 5:00 in the morning and drive for three hours. I was full of energy then. This was before windsurfing became a popular sport. A friend and I bought a surfboard secondhand and kept it down by the beach—I wonder what's become of it?

Nowadays, if I have a spare moment, pachinko's about all I can manage (laughs).* Forget oil painting! I'm the sort of person, if you get me started on something, I get all wrapped up in it. I need lots of time.

March was pretty busy for me. My area of responsibility is Kasumigaseki, so there's full-payment purchases of equipment to

---

*Pachinko is a Japanese variant of pinball. [Tr.]

balance, office budgets, huge deliveries . . . They've got to use up their allotted funds before the end of the fiscal year, so it's one of the busiest times in the whole year. The gas attack fell right between two public holidays, but I was in no position to take off a long weekend.

I rarely eat anything in the morning: coffee and a pastry and I'm out the door. I wait for a Hibiya Line train where I can usually get a seat and go in the first door of the third car. That day I must have caught the 7:53. As soon as I sit down, I'm generally out like a light. No newspaper reading for me. My eyes always pop open automatically just before Higashi-ginza, though I have overslept three times (*laughs*).

That day I woke up at Kodemmacho. An announcement came over the PA: "There's been an explosion at Tsukiji. We will wait here temporarily." So I just sat there and waited, until finally they said: "We do not foresee resuming service." What choice did I have but to get off? That's when I got a sharp smell of isopropyl alcohol. We use the stuff for wiping clean the glass in our copiers, so I know it very well. I always carry it on the job.

When I got off the train, there was a station column to my right, and next to it was something wrapped in newspaper, which seemed to be giving off the isopropyl alcohol smell—though I hardly noticed it at the time. I do remember looking down at the ground for the source of the smell. When I was sniffing I breathed deeply. Isopropyl alcohol isn't a dangerous chemical, after all.

At Kodemmacho Station, I saw only one person who was in a bad way. A man. I noticed him as I passed through the ticket barrier: back propped up against a column, foaming at the mouth and vomiting, hands trembling. But he was the only one, so I thought he'd fallen ill or something.

Outside the station, I decided to walk to Nihombashi. But then I started to feel really bad: nauseous and dizzy. My eyesight got worse, or rather it made no difference with or without my glasses. I couldn't focus. Everything was a blur. I had a headache, too. I lost my sense of direction, had no idea where I was going. I thought that walking in the same direction as everyone else would get me somewhere, so I just went along with the crowd.

I had to sit down and take a breather several times. I wanted to go home, but I knew the office was closer, so I decided to walk to work. But I lost track of where I was going and went back and forth the same way two or three times. Walking was so hard! I thought I was suffering from anemia. I thought about going into a convenience store and buying a map of Tokyo, but I was in no shape to read.

I suddenly panicked that maybe I'd burst a blood vessel. Recently it's been on the rise among people in their thirties. That's when I remembered I'd borrowed the down payment, and my wife was expecting—it looked pretty bad. What if I snuffed it there and then?

Walking blind, somehow or other I made it to Nihombashi Station. I caught the Ginza Line to Ginza, then walked to the office from there, though I don't remember a thing about this part. No memory at all. I reached the office a little after 8:45. Morning ceremonies were under way. I changed into my work clothes and joined in, but I couldn't even stand up. I'll never know how I managed to change clothes, but it shows I have a strong work ethic (*laughs*). Force of habit. Otherwise I'd never have gone to work in such a state.

I couldn't take it any longer so I went to Hibiya Hospital. I got there around 10:00. By then lots of people were already being treated. When I saw the TV news and heard them mention the frontmost door of the third car on the train stopped at Tsukiji, it all clicked: "Hey, there was that newspaper bundle when I got off at Kodemmacho." I'd been looking down, sniffing, trying to work out where the stink was coming from, so I got it much worse than the others.

I was in the hospital for a night. The problems went away after I had an IV; my eyes gradually got better.

Now there's nothing especially wrong with me. Well, maybe my memory is worse. Not things slipping my mind so much as total memory loss. It's just gone completely. So whenever anyone tells me something I make a point of jotting it down. Otherwise I'll forget.

I've used isopropyl alcohol for about ten years in my work and I'll always recognize that smell (*laughs*). But you know, later, on the news, I found out that they actually do use isopropyl alcohol to make sarin. I just knew it.

## *"In a situation like that the emergency services aren't much help at all"*

## Masanori Okuyama (42)

*Mr. Okuyama struck me as a quiet soul. Admittedly this was a first meeting and we only talked for a couple of hours, so I really can't say.*

*Born and raised in a small town in the northeast, he went to a local college. The eldest of three, he was, by his own admission, "a well-behaved child; always did what I was told."*

*A very lenient father, he hardly ever scolds his two children. When I asked if he was worried about how they would fare in the world, he answered, "I'm not so concerned."*

*He works for an interior-design-goods manufacturer, wholesaling to department stores and large supermarket chains. Unlike in most sales jobs, he doesn't need to do much entertaining or give away free gifts. These days clients are strict about not accepting favors so as to avoid collusion with suppliers, "which makes it easier to separate work from my personal life." He commutes to work via the Hibiya Line to Kayabacho.*

*On his days off, he watches TV or occasionally plays games on his PC. He doesn't go out drinking with colleagues and drinks only one bottle of beer a day at most. He knows his limit.*

● ● ●

On March 20 I wasn't especially busy at work, but it being the end of the fiscal year there was plenty to do. The next day was a holiday, so I left the house an hour earlier than usual. I wanted to get there ahead of time to tidy my files, that sort of thing. I'm pretty sure I took the 7:50 train from Kita-senju. I usually take the second car from the front.

Once the train reached Kodemmacho, there was an announce-ment telling us to get off. There'd been an explosion in the train ahead, something like that. So everyone got out. I stood waiting on the platform, thinking that sooner or later either the train would start moving again or the next train would arrive. I was there maybe one or two minutes, when suddenly a man near me started screaming. He was about twenty meters away. A strange, unfathomable sort of cry. Soon he was led away somewhere.

About the same time I realized: "Hmm, something's odd with my breathing." Not a very profound thought, just sort of "What's this now?" Then . . . that's right, a woman crouched down nearby, but again I only thought she was sick or not feeling well. Soon after that, though, there was another announcement over the PA: "Everyone please evacuate the station." They gave some reason, but I can't remember what.

The exit at Kodemmacho Station is right in the center of the platform, so people at the front of the train had to walk back to leave. I'm not too sure of the timing here, but I got back on the train and passed down through the cars because the platform was so crowded. Halfway, however, I saw someone had collapsed. That I know for sure.

On the platform again I seem to vaguely remember a puddle of something behind a column. That and the smell—similar to the sol-vents they use at construction sites . . . it gave me a stuffy feeling. I'd always had asthma since I was small, so I thought maybe that had something to do with it. Anyway, none of the passengers seemed to be in any hurry; they just strolled toward the ticket barrier.

Once outside I looked around and saw someone lying down, foaming at the mouth, and another person trying to help. Lots of people were just sitting around, their noses running, eyes streaming. It was an extraordinary sight. I had no clue what was going on. All I felt was a sense of imminent danger. "There's no way I'm going to make it to work," I thought. "This is serious, so I'd better just sit still for a while."

So I stayed there. Standing at first, then sitting down. All of a sudden my field of vision got smaller, darker. On top of which I became light-headed. The explosion and the person screaming and people falling down, none of it came together in my head. I had no inkling that these things had anything to do with me. I just sat there looking at it all and thinking, "No, I'd better stay put." Instinct.

Whereas most people, although they were in a bad way physically, still tried to get to work somehow, to go somewhere. That just seemed so strange to me. They could hardly walk—in fact, one guy near me was crawling!—it was so obvious they were in no condition to go to work. One woman was struggling to her feet and I told her, "If you're feeling ill, you'd better just sit."

Otherwise I didn't talk to anyone. I don't know what other people did, whether they talked among themselves . . . Of course, I wondered what was happening, but I didn't ask anyone else about it. I wasn't in any great pain or nauseated.

It took a long time for the ambulances to come. Finally one did—I only saw that one. So in the end, most people flagged down cabs and the drivers agreed to take them to the hospital. It was really obvious that in a situation like that the emergency services aren't much help at all.

It was some time later that I took a taxi to the hospital. Four of us traveled in one cab. We weren't too serious, so there was no great urgency. The others were salarymen. We must have talked in the taxi, but I can't recall what about. I don't know why I can't remember.

We went to Mitsui Memorial Hospital in Akihabara. I have absolutely no recollection of how we ended up there. Maybe someone directed us. When I got to the hospital, I called the office and they already knew about the gas attack. Two others from work had also been injured. Not badly, about the same symptoms as me.

I stayed in the hospital two nights. They used a drug to dilate my pupils, so that they eventually got too wide and everything was too bright. My eyesight also got weaker as a side effect. That lasted about a week. Other than that, I didn't experience much physical discomfort. Just my asthma acting up, which is torture, too, of course, but I'm used to it.

Whether my fatigue is due to the sarin or not, I can't say. It's a gray area. It could be just age . . . I'm terribly forgetful now. But again, who knows the cause? And back pains—I'd had them before—but recently they come on really strong, which is probably true of most middle-aged men.

What I find really scary, though, is the media. Especially television, it's so limited as to what it shows. And when that gets out, it really makes people biased, and creates an illusion that the tiny detail they focus on is the whole picture. When I was out in front of Kodemmacho Station, certainly that one block was in an abnormal state, but all around us the world carried on the same as ever. Cars were going by. Thinking back over it now, it was eerie. The contrast was just so weird. But on television they only showed the abnormal part, quite different from the actual impression I had. It just made me realize all the more how frightening television is.

# "Ride the trains every day and you know what's regular air"

## Michiaki Tamada (43)

*Mr. Tamada works for the Subway Authority as a conductor. He joined in April 1972. The year of the gas attack was his twenty-third year of service. His official title is chief conductor—a real veteran. His incentive for seeking subway work was somewhat unusual: he wanted a job where he'd have his "own free time, not like a nine-to-five job." A subway job offers whole days off with rotating shifts; the work schedule of subway employees couldn't be more different from the daily grind of an office. An attractive proposition for some.*

*The more I talked to him, the more I got the impression that he put a high value on individuality. There's no real hard evidence to pin that down, just something about his easygoing manner off the job.*

*He used to be a keen skier, but had a major injury six years ago and hasn't skied since. "No other interests to speak of," he says. He doesn't do anything special on his days off; he just relaxes or goes for drives somewhere by himself. He doesn't seem to mind living alone.*

*Never much of a drinker, since the gas attack he's hardly touched a drop. He took seriously his doctor's warning that sarin damages the liver.*

*He gladly responded to my request to interview him. He wants to do his bit, as he put it, to prevent the gas attack from fading in people's minds.*

•　　•　　•

I went to high school part-time, so I was 21 when I joined the subway. At first I just punched tickets, saw trains off from the platform—one year at Iidabashi Station, two years at Takebashi, I think? After that I transferred to Nakano area train duty on the Marunouchi Line.

You need to pass an exam to transfer from station duty to train duty. Then to become a driver you need to take another more difficult test and a proper written exam, a health check, an interview, this and that. In my day lots of guys took the test, so you really got the cream of the crop. I wanted to switch from station duty to train duty because of the shorter work hours. Nowadays it hardly makes a difference, but in my day that's how it was.

I joined Nakano area train duty in 1975 and for the next four years I rode on the Marunouchi Line. Then I switched to Yoyogi area train duty on the Chiyoda Line, and the year before last I changed to the Hibiya Line. When you swap lines there's lots of things you have to learn again from scratch. The specifics of each station, the layout, the structure, you have to drill those into your head, because otherwise you can never be sure what's safe. And safety, above all, is what's important. We always keep that in mind at work.

I've seen close calls any number of times. Nights when people have been drinking, some of them stray near the moving trains . . . and especially if they've been standing behind pillars, there's no way to prevent it. Then there's rush hour: everyone stands right on the very edge of the platform where the trains come in. That's really dangerous.

On the Hibiya Line, Kita-senju's especially tricky. There are just so many passengers, all of them lining up, but when it gets to the point where you can't walk down the platform behind them then you have to squeeze between the people and the trains—and that's pretty hairy.

The day of the gas attack, March 20, was supposed to be my day off, but they were short-staffed so they asked me, "Think you might work tomorrow?" Well, it's all about give and take, so without thinking too much I accepted. The shift started at 6:45 A.M. I reported to Naka-meguro Station first thing and posted the 6:55 to Minami-senju. "Posting" is what we call catching another train to where we board our train of duty. From Minami-senju Station, I headed back in the opposite direction on my train. I don't recall the exact departure time, around 7:55.

That day it was packed solid, same as ever. I didn't notice anything especially different while we were en route until word came in from Central Command: "There's been an explosion at Tsukiji Station. Please stop the train . . ."

I stopped at the next station, Kodemmacho, and read an announcement to the passengers: "We will be stopping briefly as there has been an explosion at Tsukiji Station. We will inform you of the cause of the accident as soon as we know more. Until then, we apologize for the delay."

We kept the doors open at Kodemmacho. I left the cabin and stood on the platform, just to check that there were no irregularities.

Some of the passengers asked me questions: "How long will this take?" I didn't have any detailed information, so I could only answer, "There was apparently an explosion, so it may take a while."

I think we were there about twenty minutes. Meanwhile the train after my train had stopped between Akihabara and Kodemmacho and we were in the way.

Then a message came from Central that I was to get all the passengers off my train and proceed down the line. The train behind needed to reach our platform. So I made another announcement: "This train is going out of service. All passengers please get out and find alternative transportation where possible. We apologize for any inconvenience." Then there was another message from Central saying: "This may take longer than we expected."

No word came in at all as to what had happened at Tsukiji Station, though we picked up a few hints over the radio. It didn't make much sense. Had there been an explosion? What was the extent of the damage? All we knew was the place was in complete confusion. "Quite a few people have collapsed."

There's really nothing that can explode on the subway, so I assumed a bomb had been planted. That is, terrorism. Serious stuff.

After I made my announcement and the passengers all got off, the station attendants checked inside the train. I looked in as far as I could see, then shut the doors and the train pulled out.

Lots of passengers complained: "You can't just leave us here." We explained that there was a train behind us that needed to let its passengers off at this station and apologized.

We stopped the train in a tunnel between Kodemmacho and Ningyocho Station, only the driver and me on board. After it stopped, I walked the entire length of the train and did one complete inspection. There was nothing out of the ordinary that I could see.

Only something *felt* wrong inside the train. After the second or third car I couldn't help thinking, "Something's different." It wasn't so much a smell; it was just a hunch: "Something's weird here." Everyone sweats, so the odor of their bodies, the smell of their clothes leave an indelible mark. Ride the trains every day and you know what's regular air, and you pick up on anything that's not quite the same. Call it instinct.

We waited there for about thirty minutes. I could hear the conversation going back and forth with Central all the time. It became apparent that it hadn't been an explosion after all. The tone of the conversation slowly changed.

A new message came in: "Any crew members who feel sick or strange are to report to the office." I didn't feel ill.

By then Kodemmacho Station was in uproar, though I didn't know it at the time. While we were in the station I hadn't noticed anything unusual.

The conductor's cabin is at the tail end of the train and the sarin injuries were toward the front. Quite a distance, maybe a hundred meters. I'd kept my eyes on the platform and if anyone had fallen I'd have seen them. I'd been on the lookout right up until we shut the doors and pulled out, and there was nothing out of the ordinary on the platform.

Not long after that I began to feel sick. Everything was looking dim, as if they'd turned out the lights. My nose began to run and my pulse sped up. "Strange," I thought. I didn't even have a cold. I contacted Central: "Something's wrong with me, this is my condition." "That's serious," they said, and we drove on to Ningyocho Station, where I got off while the train that had been at the station pulled out.

There was a doctor on duty at the station and I went to him and he said: "This is beyond me, go to St. Luke's or somewhere." So I rested in the Ningyocho Station office, waiting for the next change of staff. My train couldn't move until they found a replacement for me.

As I waited, my condition remained more or less constant. My nose was running and everything kept getting darker. There was no dizziness or pain, though. It was around noon when my replacement finally came and they took me by ambulance to Tajima Hospital. But there were no beds there, so they sent me on to the Self-Defense

Forces Central Hospital in Setagaya. Which was more convenient for me anyway, since I live in Machida.

I stayed in the hospital overnight. The next day my pupils were still contracted, but my nose had stopped running so it was all right for me to leave. I didn't have any real aftereffects, except maybe I'm sleeping less. Used to be I could sleep seven hours at a stretch, but now I wake up after four or five hours. Not in the middle of a dream or anything: my eyes just open.

Am I scared? I'm a subway employee; if a subway employee was scared of the subway, he couldn't work. I may feel kind of uneasy, but I try not to think about it. What's happened has happened. I try to remember that the important thing is not to let something like that happen ever again. Likewise, I'm making an effort not to bear any personal grudge toward the criminals. Grudges don't do anyone any good. I'm horrified that colleagues of mine died. We're all like one big family here, but then what can we do to help their families? Nothing. We just can't let it happen again. That's the main thing. All the more reason why we can't forget this incident. I just hope that what I'm saying, when it gets into print, will help everyone remember. That's all.

# TOKYO METROPOLITAN SUBWAY:

## HIBIYA LINE

### TRAIN A738S

*"Some crazy's probably sprinkled
pesticides or something"*

**Takanori Ichiba** (39)

*Mr. Ichiba works for a clothes designer. I may not be up on
the workings of the fashion industry, but I did recognize
the name of the boutique run by his company in the
upmarket Aoyama district of Tokyo. Come to think of it,
I'd even bought a tie at one of their stores. After the interview, I bought a pair of rust brown chinos from the bar-
gain table—and I assure you, if it's something I'd buy, they
can't be all that radical as fashions go. Their line tends
more toward casual traditional wear—what we Japanese
call "soft trad."*

*For some reason, people who work in fashion look
young. Mr. Ichiba is in his early forties now, but his face is
still youthful. He's not the type to go gently into middle
age, but then very likely his profession demands it of him
to look—and feel—young, or else. He speaks softly and
has a pleasant smile.*

*Not that he's a dreamer or anything; he's very sharp.
On hearing the announcement over the PA at Tsukiji Station, he immediately made the connection:* "Could this
have something to do with that Matsumoto incident?" *His quick wits were also in evidence when he saved a colleague who'd collapsed in front of Shibuya Station and
took him to the hospital. And it's not easy to make clear
judgments in emergencies like that.*

"What's the good of asking someone like me with
only mild symptoms?" *he said initially, and was reluctant*

*to be interviewed.* "There are far more serious cases around. I'm nothing." *No, I explained, it wasn't a question of how badly he was affected, it was his viewpoint— his experience—that mattered.*

● ● ●

I'm from Kumagaya in Saitama [about two hours northwest of Tokyo]. I went to work for a clothing manufacturer as soon as I graduated from school, then soon moved to my present company. It was your typical "one-room setup," what was then called a "condominium company." A small operation, with only about ten employees. Though we're much bigger now.

Starting a company is easy, and it's not uncommon for such a venture to grow into a big operation. It all depends on the abilities, the vision of the designers and owners themselves. On the other hand, if that vision slips, then the whole thing goes wrong. With precision machine manufacturing there's an accumulation of technical know-how, so short of some grievous error nothing's ever totally ruined. But you can't stockpile vision and creativity—they're more perishable, like fresh fruit. Making it big is no guarantee of success. There have been lots of companies that made it big, only to disappear.

I've been with my company for thirteen years, and seen it grow just like that. We now have our own direct retail outlets, with about 350 employees. My section is Business Planning: we deal with the "making" end, the actual production. Our office is in Hiro-o [southwest central Tokyo].

I live to the east in Edogawa Ward; my train station is Nishi-kasai. I got married ten years ago and bought a condominium. I like living in that old part of town. I can relax there.

March 20 coincides with our spring fashion sales peak, which keeps us pretty busy. Those happy-go-lucky people who can take a long weekend are a world apart from us. We had our weekly Monday morning meeting, same as ever, starting around 8:45. That's forty-five minutes earlier than usual, which is how I ran smack into the gas attack.

I changed at Kayabacho from the Tozai Line to the Hibiya Line for Hiro-o, but didn't notice anything out of the ordinary while I was on the train. I was in the middle, probably the sixth car. After Hatchobori there was an announcement: "Some passengers have fallen ill. We will be stopping briefly at Tsukiji, the next station."

At Tsukiji there was another announcement: "One . . . no, two of the ill passengers have fainted." Like that, very real-time. Then it was: "Three passengers down!" The conductor was in a panic. At first he seemed to be relaying information to the passengers, but gradually he got himself in a muddle. Then it was: "Hey, what is this?" The man was yelling into the mike.

I thought: "Uh-oh, sounds like trouble." But nobody seemed particularly distraught. If the same thing happened today, make no mistake, it'd be a madhouse. As for myself, for a moment I remembered the Matsumoto incident. Not that I went so far as to think it was sarin or anything, but the thought of the Matsumoto incident did carry associations of "scattering poison." The thought did cross my mind: "Some crazy's probably sprinkled pesticides or something." I didn't know anything about Aum then, however. Wasn't it a little later before Aum was implicated?

We were told to leave the station by the rear exit, there being some kind of disturbance toward the front of the train. Everyone was well behaved and slowly walked back toward the exit. I was wary, so I put a handkerchief to my mouth just in case, but no one else did. I felt like the only one who sensed any danger.

I was curious what was going on, however, so while people were still lining up at the exit, I looked at the TV monitor at the very end of the platform and saw someone lying unconscious. As I was looking, though, a station attendant shouted at me: "What do you think you're doing? Just get outside!"

When I reached the surface I saw quite a number of people squatting down, rolling over, sprawled out. They were all rubbing their eyes. I decided I had to see what was going on for myself. I couldn't just walk off and leave them. So I went up on a footbridge for a better view of the whole scene. So much for my meeting.

Soon an ambulance came, blocking off the traffic on the opposite street. They put up a big tent and carried the injured in on stretchers one after another. Eventually a crowd of onlookers gathered and squeezed me off the bridge, so I left.

After that I took the Ginza Line to Shibuya, hoping to catch a bus to Hiro-o. Good thing I remembered the bus, which I sometimes take. But the bus terminal was more crowded than usual, probably because there was no Hibiya Line. That's when I spotted a young colleague—24 or 25—leaning against a railing, and a woman from the office trying to hold him up. She didn't know anything about the trouble on the Hibiya Line at the time, however, and just thought it was anemia or something, which isn't uncommon in the morning. She was rubbing his back, saying, "You okay? You okay?" He'd apparently taken the Tozai Line, then changed to the Hibiya Line, same as me.

"What happened?" I asked, but all he could say was, "In the subway . . ." I knew, however, how many people had collapsed at Tsukiji, so it came to me in a flash: "This is no mild case of anemia. This is serious." We had to get him to a hospital quick. So I went straight to a phone booth and dialed 119, but all I got was: "All of our ambulances are out on call at the moment and cannot come to you. Please remain where you are." They were all at Tsukiji and Kasumigaseki.

So I went to the police post in front of the subway station to try to get some kind of help, but word still hadn't reached the police there; when I rushed in spouting off about an "incident in the subway" the officer had no idea what I meant and simply couldn't be bothered. I realized this wasn't going to work, so I decided to hail a taxi and take him to the hospital myself. The woman and I held him up between us and told the cabdriver to go to the Red Cross Hospital in Hiro-o. That was the closest.

My colleague was in pretty bad shape. He couldn't stand. He was in pain and could barely utter a word. He was in no condition to tell us what had happened. If I hadn't passed by, I doubt anyone would have done the right thing for him. People would have had no idea. And it would have been difficult for the woman to drag him to the taxi rank on her own.

We were the first sarin victims at the Red Cross Hospital. People there were practically shouting, "We got our first one!" It didn't occur to me at the time that I might be affected too. My nose was running, but I just thought I'd caught a cold. I wasn't aware of any other symptoms. Once he was with the doctors I called his parents to explain what had happened. Getting a call through wasn't easy, and it was after 2:00 before his parents made it to the hospital. By then the place was packed with sarin victims. People were spilling out into the corridors, all of them on IVs.

I'd been there since the morning and soon got to know all the nurses. One of them said, "You might as well get tested yourself," and I thought, "Why not?" so I had myself examined. Here I'd been in hospital half the day and still hadn't had a single test . . . Well, sure enough, my pupils were contracted, though so slightly that things didn't look any darker. Still, I got myself hooked up to an IV for an hour, just in case.

I remember a carpenter who'd cut his finger came dashing into the hospital all covered in blood, only—poor soul—he couldn't get anyone to so much as look at him. It was like, "Can't you see we're treating sarin victims here?" I couldn't help feeling sorry for him. He looked a lot worse all bloody like that.

After the IV I went back to the office. My nose was still running, but that didn't matter at work. Afterward I went home as usual. I'd been traveling in a different car from the one with the sarin, so I got off lightly. I'd only been examined as an afterthought, once I'd taken my colleague to the hospital, and for that I got my name in the newspaper.

My young colleague is no longer with our company. He left a year ago, but it was nothing to do with the gas attack. He was fine by then. I don't know what's become of him since.

I was hardly affected, so my impressions of the gas attack are much the same as the majority of the public. Of course, I don't think that sort of thing should be condoned, but above and beyond that, well . . . Afterward the Subway Authority sent me a MetroCard pass. It was bad news for the subway, too, I guess.

## "We'll never make it. If we wait for the ambulance we're done for"

### Naoyuki Ogata (28)

*Mr. Ogata works in computer software maintenance. I met with quite a few people in computer-related work in the course of compiling this book. According to Mr. Ogata, "There are lots of software companies along the Hibiya Line"—for reasons unknown. Mere coincidence?*

*Common traits among those in the software industry seem to be: (1) "they're extremely busy"; (2) "they change employment frequently." Mr. Ogata, however, has worked steadily for the same company since he graduated from school. This is quite exceptional in his field and he is much admired by his peers. Long-term employment or not, he's as busy as the next man. Not that any salaryman I talked to ever said, "Oh, we're on easy street. Loads of free time."*

*Just for the record, the people in computers I've met were never "nerds." Mr. Ogata is an average clean-cut, articulate young man—he had just turned 30 when I met him, but he hardly looked it—and a useful member of society.*

*Perhaps it was this side of his character that made him remain so long in the danger zone to help the injured, when his subway train hit disaster at Kodemmacho Station. As a result he received a big dose of sarin gas and ended up as affected as the many he'd saved. He reserves any feelings of resentment for the emergency services that were so ill-prepared to help out in a crisis of this kind.*

● ● ●

I was born in Adachi Ward [*north Tokyo*], and have always lived in the same place. Officially it's Tokyo, but it's almost all the way to Saitama. My parents, sister, and I all live together. Another sister is already married and has moved out. My work keeps me busy. I have lots of responsibility, so I work myself into a frazzle. I've complained to my boss for I don't know how long, but he doesn't listen. When the work piles up, I'm at it twelve, thirteen hours a day—that's par for the course. I work overtime, but I don't claim too much or my boss complains. But if I didn't do overtime, the work would never get finished.

So why are we so busy? Intercompany competition, I suppose. Lately whenever I go somewhere on business, there are always two or three other companies in on the act too. You can't sit around twiddling your thumbs. Weekends I just sleep, or maybe visit friends. I've got two computers at home and I use them for work, too. That's right. On my days off. I don't want to, but there's simply no end to the work. I'd never get it done otherwise (*laughs*). My parents have given up on me. "Enough is enough!" they tell me, "why is it only you have to kill yourself?" But no matter what they say, I still have to do it.

If you're over 30 in computing you're out of it. They keep coming out with new systems and standards, and it's harder to keep your head above water. The best guys in our company are mostly around 22, 23. When they're past that they'll usually leave the company. Nobody stays in this field forever.

My company's in Roppongi. I catch the bus around 7:00 to Gotanno Station, then take the 7:42 or 7:47 Hibiya Line train for Naka-meguro. It's incredibly packed. Sometimes you can't even get on. Crowded as it is, though, even more people squeeze in at Kita-senju. You're just squashed in like the filling in a sandwich. I'm talking physical harm. You feel like you'll be crushed to death, or suddenly your hip's thrown out of joint. You're all twisted out of shape and all you can think is, "It hurts!" You're just mangled up in the middle of all this, with only your feet in the same place.

It's quite literally a pain to commute like that every day. Come Monday morning I always think, "Maybe I won't go in today . . ." (*laughs*) But you know, even though your head's saying, "No way, I don't want to go!" your body just automatically sets off for the office.

If everyone had a computer hooked up to the office, there'd be no need to commute. Even now it's not impossible. You can even hold meetings by conference call. You'd only go in to the office maybe once a week—perhaps it'll happen one day.

On March 20 I missed several trains because they were delayed due to fog on the Tone River. I ended up catching the 7:50-something, which, because of the delay, was packed tight. It was terrible. The previous Friday I'd come down with a cold and had a temperature, so I'd taken the day off. But I was back on the job on Saturday. I had to change over a system for a customer. I took Sunday off and slept the whole day. On Monday I was still a bit out of things; I really wanted to take the day off, but I'd already told my boss I'd go in.

Quite a few people got off at Ueno Station, so finally I could breathe. I'd somehow held on to a handstrap. What do I do while I'm on the subway? Nothing. I'm just thinking, "Gaah, I want to sit down!" (laughs).

That day the train stopped between Akihabara and Kodemma-cho. Then there was an announcement about an explosion at Tsukiji. "The train will be stopping at Kodemmacho," it said. "Shit," I thought, "first the fog, now this accident. It's just not my day." I was already seriously late.

The train stopped just that once, then went on to Kodemmacho. I was certain it would start again sooner or later, so I waited on board. But not long afterward there was another announcement: "This train is stopping here. We do not foresee moving on again." What could I do but get off? I decided to take a taxi the rest of the way to the office. So I walked up the stairs to the ticket barrier and went above ground. Suddenly I met with the most amazing sight. People were dropping like flies all over the place.

I'd taken the third car from the back and had absolutely no idea what was happening at the front of the platform. I was just heading up above ground, swearing under my breath like everyone else, when right before my eyes I saw three people fall down and foam at the mouth, their arms and legs twitching. "What the hell's going on here?" I thought.

Closest to me was this man whose limbs were quivering, he was trembling all over and foaming at the mouth, having some kind of seizure. I just looked at him and my jaw dropped. I knew it was serious and rushed over to ask him what had happened. I could see he needed immediate care. That's when someone who was still walking by said, "Him foaming like that is dangerous, you'd better stuff some newspaper in his mouth." So we both helped him. After that all these exhausted people kept coming up from the ticket barrier below, then dropping to the ground. I couldn't work out what had happened. Some of the people sitting down suddenly just keeled over flat out.

It was a strange sight. Off toward the back of the next building, this old man—I mean really old—wasn't breathing and there was no pulse. He'd gone motionless just where he lay. "Did anyone call an ambulance?" I asked the person nearest me. "They called," he said, "but none came." Then somebody else said: "We'll never make it. If we wait for the ambulance we're done for." We decided we had to try stopping cars and asking the drivers to help move everyone out.

The traffic light had just turned red, so we all jumped in front of the cars and begged them: "Please, you have to take us to St. Luke's." That was the nearest hospital. We went for vans mostly, thinking they could carry five or six people. Everyone stopped for us, and once we'd explained the situation they were understanding and took us.

I must have been doing that for an hour, helping carry across those who'd dragged themselves up above ground. We passed them along like a relay team. We divided ourselves up between the "people carriers" and the "car stoppers."

The ambulances just didn't come. Finally one ambulance did show up, but only after about half an hour. It had come from miles away because all the others were at Tsukiji. One ambulance!

I went to the hospital by taxi too. I'd been so busy helping people, by the time I'd finished I was showing symptoms myself. The main reason was I'd gone back down to the platform. Word was that a station attendant had collapsed and another attendant came up, saying, "Can anyone give me a hand?" So I went down again together with a few others and breathed in the sarin. By that time the station was full of gas . . .

The fallen station attendant was barely conscious and muttering something about, "No, no, I have to remain here in the station." He'd somehow leaned against the ticket barrier and still he was saying, "I have to stay here." We had to drag him out of there by force.

I didn't think twice about going down to the platform. Scared or not, I wasn't even aware of it; we were too desperate. All I knew was we had to help. There were only a handful of people still on their feet, how could we not help? Going back down, there was a paint thinner–like smell. I remember thinking, "Odd, who dimmed the lights?" My pupils were contracted.

After we'd carried out all the injured and got our breath back, I was trying to get a taxi to work when I started to feel sick. My head hurt, I felt nauseated, my eyes itched. The others told me, "If you're feeling strange you'd better go to the hospital."

Three of us shared a taxi. One guy had come up from Osaka or Nagoya on business, and he was grumbling: "Why did this have to happen today? I just got here." I sat in the front seat; the two men in the back were pretty dizzy, so we wound down the windows all the way. The roads were jammed. Tsukiji was sealed off and there was no way of getting to any backstreets, so we had to head straight down Harumi Avenue, which was packed, a real mess.

They tested my eyes at the hospital and put me on a drip straight-away. The place seemed like a combat hospital, IV drips lining the corridors . . . I got two drips, then, since my symptoms weren't so bad at the time, I went home. The doctor even asked me, "Are you going home or staying?" but I was so worked up, as if I'd just left a war zone, I didn't even notice if I was tired or weak or anything.

By the time I got home my eyes really hurt. I could barely sleep for a week. I'd shut my eyes, but they still hurt—the whole night through until morning . . . that wore me out. So I went back to the hospital for more tests and was told my cholinesterase level was way down and I was showing the effects of sarin. I wish they'd told me earlier. Ever since the Matsumoto incident they knew what the symptoms of sarin were and they must have had testing procedures. And St. Luke's is one of the better places. Most of the other hospi-tals were so poorly equipped it was a joke.

The tests showed my kidney functions were down dramatically. "You're into the danger zone," they told me. And it wasn't just me; others were showing the same signs too. Apparently it had something to do with the alcohol-based solvent they used to thin down the sarin. The kidneys are what they call "silent organs," so you wouldn't even know. There's no pain. They told me to lay off alcohol com-pletely, so I didn't drink for a long time.

I ended up taking a week off from work and didn't do any over-time for the next three months. My boss understood, so that really helped.

To tell the truth, though, I have my doubts about the police and fire department. Okay, they sprang into action in the beginning at Tsukiji, but even so they were just way too late in coming to help at Kodemmacho. We'd given up on them by the time they arrived. I just wonder what would have happened if we hadn't taken it upon ourselves to do something. Granted the local police might not have any experience, but they were practically useless. Ask them which hospital to go to, and that hasn't been established so they're on the radio for ten minutes. Just a simple question: "Which hospital?"

The police showed up only after the rescue operation was practically over. Then they began directing traffic for the one ambulance that arrived. I don't know what's wrong with Japan's standby disaster arrangements. After all those sarin gas victims in Matsumoto, they ought to have learned a lesson or two. They'd identified a link between Aum and sarin at that time. If they'd followed that up this whole gas attack wouldn't have happened, or at least I'd have come away with less serious injuries.

At the hospital I saw some of the others who had helped me rescue people from Kodemmacho Station. Some were bedridden. We all inhaled sarin. I don't want to keep quiet about this thing; keeping quiet is a bad Japanese habit. By now, I know everyone's beginning to forget about this whole incident, but I absolutely do not want people to forget.

And I'm going to continue to raise objections: why hasn't any treatment policy been established for posttraumatic stress disorder? Why hasn't the Japanese government made an accurate assessment of the current health of the injured? I'm going to fight this one.

## "It'd be pathetic to die like this"

### Michiru Kono (53)

*Mr. Kono was born into a farming family in Oyama,*
*Tochigi (north of Tokyo), in 1941, the year the War in the*
*Pacific began. After graduating from high school he got a*
*job through a friend at a printing factory in Kayabacho.*
*This was back when horse-drawn carts were still rolling*
*through the old downtown warehouse districts of Tokyo.*
*You could see right across to Tokyo Station from the*
*rooftops of Kayabacho in those days. He lived in the com-*
*pany dormitory until he was 21. For recreation there was*
*the cinema, or maybe hiking in the hills with his col-*
*leagues.*

*In 1969, aged 28, he married. He and his wife now live*
*in Soka, Saitama, and have two children, both in their*
*twenties. He's strongly built and has never once been ill.*
*He swears by eating and drinking in moderation as the*
*root of all health. If he goes out drinking one night, he*
*absolutely refuses to touch a drop the next day, even if his*
*wife forgets and opens a bottle of beer. He's that strong-*
*willed.*

*Now he goes to the pool once a week and swims for an*
*hour. The gas attack sapped his strength, so he began this*
*regime.*

*He loves bonsai. Mention bonsai and his face lights up*
*and he'll talk nonstop. After the gas attack, however, he*
*was so upset and confused, he decided to get rid of his*
*cherished plants. Luckily, he changed his mind, but not*
*before a friend had taken ten of the biggest and best.*

• • •

Our company prints account ledgers. I've been working there thirty-
nine years. Ever since 1957. There was nowhere else to go (*laughs*).

Business hasn't been so good lately. Everyone's gone computerized, so there isn't much demand for accounting ledgers.

Now they just push a button and out it all comes printed. Just tear it off and stuff it in an envelope and post it. Done. So the demand for invoice forms and delivery forms, all that has gone. And it's going to get even worse from here on. There are eight of us in the company now. We used to have twenty-five.

The first thing I do when I wake up at 5:30 is water my bonsai. Before I get a drink, the bonsai get theirs. Once every three days is enough, but in summer it's every day. I've got eighty pots altogether, so it takes some doing. At least half an hour. After that I eat, dress, and leave home around 7:00. I walk to Matsubara Danchi Station and catch the 7:17. But that day, owing to circumstances, I caught a different train.

The fact is, aside from bonsai, I go freshwater fishing as a hobby. I usually take off the next day after I go fishing. You need a lot of gear: high boots, your rod, all kinds of other stuff. Well, I can't stand not cleaning each piece of equipment myself. That's just the way I am. So that's why I take the following day off.

Generally I and my friends drive up on a Saturday night from Kawaguchi as far as Niigata. We don't sleep, and as soon as morning comes we start fishing, from dawn until maybe one o'clock. We start downstream and work our way up, then we come downstream and head back to town. When the Kanetsu Expressway is busy traffic doesn't move at all, so I don't get home until about nine or ten at night. I take off the Monday after. On that weekend [*March 18/19*], we'd gone to the Daimon River in Nagano, just below Lake Shirakaba. I got back home at 8:00 on Sunday.

But the following Monday I was going to be busy, so—much as I would have liked to—I couldn't take time off. I put off dealing with the big fishing gear and settled for a quick tidy-up, which made me ten minutes later than usual leaving the house. I didn't oversleep. I never oversleep.

I change at Takenozuka for the first Hibiya Line train of the morning. I could change at Kita-senju, but it's so damned crowded. Seven or eight years ago I once had my glasses broken there. I got crushed as they all came shoving in. After that I gave up on Kita-senju. I've a much better chance of getting a seat on the first Takenozuka train. Then I read a bonsai book or a magazine.

But that day I was late, so I took a later train. I sat on the second row of seats on the right-hand side, looking in the direction of the train, by the middle door in the third car from the front. I was asked about this repeatedly by detectives, so I remember it very well. I'll never forget as long as I live (*laughs*).

Actually, the work I was doing at the time had something to do with AIDS. We were printing drug labels for a pharmaceutical company. Two-color labels to stick on the product, and we had to deliver them by March 25. We had to start printing on the twenty-second, so I had to go into work and prepare the plates.

En route—right before Akihabara, was it?—the train stopped. There was an announcement: "There's been an accident at Tsukiji Station, we will wait here briefly." But we weren't there for very long, so I wasn't bothered. That sort of thing happens all the time. Then we stopped again between Akihabara and Kodemmacho, and there was another announcement. Something about a gas explosion at Tsukiji Station. They repeated it twice. Which sent a buzz through the car.

Five or six minutes later, I can't be sure, the train we were on inched into Kodemmacho Station. Then suddenly I heard a woman scream. A loud piercing squawk like a parrot—at least I think it was a woman. It came from outside the car. "What now?" I thought, but the platform was so crowded I couldn't see a thing from inside the train.

Then came another announcement: "We will remain stopped here for a while." At this point maybe a third of the passengers got off, though I remained seated. Judging from past experience, it's usually best to stay put; the train sometimes starts again. It's stupid to get caught in the middle trying to change trains.

Well, I waited for three or four minutes, and again there was an announcement: "This train is being taken out of service." "That does it," I thought, and got up. It's two stations between Kodemmacho and Kayabacho, that's thirty or forty minutes' walk. If I hurried I might make it to the office just after 9:00. I took down the paper bag I'd put up on the shelf above my seat and stepped onto the platform.

And next to a column a little way ahead toward the front of the train, there's a man lying faceup, his arms and legs twitching like he's about to breathe his last.

I set down my bag against the wall and held his legs to keep them from kicking, but I just couldn't control them, he was trembling so bad. His eyes were tightly shut. I stayed there for six or seven minutes, just holding him, but in the end he died, I know. He was the eleventh person to die. A Mr. Tanaka from Urawa, 53 years old—the same as me.

I'm not the sort to just pass people by. Something happens and I'm right there to lend a hand. People are always telling me, "You shouldn't go looking for trouble" (*laughs*). But I just can't look the other way. Close by a woman had collapsed too, and there were about ten people around her. You can't be too careful touching a woman, but man-to-man you can help out no questions asked. Anyway they were standing around her. I was crouching, so I could see her between people's legs. Her name was Ms. Iwata, 32 years old. She died two days later.

I started shouting at everyone walking along the platform, "There's a sick man here, somebody call the station attendant!" I looked around and there wasn't a station attendant anywhere on the platform.

Soon enough one did appear, but he went straight over to the woman, not to where I was. So I yelled, "Hey, over here!" But he said, "There's only one of me and I can't be in two places at once." I heard later that this station attendant ended up in a serious condition and very nearly lost his life.

I was still crouching there, rubbing the man's legs, when suddenly I smelled this stink like rotten onions. In the train they said something about a gas explosion, so I knew it had to be gas and I had to get out of there quickly. So I stood up, grabbed my paper bag (I'm amazed I actually remembered!), and made a run for it. Every second counted, so I didn't even show my travel pass; I just jumped over the ticket barrier and dashed up the stairs, shouting the whole way, "Gas! Gas! Run for it!"

Everyone else was plodding up the stairs so slowly, completely unaware. More were coming *down* the stairs to board the train.

There were no station attendants anywhere to stop them coming down. When I started yelling, people up ahead were grumbling: "What's the hurry?" "Hey, don't push!" Maybe they were afraid I'd start a stampede. But I just pushed my way through them. I ran ahead into a narrow side street, squeezing past the parked cars. I had it in my head that the main roads would be dangerous. I even considered getting in one of the cars parked there, but it was locked. Well, of course it was locked. But I didn't even think, I was in such a state.

So off I ran again, this time to a building. I wanted to escape the gas explosion. I found somewhere with the lights on, but it was still early, so the door was locked. I went across the street, when suddenly my eyesight went funny, as if I were seeing fireworks or something. "Odd," I thought, then ten seconds later my eyes blacked out totally. It was a bright clear day, then out of nowhere this curtain descended and I couldn't see a thing.

I couldn't see, I couldn't run, but I knew I had to get across the street. I was running almost on instinct. It was a small street, it couldn't have been far, but I tripped on something and fell. "Ah! I'm going to die like this," I thought, "I don't want to die!"

Then I heard a man's voice saying, "What's wrong? What's wrong?" I vaguely remember him asking me what company I worked for. I think I held out my travel pass, because it had my company ID card in it, though I can't be certain. Then everything went black and I don't recall a thing.

I came to five or six hours later in a hospital bed.

I was this close to losing my life. Only three things saved me: (1) I smelled something; (2) I ran out of there; (3) some stranger found me and took me to the hospital long before the ambulance came. If it hadn't been for these three things, I'm sure I'd have died.

And thinking back on it now, I'm convinced that Mr. Tanaka, the man who died, said to me when I smelled gas: "It's too late for me, run!"

While the other commuters were coming out of the station, then falling like flies, I was in the hospital already getting treatment. With sarin, even a second earlier on to oxygen makes all the difference. I was the third sarin case to be hospitalized. I only heard later that when I was helping the man on the platform, the packet of sarin was just ten meters away from me.

Toward afternoon my eyes sensed a little light. I still couldn't see. It was like there were soap bubbles over my eyes. Everything was layered double, triple, and swirling around. My family had come and I could tell there was someone there, but I couldn't recognize anyone until they spoke.

It was excruciating. I vomited, but nothing came, just a little fluid. And the muscles in my legs were in spasm. The nurse and my daughter-in-law had to massage them until the evening. I'm sure I was in the same state as the man I'd helped at the station, but he could hardly speak so he must have been in unbelievable pain.

Seeing me like that, my family seemed to have resigned themselves to the fact that I might not pull through. But by the third day I was over the worst. Though I was in a bad state at first, my symptoms soon went away and I was out of there remarkably quickly. Only from the fourth day I ran a high fever of 39°C [102.2°F] that wouldn't come down for two days. My kidneys were bad. "No shape to be discharged in," they said. I was surprised to hear that. I'd had annual checkups at work and always came through 100 percent.

I was in the hospital for thirteen days, on drips the whole time. Changing the old body fluids. The biggest problem was urinating—I felt like going to the toilet every five minutes. There was nothing to pee out, just a few drops, but I found it hard to sleep when I wanted to take a leak all the time.

From the fourth day or so, I started having hallucinations. Always the same dream. Just as I'm dozing off it hits me. I'm sleeping in a white room and this white veil comes draping down over my head. It's fluttering around in the way, so I try to grab it and tear it off, but I can't reach. It's not that it's too high. I just can't get my hands on it. I dreamed that over and over again every night.

And while I'm dreaming there's this strong pressure, like someone's pressing down full force on my whole body. They say nightmares are one aftereffect of sarin. Well, it's not quite "dreaming." The fear stays lodged in the brain and these reactions just occur. But it's scary while you're dreaming; you snap awake three or four times a night, and that's what wears you out.

Another aftereffect, my eyesight's much worse. There's little chance of recovery, so I'm no good at the detailed work anymore. I have to proof layouts, which is difficult if I can't see precise alignments.

I took a week off work. The hospital said I ought to take three weeks, but if I took that long off the company would go bust (*laughs*). I'm in charge of all the plate layouts, with no one else to stand in. Two or three days we can let slide, but no more than that. So the fourth day at the hospital I had work brought in and gave instructions over the phone. I may have been sick, but I wasn't incapacitated! But you know, I think it contributed to my recovery.

Later I went back to the subway, boarded the very same train, and sat in the same seat. I even went to look at the place where I fell down. At the time I thought I'd run so far, when in fact I'd only gone about fifty meters at the most.

For a while after the gas attack I felt like throwing everything away. I'm generally good at holding on to things (I still have my plastic pencil case from elementary school). But I wanted to toss everything out. A year later that impulse has gone, but at the time it was like "Nothing's worthwhile anymore." I even felt like giving away my most precious bonsai.

When I went blind, I thought, "It'd be pathetic to die like this." I even cried out at the hospital: "I don't want to die!" Someone told me later. They heard me all the way down to the corridor from reception. It gave people goose bumps. Actually, when I was six I nearly drowned swimming in a river, and I remember thinking: "Ah, saved back then only to go blind and die like this . . ." I didn't think about my family; I just didn't want to die. Not there, not like that.

I have no feelings of hatred toward the Aum perpetrators, not now. At the time I was furious, outraged, but that anger disappeared relatively quickly. "Kill 'em, give 'em the death penalty"—I'm past all that. If you carried around all that hatred you'd never get over the aftereffects, but maybe I can say that because I don't have any really painful aftereffects . . .

### "The day of the gas attack was my sixty-fifth birthday"

## Kei'ichi Ishikura (65)

*At 55 Mr. Ishikura retired from his job with a towel man-
ufacturer, and currently works for a rubber cord company
in Ningyocho, northeast central Tokyo. The day I interviewed him at his home near Tanizuka Station on the
Tobu Isezaki Line in the northwestern suburbs of Tokyo,
the place was impressively clean. I mean spotless. Mr.
Ishikura gets up at 3:30 A.M., cleans the house from top to
bottom, has a bath, then goes to work. Amazing!*

*Not that he especially loves cleaning; he says that he
always wanted to do one thing better than anyone else,
and it turned out to be cleaning. Despite his claims to be
"impulsive by nature" and to "not really think things
through before acting," underneath it all he strikes me as
fastidious and iron-willed.*

*Mr. Ishikura did not suffer directly from being on the
platform or on any of the trains that were targeted. He just
happened to be walking past Kodemmacho Station when
he saw a victim collapse on the pavement. Concerned, he
went down into the station entrance to see what was
wrong, and that was toxic enough. A rare case among all
those I interviewed. Yet even now he suffers from aftereffects.*

•　　•　　•

I was born on March 20, so the day of the gas attack was my sixty-
fifth birthday. I was born in Ono, Fukui [on the north coast of Japan],
near Eiheiji Zen monastery. My family were dairy farmers. We had
seven or eight cows, milked them every morning, processed and bottled the milk, then delivered it to about eight hundred houses in the
town and surrounding hills.

My parents were very demanding. When we ate, they fussed over every little thing, like how we raised and lowered our chopsticks. Especially Father, who'd been in a cavalry regiment and had seen his fair share of punishment. I never did get along with Father. The reason I left home and went to Tokyo was because he wouldn't listen to anything I had to say. A real upstart I was. My big brother was in the army, and around the time he was posted to Manchuria I wanted to leave home, but my parents wouldn't let me go. "Your brother isn't here and you just disappear, what's to become of the business? You stay here and work until such time as we know for sure if your brother's dead or alive."

Then, after the war, my brother was sent from Manchuria to Tashkent in the Ukraine [*sic*], where he was forced to do hard labor. But since he was a technician, he was valued for driving cars and tractors, and he wasn't sent home for ages. It was eight years after the war ended, 1953, before he finally made it back to Japan. We didn't even know if he was still alive until a letter from him arrived in 1950.

Meanwhile I couldn't leave home. That milk delivery work, boy, how I hated it! I was coming of age, breaking out in pimples. I'd be doing my milk rounds and have to hide my face for shame every time I met a schoolgirl.

Once we knew my big brother was safe and sound, Father told me, "So now we know, you can go off wherever you want." They didn't need me around anymore, so I made straight for Tokyo. That was in 1951. I was 21.

I hadn't really thought things through before going to Tokyo, so naturally I screwed up a lot. It was always, "If only I hadn't done this, if only I hadn't said that." But as soon as I got an idea in my head, I couldn't rest until—*bam!*—I'd gone and done it. So *bam!*—I was off to Tokyo, and there I happened to meet someone from my hometown who manufactured towels and he said, "Come and work with me."

I'm ashamed to admit it, but when I came to Tokyo I'd secretly pocketed three thousand yen from my milk round (*laughs*). In those days three thousand yen was a fair amount. My train fare from Fukui down to Ueno [in Tokyo] cost only eight hundred yen. It was milk money I collected from a dozen or so families. I just stuffed it in my pocket and left.

As it turned out, I worked for that Nihombashi towel company a long, long time. It was 1984 when I retired, so that makes thirty-three years! I was in sales; I went out and got orders.

Marriage? I married the year they banned the red-light districts, so that was . . . 1958, was it? That's when the bill [*The Anti-Prostitution Act, April 1957*] was forced through . . . March 10, 1958. Army Day. I got married that day. I'd gone home for a few days and a neighbor said, "There's this girl, so how about it?" and I said, "Okay." Very simple. I thought it was about time I had a family like everyone else. We met the next day.

My father was furious. He knew about this impulsive nature of mine. "Of all the stupid things! Marrying someone you've never even met! It's not just your problem—there's the family name to consider." We had a big row. But thinking back on it now, he was right. I became a father myself, and when my daughter got married I was thinking the very same thing.

So the next day we met. She came out just once and I didn't even really get a good look at her face. We didn't have much to say. Her parents did all the talking; on my side there was just me. She came out for a moment, we exchanged greetings, and that was that. They served me sake. There wasn't much to like or dislike about her. She was a lot thinner then, and I suppose she looked pretty to me. All I thought was, "She'll do."

Anyway, about the gas attack. That day it took longer than usual to go from Tanizuka to Kita-senju. The train ran slow the whole way. I kept looking around wondering what on earth had happened. When we got to Kita-senju they announced over the PA: "There's been an explosion at Tsukiji Station, all trains are delayed." Then it was: "Alternate transport will be provided. Passengers in a hurry should take that." But I wasn't in any hurry, so I stayed on the train. Changing would have been a hassle, besides, I still had time before office hours began.

The train stayed at Kita-senju for about twenty minutes. When it did move again, it was starting and stopping all the time, crawling along. At Minami-senju or Minowa, it just stopped with the door open. En route they announced something about "injuries at Kasumigaseki." Of course, at that point we didn't know anything about poison gas, so "injuries" didn't mean much.

Yes, we were stuck at Ueno Station for ages. There was another announcement: "This train will go no farther for the foreseeable time. Passengers in a hurry should please change trains. Alternative transport is being provided." By then the train was practically empty. Everyone had gotten off, yet somehow or other it made it all the way to Akihabara. Then it stopped completely: "This service will terminate here." That was about 8:30.

I decided to walk from there. It's only two stations from Akihabara to Ningyocho. But when I got to the area around Kodemmacho Station, there were ambulances and people lying down all over the place, even on the sidewalk. "What's going on here?" I thought. I went to take a look two or three steps down into the subway entrance. But there were people lying on the steps, bent over or huddled up. One station attendant had his cap off and was clawing at his throat, groaning in agony. A businessman was shouting, "My eyes! My eyes! Do something!" Nothing made any sense.

Back up on street level, over by the Sanwa Bank, in a niche in the building, a girl was trying to help up a prostrate body. There were two or three ambulances on the scene, but that was hardly sufficient. There were bodies up and down the street, not sitting down but lying flat out, writhing in pain, struggling to loosen their collars and ties. People vomiting, too. A girl had vomited and was trying to take out her handkerchief to wipe her mouth, but she couldn't even manage that. She looked so ashamed, she tried to hide her face.

Everyone was suffering, bent over in pain, and there was no way to ask, "What's going on?" Firemen were rushing this way and that with stretchers. There was no time to talk to anyone.

One girl on the sidewalk was crying, "Help, please!" but when I asked her what had happened she didn't know. All she could say was, "Please, call somebody."

I didn't see a single policeman, just firemen with stretchers moving around, not really doing anything. Ask any of them about the situation and they couldn't tell you anything. So I decided to go on to work anyway.

I walked along Ningyocho Avenue to my company. The weather was clear that morning, yet everything looked dark and cloudy to my eyes. The day was warm; I even worked up a sweat walking, but by the time I was near the office the sun had gone dim.

I vomited as soon as I got to the office. I went inside and everything looked so dark. I had turned on the TV, then felt sick. I went straight to the toilet and vomited. A whole bucketful, really emptied out my stomach.

TV news carried first reports about the gas attack. People at the office said, "Ishikura, if you're sick you'd better see a doctor," so I went to a nearby hospital. The doctor told me, "This is just a cold." "But it's been on the TV," I said. Unfortunately the NHK News had said nothing about the attack, so he gave me two aspirins and said, "See, there's nothing on the news. It's just a cold. If your head still hurts take another of these at noon."

Well, my head did hurt. But I always have headaches, so I didn't pay much attention. I went back to the office, took the tablets, and immediately vomited again. I really retched, but there was nothing left to throw up, only water and the tablets I'd swallowed.

Soon more details came out on the TV. Two people had died at Kodemmacho, about eighty or so others had been taken to St. Luke's. I rang the police and asked them which hospital to go to, and they said Tajima in Ryogoku.

My eyes still aren't back to normal. With my left eye, the sun looks completely overcast, all fuzzy like an eclipse. It was fine before March 20. Now I wear UV filter glasses. I can't walk outside without them. I can barely see anything on TV.

I also tire more easily. There's no energy in my legs and joints. If I'm on my feet for even half a day I can't get my strength back. The doctor says, "That isn't sarin, it's just age." But do people age—snap!—just like that? It's very strange if you ask me, but there's no proof it was the attack.

My wife says my memory has gotten worse. I'll start to do something and can't remember what it was or where I put things. Also, since the gas attack, people say I ramble more. If I start to say something, everyone in the house just wanders off. I had tendencies in that direction before, but lately it's gotten terrible. I also drink more now. Before I used to drink only sake, but now I'm on whiskey. Drinking alone. I can hardly sleep, so I drink whiskey.

I get up around 2 A.M. to take a leak, then doze off until around 3:30. That's when I start dreaming. Often the same dream. I'm walking somewhere and someone bumps into me. I think, "Poor guy," but it's me who falls over. And they take me to the hospital, where the person who bumped into me apologizes. I dream that over and over again. When I wake, I'm in a cold sweat.

I don't say anything in public, but personally speaking, it's the death penalty for Asahara. I'd give anyone who did that the death penalty, no questions asked. They say the trial's going to drag on, but while I'm still alive I'd like to see them clinch it. It'd be insane if I got old and died first.

# TOKYO METROPOLITAN SUBWAY:

# KODEMMACHO STATION

### TRAIN UNIDENTIFIED

## *"I saw his face and thought:
'I've seen this character somewhere'"*

### Ken'ichi Yamazaki (25)

*Mr. Yamazaki was the young man whom Mr. Ichiba found collapsed and unconscious in front of Shibuya Station (see page 160). It took some effort to trace him, but in the course of conducting these interviews we were able to follow up various leads.*

*By pure coincidence, Mr. Yamazaki had been at high school in Kyoto with the Aum High Command's Yoshihiro Inoue. He saw his old classmate's face on TV and recognized him immediately: "Hey, that's Inoue!" He and Inoue had never gotten along, and talking to him it's not difficult to see why. Mr. Yamazaki enjoys snowboarding, basketball, fast cars (though he says he's calmed down considerably of late), and is altogether the outgoing sporty type; he would have nothing in common with the dark, introspective, even poetic sensibilities of Yoshihiro Inoue. From the moment he met Inoue on the school bus he thought to himself: "This guy's off my list. Can't even talk to him." Ten years after that initial negative impression, far away in the subways of Tokyo, he was to be visited by a very unwelcome and horrific confirmation of these doubts. Strange are the encounters of a lifetime.*

*A dedicated snowboarder, no matter how busy he is, he makes time to go to the slopes with his girlfriend at least once a week during the winter. The only good thing to come of the gas attack is that it has brought him and his*

*girlfriend closer together. It seems to have forced him to*
*grow up very quickly. He's curious as to what will become*
*of Yoshihiro Inoue.*

*Mr. Yamazaki lives with his parents and younger sister*
*in Shin Urayasu, east of Tokyo Bay.*

*   *   *

I had such trouble finding a job after college; every place was "No," straight down the list. I'd wanted to go into fashion design, but the big fashion manufacturers weren't taking anyone on. So I decided to try other fields—architecture, telecommunications, anything not food-related. In the end, I came away empty-handed. This was the year after Japan's "Bubble" burst and there was no work anywhere.

Somehow I managed to get into the clothing industry, where I worked until last March. I left because I never felt I was pushing myself to the best of my abilities. I wanted to do work where I'd be more appreciated.

I was telling my girlfriend this last October, and she'd just decided to resign too. So we were out of work and, in fact, we went to the company her father runs. It's a small firm of 15 employees. We make men's neckties, under license from an Italian maker, with three retail stores of our own in Tokyo.

Now I'm in sales there, which is great. Still, it's totally a family operation. When I entered the company I had dinner with the president—her father—and he asked me, "Do you plan to marry my daughter?" I'd been planning to ask for her hand once I'd built up a track record with the firm, but hey, what a break! (*laughs*) "Of course, sir," I told him, "I'd marry her tomorrow." And it was, "Well, well, timing aside, you're definitely the boy for our company."

About March 20, the day of the gas attack . . . Well, let me see, were we busy then? Just a second, please. I still have my Filofax from then [*goes into his room to fetch it*]. Hmm, seems we were really busy. Several new store openings, so I was getting home late, at 11:00 or 12:00 P.M. Yes and, that's right, I was going to driving school then as well.

I'd been revoked, and I was trying to get a new license. I've had

184

points against me three times running, twice for speeding in Hokkaido. And once you're revoked, they make you go back to driving school and learn everything all over again.

The morning of March 20, I left home thirty minutes earlier than usual. On Mondays there are the weekend sales figures to go through. Meetings, too. So I aim to arrive by 8:30. Thanks to which I ran into this sarin business. If it hadn't been Monday, I'd have missed it.

I was pretty spaced out that morning. It's always like that with me after a weekend. The day before, Sunday, I'd been out working in the evening. I went to a department store all the way out in Machida to talk things over with the sales staff there, deciding the layout, how to change the display. You can only do it after the store closes.

The following day was the Spring Equinox holiday, but still I had to work. I had to go to the opening of a redecorated Ginza department store. The fashion business might seem all show and glamour, but from the inside it's really tough. And the pay's not all that great either.

I always took the first or second car from the front of the train on the Hibiya Line. As soon as I changed in Hatchobori, there was an announcement: "Some passengers have been taken ill. We will stop the train at the next station, Tsukiji. Thank you for your cooperation." When the train stopped in Tsukiji, the doors opened and— *wham!*—four people fell flat out from the car right behind mine. Straight out the door.

A station attendant came over, like they do when someone faints, but they were trying to lift up the people, which seemed odd. That's when the panic started. A station attendant was shouting into a mike: "Ambulance! Ambulance!" Then it was "Poison gas! Everyone off the train! Go to the ticket barrier and head straight above ground!"

I didn't run. I wonder why? I was kind of unfocused. I did get off onto the platform, thinking I ought to sit down. I wasn't really paying much attention. There were others who didn't run. There wasn't any announcement that the train wouldn't start again, but eventually everyone filed out. Only then did it strike me, "You mean I have to leave too?" And I stood up. I was about the last.

No one seemed in any rush to get out of there. They were walking casually. It was more the station attendants who were yelling, "Please walk faster! Get outside!" I couldn't see any danger. No explosion or anything. The station attendants were all in a panic, but not the passengers. There were still a lot of people lingering in the station trying to decide what to do.

The people who'd collapsed didn't even twitch. Had they passed out? Were they dead? Some had their feet in the train and their bodies on the platform, and had to be dragged out. I still didn't sense any real danger. I don't know why. In retrospect that seems odd—why wasn't I afraid?—but then neither was anyone else.

I didn't go over to the injured people. I went toward the Tsukiji Honganji temple exit. Suddenly I got a whiff of this sweet smell, really sweet, like coconut. I was climbing the steps, thinking, "What's that?" when gradually it became difficult to breathe. Then I remembered that I had to call the office and tell them I was going to be late. There was a convenience store by the exit where I used the telephone. But it was still too early to call in to work, so I called home instead. My mother answered and I told her, "For some reason the train's stopped at Tsukiji and I'll never make it to work by 8:30."

Even in the short span of that telephone call, my breathing became worse. It wasn't like my throat was blocked or anything, I could breathe all right, but I wasn't getting enough oxygen; I'd inhale and inhale, but it was as though my lungs weren't working. It was strange. Like what happens when you wind yourself.

Only then did I begin to think things were a bit odd, that there might be some connection with the people who'd collapsed on the platform. After finishing my call, I went back to see the exit where I'd come up. I was gasping, but I had to know what was happening. Right at that very instant some Self-Defense Force soldiers or who-knows-who in gas masks and special combat gear went down the steps. There were station attendants being carried up on stretchers. They looked totally rabid: drooling, and their eyes completely white. One of them wasn't responding to anything, and another seemed to be having a fit—he couldn't walk straight and was groaning in pain. By then the roads were blocked off, and there were police cars and fire department cars all over the place.

I decided to walk to Yurakucho Station, take the Yamanote Line to Shibuya, then go by bus to Hiro-o, but the more I walked, the worse I felt. By the time I boarded the Yamanote Line train I felt I was done for. Everything was such an effort. The smell had penetrated my clothes. But somehow I had to make it to the Shibuya bus terminal. I knew for certain I'd run into someone from work there. Lots of our people commute by bus from Shibuya. But if I collapsed on the train, no one would help me. I had to get to the Shibuya bus stop even if I had to crawl all the way.

I got off the train at Shibuya and somehow managed to cross at the lights and reach the bus stop, where my legs just gave out. I sat on the sidewalk and leaned back against the handrail with my legs stuck out. Nobody looks that wasted in the morning, do they? Nobody except drunks, maybe. Which is why no one spoke to me. They saw me lying there and just assumed I'd been out on the town all night in Shibuya.

Finally, someone from work came along and spoke to me, but I couldn't speak. I could barely breathe. My voice was like some old alcoholic's with a paralyzed tongue. In any case, I couldn't translate my thoughts into words. I'd try to speak, but nothing came across. Since I couldn't explain, I just wanted any kind of help at all, but no one seemed to understand. I was getting a chill, colder and colder, just unbearable. Then another older colleague came by [*Takanori Ichiba*], and as fate would have it, he'd taken the Hibiya Line as well. He asked me, "Hey, did you get caught up in all that business at Tsukiji?" He put two and two together.

I was very lucky. If it hadn't been for him, no one would have known how serious things were. He immediately went to phone for an ambulance, but all the ambulances were out on call. So he hailed a taxi and lifted me into it with the help of two other people from work. We all got in and went to the Red Cross Hospital in Hiro-o. In the taxi, one of them said, "What's that sweet smell?" My clothes were soaked with sarin.

Breathing was the hardest thing, but aside from that I felt numb all over, and I couldn't keep my eyes open, as though all the strength had drained out of my body and I was drifting off into a deep sleep. I really thought I was going to die. I couldn't move. Still, I wasn't frightened. It wasn't painful. I thought, "Maybe this is what it's like to die of old age. If I have to die, let me at least see my girlfriend's face." More than even my parents, she's the one who came to me, in the end. Like, "Just tell her I wanted to see her face."

I don't remember how long it was before my work colleague found me, but I do remember being furious at all the people who pretended not to see me lying there. Assholes! How can human beings be so cold? Someone's in agony right there in front of them and they don't say a word. They just avoid you. If I'd been in their place, I'd have said something. If there's someone looking ill on the train I always say, "Are you okay? Want to sit down?" But not most people—I really learned that the hard way.

I was hospitalized for two days. They told me to stay longer, but I felt like I was some kind of guinea pig for testing a rare disease, so I went home. The doctor said, "You ought to stay here so that we have examples for other cases like yours." No thank you! On the train back, I was still wheezing, but I just wanted to get home, eat some good food, and take it easy. Strangely enough, my appetite was unaffected. Alcohol and cigarettes were completely out of the question for a long time, though.

The lethargy persisted for about a month. I took off another week from work, but for a very long time I wasn't on top of things physically. I still had difficulty breathing and I couldn't concentrate on my work. In sales, I have to talk like I am now—but the thing is, for every word I spoke I'd have to make an effort—*aah, ahh*—to draw in enough oxygen. Climbing the stairs was simply impossible. I often had to take time off. I just wasn't up to sales.

Honestly, it would have been better for me to take some time off with sick pay, but the company wasn't that generous. It was nine to five, plus overtime just like always. It was hard for me, but on the other side of the coin I suppose it had its interesting moments for others. In a funny kind of way. I'd go to clients and they'd say, "Yamazaki, I hear you got gassed with sarin." Everyone knew. I tried not to think too deeply about it, but the hardest thing was that no one really understood what I'd gone through. No, my changing jobs had nothing to do with the attack.

Even now I can't take too much strenuous exercise. I used to be able to snowboard for two hours straight without stopping, but now it's one and a half hours at the very most.

For a while after returning home I used an oxygen bottle when I had trouble breathing. You know, like the ones the baseball players use at the Tokyo Dome. No bigger than a can of insect spray, with a nozzle. My girlfriend bought it for me.

For me, the only good thing that came of the gas attack was coming to more of an understanding with my girlfriend. Until then we argued all the time. We didn't really consider each other's feelings. I was never quite sure how she felt about me. So I was really surprised when she came rushing to the hospital in floods of tears. "I thought you were going to die," she said, she was really upset. My boss was beside me at the time, and in plain view of him she held my hand and wouldn't let go. She came to the hospital every single day and when I checked out and went home, she came with me too. We'd always kept our relationship a secret at work, so to have her squeeze my hand in front of the boss . . . (*laughs*) That blew our cover!

I was in the same class as Yoshihiro Inoue at Rakunan High School in Kyoto. We never took any of the same courses, but we were in the same grade level. We took the same bus to school from Hankyu Omiya Station, so I got to know him fairly well. A good friend of mine took the same courses as Inoue, which is why we traveled together. I never got friendly with him.

And yet I still remember him extremely vividly. My first impression was that he was incredibly strange. Weird. Twisted. I disliked him from the start. That's why I never talked to him. You can tell whether you'll get along with someone from just a few words; well, I never got along with him. I'd listen to my friend's conversations with Inoue and I thought: "This guy gives me the creeps." I went to a school in Tokyo in my junior year, but I heard later from my friend that Inoue had been doing *zazen* in class, meditating for hours.*

I had lots of friends. I was into bikes, and we'd all go out riding. I liked being outdoors, but Inoue didn't.

About two weeks after the gas attack, when they showed the Aum people in the papers and on TV, I saw his face and thought: "I've seen this character somewhere." I rang up my old school friend and he said, "Yep, it's Inoue, all right."

I was furious. I remembered the unpleasantness I had felt back

*Zazen* is a form of seated meditation. [Tr.]

in high school. I was just outraged. I'd changed high schools, but I still had some pride in the old place. I couldn't believe any graduate from Rakunan could do such a terrible thing. It was such a shock, a real letdown.

I'm still keeping an eye out for news of him. I just want to see what they'll do with him, how far his so-called sincerity goes.

## "He was such a kind person. He seemed to get even kinder before he died"

### Yoshiko Wada (31)
*wife of the late Eiji Wada*

*Mrs. Wada was pregnant when her husband died. A daughter, Asuka, was born not long afterward. Mrs. Wada was often in the media spotlight after the gas attack, and many Japanese now know her face. Before meeting her I glanced over all the magazine and newspaper articles I could find, but the difference between the image I'd invented and the person I actually met was startling. Of course, that image was a complete fabrication on my part and no one was to blame, but it did make me pause to consider how the media works—how they make up whatever image they want.*

*The real Yoshiko Wada (as opposed to the media invention) was bright, articulate, and smart. By "smart" I mean she chose her words as carefully as she had chosen her way of life. Although I had never met her late husband, somehow I knew that anyone who had chosen her as a mate had to have been an all-right guy.*

*The shock of losing her husband must have been great. I doubt if one can ever recover from such a thing. But throughout the three hours I interviewed her, she never once lost her composure or her smile. She was very open with her replies, however indelicate my line of questioning, and only once became tearful, at the very end. I apologize for putting her through so much.*

*She met me with Asuka in her arms and even saw me off at the station afterward. The streets were almost deserted in the summer heat. Walking outside, she looked like any other happy, young suburban housewife. My parting words were pretty lame—"Please be healthy and happy" or something like that—I couldn't think of any-*

*thing else to say. Words can be practically useless at times, but as a writer they're all I have.*

* * *

I was born in Kanagawa [southwest of Tokyo], but we moved to Yokohama [south of Tokyo] when I was in elementary school and I've lived here ever since. I went to school in Yokohama, worked in Yokohama. I'm a Yokohama girl, so of course I love the place. Last year when I had my baby, I spent a long time at my in-laws' up in Nagano. The air was much cleaner, a complete change of environment, which was great and all, but when I got back here I was so happy I cried.

Most of my friends are here in Yokohama. Friends from high school, from work, skiing friends, we all go back ten years . . . Friends really helped me a lot. They're all married now, but still we get together from time to time and have a barbecue or go bowling or something.

When I left high school, I went to work for the Yokohama Savings and Loan as a clerk. I left soon after I got married. Before that I lived with my parents. I'm an only child, but I was always arguing with them, especially with my dad. Over stupid little things, really. "You said this." "No, I never said that!" (*laughs*) I was pretty selfish. I'm living with Dad now, but we don't argue anymore.

I met my husband skiing. Another girl at work had a boyfriend working for Japan Tobacco, and he just happened to bring him along. This was in February 1991.

My husband was really into skiing. I'd only begun to ski at 20, so I was nowhere near his level. Still, I'd go skiing maybe five times a season. Though my parents didn't want to let me go. They said it was too dangerous (*laughs*). They were so overprotective. I had a curfew until I was 25. Had to be home by ten (*laughs*). Sometimes I'd get back late and find myself locked out, so I'd end up sleeping at a friend's house. Thinking back on it I suppose I was pretty bad. Now that I have my own child, I know, you get angry because you care.

My mother died of breast cancer four years ago. It spread all over her body. Dad stopped working to stay by her side. It was hard on him, I know. But even then, he and I, we were arguing the whole time. I feel terrible about it now, but at the time I just couldn't help it. On the other hand, it's because we argued so much then that we can get along together now.

My dad tells me I've changed a lot. Mellowed a bit. Maybe I'm more of an adult. Asuka's the big reason, probably. I look at the baby and even if I'm worked up I have to smile.

As first impressions go, my husband didn't seem like much when he was skiing. No charm whatsoever. He wore glasses behind his goggles. I tried talking to him, but it was like, "What's with this guy?" He was so unfriendly. He was just so wrapped up in his skiing he couldn't be bothered with anyone else. He couldn't rest unless he was skiing in front. He barely spoke.

But in the evening when we went out drinking suddenly he changed completely, I mean, he really opened up, even told jokes. He was like a different person. We stayed at the ski resort three days, but we never got close personally, though I guess we were attracted to each other.

To be honest, when I first met him, I instinctively felt: "Here's someone I could go out with, maybe even marry." It was like, well, a woman thing. So I thought, "Might as well give him my phone number." I was pretty sure of myself (*laughs*).

We were both 26 and we both drank a lot: beer, whiskey, sake, wine, you name it. He really liked having a good time.

We saw each other a lot after that ski trip. He was living in a single men's dorm in Kawaguchi, so we'd generally meet somewhere in the center of Tokyo. We often went to the cinema, saw each other every week, and if possible at weekends, too.

Yeah, it really seemed we were made for each other. Like it was fate or something. We courted for a year and never once was I bored.

He mentioned marriage to my dad even before saying anything to me. He said to my dad: "I'd like to ask your permission to see Yoshiko socially with the understood intention of marriage." Of course I liked him and all, but the two of them talking among themselves like that before I knew anything about it really got on my nerves.

We were married in June the following year. My mom had died that February and we were in mourning, so we put off the wedding until then. I guess I really wanted to wear a wedding dress and every-thing. We planned to live with my dad in Yokohama after getting mar-ried. We didn't want to leave him all alone . . . it was my husband who suggested it. So he ended up commuting from Yokohama to Oji, two hours each way. Every day, he'd leave the house at six in the morning. I was fighting with Dad the whole time then and my hus-band always had to settle things between us. He had it hard. He'd come back home at 11:00 or 12:00 at night, dead tired.

We lived with Dad for ten months, then we moved to Kita-senju. Japan Tobacco happened to have some company housing there, but that now put me an hour and a half away from my job in Yokohama. After a year of commuting, I was worn out. My husband said, "Why kill yourself like that? You do what you want."

So I became a housewife. Three meals a day plus afternoon nap? Not bad if you ask me (*laughs*). You can watch TV all day. I'd never watched daytime TV before, so at first I was—*happy!* And by July, I was expecting. Kita-senju was a nice place to live. Lots of shops, near the station, and the company housing was spacious. I had friends there too.

In November 1994, my husband got transferred from Oji to the main plant in Shinagawa [closer to Yokohama]. Then he had to work on-site at the new head office they were building in Toranomon [cen-tral Tokyo]. The building was scheduled for completion in April 1995 and he had to look after installation work and construction. He was an electrical specialist, so he was in charge of the elevators and light-ing and air-conditioning systems. I could tell he was happy to get away from desk work.

He'd come home and tell me about his day over a beer. That was the best part, hearing him talk about the company, about his col-leagues, like, "There's this guy who's this or that, what do you think I should do?" He usually joked most of the time, but at work he could concentrate, real serious, just like that. He was so reliable.

Both of us wanted children. We wanted about three. Especially me, probably because I was an only child. I was so overjoyed when I found out I was pregnant. We settled on my daughter's name before she was born. I heard it in a dream. I dreamed this child was running off somewhere and I was chasing her, calling out that name. I couldn't remember it myself, but my husband told me he heard me shouting, "Asuka! Asuka!"

We hardly ever quarreled. Still, I was irritable while I was pregnant. I'd get at him for the most trivial things but he just took it all in his stride. He usually just laughed it off. He was such a kind person. He seemed to get even kinder before he died.

If he got home from work and the cooking had gone wrong he'd just say, "It's all right, I'll get takeout." He even asked around at work about what I should be eating during pregnancy. He really cared for me. And when I had morning sickness and could only eat sandwiches and grapefruit jelly, he'd always buy them for me on the way home from work.

The Sunday before March 20 we went shopping together. Something he'd ordinarily never do.

It was raining that morning so we slept in, but it had cleared up by the afternoon so I said, "Let's go shopping," and for once he said, "Fine."

We went to buy baby clothes and diapers, stuff like that. My belly was already big by then and I had a hard time walking, but the doctor was always telling me: "Move! Move! Move!"

After that we ate dinner. He was eager to go back to work the next day. He'd taken Friday off, but the April 1 office completion date was looming and it was preying on his mind. Also that particular Monday they had a welcoming party of some sort, which he was looking forward to.

He always got off at Kasumigaseki on the Hibiya Line to go to the Toranomon office. He'd generally get up at 7:00 and leave home by 7:30. That day he got up really early, around 5:30. Usually I didn't have time to make him breakfast, but the night before he'd said: "On occasion, it'd be nice to be pampered and woken up to a real breakfast." "Well, if that's what he wants," I thought, and I forced myself to get up early and cook for him. He just seemed to crave a little pampering.

I've never been a morning person, I usually forget breakfast. And he wasn't a morning person either, so it was always "Never mind," up and out the door at the last minute, catch a quick bite on the way to work. But that morning I set two alarm clocks, got up bright and early, made toast and coffee and fried eggs and sausages for him. He was so happy he shouted: "Wow! Breakfast!"

It was as though he had some kind of premonition. Besides saying he wanted me to make him breakfast, I remember him saying something like, "If anything ever happens to me, you know you have to hang on in there and fight." It was right out of the blue, caught me completely off guard, and I asked him, "What makes you say a thing like that?"

It turned out that at the new office there would be a shift system, so he'd have to sleep over for two nights. There'd be days he wouldn't be coming home, so he wanted to make sure I could handle things on my own. But then if he stayed over two nights, he'd get three days off and that would give him more time with the baby, which was a pleasant prospect.

He left the house around 7:30. I understand he caught the 7:37 Hibiya Line train departing from Kita-senju. I sent him off, washed up, then puttered around a bit before settling down to watch the *Morning Wide Show*. Across the TV screen they ran subtitles: "Such-and-such happened at Tsukiji Station," but I didn't worry because I thought he said he commuted by the Marunouchi Line.

At 9:30 a call came from the company saying, "He seems to have gotten mixed up in this mess. We'll call back later." Then ten minutes later, it was, "He's been taken to Nakajima Hospital. We'll fax you the details so you can get in touch directly." So I called them up, but they were in total confusion. "We can't even keep track of who's here," they said, and hung up. So all I could do was be patient and wait.

It was just before 10:00 when the call came: "It looks pretty bad, so come to the hospital as quickly as possible." I was getting ready to leave when the phone rang again with the message: "He just died." I think it was his boss. He was saying, "Keep calm, Mrs. Wada, keep calm!"

Well, leaving the house was okay, but I had no idea where I was going. I didn't even know which subway line to take. Both the Hibiya and Marunouchi lines were canceled. I went to the taxi stand at the station, but there were about fifty people lined up. "This is no good," I thought, so I made straight for a cab company nearby. All the cars were out on call. They radioed, but I waited and waited and still nothing came. Luckily the man at the cab company spotted a taxi sitting empty over by the train crossing, so I took that.

By then the body had been transferred from the hospital to the central police station in Nihonbashi. I took another taxi to Nihonbashi, but traffic was jammed from an accident on the expressway. We left Kita-senju at 10:10 and reached the police station around 11:30. In the taxi I heard my husband's name. The driver had the news on and they were reading out the names of the deceased. "That's me," I said. "My husband's died." The driver asked me, "Should I turn off the radio?" but I said, "No, keep it on. I want to know what's happening."

That hour in the taxi was torture. My heart was pounding, I thought it was going to leap out of my mouth. What if I went into labor right there and then? But I also thought: "I can't be sure until I see his face. I won't believe until I see his face for myself. There's absolutely no way it could happen, there has to have been some mistake. Why, oh why would my husband be the one to die?" That's all that kept spinning through my head: "I won't cry until I know for sure" . . . I just hoped against hope.

They were examining the body, so it was 1:30 before I got to see him. I had to hang around in the police station all that time. The telephone was ringing nonstop and everyone was running about in a blind panic. Total confusion. My husband's boss and a police officer explained everything to me, though at that point many details still weren't clear. It was only the most sketchy explanation: "He inhaled something and that's what killed him."

I called my dad immediately. "Just come," I told him. As soon as I saw Dad's face, I couldn't fight back the tears. My husband's parents are farmers; if the weather's good, they're always working outdoors, so I couldn't get through to them. His boss kept trying to phone them, but no one answered. I wanted to see my mother-in-law as soon as I could. I just sat there, unable to speak, thinking: "What am I doing here?" It was all I could do just to nod at the detective's questions.

I finally got to see my husband face-to-face downstairs. Upstairs was the police station, the ground floor was the morgue. That's where I got to see him. In a tiny room not more than two tatami mats in size, if that. They'd laid him out, covered with a white sheet. Completely naked and covered with a white sheet. "Don't touch him," they told me. "Don't go too near." There was something on him and if I touched him, it would penetrate my skin.

But before they'd warned me not to, I'd already gone and touched him. He was still warm. There were bloodied bite marks on his lips. Scabs, as if he'd bitten down really hard. And on his ears and nose, too, crusted, where he'd bled. His eyes were shut. It wasn't a suffering face. But those scars, those blood marks, they looked so painful . . .

They didn't let me stay very long because it was "dangerous." I was in there maybe a minute . . . no, not even a minute. "Why did he have to die?" I said. "Why did he leave me here?" And I broke down.

The body was transferred to Tokyo University Law Medical Department at 4:30. Dad tried to give me courage, but his words didn't even reach me. I couldn't do anything. I couldn't think. "What am I going to do now? What am I going to do now?" was all I could manage.

The next day, I bid him a final farewell at Tokyo University. They didn't let me touch him then, either, nor my mother-in-law, who came down from Nagano. We could only look. I couldn't believe they'd left him overnight in such a lonely place. Even the police department would have been better. His parents came all the way to Tokyo and they wouldn't even show them Eiji's body at the police station. Talk about cruel.

My husband's elder brother took the body back to Nagano by car. My in-laws and Eiji's grandfather, I, and my dad went by train. I cried the whole way. I told myself, "Control yourself." I had to see the funeral through; after that I didn't care. My in-laws were trying their hardest, after all, so I should. Like they say, the Buddha doesn't like to see weeping. But I just couldn't . . .

The baby moved inside me. As soon as I cried, it was rolling this way and that. After the funeral, my stomach bulge sank lower and lower. Everyone was worried for me. They said that births often follow quickly after a shock.

We keep a little picture of the deceased on the Buddhist altar, right? I put that by my bedside in the labor room, and it gave me strength. My mother-in-law and my husband's friend's mother were also there to cheer me on. It took thirteen hours in all. "Quite normal," they told me. "This is normal?" I thought (*laughs*). The baby weighed six pounds, eleven ounces, heavier than expected. During the birth I was so preoccupied I completely forgot about my husband. It was that painful. I almost passed out, but my mother-in-law came into the delivery room and slapped me on the cheeks: "Hold on!" I don't remember any of this, though.

When it was all over I was so tired, all I wanted to do was sleep. Most women probably think, "How wonderful" or "What a cute baby"—but not this one. After pushing so hard, I just had to let go . . .

It took forever to lose weight after the birth, but my mother-in-law took care of everything. She looked after Asuka. I was without a mother of my own, and Dad wouldn't have had a clue what to do. My mother-in-law was a real veteran, having helped my brother-in-law's wife with her children, so I felt like I was safe on board a luxury liner. If it had been just me, I might have gone mad. That's the good thing about extended families.

Eiji's brother had two children (and a third one around the same time as mine) and whenever I started sobbing those kids came and asked, "Auntie, you okay?" or "Is it because Eiji died?" I couldn't keep crying with children around. They were a great consolation.

I returned to Yokohama that September, after living about half a year with my in-laws. It practically became a second home (*laughs*). I still go there a lot. I enjoy it. Everyone welcomes me, and my husband's grave is there.

A year on, I've managed to put things behind me a bit. It's gradually sunk in that he's not around anymore . . . My husband used to go to America on business trips for two or three months at a time, so on one level it seemed normal, him not being here. Even after he died I'd think, "Ah, he's off again on one of his trips." The whole year was like that, as if he'd suddenly step through the door and say, "I'm home!" I'd wake up in the morning and think, "He's away," but then I'd see his picture on the altar. Some part of me still couldn't accept what had happened. I seemed to be living a mixture of reality and fantasy. Like I'd be thinking, "He'll be coming home soon" even while visiting his grave. But now, a year later, I'm much clearer in my own mind: "Yes, he's dead."

That was the hardest part. Going on walks, seeing a father carrying a baby on his shoulders was almost too much to bear; or overhearing a young couple's conversation—I just didn't want to be there.

I've read what they said about me in the papers, but they never write what's really important. For one reason or another I once appeared on TV. Afterward the man from the TV station told me there was "lots of response" and "many letters," not that they sent me anything. What a shabby operation (*laughs*)! I don't want to be on TV anymore. Never again. They just don't tell the truth. I'd hoped for a little truth, but the station's got its own agenda about what it broadcasts. They never showed what I really wanted to say.

For example, when that lawyer Sakamoto disappeared, if the Kanagawa police had been allowed to investigate in depth like they were supposed to, the gas attack would never have happened.* All the victims would have been spared. That's what I wanted to say, but they cut all that out. When I asked why, they said they'd be under pressure from advertisers if they broadcast that. And the same goes for newspapers and magazines.

When we took the coffin to Nagano there were TV crews ready with their cameras. Talk about insensitive!

When I came home to Yokohama, everyone knew all about me. I'd walk down the street and people would point at me: "Look, there she is. That sarin widow." My back tingled, I felt like I was being stabbed. I couldn't stand it, so I moved.

The first time I went into the Public Prosecutor's Office for a hearing, they had the testimony of the person who had carried my husband out of the station. They also had testimonies from the station attendants. The prosecutor asked me did I want to know how my husband had died? "Of course," I said, and they read them to me. "What? Do you mean to say he died in such agony?" I thought. I wanted to give the ones who did it a taste of their own medicine.

*In November 1989 anti-Aum lawyer Tsutsumi Sakamoto was murdered, along with his wife and their baby son. It was not until October 1998 that cult member Kazuaki Okazaki was sentenced to death for murdering the Sakamotos. He had crept into the family home and injected them with lethal doses of potassium chloride, then strangled them. Shoko Asahara has also been charged with murdering the Sakamotos. [Tr.]

Why were we even keeping them alive? Give them the most extreme punishment, the sooner the better, that's what I think. I always will. The trial proceedings just irritate me. What possible reason was there to kill my husband? What am I supposed to do with this emptiness now that our future's been destroyed?

I'd like to kill Asahara with my own two hands. If it were allowed, I'd like to kill him slowly and painfully. Hayashi, the culprit who gassed the Hibiya Line train, is still on the loose.*

I just want to know the truth. The truth, and not a minute too soon . . .

Even the media, they didn't say a thing about how the victims died in agony. Not a word. There was a little at the time of the Matsumoto incident, but with the gas attack, nothing. Strange. So I'm sure the majority of people out there probably imagine they just keeled over and died "normal" deaths. The same with all the newspaper articles. I only learned how painfully my husband died when the prosecutor read me those testimonies. I want more people to know the truth about just how horrible it was . . . Otherwise, it all becomes somebody else's problem.

The only good thing is Asuka. When she spoke her first words . . . Some little gesture, some food she likes will remind me of him. I'm always telling Asuka, "Dada was like this." If I didn't tell her, she'd never know. When Asuka asks, "Where's Dada?" I point to the photo on the altar and say, "Dada, Dada." She says, "Nighty-night" to the photo before going to sleep. It makes me want to cry.

I still have a few videos from ski trips, our honeymoon. You can hear his voice, so I'll play them for her when she gets a bit older. I'm *so* glad we took those videos. Even I'm starting to forget his profile. At first, I could still feel every part of his face in my fingers, but gradually it's all going away . . .

Forgive me . . . It's just that, without the body, it all starts to fade.

I'm thinking of teaching Asuka to ski. My husband always said he would. I'll wear my husband's gear and teach her. My husband and I wore the same size. I think I'll start next season. It's what he would have wanted.

---

*He was finally arrested in December 1996. [Tr.]

### "He was an undemanding child"

## Kichiro Wada (64) and Sanae Wada (60)
*parents of the late Eiji Wada*

*Kichiro and Sanae Wada live in Shioda-daira in the coun-
tryside on the outskirts of Ueda, not far from Bessho Hot-
springs. The autumn leaves were falling when I visited the
Wada household, the hills were tinged crimson and gold,
the apple trees in the orchards were laden with ripe red
fruit. It was an idyllic picture of the mountainous Nagano
Prefecture at harvesttime.*

*The area had once been the center of silk production,
with vast tracts of mulberry trees whose leaves were used
to feed the silkworms. After World War II the land was
converted to rice fields, which brought the local silk
industry to a sudden halt.*

"Government's way of doing things don't make much
sense for a farming village as small as ours," *says Mr.
Wada. He is a man of few words—though there are plenty
of things he could say if he wanted to. His wife, Sanae, by
contrast, is your affable, talkative "mother" type.*

*The Wadas have about two and a half acres in rice, as
well as vegetables and apples. As I was leaving for Tokyo,
they gave me an armful of apples fresh from their orchard—
they were delicious!*

*For the first few years after they married the Wadas sur-
vived by farming alone, but as times got tougher Mr. Wada
was forced to work in a factory to make ends meet, only
tending the fields on his days off. The double workload
really wore him out. When their son died in the gas
attack, he could scarcely recover from the shock and he
left his factory job.*

*I asked him what sort of child Eiji had been.* "Didn't
have much to do with raising the boy," *he told me,* "best
ask my wife." *He had too much on his hands to deal with*

*the children, I suppose, and yet, at the same time, I got the distinct impression he found the subject of his dead son too painful to talk about.*

*"He was an undemanding child." Comments to that effect were repeated over and over again in the course of the interview. Eiji had been a strong, independent young man who never caused his parents any worry. Not until the day his body was sent home without a word of explanation . . .*

●  ●  ●

MOTHER: Eiji was born at 5:40 in the morning on April 1. I just knew I couldn't hold out until morning, so when dawn came we went to the midwife's place. That was around 4:00. I gave birth almost immediately.

It was an easy birth. He only weighed five pounds. The older one was eight pounds, so Eiji was a lot smaller. It was a natural birth, over in an hour and a half, no need to call in the doctor. With his big brother, though, what an ordeal!

We didn't have any choice but to raise goats. Had lots of grass all around anyway. So I'd milk the goats and drink their milk to give me lots of milk so I could breast-feed Eiji. That's how I got Eiji to grow up healthy. Always stayed a little skinny, though, never put on much weight. But we never once had to put him in the hospital.

He was an undemanding child. Whatever it was, he could always do it for himself. When he went for an interview with Japan Tobacco, we asked, "Would you like one of us to go with you?" which only annoyed him: "Who's gonna come with me? I'll go alone!" (laughs) Or when he was living alone, I'd say, "Shall I come and houseclean for you?" and he'd say: "Housecleaning I can do for myself!" These last ten years there's been only three times I had to go out of my way for Eiji: when he got engaged, then for the wedding, and then when we had to bring back his body.

The older boy, he's more the quiet type, but Eiji was active, a whiz-bang do-it-yourselfer. Even did his own cooking. That's why we never had any problem bringing him up. He'd decide everything for himself.

When it came time for high school, we told him, "Why not try and go on to university?" But he said, "I like electrical stuff, so I'll go to a vocational school and not go any higher." The boys had talked it over. The elder one said, "It'll be easier if I just stay on here and take on the family farm," and Eiji said, "I don't expect anything from here, so I'll go off on my own." The two of them decided it between themselves.

The older boy did try going to university in Tokyo, but said he couldn't see himself living in that crazy mixed-up place and came back to agricultural school here. But not Eiji. That boy could make it anywhere. He took to city life straightaway. After graduating from the electrical program, he went to work for Japan Tobacco in 1983. My sister's husband worked there already. When he was about to retire, he said, "Why doesn't Eiji join Japan Tobacco?" This was just around the time they were computerizing the machines, and when Eiji went in for the interview, he said, "I want to join so I can learn these computer systems," so maybe that's why they gave him the job. At the training in Nagaoka everyone else was a university graduate, he told me, only two out of twelve were straight out of high school.

He said that in Nagaoka the snow piled up a meter deep. So the next thing he's saying he wants to learn to ski. He needed equipment so could I send him money? Which I did. So then he really got into skiing, was skiing all the time. It was on a ski slope that he met Yoshiko.

At Nagaoka he was away from home, starting a new life alone, but he didn't seem lonely. He made lots of friends, he was making money for himself and was free to have fun with it.

When they told us Eiji had died, honestly, my head went totally blank. You hear about people "blanking out," but it really did happen. Didn't know what was what.

Wasn't anybody home at the time. His company and the police rang up, but everyone was out. Before that I'd been putting up miso, like I always make up a batch in April, but since I had to go and help with Eiji's baby, I put it up a month ahead of time. That kept me busy. On the twentieth the weather was clear, so I washed the laundry that had been piling up, ran all sorts of errands. Father had gone to prune the apple trees in the orchard that morning, and my blood pressure was up a little, so I went to the hospital for medicine, which is why nobody was at home.

Eventually they got through to my elder sister, who said, "I call you a thousand times and there's no one there. Haven't you seen TV?" On the way back from the hospital I was going to buy some flowers, it being Higan [the Buddhist equinox], but first I went home for a bit. That's when the phone rang.

"Such good weather, why would anyone be watching TV? If it rains I'll watch, but now I'm just too busy." That's when she said, "Listen, don't get alarmed. Brace yourself." And I was like, "Brace myself? What's this all about?"

And it was, "Just now on the TV, they said Eiji's dead." That's when everything went blank. That was it. I can't recall another thing. It came that hard. The shock, it just wiped out everything . . .

It was a year before they married that he brought Yoshiko home. Brought her in the wintertime. Eiji only ever came home twice a year, at Obon [the Buddhist festival of the dead, in August] and at year-end, and this was in the winter. Because we'd just finished all our winter preparations. As I recall, Yoshiko didn't stay with us that time, she went back home the same day.

All along I'd been saying, "Wouldn't it be better to get a bride from the country? So it'd be easier to come up here, it being home country to you both." And Eiji would say, "No, a country girl would be just as much a bother. I'll find my own, don't you worry, Mother. I'll worry about that myself."

FATHER: That was fine by me. Let him choose who he likes and stay with her, that's all that matters. A parent has no right to interfere in a child's marriage. Let them do it for themselves, is what I say.

MOTHER: Their wedding was at a chapel in Aoyama. A small ceremony. "Dozens of people wouldn't fit in the hall," he told us, so only really close relations attended. But when I said, "We'll have to throw another ceremony again when you come up to the country," he told me, "I'm the second son. Brother's the one going to carry on the family line. Me, who knows whether I'll even end up back here or not, so there's no need to do anything special for me."

We heard that Yoshiko was expecting when they came to visit at New Year. I'd somehow sensed it when they came up in August. The color in her cheeks hadn't looked so good then, and I thought to myself, well, just maybe. So I asked her and she said, "I suppose I could be."

FATHER: On March 20, like my wife said earlier, I was pruning the apples out back. Been at it since morning. Have to finish before the end of March. We got forty apple trees in all.

Our eldest lives with us, but under a separate roof. Meals and everything we take separate. He's got his wife and kids with him. So if our phone rings, you can't even hear it over there. And anyway his wife was pregnant then too, and she was out getting medicine at the birth clinic.

But it just so happens the older boy was listening to the radio at work when the name "Eiji Wada" came out. Then he flew over to our place. He'd called and called on the phone but nobody answered, so he guessed we were out in the field. But even before him, my wife'd come home and got that phone call first.

Word came from the police, too. Headquarters had phoned the local police post, told them to go straight out and find us, is what happened. And just when my wife was on the phone, the police came driving up.

MOTHER: I didn't want Father to keel right over in the field if he suddenly heard about it, so we went out to the apple orchard and told him, "Come here a second." Four of us went to Tokyo. Father, me, our eldest boy, and my sister's husband, who pushed Eiji to join Japan Tobacco. We caught the 2:00 train from Ueda, and we got into Ueno Station around 5:00. It was still light out. Someone from Japan Tobacco came to meet us and took us by taxi to the Central Police Headquarters. No one breathed a word on the way. It was dead silence. We just kept quiet in the car and got out when we were asked.

But by then the body was no longer with the police. It had been sent over to Tokyo University Forensics. So after all that we couldn't even see our Eiji that day and we were put up overnight in the Japan Tobacco guest house. I couldn't sleep that night. The next morning at 9:00 we all went to Tokyo University Hospital and finally got to see him. Without thinking, I touched Eiji and they yelled at me.

How was I supposed to know you weren't supposed to touch him? I just couldn't help myself. Apparently Yoshiko touched him and they shouted at her, too. But to a mother, she's got to touch him and feel he's cold before she finally admits to herself, "It's too late." Otherwise nothing's going to convince her.

Everything in my head was just wiped clean away. I couldn't understand anything. But I kept control, you know, so I didn't cry. I was reduced to a complete idiot, my body still moving but that was it. We had to send him to meet Lord Buddha and give him a funeral. When your head goes empty, even tears don't come.

It's strange, but in my head all I could think about was preparing the rice fields. Two children . . . grandchildren on the way, rice planting to do, gotta do this, gotta do that, my mind was keeping me busy. So there I was, getting ready to transplant the rice seedlings when the TV crew showed up.

FATHER: I didn't answer nothing to the reporters. I got so mad at them. They even followed us to the crematorium. Even took pictures of the birthing clinic. I told 'em please go away, but no matter what I said they just wouldn't go. They pushed themselves on the neighbors. And they asked us, "They want us to talk, so what should we do, Mr. Wada?" but I told them, "Don't say nothing."

Just once, when I was riding my tractor and they came up shoving a mike at me, saying, "Mr. Wada, any comment?" just once I answered. I said: "I'd like to see the killers get an immediate death penalty for their crime. And they'll have to amend Japan's Constitution. That's all. Now please go home." I just wouldn't have anything more to do with them and I went straight back to the field. The TV station set up a camera in front of our house, aiming for when I came home. So I just scooted around back on my bike. At the time, there was just so many people come to report on us. Saying they were writing something for magazines or whatever.

I just barely hung on, knowing the rice planting had to get done or else. And when rice planting was done, I just collapsed. All sorts of thoughts were in my head, but think and think there's just no end to it. No matter how much you think, the dead boy's not coming back. I had to tell myself, can't keep feeling this way forever. Still, there's no forgetting, either. Every time I think back over it all, I get these feelings stewing again in my gut.

I'm not much of a drinker, but I like my sake. So whenever Eiji came home, us three'd drink together, father and sons. That sake always tasted the best, like nothing else. A little drink in us and the talk'd just spring to life. We'd put away a *sho* [1.8 liters] in an evening. We're a close family. Never once argued.

MOTHER: He was a kind child. When he got his first pay, he bought me a watch. And also whenever he came back to visit, he'd always bring something for his big brother's kids. When he went to America and Canada on business, he bought us souvenirs.

He even bought souvenirs for Asuka before she was born. A while back, when Asuka came up to visit, she was wearing clothes that Eiji had bought her in America. That's how much he looked forward to the child being born. I mean he really was looking forward to it, and yet . . . when I think how those idiots went and killed him, it's so pathetic.

FATHER: At the time of the Matsumoto incident, why didn't the police do a better job of investigating? If they'd done that, this whole mess would never have happened. If only they'd pushed harder on the case back then.

MOTHER: Still, his wife and baby are fine; she bore us a splendid grandchild. I try to remember that. If I hung around here sobbing all the time, I'd be no good helping her after the birth, so I had to pull myself together, and it's gotten me through this far.

FATHER: There's farming to be done, what we've always done. Once the rice seedlings are set it's time to transplant them to the rice fields, once that's done it's picking the apple buds, then it's pollinating the blossoms . . . there's no rest, the work keeps on coming. Working like that wears you down physically and when you're tired out you sleep like a log. We've got no time for neuroses or tranquilizers. That's just how it is for farmers.

## "Sarin! Sarin!"

### Koichiro Makita (34)

*Mr. Makita works in film production. From 1988 to 1994, he had his own company and was doing independent production, but when the recession set in he went to work for his present company. He's in charge of visual development for computer-game software.*

*In compiling this book, I laid down a rule for myself not to interview anyone more than once—no later additions—but Mr. Makita was an exception. My tape recorder wasn't working properly and wouldn't play back what we recorded the first time, so unfortunately I had to beg for a second attempt—in order to "get more detail." Maybe the mishap with the tape recorder was some kind of message; the second time around, Mr. Makita gave me a long, in-depth interview.*

*Mr. Makita was not reluctant to speak, but neither is he the type to volunteer information about himself. His answers generally stayed within the bounds of the questions asked. Not one to pry, I found it hard to ask directly about the effects of the gas attack on his family. Although sometimes, afterward, I regretted my own reticence.*

●   ●   ●

I commute to work on the Hibiya Line. It's incredibly crowded, especially at Kita-senju Station, where lots of people transfer and they've been doing all these repairs that have cut into the platform space—it's really dangerous. One little push and you could easily fall onto the tracks.

When I say it's crowded, I was boarding a train once when my briefcase got swallowed up in the torrent of people and swept away. I was holding on, trying not to let go, but I just had to or my arm would have broken. The case just disappeared. I thought I'd never see it again (*laughs*). I had to wait until the crowd thinned out to find it. At least there's air-conditioning now. Summers were just unbearable in the past.

Some people get off at Akihabara, so finally there's a little breathing space. At Kodemmacho, there are no longer people rubbing up against you, and at Kayabacho you might even find a seat. On past Ginza, there's room to read a magazine.

My wife and I have a daughter, four years old. We've been married five years. We rent our house. It's where my family lived when I was small, but while I was still in school my parents and brother all died one after the other, so I'm the only one left. Now I have my own family and we've taken the place on. It's in a residential area, a little on the small side, but there are all the modern conveniences.

I originally wanted to be in music. I was in a college band, and for three years after that, too. Strictly amateur, mostly techno stuff. I didn't even have space to set up my instruments.

Once out of college I became a typical salaryman. But that just wasn't me. I barely survived the office environment. I was working for a computer company, but I hated it. The work kept me very busy. Hardly any time off. It was going nowhere, so I resigned after a year and a half.

Then after a while I got a job with an audiovisual company, which went bust after a few years, so I formed my own company. I never really wanted to be self-employed, but it proved necessary for tax reasons. There were three of us at its peak, but as the economy worsened less work came in, and for the last year it was just me.

March 20 was a Monday. I had an appointment with my boss, so I went to work early. If I'd waited a few trains at Kita-senju, I might have gotten a seat, but I'd have lost fifteen minutes, so I hurried onto the first train that came. Sit or stand, you're still packed in face-to-face, so sitting's not all that comfortable anyway. That day, the train was packed. Monday mornings are the worst.

I always take the fourth car from the front, by the rear door. The time is fixed, so it's generally familiar faces, but that day it was a different train, so I didn't know anyone. I remember that impression, of how things were a little different.

There was absolutely no chance of getting a seat until Tsukiji.

That was unusual. I can usually get a seat around Kayabacho . . . So anyway I finally got a seat, when there came an announcement, "One passenger has collapsed. The train will make a temporary first-aid stop at this station." I sat and waited, but then after about two minutes the message changed to "Three passengers have collapsed."

Out on the platform there was this wall of people. It was all happening in the next car where the packet of sarin was. What's going on? I wondered and stuck my head out the door, but I couldn't see what was wrong. Then a middle-aged man came walking from that direction saying, "Sarin! Sarin!" I distinctly remember him saying, "sarin," but he sounded drunk.

Hearing that, several people around me stood up, though they didn't seem in any particular hurry. They weren't running to escape or anything.

A little while after that there was another announcement: "Poison gas has been detected. It is dangerous underground. Please head for safety above ground." At that all the passengers stood up and got off the train, but still there wasn't any panic. They walked a little faster than normal, but there was no pushing or anything. Some put handkerchiefs to their mouths or were coughing, but that's all.

The wind was blowing through the station from the back toward the head of the train. Which is why I thought, "I'm all right, the trouble's in the next car up, upwind from here." And the way out was also upwind, toward the exit at the back of the train. Meanwhile, I felt a strange tickle in my throat. You know when the dentist gives you anesthetic and it's seeping back into your throat? Just like that. To be honest, I was scared. The realization that I might be gassed to death suddenly hit me. If it was sarin, it was serious. I saw what it did in Matsumoto; you breathed it in and you died.

I went out the exit and up the stairs. Outside, I wanted to have a cigarette, but I could barely draw air into my throat before I was coughing hard. That's when I knew I'd breathed the gas. "I'd better call the office," I thought. There were two phone booths outside the station, but both had long lines. I had to wait fifteen or twenty minutes for my turn. It was still before office hours, but I told the girl who answered: "There's been some terrorist activity. I'm going to be late."

After I finished my call, I looked around and saw that there were lots of people crouching on the ground, dozens of them. Some looked unconscious, some had been carried up the stairs. Before I'd made my call there had only been a few, but in only fifteen or twenty minutes the place was in an uproar, though not yet the war-zone atmosphere they showed on TV.

This detective person was walking around asking out loud, "Did anyone see the culprit who planted the poison gas?" Then straightaway an ambulance arrived.

They still hadn't sealed off the entrance to the subway and quite a few people were going down for a look. I was thinking, "That can't be safe." But eventually I remember a station attendant appeared and shut the entrance.

I knew I'd inhaled poison gas, so I was concerned, but I didn't know whether to leave the area or not. It'd be better if I got tested, right? It's only asking for trouble to avoid the issue and take another train to work, then collapse midway.

On second thought, though, I could still walk—unlike the ones they carried up—so that must mean I wasn't in such a bad way. When the first-aid team came and said, "Everyone who's feeling ill, please get in the ambulance," I didn't. I thought I was okay.

So I walked to Shintomicho Station and took the Yurakucho Line to get to work. When I got there, the executive director contacted me to ask if I was all right. I explained the situation, and he told me, "They're saying it was sarin, so you'd better get to a hospital quick and have some tests."

The hospital was nearby. Actually, things had started to look dim the moment I'd entered the subway at Shintomicho, but at the time I thought it was because of the brightness of the sun outside. I later learned it was due to the sarin. The tickle in my throat was almost gone; I could smoke. Anyway, I wanted them to test me.

But they told me, "We can't test for sarin here." The doctors can't have been watching the news. They had absolutely no idea what had happened. This was around 10:30. Naturally they'd never tested for sarin before and had no idea how to go about it. After making me wait for an hour while they looked it up, they told me, "Well, it's like a pesticide, so the thing to do is drink a lot of water and flush it out of your system. But for now you're okay." All right, I'm okay for now, I thought, and went to the reception area to pay the bill. Then a nurse who'd been watching television came and told me, "We can't treat for sarin here. The TV said they can do a full treatment at St. Luke's Hospital. Over there they've got the medicines and they can run a proper test. You'd better go check with the police."

I was still unsure, so I went to the police post in front of the hospital and asked the officer there to tell me which hospital to go to for sarin testing. He must have thought I was a serious case and immediately called an ambulance. They took me straightaway to a hospital about twenty minutes away.

As I was a "serious case," three doctors were waiting for me. I was so embarrassed I had only light symptoms. "You're not so bad. If no further irregularities show up today, then you're all right," they told me. No drip, no drugs.

So I was right back into the swing of things. My pupils weren't badly contracted—I scarcely remember how long the condition lasted.

After the gas attack the police somehow became convinced I was one of the culprits. Two detectives came to my home and gave me a grilling. One of them looked me in the eyes and said: "Have you always worn your hair like that?" After I went over the events of that whole day, they showed me two likenesses, one of which looked quite like me. "During the gas attack, did you happen to see anyone like either of these?" No, I answered, I hadn't, but I really felt they suspected me. According to these detectives, there was a high probability that the culprits had been contaminated themselves and had gone to a hospital for treatment.

Two or three weeks later the phone rang: "Mr. Makita?" came this voice. "Yes?" "Police. We take it you're back home now." It seems they wanted to obtain a statement, so I was to report to the precinct. It occurred to me that I'd been under surveillance, probably tailed. They still hadn't positively linked the thing to Aum and everyone was on edge.

More than any anger toward Aum, I feel disgust. I despise people who turn a blind eye to the dangers of that kind of religion. I especially dislike the ones who try to recruit new people to their organization.

When I was in college, in the course of only three years, I lost my parents and my younger brother. Father had been in and out of hospitals, so it was no great shock when he died. But my mother had a heart murmur and was going in for observation, then died two days later. They hadn't even operated. I was totally floored. No one had even imagined she might die. Then my brother died in an accident. By that point I couldn't help thinking, "People can die at any moment." I almost felt as if it were my turn next.

I just slept and slept. Twelve hours at a strech. Sleep that long and your sleep becomes very shallow. I dreamed a lot.

Around that time, I was approached by one of these new religions. This recruitment type came on to me, saying, "That kind of misfortune just keeps repeating, so you had better change your fate here and now. Shouldn't you accept a faith . . . ?" Truly tasteless as far as I was concerned. Maybe that's why I'm so down on religion.

## "The very first thing that came to mind was poison gas—cyanide or sarin"

### Dr. Toru Saito (b. 1948)

*Dr. Saito has worked at Toho University's Omori Hospital Emergency Care Center for twenty years. The staff are real professionals. The center is where they bring in life-or-death cases and where split-second decisions are critical. In most instances, there is no time to wonder "What shall we do?" That's where Dr. Saito's experience and intuition come into play. His knowledge of symptoms is encyclopedic.*

*Coming from such a background, his speech is succinct, clear, and authoritative. To see him on the job is singularly impressive: it's hard work every day with not a moment's rest to calm his nerves. I'm grateful he could spare time in his busy schedule to talk to me.*

● ● ●

I am a circulatory specialist with Internal Medicine Ward 2. Hence my duties at the Emergency Care Center mainly concern arterial valve and heart irregularites. The center here has brought together a rather special team of veteran doctors from several different hospital departments. There are some twenty doctors in total, working in twenty-four-hour shifts.

The day before the gas attack, I was on supervisor duty, responsible for overseeing the running of the hospital. Sunday supervisor duty runs from nine to nine, Sunday morning to Monday morning. During the daytime I'm generally in the ward examining patients.

That morning I was in the doctors' lounge watching TV with a cup of instant ramen for breakfast. The first reports came in about 8:15: "Poison gas at Kasumigaseki Station. Heavy casualties." "What's this?" I thought. The very first thing that came to mind was poison gas—cyanide or sarin.

MURAKAMI: *So city gas pipes or any other possible gases simply did not occur to you?*

It's unlikely inside a subway station. From the very first, I thought there probably had to be a criminal involvement. Already with the Matsumoto incident there had been talk that just maybe it was Aum, so almost automatically it all clicked: "Poison gas—crime—Aum—sarin or cyanide."

It was likely the victims would be brought to our hospital, so I thought we had better be prepared to deal with either cyanide or sarin. Actually, for cyanide poisoning we always keep a treatment kit to hand. For sarin, however, there are two remedies—atropine and 2-Pam—both of which we've used before.*

Actually, up until the Matsumoto incident I knew virtually nothing about sarin. There was no need for me to be up on such a specialist military weapon. But with Matsumoto, there were symptoms like low blood cholinesterase and visible contraction of the pupils, enough to make us doctors think it must be due to some kind of organophosphate.

Now, phosphates have long been used in fertilizers and pesticides, and sometimes people have ingested them to commit suicide. In twenty years here I've treated about ten of these phosphate poisoning cases. To put it simply, sarin is phosphate in gaseous form.

MURAKAMI: *So whether one ingests an organophosphate fertilizer or sarin gas, one gets the same lowering of cholinesterase and contracted pupils?*

Exactly the same symptoms. But these agricultural chemicals have up to now been liquids that don't usually evaporate. That's why we can spray them on roses and stuff. But since ultimately sarin is a gaseous organophosphate, doctors in Emergency Care basically know we can treat sarin poisoning cases the same way we treat organophosphate poisoning. It was only thanks to the Matsumoto incident that we discovered this.

Atropine is used in cases where the pulse is slow or as a preliminary to anesthetic, so it's used both in emergency care and out-

*Sarin inhibits the action of cholinesterase, an enzyme produced by the liver. 2-Pam (Protopam or pralidoxime chloride) is a cholinesterase reactivator, also used as an antidote in cases of organophosphate pesticide poisoning. [Tr.]

patient wards in most hospitals. 2-Pam, however, is a specialized antidote to organophosphates. The pharmaceutical department might stock just a little of it.

As the gas attack was televised there was some discussion about it being either sarin or cyanide. There were interns in the lounge at the time and I told them, "Get some background on sarin." Actually we had studied the Matsumoto incident in my university toxicology lectures. We'd put together a ten-minute videotape of TV news footage as a teaching aid, so I told them, "Look at that." And all the interns saw what I was saying. "Now you understand about sarin. Otherwise, here are the kits in case it's cyanide." So we prepared ourselves and waited for the victims to come in.

Around 9:30 the TV reported that the Tokyo Fire Department had detected acetonitrile. The fire department has a special Chemical Alert Brigade car for on-site gas detection. And their report showed acetonitrile, which meant a hydrocyanide compound—cyanide.

A call came in to our hotline: "Be prepared to take a victim from the subway." So we got ready the cyanide-poisoning kit and waited in Emergency. It was 10:45 when they brought in the patient. His pupils were contracted and he was in a fairly serious comatose state. He'd move if pinched, but otherwise there was no response. If this was cyanide, it would be what's called acidosis: blood acidity. Acidosis indicated cyanide, but contracted pupils were an indication of sarin. That was the critical point of differentiation.

Blood tests showed no acidosis. Reflexes were way down. All symptoms of sarin poisoning. Everyone was shaking their heads: "Doctor, this just has to be sarin." "Yes, it looks like sarin, but then the news report did say acetonitrile. Let's try half the cyanide kit just to be on the safe side."

About thirty minutes later there was a gradual recovery of consciousness, so we thought the cyanide kit had done the trick. His condition improved dramatically after injection. We don't really understand why. I would guess that the perpetrators had mixed acetonitrile into the sarin in order to slow evaporation, giving them time to escape. Pure sarin would have evaporated much too quickly and in all probability killed them straightaway.

Around 11:00 the police department confirmed it was sarin. Again I found this out on TV. Did anyone think to contact us? Not a word. All our information came from TV. But by that time all the patients showed sarin-related symptoms, so we'd already begun using atropine.

About then a call came in from Shinshu University Medical Department. It was the doctor who'd treated the patients of the Matsumoto incident. He'd been calling around all the emergency care centers and hospitals in Tokyo saying, "If you want, I'll fax you our data on sarin treatment." "Fire away," I said, and the faxes piled up.

Looking over the data, the most critical thing we learned was how to tell those patients who required hospitalization from those who didn't. Without direct experience we lacked any practical basis for making a judgment. According to the data, there was no need to hospitalize patients with contracted pupils who could still walk and talk. Fine. People whose cholinesterase levels were normal did not need immediate treatment. That was helpful. If we'd had to take in everyone who came to us, we'd have been in a real fix.

MURAKAMI: *Could you explain briefly about cholinesterase?*

If you want to move a muscle, the nerve endings send out an order to the muscle cells in the form of a chemical, acetylcholine. It's the messenger. When the muscles receive that they move, they contract. After the contraction, the enzyme cholinesterase serves to neutralize the message sent by the acetylcholine, which prepares for the next action. Over and over again.

However when the cholinesterase runs out, the acetylcholine message remains active and the muscle stays contracted. Now muscles work by repeated contraction and expansion, so when they stay contracted we get paralysis. In the eye, that means contracted pupils.

The faxes from Matsumoto told us that a cholinesterase level of 200 or below meant the patient required hospitalization. Usually those hospitalized made a full recovery and were discharged in a few days. Unless the cholinesterase level is very low, we don't get anything approaching paralysis. Even among our own outpatients, there were those whose readings were way down yet seemed otherwise fine. The pupil contraction persisted three or four more days, but it didn't paralyze the breathing.

Most of the seriously injured regained consciousness within a day. The ones we couldn't save were those whose heart or lungs had stopped before they got to the hospital. Either that, or they were infibrillated on arrival to restart their heartbeat, but became "vegetables" as a result.

MURAKAMI: *Did any remedial information come in from either the fire department or the police? With such unusual symptoms you'd think that broadcasting agreed medical guidelines from a central source would be the fastest way to reach the most people.*

No, nothing of the sort came in straight after the event. There was a bulletin from the Tokyo Bureau of Health in the early evening, around 5:00 (*pulls out a file and reads*): "We greatly appreciate your looking after patients from this morning's incident. We have obtained some sarin-related information. Sarin is a . . . etc., etc." By the time this came in, we'd more or less dealt with the situation. The only ones who contacted us early on and sent us the necessary information were the Shinshu University Medical Department. That was of real practical help.

MURAKAMI: *So it was as if each medic team, each hospital was told, "You're on your own"?*

Well, yes, in effect. Knowledge about sarin was inadequate. For instance, at one hospital the doctors and nurses examining and treating the patients began to feel dizzy. Their clothes were impregnated with the gas. They became secondary casualties. Even we weren't aware that we should have asked the patients to undress first thing. We just didn't even think about it.

**Dr. Nobuo Yanagisawa** (*b.* 1935)
*Head, School of Medicine, Shinshu University,*
*Nagano Prefecture*

March 20, when the Tokyo gas attack happened, was in actual fact our graduation day at Shinshu University. As head of the hospital I was obliged to attend the ceremonies and had changed especially for the occasion. That day I also had an Admissions Committee meeting, so I'd scheduled absolutely nothing else. That was the stroke of luck in the midst of misfortune.

Another thing: I'd researched the Matsumoto incident and edited the findings, which were supposed to be published that day [March 20] as well. That's how things just happened to work out.

Well, that morning, a reporter from the *Shinano Daily News* rang my secretary saying, "Something strange has happened in Tokyo. Seems kind of like the Matsumoto sarin business." I got that message around 9:00. "What now?" I thought, and switched on the TV and all the victims seemed to be reporting acute symptoms of organophosphorus toxicity: eye pain, tears, blurring vision, running noses, vomiting . . . that sort of thing. Not enough, however, to single out sarin as the cause.

But one victim among them reported a contraction of the pupils. This person came on camera saying: "When I looked in the mirror my eyes were so small." Which all added up to organophosphorus toxicity. And since people in the subway were reporting such intense symptoms, it had to be a gas. Now, as for organophosphorus compounds used in chemical warfare, that could only mean sarin, soman, tabun, that line of compounds. The same as in Matsumoto.

By the time I had my TV on over a thousand people had been taken to St. Luke's Hospital. I just knew the staff must be having a hell of a time, maybe even panicking. And that got me worrying.

We ourselves were really in a pinch when Matsumoto happened. Seeing all those patients coming in with unaccountable symptoms.

We'd guessed that it was probably organophosphorus intoxification and treated them accordingly; but none of us had the slightest clue it was sarin.

I immediately called in two doctors from Neuropathology and Emergency, and told them to contact St. Luke's and any other hospitals that were thought to have taken in these patients. We faxed information to every single hospital they mentioned on TV: "Treat with sulfuric atropine and 2-Pam as antitoxin, etc., etc."

First thing, I called St. Luke's. This was between 9:10 and 9:30. I couldn't get through, but I managed to get a line straightaway on my mobile. "Get me the person in charge of Emergency," I said, and gave a general rundown: "Do this and this and this to treat your cases." Then I told them I'd fax in more detail. Ordinarily I ought to have cleared all this through the head of the hospital, but I thought talking directly to the doctors in the wards would be faster. But there was a mixup somewhere. I heard later from someone at St. Luke's that they were scouring the library until 11 A.M. trying to determine the toxin.

We started sending the faxes around 10 A.M. I still had to attend the graduation ceremony, so I left the two doctors from Neuropathology and Emergency in charge and went. There was a final proof of the *Matsumoto Sarin Incident Report* on my desk outlining the symptoms, diagnosis, and treatment of sarin gas poisoning, so they just kept faxing out copies. I keep thinking in retrospect how lucky we were to have had that on hand. But even so, there were so many pages, so many places to send to, it took an amazing effort.

The most important thing in a mass disaster is triage: the prioritizing of patients to receive treatment. In the Tokyo gas attack, serious cases had to get first treatment, while lighter cases were left on their own to naturally get well over time. If the doctors treated everyone who came in, in the order they came in, lives may have been lost. If you don't have a good grasp of the situation and people come in screaming, "I can't see!" the whole scene can easily descend into a state of panic.

The doctor's dilemma is having to decide who gets priority: the patient who can't breathe, or the one who can't see? Difficult judgments come with dangerous situations. It's the hardest thing about being a doctor.

MURAKAMI: Is there some sort of practical manual on what to do in a mass disaster, a guide doctors can all refer to?

No, nothing like that. Even with us, until the Matsumoto incident we had almost no idea what to do.

When I came back at noon, the phones were ringing everywhere. Requests were coming in from clinics all over the place saying, "Send us information too!" I mean, they had sarin victims in over a hunded facilities. That whole day was one big uproar. We were faxing nonstop.

If it had been an ordinary day with no graduation ceremony, I'd have been up to my neck in hospital work from 8:30 A.M. straight through, snowed under with one thing after another. Even if someone had told me, "Something strange has happened in Tokyo," I wouldn't have had the time to watch anything on TV until lunchtime. We probably wouldn't have been able to respond so quickly. It was just a very, very lucky coincidence.

Actually the most efficient thing to do would've been to get in touch with the fire department and let them get the word out to all these places. Well, we did try to contact the fire department, but we couldn't get through.

The biggest lesson we learned from the Tokyo gas attack and the Matsumoto incident was that when something major strikes, the local units may be extremely swift to respond, but the overall picture is hopeless. There is no prompt and efficient system in Japan for dealing with a major catastrophe. There's no clear-cut chain of command. It was exactly the same with the Kobe earthquake.

In both the Matsumoto incident and the Tokyo gas attack, I think the medical organizations responded extremely well. The paramedics were also on top of things. They deserve praise. As one American expert said, to have had five thousand sarin gas victims and only twelve dead is close to a miracle. All thanks to the extraordinary efforts of the local units, because the overall emergency network was useless.

We sent faxes to at least thirty medical facilities. On the seven o'clock news the next morning they reported seventy people seriously injured. The thing about sarin poisoning is that even really serious cases can recover in a few hours if properly treated. Knowing what to do can make a huge difference.

I really thought I had to get word out, so I called the Tokyo Health Bureau, but nobody answered. It was after 8:30 by the time I got through. The person who came on the line said something like, "Well, we all have our jobs to do"—where's the sense in that?

The fire department ought to have been quicker in getting to the scene, monitoring the whole situation, and stationing triage teams to give precise instructions. That way, the ambulance crews could respond on the spot. And probably emergency medics ought to go with them too. Active input from the medical side is vital if you want to stop people panicking.

To be perfectly honest, the way things are with us doctors in Japan, it's almost unthinkable that any doctor would go out of his way to send unsolicited information to a hospital. The first thought is never to say too much, never to overstep one's position.

But with the gas attack I had other motives too. One of the seven people who died in the Matsumoto incident was a medical student here at Shinshu University. A coed, extremely bright, who by rights ought to have been at that day's graduation ceremony. That simple fact kept me going.

# BLIND NIGHTMARE:

# WHERE ARE WE JAPANESE GOING?

• • • •

## What Happened in the Tokyo Subway on March 20, 1995?

The morning of March 20, I was at my house in Oiso, two hours due south of Tokyo. I was living in Massachusetts at the time, but had returned to Japan for a fortnight during the spring holidays. With no TV or radio in the house, I was completely unaware that a major cataclysm was taking place in the city. I was indoors listening to music, leisurely straightening up my bookshelves. I remember that peaceful morning very well. Not a cloud in the sky.

Around 10:00 I received a phone call from an acquaintance working in the media: "Something crazy's happened in the subway; lots of people hurt." His voice was tense. "Poison gas. This is Aum's doing, no mistake. Better steer clear of Tokyo for the time being. They're dangerous."

What was he saying? Poison gas in the subway? Aum? I'd been away from Japan for some time and hadn't kept up on current affairs. I'd missed the *Yomiuri Shimbun* scoop on New Year's Day when they'd discovered sarin residue near the Aum headquarters in the village of Kamikuishiki. This linked the cult to an earlier outbreak of poisoning in nearby Matsumoto, three hours northwest of Tokyo. Little did I know the Aum cult had been implicated in strange dealings surrounding a number of crimes, that it was an extremely hot topic in Japan.

From today's perspective, I now realize that few people—in the media at least—thought it far-fetched that Aum might be involved in such a major act of terrorism. Anyway, as I had no plans to go into

Tokyo that day, I went back to sorting out my books as if nothing had happened.

That was my March 20.

Yet somehow the perplexity I felt that morning—a sense of estrangement or displacement—stayed with me. I remained "out of phase."

For many months thereafter, the media overflowed with "news" of all kinds about the cult. From morning till night Japanese TV was virtually nonstop Aum. The papers, tabloids, magazines all devoted thousands of pages to the gas attack.

None of which told me what I wanted to know. No, mine was a very simple question: *What actually happened in the Tokyo subway the morning of March 20, 1995?*

Or more concretely: What were the people in the subway cars doing at the time? What did they see? What did they feel? What did they think? If I could, I'd have included details on each individual passenger, right down to their heartbeat and breathing, as graphically represented as possible. The question was, what would happen to any ordinary Japanese citizen—such as me or any of my readers—if they were suddenly caught up in an attack of this kind?

High-flown excesses aside, the polemic put forth by the media was quite straightforward in structure. To them, the moral principle at stake in the gas attack was all too clear: "good" versus "evil," "sanity" versus "madness," "health" versus "disease." It was an obvious exercise in opposites.

The Japanese were shocked by this macabre incident. From every mouth it was the same outcry: "The sheer lunacy of it all! What on earth's become of Japan, when such mass insanity walks among us? Where were the police? It's the death penalty for Shoko Asahara no matter what . . ."

Thus, to a greater or lesser degree, people all jumped onto the "right," "sane," "normal" bandwagon. There was nothing complicated about it. That is, placed alongside the likes of Shoko Asahara and the Aum cult, compared to the deeds they had done, the overwhelming majority of Japanese were indeed "right," "sane," and "healthy." It could hardly have been a more open-and-shut case. The media merely played along with this consensus and accelerated its force.

There were a few lone voices that bucked the trend. "Shouldn't the crime be punished as a crime, without all this talk of 'goodness' or 'sanity'?" they insisted, but were largely ignored in the general furor.

Only now, several years after the event, just where has this ramshackle bandwagon of mass consensus delivered us Japanese with "right on our side"? What have we learned from this shocking incident?

One thing is for sure. Some strange malaise, some bitter aftertaste lingers on. We crane our necks and look around us, as if to ask: where did all *that* come from? If only to be rid of this malaise, to cleanse our palates of this aftertaste, most Japanese seem ready to pack up the whole incident in a trunk labeled THINGS OVER AND DONE WITH. We would rather the meaning of the whole ordeal was left to the fixed processes of the court and everything was dealt with on the level of "the system."

Certainly the legal process is valuable and will bring to light many truths. But unless we Japanese absorb those facts into our metabolism and integrate them into our field of vision, all will be lost in a mass of meaningless detail, court-case gossip, an obscure, forgotten corner of history. The rain that fell on the city runs down the dark gutters and empties into the sea without even soaking the ground. The legal system can deal with only one facet of the issue on the basis of the law. There is no guarantee that this will settle the matter.

In other words, the shock dealt to Japanese society by Aum and the gas attack has still to be effectively analyzed, the lessons have yet to be learned. Even now, having finished interviewing the victims, I can't simply file away the gas attack, saying: "After all, this was merely an extreme and exceptional crime committed by an isolated lunatic fringe." And what am I to think when our collective memory of the affair is looking more and more like a bizarre comic strip or an urban myth?

If we are to learn anything from this tragic event, we must look at what happened all over again, from different angles, in different ways. Something tells me things will only get worse if we don't wash it out of our metabolism. It's all too easy to say, "Aum was evil." Nor does saying, "This had nothing to do with 'evil' or 'insanity'" prove anything either. Yet the spell cast by these phrases is almost impossible to break, the whole emotionally charged "Us" versus "Them" vocabulary has been done to death.

No, what we need, it seems to me, are words coming from another direction, new words for a new narrative. Another narrative to purify this narrative.

## 2
## Why Did I Look Away from the Aum Cult?

What alternative is there to the media's "Us" versus "Them"? The danger is that if it is used to prop up this "righteous" position of "ours" all we will see from now on are ever more exacting and minute analyses of the "dirty" distortions in "their" thinking. Without some flexibility in our definitions we'll remain forever stuck with the same old knee-jerk reactions, or worse, slide into complete apathy.

A little while after the events, a thought occurred to me. In order to understand the reality of the Tokyo gas attack, no study of the rationale and workings of "them," the people who instigated it, would be enough. Necessary and beneficial though such efforts might be, wasn't there a similar need for a parallel analysis of "us"? Wasn't the real key (or part of a key) to the mystery thrust upon Japan by "them" more likely to be found hidden under "our" territory?

We will get nowhere as long as the Japanese continue to disown the Aum "phenomenon" as something completely other, an alien presence viewed through binoculars on the far shore. Unpleasant though the prospect might seem, it is important that we incorporate "them," to some extent, within that construct called "us," or at least within Japanese society. Certainly that is how the event was viewed from abroad. But even more to the point, by failing to look for the key buried under our own feet, where it might be visible to the naked eye, by holding the phenomenon at such a distance we are in danger of reducing its significance to a microscopic level.

This thought has a history. I trace it back to February 1990, when Aum stood for election in the Lower House of the Japanese Diet. Asahara was running in Shibuya Ward, the Tokyo district where I was living at the time, and the campaign was a singularly odd piece of theater. Day after day strange music played from big trucks with sound systems, while white-robed young men and women in oversize Asahara masks and elephant heads lined the sidewalk outside my local train station, waving and dancing some incomprehensible jig.

When I saw this election campaign, my first reaction was to look away. It was one of the last things I wanted to see. Others around me showed the same response: they simply walked by pretending not to see the cultists. I felt an unnameable dread, a disgust beyond my understanding. I didn't bother to consider very deeply where this dread came from, or why it was "one of the last things I wanted to see." I didn't think it was all that important at the time. I simply put the image out of mind as "nothing to do with me."

Faced by the same scene, no doubt 90 percent of people would have felt and behaved the same way: walk by pretending not to see; don't give it a second thought; forget it. Very likely German intellectuals during the Weimar period behaved in a similar fashion when they first saw Hitler.

But now, thinking back on it, the whole thing seems very curious. There are any number of new religions out there proselytizing on the street, yet they don't fill us—or at least me—with an inexplicable dread. No, it's just "Oh, them again," and that's it. If you want to talk aberrations, then shaven-headed Japanese youths dancing around chanting "Hare Krishna" are a departure from the social norm. Still, I don't look away from Hare Krishnas. Why, then, did I automatically avert my eyes from the Aum campaigners? What was it that disturbed me?

My conjecture is this. The Aum "phenomenon" disturbs precisely because it is not *someone else's affair*. It shows us a distorted image of ourselves in a manner none of us could have foreseen. The Hare Krishnas and all the other new religions can be dismissed at the outset (before they even enter into our rational mind) as having no bearing on us. But not Aum, for some reason. Their presence—their appearance, their song—had to be actively rejected by an effort of will, and that is why they disturb us.

Psychologically speaking (I'll wheel out the amateur psychology just this once, so bear with me), encounters that call up strong physical disgust or revulsion are often in fact projections of our own faults and weaknesses. Very well, but how does this relate to the feeling of dread I felt in front of the train station? No, I'm not saying "There but for the grace of—whatever—go I. Under different circumstances, you and I might have joined the Aum cult and released sarin gas in the subway." That doesn't make any sense realistically (or logistically). All I mean to say is that something in that encounter, in their presence, must also have been present in us to necessitate such active conscious rejection. Or rather, "they" are the mirror of "us"!

Now of course a mirror image is always darker and distorted. Convex and concave swap places, falsehood wins out over reality, light and shadow play tricks. But take away these dark flaws and the two images are uncannily similar; some details almost seem to conspire together. Which is why we avoid looking directly at the image, why, consciously or not, we keep eliminating these dark elements from the face we want to see. These subconscious shadows are an "underground" that we carry around within us, and the bitter aftertaste that continues to plague us long after the Tokyo gas attack comes seeping out from below.

### 3
### The Handed-Down Self: the Allocated Narrative

To quote from the Unabomber manifesto, published in *The New York Times* in 1995:

> The system reorganizes itself so as to put pressure on those who do not fit in. Those who do not fit into the system are "sick"; to make them fit in is to "cure." Thus, the power process aimed at attaining autonomy is broken and the individual is subsumed into the other-dependent power process enforced by the system. To pursue autonomy is seen as "disease."*

*The document that became known as the Unabomber manifesto was sent to *The New York Times* and *The Washington Post* in April 1995 by a person called "FC," identified by the FBI as the Unabomber and implicated in three murders and sixteen bombings. The author threatened to send a bomb to an unspecified destination "with intent to kill" unless one of the newspapers published this manuscript, entitled "Industrial Society and Its Future." The attorney general and the director of the FBI recommended publication and it appeared in a special supplement in both papers in September 1995. This led David Kaczynski to draw a comparison between the Unabomber and his estranged brother Theodore, who was arrested in April 1996. He was sentenced to life imprisonment in 1998. [Tr.]

Interestingly enough, while the Unabomber's modus operandi almost exactly parallels Aum's (when, for instance, they sent a parcel bomb to Tokyo City Hall), Theodore Kaczynski's thinking is even more closely linked to the essence of the Aum cult.

The argument Kaczynski puts forward is fundamentally quite right. Many parts of the social system in which we belong and function do indeed aim at repressing the attainment of individual autonomy, or, as the Japanese adage goes: "The nail that sticks up gets hammered down."

From the perspective of the Aum followers, just as they were asserting their own autonomy, society and the state came down on top of them, pronouncing them an "antisocial movement," a "cancer" to be cut out. Which is why they became more and more antisocial.

Nonetheless, Kaczynski—intentionally or unintentionally—overlooked one important factor. Autonomy is only the mirror image of dependence on others. If you were left as a baby on a deserted island, you would have no notion of what "autonomy" means. Autonomy and dependency are like light and shade, caught in the pull of each other's gravity, until, after considerable trial and error, each individual can find his or her own place in the world.

Those who fail to achieve this balance, like Shoko Asahara perhaps, have to compensate by establishing a limited (but actually quite effective) system. I have no way of ranking him as a religious figure. How does one measure such things? Still, a cursory look at his life does suggest one possible scenario. Efforts to overcome his own individual disabilities left him trapped inside a closed circuit. A genie in a bottle labeled "religion," which he proceeded to market as a form of shared experience.

Asahara surely put himself through hell, a horrific bloodbath of internal conflicts and soul-searching until he finally arrived at a systematization of his vision. Undoubtedly he also had his satori, some "attainment of paranormal value." Without any firsthand experience of hell or extraordinary inversion of everyday values, Asahara would not have had such a strong, charismatic power. From a certain perspective, primitive religion always carries its own associated special aura that emanates from some psychic aberration.

In order to take on the "self-determination" that Asahara provided, most of those who took refuge in the Aum cult appear to have deposited all their precious personal holdings of selfhood—lock and key—in that "spiritual bank" called Shoko Asahara. The faithful relinquished their freedom, renounced their possessions, disowned their families, discarded all secular judgment (common sense). "Normal" Japanese were aghast: How could anyone do such an insane thing? But conversely, to the cultists it was probably quite comforting. At last they had someone to watch over them, sparing them the anxiety of confronting each new situation on their own, and delivering them from any need to think for themselves.

By tuning in, by merging themselves with Shoko Asahara's "greater, more profoundly unbalanced" Self, they attained a kind of pseudo-self-determination. Instead of launching an assault on society as individuals, they handed over the entire strategic responsibility to Asahara. We'll have one "Self-power versus the system" set menu, please.

Theirs was not Kaczynski's "battle against the system to attain the power process of self-determination." The only one fighting was Shoko Asahara: most followers were merely swallowed up and assimilated by his battle-hungry ego. Nor were the followers unilaterally subjected to Asahara's "mind control." Not passive victims, they themselves actively sought to be controlled by Asahara. "Mind control" is not something that can be pursued or bestowed just like that. It's a two-sided affair.

If you lose your ego, you lose the thread of that narrative you call your Self. Humans, however, can't live very long without some sense of a continuing story. Such stories go beyond the limited rational system (or the systematic rationality) with which you surround yourself; they are crucial keys to sharing time-experience with others.

Now a narrative is a story, not logic, nor ethics, nor philosophy. It is a dream you keep having, whether you realize it or not. Just as surely as you breathe, you go on ceaselessly dreaming your story. And in these stories you wear two faces. You are simultaneously subject and object. You are the whole and you are a part. You are real and you are shadow. "Storyteller" and at the same time "character." It is through such multilayering of roles in our stories that we heal the loneliness of being an isolated individual in the world.

Yet without a proper ego, nobody can create a personal narrative, any more than you can drive a car without an engine, or cast a shadow without a real physical object. But once you've consigned your ego to someone else, where on earth do you go from there?

At this point you receive a new narrative from the person to whom you have entrusted your ego. You've handed over the real thing, so what comes back instead is a shadow. And once your ego has merged with another ego, your narrative will necessarily take on the narrative created by that other ego.

Just what kind of narrative?

It needn't be anything particularly fancy, nothing complicated or refined. You don't need to have literary ambitions. In fact, rather, the sketchier and simpler the better. Junk, a leftover rehash will do. Anyway, most people are tired of complex, multilayered scenarios—they are a potential letdown. It's precisely because people can't find any fixed point within their own multilayered schemes that they're tossing aside their self-identity.

A simple "emblem" of a story will do for this sort of narrative, the same way that a war medal bestowed on a soldier doesn't have to be pure gold. It's enough that the medal be backed up by a shared recognition that "this is a medal," no matter that it's a cheap tin trinket.

Shoko Asahara was talented enough to impose his rehashed narrative on people (who for the most part came looking for just that). It was a risible, slapdash story. To unbelievers it could only be regurgitated tripe. Still, in all fairness, it must be said that a certain consistency runs through it all. It was a call to arms.

From this perspective, in a limited sense, Asahara was a master storyteller who proved capable of anticipating the mood of the times. He was not deterred by the knowledge, whether conscious or not, that his ideas and images were recycled junk. Asahara deliberately cobbled together bits and pieces from all around him (the way that Spielberg's ET assembles a device for communicating with his home planet out of odds and ends in the family garage) and brought to them a singular flow, a current that darkly reflected the inner ghosts of his own mind. Whatever the deficiencies in that narrative, they were in Asahara himself, so they presented no obstacle to those who chose to merge themselves with him. If anything, these deficiencies were a positive bonus, until they became fatally polluted. Irredeemably delusional and paranoiac, a new pretext developed, grand and irrational, until there was no turning back . . .

Such was the narrative offered by Aum, by "their" side. Stupid, you might say. And surely it is. Most of us laughed at the absurd off-the-wall scenario that Asahara provided. We laughed at him for concocting such "utter nonsense" and we ridiculed the believers who could be attracted to such "lunatic fodder." The laugh left a bitter aftertaste in our mouths, but we laughed out loud all the same. Which was only to be expected.

But were we able to offer "them" a more viable narrative? Did we have a narrative potent enough to chase away Asahara's "utter nonsense"?

That was the big task. I am a novelist, and as we all know a novelist is someone who works with "narratives," who spins "stories" professionally. Which meant to me that the task at hand was like a gigantic sword dangling above my head. It's something I'm going to have to deal with much more seriously from here on. I know I'm going to have to construct a "cosmic communication device" of my own. I'll probably have to piece together every last scrap of junk, every weakness, every deficiency inside me to do it. (There, I've gone and said it—but the real surprise is that it's exactly what I've been trying to do as a writer all along!)

So then, what about you? (I'm using the second person, but of course that includes me.)

Haven't you offered up some part of your Self to someone (or something), and taken on a "narrative" in return? Haven't we entrusted some part of our personality to some greater System or Order? And if so, has not that System at some stage demanded of us some kind of "insanity"? Is the narrative you now possess *really and truly* your own? Are your dreams *really* your own dreams? Might not they be someone else's visions that could sooner or later turn into nightmares?

# 4
## Memory

I began researching this book nine months after the gas attack and then worked at it for another year.

A certain "cooling period" had passed by the time I set about gathering stories. But the event had such an impact that memories were still fresh. Many interviewees had previously told and retold their experiences to people around them. Others had never admitted to anyone certain details about the attack, but even so, they surely went over and over the events in their own minds and thereby objectified them. In most cases the descriptions were extremely real and highly visual.

Nevertheless, they were all, strictly speaking, just memories.

Now, as one psychoanalyst defines it: "Human memory is nothing more than a 'personal interpretation' of events." Passing an experience through the apparatus of memory can sometimes rework it into something more readily understood: the unacceptable parts are omitted; "before" and "after" are reversed; unclear elements are refined; one's own memories are mixed with those of others, interchanged as often as necessary. All this goes on perfectly naturally, unconsciously.

Simply put, our memories of experiences are rendered into something like a narrative form. To a greater or lesser extent, this is a natural function of memory—a process that novelists consciously utilize as a profession. The truth of "whatever is told" will differ, however slightly, from what actually happened. This, however, does not make it a lie; it is unmistakably the truth, albeit in another form.

During the course of my interviews I endeavored to maintain the basic stance that each person's story is true within the context of that story, and I still believe so. As a result, the stories told by people who simultaneously experienced the very same scene often differ on the small details, but they are presented here with all their contradictions preserved. Because it seems to me that these discrepancies and contradictions say something in themselves. Sometimes, in this multifaceted world of ours, inconsistency can be more eloquent than consistency.


## 5
## What Can I Do?

I decided to write this book because, in short, I have always wanted to understand Japan at a deeper level. I'd been living abroad, away from the country, for a long time—seven or eight years—first in

Europe, then America. I left after writing *Hard-Boiled Wonderland and the End of the World* and, apart from brief visits, I did not return until I had finished *The Wind-Up Bird Chronicle*. I regarded it as a period of self-imposed exile.

I wanted to broaden my experience of other places, plant myself down, and write. By getting away from Japan—which stood *a priori* both to the Japanese language and to my own being—I forced myself to map out the various methods and postures I assumed, phase by phase, when dealing with the language and all things Japanese.

To my surprise, it was only during the last two years of my "exile" that I discovered anything I urgently wanted to know about "that country called Japan." The time I spent abroad, wandering about trying to come to terms with myself, was coming to an end—or so I gradually realized. I could feel the change inside me, an ongoing "revaluation" of my values. I was, to understate the obvious, no longer that young. And by the same token, I suddenly knew I was entering the ranks of that generation with a "vested duty" toward Japanese society.

"Time for me to be heading back to Japan," I thought. Go back and do one solid work, something other than a novel, to probe deep into the heart of my estranged country. And in that way, I might reinvent a new a stance for myself, a new vantage point.

Now then, how do you go about understanding Japan any better?

I had a fairly good idea of the stuff I was looking for. The bottom line was, after doing one good clean sweep of my emotional accounts, I needed to know more about Japan as a society, I had to learn more about the Japanese as a "form of consciousness." Who were we as a people? Where were we going?

Yes, but what *specifically* did I have to do? I had no idea. I spent my last year abroad in a sort of fog when two major catastrophes struck Japan: the Kobe earthquake and the Tokyo gas attack.

In the end, my extended research into the Tokyo gas attack did indeed turn into a decisive exercise in "more deeply understanding Japan." I met a great many Japanese, listened to their stories, and *as a result* was able to see what it meant to be Japanese when confronted by a major shock to the system like the gas attack. Thinking it over now, I admit to injecting a degree of authorial ego into it. I did in one sense use the exercise as a "convenient vehicle" for my own ends. Not to recognize this would be hypocritical.

Even so, certain other aspects of my ego were nicely snubbed over the course of conducting these interviews. Meeting the victims face-to-face and hearing so many raw, firsthand accounts, I had to pull myself together. It wasn't a topic you merely toyed with. What transpired was more profound, more compounded with meanings than anything I could have imagined. It was humbling to know how completely ignorant I was about the gas attack.

For me, as a novelist, hearing all these people tell their "narratives"—told from "our" side, it should go without saying—had a certain healing power.

Eventually I stopped making judgments altogether. "Right" or "wrong," "sane" or "sick," "responsible" or "irresponsible"—these questions no longer mattered. At least, the final judgment was not mine to make, which made things easier. I could relax and simply take in people's stories verbatim. I became, not the "fly on the wall," but a spider sucking up this mass of words, only to later break them down inside me and spin them out into "another narrative."

Especially after conducting interviews with the family of Mr. Eiji Wada—who died in Kodemmacho Station—and with Ms. "Shizuko Akashi"—who lost her memory and speech and is still in the hospital undergoing therapy—I had to seriously reconsider the value of my own writing. Just how vividly could my choice of words convey to the reader the various emotions (fear, despair, loneliness, anger, numbness, alienation, confusion, hope . . . ) these people experienced?

Also, I'm quite sure I carelessly hurt a few people in the course of my interviews, whether through my insensitivity or my ignorance or purely because of some flaw in my character. I've never been a good talker, and sometimes I don't put things very well. I would like to borrow this opportunity to sincerely apologize to all those I may have hurt.

I came to them from the "safety zone," someone who could always walk away whenever I wanted. Had they told me, "There's no way you can truly know what we feel," I'd have had to agree. End of story.

# 6
## Overwhelming Violence

The Kobe earthquake and the Tokyo gas attack of January and March 1995 are two of the gravest tragedies in Japan's postwar history. It is no exaggeration to say that there was a marked change in the Japanese consciousness "before" and "after" these events. These twin catastrophes will remain embedded in our psyche as two milestones in our life as a people.

That two such cataclysmic events should come in quick succession was as startling as it was coincidental. Yet, arriving as they did at the time when Japan's "Bubble economy" burst, marking the end of those times of rampant excess, they ushered in a period of critical inquiry into the very roots of the Japanese state. It was as if these events had been lying in wait to ambush us.

Common to both was an element of overwhelming violence: the one an inescapable natural calamity, the other an avoidable man-made disaster. A tenuous parallel perhaps, yet to those most affected the suffering was frighteningly similar. The source and nature of the violence may have differed, but the shock in both cases was equally devastating. That was the impression I got, talking to the survivors of the gas attack.

Many of them remarked how intensely they "hated those Aum thugs," yet they found themselves deprived of any outlet for their "intense hatred." Where could they go? Where to turn? Their confusion was compounded by the fact that no one could pinpoint the sources of the violence. In this sense—having nowhere to direct their anger and hatred—the gas attack and the earthquake bear a striking formal resemblance.

In some ways, the two events may be likened to the front and back of one massive explosion. Both were nightmarish eruptions beneath our feet—from underground—that threw all the latent contradictions and weak points of our society into frighteningly high relief. Japanese society proved all too defenseless against these sudden onslaughts. We were unable to see them coming and failed to prepare. Nor did we respond effectively. Very clearly, "our" side failed.

That is, the narrative that most Japanese embrace (or imagine they share) broke down; none of these "common values" proved the least effective in warding off the evil violence that erupted under us.

Granted, a sudden emergency on such a scale will inevitably result in a level of confusion and oversights. As is clear from these testimonies, people at all levels of society—in the Subway Authority, in the fire department, in the police, in the various medical facilities—were all subject to lapses of judgment and mixups large and small.

It is not my intention, however, to point fingers or lecture anyone over individual errors. I'm not saying "It couldn't be helped," nor am I suggesting that each and every error be made right at this late date. More to the point, what I hope should sink in is the recognition that Japan's crisis-management system itself is erratic and sorely inadequate. The immediate on-the-ground errors of judgment were the result of existing holes in the system.

Even more dangerous, little if anything has been learned about what actually happened *as a result* of those failings, because the information is classified. Japan's institutions remain inner-circle-upon-inner-circle, acutely sensitive to any public "loss of face," unwilling to expose their failings to "outsiders." Efforts to investigate what happened were greatly limited for all the usual hazy, accepted reasons: "It's already on trial . . ." or "That's government business . . ."

Then there were those interviewees who were curiously reticent: "I myself would like to cooperate, but the people upstairs aren't so keen . . ." Very likely it was felt that if people revealed too much, someone would have to take responsibility. Typically in Japan, the order to keep mum is never a direct order, but rather a sort of soft-pedaling from above: "Well, it's over and done with anyway. Probably best not to say any more than we have to . . ."

In preparing to write my last novel, *The Wind-Up Bird Chronicle*, I did in-depth research into the so-called 1939 Nomonhan Incident, an aggressive incursion by Japanese forces into Mongolia. The more I delved into the records, the more aghast I became at the recklessness, the sheer lunacy of the Imperial Army's system of command. How had this pointless tragedy gone so wantonly overlooked in the course of history? Again, researching the Tokyo gas attack, I was struck by the fact that the closed, responsibility-evading ways of Japanese society were really not any different from how the Imperial Japanese Army operated at that time.

In essence it was the foot soldiers with guns in their hands who risked the most, suffered the most, faced the worst horrors, and were the least compensated in the end, whereas the officers and intelligence behind the lines took no responsibility whatsoever. They hid behind masks, refused to admit defeat, whitewashed over their failure with jargon and rhetoric. For if such glaring ignominy on the front line were to be exposed, they as field commanders would be subject to swift and severe punishment. Typically, this meant *harakiri*. Thus the truth of the matter was nominally classified as a "military secret," sealed away from public scrutiny.

In this way, countless soldiers were sacrificed to an insane stratagem in a bitter fight to the death at the front line (worse than anyone expected). Even after more than fifty years, I was still shocked to learn that we Japanese had embarked on such a patently idiotic maneuver. And yet here in today's Japan we were repeating the very same thing. The nightmare continues.

Ultimately, the reasons for our defeat at Nomonhan were never properly analyzed by the Army High Command (aside from some rather hasty studies), so that absolutely nothing was learned. No lessons were passed on, and with the replacement of a few figures in the Kanto Army, all information about the war on that distant front was effectively kept under wraps. Two years later, Japan entered World War II, and the same insanity and tragedy that happened at Nomonhan was repeated all over again on a massive scale.

# 7
## Underground

Another personal motive for my interest in the Tokyo gas attack is that it took place underground. Subterranean worlds—wells, underpasses, caves, underground springs and rivers, dark alleys, subways— have always fascinated me and are an important motif in my novels.

The image, the mere idea of a hidden pathway, immediately fills my head with stories . . .

Underground settings play particularly major roles in two of my novels, *Hard-Boiled Wonderland and the End of the World* and *The Wind-Up Bird Chronicle*. Characters go into the World Below in search of something and down there different adventures unfold. They head underground, of course, both in the physical and spiritual sense. In *Hard-Boiled Wonderland* a fictional race called INKlings have lived beneath us since time immemorial. Horrible creatures, they have no eyes and feed upon rotting flesh. They have dug a vast underground network of tunnels beneath Tokyo, linking their "nests." Ordinary people, however, never even suspect their presence. The protagonist for one reason or another descends into this mythic landscape below, encounters chilling traces of INKling infestation, somehow makes his way through the black depths, and emerges unscathed into Aoyama Itchome Station on the Ginza Line.

There were times, traveling on the Tokyo subway after writing this novel, when I'd fantasize seeing INKlings "out there" in the darkness. I'd imagine them rolling a boulder into the path of the train, cutting off the power, breaking the windows and overrunning the cars, ripping us to shreds with their razor-sharp teeth . . .

A childish fantasy, admittedly. Yet, like it or not, when news of the Tokyo gas attack reached me, I have to admit those INKlings came to mind: shadowy figures poised waiting just beyond my train window. If I were to give free rein to a very private paranoia, I'd have imagined some causal link between the evil creatures of my creation and those dark underlings who preyed upon the subway commuters. That link, imaginary or not, provided one rather personal reason for writing this book.

I don't mean to cast the Aum cultists in the role of monsters straight out of the pages of H. P. Lovecraft. That I worked INKlings into *Hard-Boiled* surely says more about the primal fears latent inside me. Whether from my own mind or the collective unconscious, they were a symbolic presence, or else represented danger pure and simple. Never to be disassociated from the dark, always just out of our field of vision. Yet there are times when even we children of sunlight may find comfort in the gentle healing embrace of darkness. We need the sheltering night. But under no circumstances do we venture further, to open that locked door leading down to the deepest recesses. For beyond unfolds the impenetrably dark narrative of the INKling world.

Thus, in the context my own narrative, the five Aum "agents" who punctured those bags of sarin with the sharpened tips of their umbrellas unleashed swarms of INKlings beneath the streets of Tokyo. The mere thought fills me with dread, no matter how simplistic. Yet I have to say it out loud: they should never have done what they did. For whatever reason.

# PART TWO

# THE PLACE THAT WAS PROMISED

• • •

## "An Old Man Awake In His Own Death"

### by Mark Strand

This is the place that was promised
when I went to sleep,
taken from me when I woke.

This is the place unknown to anyone,
where names of ships and stars
drift out of reach.

The mountains are not mountains anymore;
the sun is not the sun.
One tends to forget how it was;

I see myself, I see
the shore of darkness on my brow.
Once I was whole, once I was young . . .

As if it mattered now
and you could hear me
and the weather of this place would ever cease.

# Preface

• • •

When I wrote *Underground* I made it a point of principle to avoid reading any of the reports in the media about Aum. I put myself as much as possible in the same situation the victims of the attack found themselves that day: taken totally unaware by some unknown, deadly force.

For this reason I deliberately excluded any Aum viewpoint from *Underground*. I was afraid it would only throw the book out of focus. Above all I wanted to avoid the kind of wishy-washy approach that tries to see the viewpoint of both sides.

Because of this, *Underground* was criticized by some as one-sided, but I had, after all, intentionally set up my camera at one fixed spot. What I was after was a book that brought one closer to the interviewees (this doesn't always mean one is on their side, however). I wanted a book that made you feel what these people felt, think what they thought. That isn't to say I was totally oblivious to the social significance of Aum Shinrikyo.

After *Underground* was published, and various repercussions from the events had settled down, the question "What was Aum Shinrikyo?" welled up inside me. After all, *Underground* was an attempt to restore a sense of balance to what I saw as biased reporting. Once that job was over, I had to wonder whether we were receiving true and accurate accounts of the Aum side of the story.

In *Underground*, Aum Shinrikyo was like some unidentified threat—a "black box" if you will—which suddenly, from out of nowhere, made an assault on the everyday. Now, in my own way, I wanted to try to pry open that black box and catch a glimpse of what it contained. By comparing and contrasting those contents with the viewpoints gathered in *Underground* I hoped to gain an even deeper understanding.

I was also motivated by a strong sense of fear that we had still not begun to deal with, let alone solve, any of the fundamental issues arising from the gas attack. Specifically, for people who are outside the main system of Japanese society (the young in particular), there remains no effective alternative or safety net. As long as this crucial gap exists in our society, like a kind of black hole, even if Aum is suppressed, other magnetic force fields—"Aum-like" groups—will rise up again, and similar incidents are bound to take place.

Before I began working on *The Place That Was Promised* I felt uneasy; now it is finished I have an even stronger sense of foreboding. It wasn't always easy finding victims of the gas attack willing to be interviewed and, for different reasons, it wasn't an easy task finding Aum Shinrikyo members, or even former members, to interview. What sort of criteria could one possibly use to choose interviewees? How could you come up with a representative sample? And who could say it was truly representative? I was also worried that, even if we could find such people and listened to what they had to say, it would turn out to be just a lot of religious propaganda. Would we be able to interact in any meaningful way?

The editorial staff of the magazine *Bungei Shunju*, where these interviews were first published, found the Aum members and former members for me. In general the interviews follow the same style and format as the ones in *Underground*. I decided to be as indulgent as possible over each one, letting the interviewees take as much time as they wished to respond. Each interview lasted three or four hours. The tapes were transcribed and the interviewee was asked to go over the manuscript. They could omit parts that, upon reflection, they didn't want to see in print, and add statements they thought were important that they had forgotten to make at the time of the interview. When I had their final go-ahead, the interview was published. As much as possible I wanted to use their real names, but it was often a condition of the interview that no indication would be given when a pseudonym was used.

Generally few attempts were made to check whether the statements made in the interviews were factually accurate or not, other than when they obviously contradicted known facts. Some people might object to this, but my job was to listen to what people had to say and to record this as clearly as possible. Even if there are some details inconsistent with reality, the collective narrative of these personal stories has a powerful reality of its own. This is something novelists are acutely aware of, which is why I regard this as fitting work for a novelist.

Yet the interviews in *Underground* and those collected here do not follow the exact same format. This time I often interjected my own opinions, voiced doubts, and even debated various points. In *Underground* I tried to keep myself in the background as much as possible, but this time I decided to be a more active participant. Sometimes, for instance, the conversation began to swerve too much in the direction of religious dogma, which I felt was inappropriate.

I am by no stretch of the imagination an expert on religions, nor a sociologist. I am nothing more than a simple, not very refined novelist. (This is not false modesty, as many will testify.) My knowledge of religion is not much above the level of a rank amateur, so there was little chance I'd be able to hold my own if I got into the ring to debate doctrine with some devout religious believer.

This was my concern when I began these interviews, but I decided not to let it hold me back. When I didn't understand something, I just went ahead and exposed my ignorance; when I thought that most people would not accept a certain viewpoint, I challenged it. "It might hold a certain logic," I'd say, "but your average person wouldn't buy it." I'm not just saying this to defend myself or show how bold I am. I wanted to take the time to clarify basic terms and ideas—to say, "Wait a second. What does that mean?"—rather than simply nodding my head and letting a lot of technical terms fly by.

At a commonsense, everyday level, we were able to get our points across, and I feel I was able to understand the basic ideas the interviewees tried to convey. (Whether or not I accept them is another story.) This was more than enough for the type of interview I was conducting. Analyzing the interviewee's mental state in detail, evaluating the ethical and logical justifications for their positions, etc., were not the goals I laid out for this project. I leave deeper study of the religious issues raised, and their social meaning, to the experts. What I've tried to present is the way these Aum followers appear in an ordinary, face-to-face conversation.

Still, talking to them so intimately made me realize how their religious quest and the process of novel writing, though not identical, are similar. This aroused my own personal interest as I interviewed them, and it is also why I felt something akin to irritation at times as well.

I have an abiding anger toward the Aum Shinrikyo members involved in the gas attack—both those who are under arrest and those who were involved in other ways. I have met some of the victims, many of whom continue to suffer, and I have personally seen those whose loved ones were stolen from them forever. I'll remember that for as long as I live, and no matter what the motives or circumstances behind it, a crime like this can never be condoned.

However, opinion is divided over the extent to which the entire Aum Shinrikyo organization was committed to the gas attack. I will leave any judgment here to the reader. I did not undertake these interviews with present and former members of the cult in order to criticize them or denounce them, nor in the hope that people would view them in a more positive light. What I am trying to provide here is the same thing I hoped to convey in *Underground*—not one clear viewpoint, but flesh-and-blood material from which to construct *multiple* viewpoints; which is the same goal I have in mind when I write novels.

As a novelist, I will be sifting through what remains within me, bit by bit, investigating, putting things in order as I pass through the time-consuming process of shaping this into narrative form. It's not the sort of thing that takes shape easily.

These interviews were published in monthly installments in *Bungei Shunju* from April to October 1997, and were published serially under the title *Post-Underground*.

# "I'm still in Aum"

## Hiroyuki Kano (b. 1965)

*Mr. Kano was born in Tokyo, but soon moved to a neigh-
boring prefecture where he grew up. In college his health
declined and he began attending classes at a yoga training
center run by Aum. After just twenty-one days Shoko Asahara advised him to become a renunciate, which he did
five months later.*

*At the time of the gas attack Mr. Kano was a member
of Aum's Ministry of Science and Technology, where he
was involved mainly in computer-related work. Until the
attack, his six years in Aum had been wonderful and fulfilling and he had made many friends.*

*Though he has not officially left Aum, he no longer
lives communally with the other members, and keeps his
distance from them. He lives alone in Tokyo, doing computer work at home, while still following his own regime
of ascetic training. He is deeply interested in Buddhism,
and his dream remains to construct a theoretical framework for Buddhism. Many of his friends have left Aum. At
32, he wonders what the future has in store for him.*

*Our interview lasted a long time, but not once did he
mention the name Shoko Asahara. He avoided referring to
Asahara directly, using the terms "leader" or "guru," or,
once as I recall, "that person."*

●　　●　　●

In elementary school I was healthy, taller than the other kids. I loved
sports and was into all kinds of things. But in junior high I stopped
growing and now I'm a little bit shorter than average. It's like my
physical development responded to my emotional state, and went
downhill along with my health.

I was a pretty good student, but I felt a kind of resistance to the whole idea of studying. For me, studying meant gaining wisdom, but schoolwork was just rote memorization, things like how many sheep there are in Australia or something. You can study that all you want, but there's no way it'll make you wise. To me, that's what being an adult meant. To be able to have that kind of calm, that sense of intelligence. There was a huge gap between the image I had of what an adult should be and the actual adults around me.

You get older, gain knowledge and experience, but inside you don't grow as a person one little bit. Take away the outer appearance and the superficial knowledge and what's left is no better than a child.

I also had some major doubts about love. When I was around 19 I thought long and hard and came to the following conclusion: pure love for another person, and what people call romantic love, are two different things. Pure love doesn't manipulate the relationship to one's advantage, but romantic love is different. Romantic love contains other elements—the desire to be loved by the other person, for instance. If purely loving another was enough, you wouldn't suffer because of unrequited love. As long as the other person was happy, there wouldn't be any need to suffer because you weren't being loved in return. What makes people suffer is the desire to be loved by another person. So I decided that romantic love and pure love for a person are not the same. And that by following this you could lessen the pain of unrequited love.

MURAKAMI: *It seems to me an overly logical approach. Even if they experienced unrequited love, most people wouldn't carry the idea that far.*

I suppose so. But since I was about 12 I've always approached things in a philosophical way. Once I started thinking about something I'd sit there for six hours. For me, to "study" something meant precisely that. School was just a race to gain the most points.

I tried talking with my friends about these things, but got nowhere. Even my friends who were good students would only say something like, "Wow. Pretty amazing stuff you come up with," and that'd be the end of it. The conversation would hit a dead end. I couldn't find a single person who wanted to talk about the things that I cared about.

MURAKAMI: *Most adolescents, when they worry about those kinds of things, really get into reading books. To find some helpful advice.*

I don't like reading. When I read something I just see what's wrong with the book. Especially philosophy books—I only read a few and couldn't stand them. I always thought philosophy was supposed to provide you with a deeper consciousness so you could find a "remedy" to life's problems. To really understand the purpose of living, to find fulfillment and happiness, and to decide what your life's goals should be. Everything else was just a means to that end. But the books I read all seemed to be excuses for famous scholars to flaunt their linguistic skills: "Hey, look how much I know!" I could see right through this, and couldn't stand those books. So philosophy never did anything for me.

There was one other reality I came to ponder when I was in the sixth grade. I was staring at a pair of scissors in my hands and the thought suddenly struck me that some adult had worked very hard to create them, but that someday they would fall apart. Everything that has form will eventually fall apart. Same with people. In the end they die. Everything's heading straight for destruction and there's no turning back. To put it another way, destruction itself is the principle by which the universe operates. Once I reached that conclusion I started to look at everything in a very negative way.

For instance, if my own life is headed toward destruction it doesn't matter if I become prime minister or end up just one of the homeless, right? What's the point of struggling? The horrible conclusion I came to was that if suffering outweighs joy in life, it would be much wiser to commit suicide as quickly as possible.

There's only one way out, namely the afterlife. That's the sole remaining hope. The first time I heard that expression "afterlife" I thought it was stupid. I read Tetsuro Tanba's book *What Happens After Death?* just to see what kind of idiotic things were written in it. I'm the kind of person who has to pursue an idea to the bitter end once it takes hold of me. I'm not the type to just think, "What the hell, it'll work out somehow." I have to clearly differentiate what I understand from what I don't. The same holds true for studying. For every new thing I learn, ten more questions will pop into my head. Until I can answer those, I can't go on.

Anyway, Tanba's book was worthless, but he mentioned Swedenborg's work, which I read and was amazed by. Swedenborg is a famous scholar, a physicist of Nobel Prize caliber, but after he turned 50 he became like a psychic and wrote down a lot of records of the afterlife. I was struck by how extremely logical his work was. Compared to other books on the subject, everything fit together logically. The relationship between his premises and his conclusions was utterly convincing and believable.

I thought I should look a bit further into the afterlife, so I read a lot of material on near-death experiences. I was bowled over. The testimonies were strikingly similar. These were actual testimonies with the people's real names and photographs. "They can't all be conspiring to tell the same lie," I thought. Later on I learned about the Law of Karma, and it was like a veil had lifted, and many of the doubts and questions I'd had since I was little were solved.

I also learned that the basic Buddhist tenet of impermanence is the same as the idea I had about the law of the universe tending toward destruction. I'd always looked at this in a more negative way, but this made it very easy for me to get into Buddhism.

MURAKAMI: *Did you read books about Buddhism as well?*

Not real studies of Buddhism. The ones I read didn't seem very direct in their approach. I couldn't discover the "remedy" I was searching for. They talked about various sutras, but never got to the heart of the matter, the part I really wanted to find out about. Records of people's actual experiences had more of what I was looking for.

Of course, there were parts I couldn't believe. I don't know why, but for some reason I was convinced I could distinguish which parts of people's stories could be believed and which parts couldn't. Call it experience, or intuition. Anyway, I had a strange confidence that I could do this.

MURAKAMI: *It sounds to me like you exclude everything that goes against your own theories or feelings. There are many things in the world that run counter to one's viewpoint, that challenge one's cherished ideas, yet I don't get a sense that you tried to engage with these.*

Ever since I was in elementary school I hardly ever lost an argument to an adult. I know it's not true, but the adults all seemed like idiots to me. Now I regret having thought this way. I was immature then. If I brought up a certain point, I knew, I'd lose the argument, so I'd make a detour around it. That way I never lost. I got a bit big-headed.

I got along with my friends okay. I'd adjust whatever I said to fit the person I was talking to. I always knew just the right thing to say at any point to smooth things over. So I had a lot of friends. I lived that way for about ten years, enjoying entertaining my friends. But when I got home and was alone I wondered what my life would be like if I continued this way. In the final analysis I didn't have a single friend who was interested in the same things I was.

I didn't take the entrance exams for college, but went instead to an electricians' school. I studied engineering, but that wasn't what I really wanted to do. I still wanted real wisdom. One ideal I had was to scientifically systematize Eastern philosophy.

Take biophotons, for example, the light that living things give off. If you compiled detailed statistics on the relationship between that and illness, you might be able to discover the physical properties involved. For instance, there must be some physical properties you could discover by connecting biophotons and the movements of the heart. This is something I believe from my experiences with yoga.

MURAKAMI: *So it was very important for you to be able to measure the amounts of the force or to be able to map it visually.*

That's right. If you systematize things this way, your arguments will ring true. In this sense modern science is an amazing system. In Aum, too, there are many valuable parts. I want the meat of it to remain. Aum's finished as a religion. It has to be theoretized as a natural science.

I'm not much interested in things that can't be measured scientifically. What cannot be measured has no persuasive power, so whatever value it might have can't be transmitted to other people. If things that can't be measured acquire power, you end up with something like Aum. If you're able to measure things, you can exclude the potential danger.

MURAKAMI: *Okay, but how much reality would these measurements have? And wouldn't they differ depending on your viewpoint? There's also the danger that data could be manipulated. You'd have to decide at what point your measurements are sufficient, not to mention the question of the reliability of the instruments used to do the measuring.*

As long as the statistical structure you use is the same as that used in medical science, then it's okay. These symptoms mean this, this is how you treat them, that sort of thing.

MURAKAMI: *I don't imagine you read novels.*

No, I don't. Three pages is about the most I can manage before I give up.

MURAKAMI: *Since I'm a novelist I'm the opposite of you—I believe that what's most important is what* cannot *be measured. I'm not denying your way of thinking, but the greater part of people's lives consists of things that are unmeasurable, and trying to change all these to something measurable is realistically impossible.*

True. It's not that I believe all these things that can't be measured are worthless, it's just that the world seems filled with unnecessary suffering. And the causes of suffering are increasing—uncontrollable desires are causing people to suffer. The appetite for food, for instance, or sex.

What Aum did was reduce that type of psychological stress, and by doing so increase each individual's power. Ninety-nine percent of the image that Aum followers have of Aum Shinrikyo is exactly this—a way of looking at spiritual and physical phenomena, and a remedy or solution to these. The organization or some eschatological philosophy, or whatever is just an image of Aum created by the media. I didn't know anybody who cared about Nostradamus's *Prophecies*. Nobody's going to be convinced by something like that.

What I really want to do is scientifically systematize Eastern philosophical ideas such as transmigration and karma. If you visit India you'll find that people there believe these things intuitively, they're an integral part of their daily lives, but in advanced countries we live in an age when it's necessary to put these on a theoretical basis in order for people to understand and accept them.

MURAKAMI: *Before the war some Japanese believed the Emperor was a deity, and they died for this belief. Is this acceptable to you? That things are fine as long as you believe in them?*

If that were the end of it, that would be okay, but if you consider the afterlife, it's better to live a Buddhist life.

MURAKAMI: *But that's just a question of different objects of belief—whether you believe in the Emperor or in Buddhist transmigration.*

But the results are different. What you attain after death if you believe in the Emperor is not what you get after death believing in Buddhism.

MURAKAMI: *That's just what Buddhists say. People who believed in the Emperor thought that if you died for him your soul would rest in Yasukuni Shrine and find peace. So you're saying this is okay?*

That's why I'm so concerned about a method to prove Buddhism mathematically. That method doesn't exist yet, which is why we get into these sorts of debates. There's nothing more I can add.

MURAKAMI: *So if a method was found to measure the Emperor theoretically you wouldn't mind this?*

Correct. As long as this was beneficial to that person after death, I wouldn't mind.

MURAKAMI: *What I'm getting at is that if you examine the history of science you can see that it has been manipulated in the name of politics and religion. The Nazis did this. There's been lots of sham science that in retrospect was misguided. And this has brought untold harm to society. Granted you're a person who closely gathers evidence, but most people, told by authority figures that something is "scientific," swallow it whole and go along with whatever they say. And to me that's very frightening.*

I just think our present situation is frightening. But people in the world today are suffering needlessly. That's why I'm trying to think of ways this can be avoided.

MURAKAMI: *By the way, how did you come to join Aum Shinrikyo?*

I read a book about easy meditation you can do at home and when I tried it something very weird happened to me. I didn't practice it all that seriously, but when I attempted to purify my chakras, my chi [life force] got that much weaker. What you're supposed to do when you purify your chakras is simultaneously strengthen your life force. But I didn't. And my chakras were out of balance. I felt like I was burning up one minute, freezing cold the next. My energy level was way down, and I was always anemic. It was a dangerous situation. I couldn't eat anything and I lost a lot of weight. I felt sick whenever I attended classes at college, and I couldn't study at all.

Around that time I went to the Aum dojo at Setagaya. They explained my situation to me and told me right then and there how to treat it. I tried the breathing exercises they taught me, and I couldn't believe how quickly I got better.

For two months after that I didn't go to the dojo very much, but then I started going regularly, doing volunteer work, folding leaflets and stuff. Soon after that there was a "Secret Yoga" session where you could talk directly to the Leader [Shoko Asahara], and I asked him what I should do about my poor health. "You need to become a renunciate," he told me. It was like he saw the real me at a glance. People were amazed because he'd never said that to anyone before— so I felt I had no choice but to leave school and become a renunciate. I was 22.

There were very few people who started out as renunciates. It's rare. But I was so weak I couldn't walk properly and I was sure if things continued as they were I wouldn't be able to live a normal life. "You don't fit this transient world," I was told [by Asahara], and I certainly agreed—no need to convince me of that. We didn't really have a conversation, he just came out with it. He usually didn't say anything, but would be able to tell a lot about a person just by looking at his face. Like he knew everything about you. That's why people believed in him.

MURAKAMI: *Of course, one might suspect that before he met a person he'd have a file on him, with all kinds of data.*

Sure, that's possible. At the time, though, it didn't seem like that. I became a renunciate in 1989, and at that time there were only about two hundred renunciates. At the end I think there were about three thousand.

When he was kind to you, that man [Asahara] was kinder than anyone I've ever met. But when he was angry, he was the scariest person in my life. The difference was so marked just talking to him made you convinced he was somehow inspired.

It was tough on me being told to become a renunciate. I didn't want to worry my parents, and I hated the idea of new religions. I explained things to them as best I could but they cried a lot, which upset me. My parents aren't the type to argue, they just cry. My mother passed away not long after this, which hurt terribly. She had a lot of stressful things happen to her around then, and this business with me might have been the last straw. My father probably thinks I'm the one who killed her. I'm sure he does.

[*Not long afterward, there was an election for the Lower House of the Japanese Diet, and Aum Shinrikyo had several candidates. Mr. Kano was convinced that Asahara would be elected. Even now he finds it hard to believe that almost no one voted for him. Many followers think the election was rigged. After this, Mr. Kano was assigned to the Construction Division of Aum and worked on Aum facilities at Naminomura in Kumamoto Prefecture.*]

I was in Naminomura about five months, where I worked as a long-distance truck driver. I drove all over Japan gathering materials. It wasn't so bad. At the construction site you'd be working under the intense sun, so compared to that driving a truck was a breeze.

Life in Aum was much tougher than secular life, but the tougher it was, the more satisfying it felt; my inner struggles were over, for which I was grateful. I made a lot of friends, too—adults, kids, old ladies, men, women. Everyone in Aum was aiming for the same thing—raising their spiritual level—so we had lots in common. I didn't have to change myself to get along with others.

No doubts remained, because all our questions were answered. Everything was solved. We were told: "Do this, and this will happen." No matter what question we had, we got an answer straightaway. I was completely immersed in it [*laughs*]. The media never reports that aspect. They label it all mind control. But actually it isn't. That's just what they say to boost talk-show ratings. They don't even try to report the facts.

I went back to the Mt. Fuji headquarters after Naminomura and worked with computers. Hideo Murai was my superior. I had some things I wanted to investigate, and Murai said, without much interest, "Just go ahead." He was doing all he could to carry out orders from above.

MURAKAMI: *When you say "from above" you mean Asahara?*

Yes. Murai was trying to suppress his own ego as much as possible. The last thing he cared about was someone below him coming up with an idea. But he didn't mind it if we had something we wanted to investigate on our own.

My position was "assistant master," the highest rank you could attain below the Aum leadership itself, something like the head of a section in a company. Not all that impressive, really. I had nobody directly below me. It was like I was working on my own, with no restrictions. I knew a lot of people like that. If you believe the media reports, everyone was under strict control like they were living in North Korea, but actually many people were free to do what they wanted. And of course we were free to come and go. We didn't have our own cars, but we could borrow one whenever we wanted.

MURAKAMI: *But later on there was systematic violence—the murder of the lawyer, Mr. Sakamoto, and his family, fatal beatings, the Matsumoto incident. Didn't you have any inkling that these things were taking place?*

There seemed to be more activity than usual, secretive, suspicious goings-on. But no matter what I might have seen, I'm sure I would have stubbornly insisted first and foremost that the personal benefits of what we were doing outweighed anything bad. I couldn't believe all the reports in the media. However, since about two years ago [1996], I've started to think that maybe those kinds of things really did take place.

I was sure that there was no way our group could hide something like the Sakamoto affair for so many years. Because the whole organization was so haphazard. It was like communism: if you made a mistake, you wouldn't get fired, and though we say we had "jobs" in Aum, it's not like we were drawing a salary or anything. I wouldn't call it irresponsible, exactly, there was just no sense of *individual* responsibility. Everything was sort of unclear and random. There was a sense that as long as your spiritual level was advancing, nothing else mattered. Most people in the secular world have a wife or family, so they have a certain sense of responsibility and work as hard as they can, but in Aum this was completely missing.

Say, for example, you're at a construction site and a steel frame has to arrive by tomorrow for work to continue. If it doesn't get there the person in charge just says, "Oh, that's right, I forgot about it." And that's the end of that. He might be scolded a little, but he doesn't care. Everyone has reached a stage where the harsh realities of everyday life don't affect them. Even if something bad happens, they just say it's bad karma dropping away, and everybody's happy. Making mistakes, getting yelled at—they just view these as so many personal impurities falling away [*laughs*]. They're pretty tough people when you think about it. No matter what happens, it doesn't bother them. Aum members looked down on ordinary people in the secular world. Like: "Look how they're all suffering, but we're not bothered."

MURAKAMI: *You were involved with Aum for six years, from 1989 to 1995. Did you have any problems or doubts during that time?*

I felt gratitude, fulfillment. Because even if something painful happened, they would explain the meaning of it to me in great detail. As you advanced to a higher stage, everyone was amazing. Fumihiro Joyu is a good example, but there were many people like him who were just as eloquent. Something in Aum definitely operated on a different level from the secular world. The higher up you advanced, the less sleep you needed; lots of people only slept three hours a day. Hideo Murai was like this. Spiritual power, discernment—these higher-ups were pretty astounding in everything.

MURAKAMI: *Did you have times when you could meet Shoko Asahara and talk to him directly?*

Yes, I did. In the past, when there were fewer followers, people often went to him with silly problems—like the fact that they were always feeling sleepy, etc., but as the organization grew we didn't have as many opportunities. We couldn't approach him on a one-to-one basis anymore.

I went through many kinds of initiations. Some of them were pretty hard. The one they called "Heat" was really bad. They involved drugs, too. I didn't know it at the time but it was LSD. You take that and it's like only your mind is left. You have no sense of your body, you're face-to-face with your deepest subconscious. Not an easy thing to confront, believe me. You feel completely listless, like this is what it must be like after you die. I didn't know I was doing drugs—I just thought it was a medicine that made me more inward to help me in my ascetic training.

MURAKAMI: *But it appears some people experienced some pretty bad trips and ended up with deep emotional scars.*

That's when the dose is too strong, and when other methods didn't work. There was a division in Aum called the Medical Ministry, run by Ikuo Hayashi, but it was a pretty random affair. I think that if they'd done it more scientifically, there wouldn't have been any problems. You have to remember that in Aum there was the idea that you should be given all types of tough challenges and overcome them. With the drugs, though, a bit more consideration would have helped.

MURAKAMI: *In March 1995, when the gas attack occurred, where were you and what were you doing?*

I was in my room at Kamikuishiki alone, using my computer. I had Internet access and I often read the news that way. We weren't supposed to, but I just went ahead anyway. Occasionally I went out, bought a newspaper, and passed it around to others. If you were found out they'd warn you, but it was no big deal.

So I was on the Internet reading the news flashes when I learned about the incident in the Tokyo subway. But I didn't think Aum was involved. I didn't know who did it, but I was certain it wasn't Aum.

After the attack Kamikuishiki was raided. We thought that members of the Science and Technology Ministry would all be arrested on trumped-up charges and it looked like it was best to get out, so I took a car and drove around while the police searched the place. I was certain it wasn't Aum.

Even after he [*Asahara*] was arrested, I didn't feel any anger. It seemed unavoidable. Aum followers believe that anger is a sign you are still spiritually immature. Instead of getting angry, we thought it was more virtuous to see deeper into the reality of a situation, then consider what actions to take.

We talked about what we should do, and we all agreed that as much as possible we should continue our training. We certainly didn't have any tragic sense of being driven into a corner or anything. Inside Aum it was like the eye of a hurricane, very calm.

I began to suspect Aum was the real culprit only after people were arrested and confessed. They were almost all friends of mine from long ago. Still, for the average Aum follower, whether they did it or not is beside the point; what was important was whether you would continue your ascetic training. How you developed your inner Self was more important than whether or not Aum was guilty.

MURAKAMI: *But the teachings of Aum Shinrikyo went in a certain direction, resulting in these crimes where many people were killed or injured. How do you feel about this?*

You have to understand that that part—Vajrayana Tantra—is clearly differentiated from the rest.*

Only those people who have reached an extremely high stage practise Vajrayana. We were told over and over that only those who have completed the Mahayana stage can carry that out. We were many levels below that. So even after the gas attack we didn't question the training or activities we were involved in.

MURAKAMI: *Setting aside the question of high or low stages, Vajrayana is an important part of Aum doctrine, so it has great significance.*

I can understand your saying that, but from our standpoint it was pie in the sky—completely unconnected with what we normally did or thought. It was just too far away. There were tens of thousands of years' worth of things you had to accomplish before you reached that level.

MURAKAMI: *So you felt it had nothing to do with you? For the sake of argument, though, let's say that your level shot way up to the level of Vajrayana, and you were ordered to kill someone as part of your path to reach Nirvana. Would you do it?*

Logically, it's a simple question. If by killing another person you raised him up, that person would be happier than he would have been living his life. So I do understand that path. But that should only be done by someone who has the ability to discern the process of transmigration and rebirth. Otherwise, you'd better leave it alone. If I'd been able to perceive what happens to a person after their death, and help them rise to a higher level—then maybe even I would have been involved. But there was no one in Aum who had risen that high.

MURAKAMI: *Yet those five people did it.*

But *I* wouldn't have. That's the difference. I couldn't take responsibility for that kind of action. It scares me, and there's no way

---

*Vajrayana is very similar to conventional Buddhism, with the crucial difference that it offers followers a "fast path" to salvation instead of the slow path like the Mahayanas. This faster path is also interpreted by some as condoning murder as an aid to liberation. [Tr.]

I could do it. Let's make one thing very clear. A person who cannot discern the transmigration of another does not have the right to take their life.

MURAKAMI: *Was Shoko Asahara qualified to do that?*

At the time I think he was.

MURAKAMI: *But can you measure that? Do you have any objective proof?*

No, at the moment I don't.

MURAKAMI: *So having him judged by our society's laws, no matter what judgment is handed down, is unavoidable?*

Right. I'm not saying that everything about Aum is correct. I just feel there's a lot of value in it, and I want to use it somehow to benefit ordinary people.

MURAKAMI: *On a very commonsense level, though, ordinary people were murdered. If you aren't able to work that into the equation who will listen to you?*

That's why I don't think we can talk about it in the framework of Aum anymore. I'm still in Aum, because the benefits I've received are so great. I'm trying to sort all this out, on an individual level. I still believe there are a lot of possibilities there. It requires a kind of logical reversal. There are hopeful elements, and I'm trying to clearly distinguish what I understand from what I don't.

I'm going to wait about two years, and if Aum is still in the same shape it is now, I plan to drop out. Until then I've got a lot to think over. But one thing is certainly true—Aum Shinrikyo doesn't learn from experience. It turns a deaf ear—no matter what other people say. It doesn't affect it a bit. No sense of regret. It's like what Aum members say about the gas attack: "That was a mission for other people. Not me."

I'm not like that, since I think the attack was a terrible event. It should never have been carried out. So inside me this dreadful event is at war with all the good things I've experienced. People who have a stronger sense of the awful things that happened left Aum, those for whom the "good things" are stronger remain. I'm stuck somewhere in the middle. I'm going to wait and see.

# "Nostradamus had a great influence on my generation"

## Akio Namimura (b. 1960)

*Mr. Namimura was born in Fukui Prefecture. He wanted to study literature and religion, which he'd been interested in before college, but he and his father, who was a stubborn man, clashed over what he should major in, and he gave up college to go to work. He got a job in an auto-parts factory in Fukui City. In high school he hated studying, and just read books on his own, always feeling alienated from his environment. Most of the books he read then were on religion or philosophy.*

*He has had a number of jobs, and continues to read, reflect, and write and to be interested in religions. Throughout his life he has had a clear sense that he and the world are out of sync. That's why he sought connections with people who were living outside the mainstream. In the midst of his searching, though, he can never completely rid himself of doubts that what he discovers is not the answer he seeks. He finds it impossible to throw himself heart and soul into any one group, even when he was a member of Aum.*

*At present he is back in his hometown, working for a haulage company. He has always loved the sea and often goes swimming. He's crazy about Okinawa. Hayao Miyazaki's films make him cry.\* "That proves I have normal human feelings," he says.*

●   ●   ●

When I graduated from high school I felt like I would either renounce the world, or die—one of the two. The idea of getting a job made me

---

\*Hayao Miyazaki is a successful manga cartoonist, animator, and director. His films include *Nausicaä of the Valley of Wind*, *Princess Mononoke*, and *Porco Rosso*. [Tr.]

sick. If I could, I wanted to live a religious life. Since living meant accumulating sin, I thought dying would be much better for the world.

These ideas went through my head as I worked selling tires for an auto-parts company. At first I was a useless salesman. I'd walk into a gas station or repair shop, say "Hello," then freeze up, unable to say another word. It was hard on me, and for my potential customers, too. In the beginning my sales record was zero.

Later I grew more sociable and was able to rack up some sales. It was good training for life. I worked there for two years. The reason I left was I lost my driver's license.

One of my relatives happened to be running a cram school in Tokyo, and he said I could work there. I was thinking about becoming a novelist, and when I mentioned this he said, "You can study to be a novelist while you're correcting essays."

Sounds good, I thought, so I moved to Tokyo at the beginning of 1981 and started work at the school. But things weren't as promised. My relative was suddenly very cold to me: "You want to be a novelist? Stop dreaming. The world's not some fairyland, you know." I wasn't even allowed to help correct compositions. "You're incompetent," he said, and I had to settle for odd jobs—keeping the students quiet, cleaning the rooms, stuff like that. I put up with it for a year and a half, then threw in the towel.

I'd saved a bit of money while I was working in Fukui, so I decided to live on my savings for the time being and study to be a writer. So for three years I was unemployed. I kept my expenses down to a minimum. I didn't buy anything, just food. I'm generally a pretty frugal guy, anyway. I just read, and wrote. The area I lived in was great since there were five public libraries a short distance away. It was a lonely life, but loneliness doesn't bother me. Most people couldn't have stood it, I imagine.

I mostly read surrealist fiction—Kafka, Breton's *Nadja*, and the like. I went to university festivals, read all the little magazines they published, and made friends I could talk about literature with. One guy I became friends with was in the philosophy department at Waseda University, and he introduced me to a lot of writers: Wittgenstein, Husserl, Shu Kishida, Shoichi Honda. I was impressed by the fiction this guy wrote, but now that I think about it, his stories were really derivative.

This guy from Waseda had a friend named Tsuda who was a follower of Soka Gakkai.* He tried his hardest to get me to join. We debated religion back and forth, but finally he said: "Look, talking about it won't get you anywhere. If you don't actually experience it your life won't change, so just take my word for it and give it a try." So I joined his Soka Gakkai group, living with them for about a month, but I realized it wasn't for me. They're one of these religions that aim to help people become successful in this world. I was looking for a purer kind of doctrine. Like Aum. Aum was closer to the original teachings of Buddhism.

When my money ran out, I started working for a company transporting department-store goods. I did that for two years. It was a tough job, but I'd always been into the martial arts and liked to work out, so physical labor didn't faze me. It was a part-time job, so the pay was low, but I worked three times harder than anyone else. I attended night classes at a place called the Japan Journalist Technical School. I thought I could write reportage.

Just around that time, though, life in Tokyo started to exhaust me. My mind was getting messed up. I was more violent, hot tempered. I was interested in nature then, and thought getting back to nature or moving back to my hometown sounded like a good idea. Once I get into something I really get into it. At the time it was ecology. Any way you cut it, the concrete jungle had burned me out and I longed to see the ocean in my hometown.

So I moved back to my parents' house and started working on the construction of the Monju high-speed nuclear reactor. I put up scaffolding. I considered this training too, but it was extremely dangerous work. After a while you get used to heights. I fell a number of times, and came close to dying. Let's see—I must have been there about a year. From the Monju reactor you have a fantastic view of the ocean. That's why I chose that job. So I could see the ocean while I

*Soka Gakkai is a lay Buddhist association that embraces the philosophy and teachings of Nichiren, a thirteenth-century Japanese Buddhist sage and scholar. There are more than ten million members of Soka Gakkai in Japan and seventy-six worldwide organizations that make up Soka Gakkai International. [Tr.]

worked. The ocean where the Monju was built is the most beautiful area around.

MURAKAMI: *But should someone into ecology work on a nuclear reactor?*

I was planning to write reportage on it. I thought that by writing about it I could cancel out my participation in building it. Wishful thinking, perhaps. You know the film *The Bridge on the River Kwai?* My idea was something like that. You work hard to build something, then in the end destroy it yourself. Of course I wasn't going to plant a bomb or anything. How should I put it? Since the sea that I loved so much was going to get polluted anyway, I might as well be the one to do it. Mixed-up emotions, I know. My mind was torn in different directions.

After a year I finished work on the Monju and went to Okinawa. I used the money I'd saved from the construction job to buy a used car, and I took the ferry to Okinawa and lived in my car for a while. I took a leisurely trip from one beach to the next. That took about two months. I fell in love with the great outdoors. What's great about Okinawa is that each place you go to has its own distinct personality. Every summer I'd come down with "Okinawa Fever" and couldn't sit still. I'd have to go. It made it hard for me to hold down a job. Come summer I'd just take off for Okinawa without a word.

In the meantime my father passed away, just before I turned 30. We didn't get along. No one in the family liked him. People thought of him as a good person, but at home he was a tyrant. He got violent when he drank. He used to hit me when I was a kid. Later on I was physically stronger so I'd hit *him* first. I'm not proud of that. I should have been a better son.

I was always drawn to religion, but my father was materialist, a rationalist. This caused problems between us. I'd come out with some religious opinion and he'd laugh at me, saying, "Enough of this God nonsense!" He'd get furious. This made me so sad: "Why does he have to say such terrible things? And why doesn't he accept anything I do?"

I was in Okinawa when my father's condition got worse. I rushed back to Fukui, but he passed away soon afterward. He had cirrhosis of the liver, a horrible way to die. In the end he didn't eat a thing, just drank and wasted away. On his deathbed he said to me, "Let's have one good talk," but I said, "Give me a break. Just go ahead and die, why don't you?" In a sense, I think I killed him.

After the funeral I went back to Okinawa. I was working on a construction site. But being away from Fukui and my family, I got terribly depressed. I was fine after my father died. The whole family got together and we had a pretty lively old time. But suddenly after I returned to Okinawa I took a nosedive. It felt like I was being dragged down to hell, kicking and screaming. "I'm done for," I thought. I'll definitely end up in hell. No way I can go back. That kind of feeling. It was a severe case of clinical depression. I was steadily going mad. On rainy days when we couldn't work I'd just lie curled up in bed. The others would go out to play pachinko, but I'd just stay there alone, completely blank.

One day, about three in the morning, I woke up and felt so terrible I thought, "This is it, I'm a goner." I felt like I was going to lose consciousness. I called my mother and she told me to come back home. But my mental problems persisted even in Fukui. Nothing cheered me up. I spent the first month at home doing absolutely nothing.

What rescued me from this situation was a female *yuta* in Okinawa.*

Actually I'd read Lyall Watson's book *Lightning Bird: One Man's Journey into Africa* and I was quite moved by it.

MURAKAMI: *That's an interesting book, isn't it?*

The main character, Boshier, is an epileptic and a schizophrenic. But he and others like him were able to meet a teacher, go through training, and become sorcerers. In other words, they could turn negative elements into something positive. And people would look up to them. I read that and thought: "Hey! That's me they're talking about." I started checking into it and found out that the same things are said about the *yuta* in Okinawa. In Okinawa that path to salvation still remains. So maybe I could become a *yuta*. I'm qualified, right? That's what I thought. That was one way out for me.

So I went to Okinawa and was able to see a famous *yuta*. I met

*Yuta is a southern-island term for a kind of shaman. [Tr.]

her along with several dozen other people, but she singled me out in the crowd, telling me I was troubled by something. It was like she could see right into my soul. "You're troubled because of your father, aren't you?" she said. "You're clinging to your father and have to rid yourself of that attachment. Put your father behind you and take a step in a new direction. If your mother is still alive you must take good care of her. Living an ordinary life is the most important thing."

Hearing this, I felt like a weight had lifted: "Ah, I'm saved!" And after that I stayed with just one company. In the summers I no longer took off for Okinawa. I decided to take good care of my mother and work hard, sticking to one job.

MURAKAMI: *In Adrian Boshier's case he had to enter that other world, but in your case you could still return to this world. You were told, in fact, to return.*

That's right. That's what happened. Having a normal life—marriage, kids—that's all a kind of training, I was told. In fact, it's the most difficult sort of training.

I'd been keeping an eye on religions for some time, checking them out. I was pretty involved in Christianity, and Soka Gakkai, as I mentioned. Even now I attend a Christian church. So Aum was just a tiny part of my life. Still, even now I feel Aum was something special. That's how much power it had.

In 1987 when Aum first appeared I wrote asking for some introductory literature. A heap of pamphlets arrived. I was amazed how professional they were, that a brand-new religion had the money to publish such slick stuff.

At the time there wasn't an Aum branch in Fukui, but there was one in nearby Sabae, where a man named Omori allowed Aum members to use his apartment as a meeting place once a week. They invited me and I went every once in a while. They showed a video clip about Aum that had appeared on the *All-Night Live TV!* show, and I was impressed. Joyu spoke so eloquently.*

He explained that Aum followers were using primitive Buddhism as a base to develop kundalini through ascetic practice. He

*Fumihiro Joyu was a senior member of and spokesman for Aum Shinrikyo. In 1997 he was sentenced to three years in prison on charges of forgery and perjury and was released in December 1999. He has since rejoined the cult. [Tr]

could answer any question clearly and simply. "This is really something," I thought. "What an impressive guy, and what an amazing group."

All the people there were Aum followers except me. I was just an observer. One practical reason kept me from going in further at the time: Aum costs money. They had a course you could take—ten tape cassettes for 300,000 yen. They were sermons by Master Asahara, so they were very effective. That's a cheap price to pay to get power, everyone thought, and shelled out 300,000 yen. But that only made me afraid. I was poor, and stingy to boot, so maybe I was even more sensitive to this.

We all took a bus together to Nagoya. It was the first time I saw Shoko Asahara. I wasn't a member yet, so I wasn't allowed to ask him any questions. In Aum you have to rise up through the ranks if you want to do anything, and that cost money. Once you got to a certain level you were allowed to ask Asahara questions. A step up from that and you were given a flower garland. I saw this in Nagoya and thought it was pretty silly. Also Asahara was gradually being deified, which disturbed me.

I subscribed to the Aum journal *Mahayana* from the very first issue. In the beginning it was a good magazine. They took great care in presenting the experiences of actual believers, and had stories on "How I Became an Aum Member," using people's real names. I was impressed by their honesty. After a while, though, the magazine didn't focus on individual members but solely on Asahara, raising him higher and higher with everyone worshipping him. For instance, when Asahara was going anywhere believers would lay their clothes on the ground for him to walk on. That's a bit much. It's scary—worship one person too much and freedom goes out the window. On top of that, Asahara was married and had a lot of children, which I found strange in light of the original tenets of Buddhism. He got around this by saying that he was the Final Liberated One and those kinds of things would not accumulate as karma. Of course no one really knew if he was or not.

I had no compunction about making my doubts known to people. One thing I found strange was that a lot of Aum followers died in car accidents. I asked a woman I knew well—Ms. Takahashi—about it. "Don't you think it's unusual that this many believers have died?" I asked her. "No, it's all right," she replied, "because four billion years in the future the Master will return as the Maitreya Buddha and will raise up the souls of those who died." "What rubbish!" I thought.

Also, Aum violently attacked Taro Maki, the editor of the *Sunday Mainichi* magazine, which had continued to criticize Aum. When I asked them why they just said: "Whether we're attacked or whatever happens to us, people who have a relationship with the Master are blessed. Even if we fall into hell, he will save us later."

For a long time my relationship with Aum Shinrikyo was an on-off affair. One day in 1993, though, an Aum man named Kitamura came to my door. He'd called saying he wanted to talk to me, so I said okay. I'd been away from Aum for a while and wanted to catch up on the latest news. But the more he talked, the crazier he got. He talked about what would happen if World War III broke out, laser weapons, plasma weapons—like something out of science fiction. It was interesting, admittedly, but it made me think that Aum was getting into some pretty intense things.

At the time Aum was putting a lot of pressure on me to become a member. The reason I ended up joining had to do with the woman I mentioned, Ms. Takahashi. My grandmother had just passed away and I was feeling sad about it. Ms. Takahashi called me and said she had something she wanted to talk over with me. "Actually," she said, "I've just joined Aum myself, and would like to discuss it with you." So we got together. She was 27, six years younger than me. It was like destiny. I felt it at a gut level. After that, she and I really opened up to each other. And in April 1994 I joined.

My grandmother's death must have had an influence. Also the company I was working for was starting to lay off people. To top it all, the illness I talked about before was still with me. I hoped that joining Aum might help clear it up once and for all.

I'll admit I was interested in Ms. Takahashi. Not in a romantic sense—but somehow I couldn't get her out of my mind. I could see she was absorbed by Aum—but was it good for her to be so totally immersed in it? I was skeptical about Aum, and thought it best to raise these doubts with her. The fastest way to do so, I concluded, was for me to join Aum as well, in order to be able to see her and have opportunities to talk to her. I know it sounds a bit altruistic.

Fortunately the entrance fee to join had gone down drastically to only 10,000 yen. Half a year's dues came to 6,000 yen. And they gave us ten free tapes. After joining, in order to go through the initiation rite you have to watch ninety-seven Aum videos and read seventy-seven Aum books. A huge amount, but somehow I made it through them. The last thing you had to do was chant your mantra. We got a printed sheet and read it aloud over and over using a counter to click off the times. That's why all Aum members have counters. We had to do that seven thousand times. I tried it for a while, but thought it was stupid and gave up. To my mind, it wasn't any different from a Soka Gakkai service.

They tried very hard to get me to become a renunciate. At this point Aum was struggling to increase its numbers. I still hadn't undergone the initiation rites, but they said it didn't matter. Still I resisted. Ms. Takahashi became a renunciate at the end of that year. She called me at work on December 20 and said, "I'm going to do it." That was the last time we ever spoke. She became a renunciate and went away.

When the gas attack occurred I was already distancing myself from Aum. There was a person Ms. Takahashi had proselytized and I was trying to convince that person not to join. Everyone knew I was critical of Aum's methods. But a follower is a follower and in May 1995 the police took me in for questioning. By this time they knew who had been members. They probably had a list of names. Their methods were pretty archaic. "Can you trample on a photo of Shoko Asahara?" they demanded, like it was in the Edo period when they made the Japanese Christians renounce their faith by stepping on a drawing of Jesus. I had a direct experience of how frightening the police can be.

The police came to question me again in 1995, when an ANA [All Nippon Airways] plane was hijacked in Hokkaido. "You know something about it, right?" they insisted. They came all the time. It was like being stalked. No matter what I did, someone was always watching me. A spooky feeling. The police are supposed to protect citizens, but here they were frightening me to death. I hadn't done anything wrong, but still I was afraid all the time that I might be arrested. They were picking up Aum believers one after another for petty offenses. They'd trump up some charges like forgery or something, and I was sure they'd do the same to me.

They phoned me all the time, asking if anyone in Aum had been in touch. I should have just put up with it, but I was stupid enough to let my curiosity about what was happening inside Aum get the best of me and I went all the way to a satyam in Osaka to see another woman renunciate I knew. I wondered how she felt in the midst of this police crackdown.

I bought a few issues of the Aum magazine *Anuttara Sacca* to take back with me. You couldn't get Aum books and magazines in bookstores anymore, and I wanted to see what was in them. Just as I left the satyam two policemen stopped me for questioning, asking me what I was up to inside. I was afraid, and also didn't want to be bothered, so I somehow brushed them off and hightailed it out of there. No wonder the police kept an even closer eye on me.

MURAKAMI: *At the time did you believe that the gas attack on the subway was the work of Aum?*

I did. I was positive they did it, but still I couldn't suppress my curiosity about Aum. I was interested in the essence of this religious group that had been attacked by society, whose books no bookstore would stock, yet which still actively published its journals—this strange kind of life force that sprang back every time no matter how much you tried to crush it. What was going on in Aum? What did the followers really think? That's what I wanted to know. A journalist's viewpoint, I suppose. Nothing like what was ever shown on television.

MURAKAMI: *How do you feel about the gas attack itself?*

It's completely wrong and cannot be condoned. No doubt about that. But you have to distinguish Shoko Asahara from the ordinary rank-and-file believers. They aren't all criminals, and some of them have truly pure hearts. I know many people like that and I feel sorry for them. They don't fit into the system because they're not comfortable with it, or because they've been excluded from it. That's the kind of people who join Aum. And I like them. It's easy for me to be friends with them. I feel much closer to them than to people who are well adjusted. The real culprit is Asahara himself. He was tremendously powerful.

What's funny is that being with the police so much I started to make friends with them. At first I was scared, but gradually we got to be friendly. They'd ask me if any mail had come from Aum and I'd show them everything. Once I cooperated, the police became much more open and kinder to me. "Well now," I thought, "even the police can be pure and honest sometimes. They're all working as hard as they can. So if they make a reasonable request of me, I'll cooperate."

New Year rolled around and I got a card from Ms. Takahashi's mother. She wrote, "We were completely wrong." She'd been a devout Aum follower herself, at first. She'd gone through the initiation. I wanted to see Ms. Takahashi, no matter what. There was so much I wanted to talk to her about. I mentioned this to the police and showed them the card.

That's probably what gave them the idea that they could use me as a spy. They called me in and sounded me out about the idea. Whether they actually used the word "spy" or not I can't recall, but that was the gist of it. In other words, would I go into the Aum organization to gather information and report back to them? Naturally the idea of being a spy wasn't appealing. I just wanted to find a way to be with Aum followers. I was already friends with the police, I thought, so what the hell. I'll give it a try.

I'm the type who just goes with the flow. A loner, basically, with no friends. The type who's stuck at the bottom of the company ladder and is always getting yelled at. Nobody would ever take me seriously. So when the police said to me in all sincerity, "Do your best and try to get some information for us," I was very happy. Even if it's the police, I just felt happy being able to communicate with someone. At my company, I never made any friends. My Aum friends were all gone, and Ms. Takahashi had become a renunciate and disappeared. So, "If it's for a short time, okay," I thought. And that's what I told them. I shouldn't have.

MURAKAMI: *Was being a police spy a valuable experience?*

All I wanted was to get in touch with Ms. Takahashi, to bring her back. Not as a spy or anything, I just wanted to be in contact with Aum members. But if I tried that on my own, without cooperating with the police, I would have been pegged as an Aum person, and I was afraid of that. They would have treated me as a criminal. Having the police back me up would make the whole thing go more smoothly. Also I thought I might be able to persuade a few members to quit Aum. But that was dishonest. Don't you think?

MURAKAMI: *Dishonest or not, it's a convoluted story.*

It is indeed. I felt sorry for Ms. Takahashi, and felt I had to do *something.* That's all I was thinking about. If things continued as they were, she'd be treated like a criminal. I had to try to persuade her, but I had no idea where she was. If I cooperated with the police, I might get some information. But I never did find out her whereabouts. I asked all the time, but the police couldn't track her down. All they knew was that she was still a renunciate. Maybe they did know but just didn't tell me.

At any rate, since the Fukui and Kanazawa branches were shut down, the plan to have me infiltrate Aum fell through.

MURAKAMI: *So it ended up well for you, didn't it? By the way, are you interested in Nostradamus's prophecies?*

Very much so. Nostradamus had a great influence on my generation. I'm planning my life's schedule around his prophecies. I have a desire to kill myself. I want to die. I don't mind dying very soon. But since the end is coming in two years, I think I might be patient for a bit longer. I want to see with my own eyes what will happen at the end. I'm interested in doomsday religions. In addition to Aum, I have contacts among Jehovah's Witnesses. What they talk about is nonsense, though.

MURAKAMI: *When you say "the end," is that when the present system will be wiped out?*

I prefer to think of it as being reset. It's the desire to push the reset button on life. I imagine it as a catharsis, very peaceful.

# "Each individual has his own image of the Master"

## Mitsuharu Inaba (b. 1956)

*Mr. Inaba is still an active member of Aum Shinrikyo. He lives with several other Aum members in a two-story apartment building in Tokyo. It's difficult to rent anywhere if you're in Aum, but the landlord of this particular place was very understanding: "If you have no other place to stay as you make the transition back to normal life, then go ahead." Cockroaches seem to spring up wherever Aum followers live, and during our interview I saw quite a few of them crawling across the tatami mat. This must be a worry for the landlord. Neighbors are aware they're in Aum and give them the cold shoulder.*

*Mr. Inaba was born in Hokkaido in 1956. He seems to have been a quite ordinary child, but according to him he was always brooding over the meaning of life. This tendency is present in many Aum believers. His intellectual pursuits took him from philosophy to Buddhism, then to Tibetan Buddhism, and finally to Aum Shinrikyo. An elementary and junior high teacher, he became a renunciate at 34. At the time of the gas attack he belonged to the Aum Defense Ministry and worked maintaining Cosmo cleaners.\**

*Now he scrapes by tutoring once a week. Life is hard. "Do you know any students you can introduce to me?"* he asks with a smile. *He's a very serious, calm person, and I imagine he's a good teacher. He lights up when he recalls teaching the children of renunciates inside Aum.*

*In his room there is a small altar with a photograph of Master Asahara and one of His Holiness Rinpoche, the new leader of Aum.*

●   ●   ●

---

\*Cosmo cleaners: air filtration equipment designed by Aum members to thwart poison gas attacks, among other things. [Tr.]

I didn't want to be a teacher, but according to my mother, that was the only path open to me [laughs]. I spent two years after high school studying for the college entrance exams before I got in. One whole year I was ill. I had some sort of philosophical struggle going on in me, a period of great discontent. I went to the hospital and it turned out my blood pressure was 180. After this I stayed at home to get better. I took medicine to lower my blood pressure. I was the kind of person who broods over things, and is too sensitive to his surroundings. By "philosophical struggle" I mean that I realized I had to do certain things in a certain way, and knowing I couldn't manage it made me hate myself. I was young and hardheaded.

I majored in elementary education in college, with a concentration in educational psychology. I chose the elementary level because I like children. Still, I was plagued by the question of what I should do with my life. I had the notion that there were things the children would teach *me*. I would both teach, and be taught at the same time.

I graduated from college and found a job in an elementary school in Kanagawa Prefecture. It wasn't so hard for me to leave home. I was used to moving, and was sure I could make friends no matter where I went.

I was put in charge of my own class from the very first year. Forty kids to a class, and it wasn't easy in the beginning, believe me. It totally occupied me for a while. Actually it was a lot of fun. I was a teacher for a total of ten years, and the five or six years I was in elementary school were the best. I got on well with the parents, too. We'd get together sometimes to sing, eat homemade cakes, and so on. I never had any bad experiences with the rest of the staff.

People tried to find someone for me to marry. My parents even tried to set me up. And I did go out with a few women for a while. But all the time I knew that eventually I was going to renounce the world.

MURAKAMI: *So you were already thinking about that?*

Yes, I was. It was before I found out about Aum, but what I had in mind was more becoming a traditional renunciate. The image I had was of quietly retiring from the world at 60 and living a simple life.

When I was in college I was really into Nietzsche and Kierkegaard, but gradually my interests turned to Eastern thought, especially Zen. I read all kinds of Zen books, and did the kind of do-it-yourself practice called "lone wolf Zen." But I couldn't bring myself to follow the ascetic aspects. So next—chronologically, about the time I got my job—I started to get interested in esoteric Shingon Buddhism, particularly Kukai. I climbed Mt. Koya, did a pilgrimage around Shikoku during summer vacation, visited Toji Temple when I went to Kyoto— that sort of thing.

People put down Japanese Buddhism as "Funeral Buddhism," saying all it's concerned with is conducting funeral ceremonies, but I think you should look at it in a more positive way, at its staying power over many centuries. Surely within those traditions there's got to be some place where authentic Buddhism is practiced. I didn't pay much attention to the so-called new religions. No matter how wonderful they might be, I thought, they had at most a history of thirty or forty years. I'd stick to Shingon Buddhism.

After four years teaching in elementary school I was asked all of a sudden if I would move over to junior high.

I was about four years into teaching at the junior high when I came across some Aum books. The bookstore carried a small magazine called *Mahayana*, which I bought and read. This was when it first came out, maybe the fourth or fifth issue. There was a special section devoted to esoteric yoga, which I didn't know much about. I wanted to learn more.

One Sunday a colleague of mine and I went to Shinjuku to buy some teaching materials. We took the Odakyu Line on the way back, and near Gotokuji Station there was an Aum dojo in Setagaya. We had some time to spare, so I thought I'd just drop by. Joyu happened to be giving a talk entitled "The *Po-a* Gathering." *Po-a* here meaning the raising of one's spiritual level.

I was really impressed by what he said. It was so clearly stated— the way he used metaphors, for instance. It was very appealing, especially to young people. After the sermon he took questions, and his answers were extremely precise, each one perfectly tailored to the person who asked it.

A month later I joined. I made it very clear it was for three months or half a year, just for me to check it out. It was about 3,000 yen to join, and yearly fees were 10,000 yen, quite cheap. Once you join you receive these periodicals, and can attend all the sermons. Sermon meetings were divided into those for the general public, those for lay followers, and those for anyone who had taken vows. I went to the dojo once or twice a month.

When I became a member I didn't have any personal problems or anything. It was just that, no matter where I found myself, I felt like there was a hole inside me, with the wind rushing through. I never felt satisfied. From the outside you wouldn't imagine I had any troubles. When I became a renunciate people would ask me, "What could possibly be troubling you? How could you have any problems?"

MURAKAMI: *In everybody's life there are times when you feel pain, sadness, depression. Something that shakes you to the core. You never experienced anything like this?*

Nothing extreme, no. Not that I can recall anyway.

In the summer I spent three days at the newly built head-quarters at Mt. Fuji. But it wasn't until autumn 1989 that I began to get serious about attending the dojo. I'd go every Saturday night and return on Sunday. During the week I trained on my own at home, especially when I got to the point where I received *sakti-pat*—I had to get in shape for that. The introduction of energy there is very delicate; you have to concentrate on training for it. I did *asana* [yoga], breathing exercises, simple meditation; there were three-hour courses and you had to get twenty units. As you continue to train you feel a transformation come over you. Your mental outlook grows more upbeat, more positive. You're like a new person.

The members at the dojo were sober, resolute types. The masters and the instructors were all quite sincere and appealing. However, the way they responded to people from the outside—how shall I put it?—I think they could have done a better job. It's like when a student graduates and gets his first job and he's overly serious about it. He still doesn't have any experience in society. Aum gave the same strong impression of immaturity—of students who know nothing about the world.

In order to become a renunciate I'd have to leave my teaching job. I met with the principal and told him I'd like to finish in March, at the end of the school year. I also talked it over with my "elder brother" in Aum. He told me, "There's no need to rush. Wouldn't it be best if you worked for another year, fulfilled your obligations, and then took vows?" I worried about it, but decided I'd work for another year.

However, as I continued my training I got immersed in astral, my subconscious began to emerge, and my sense of reality grew faint.*

When that happens you're supposed to be apart from the world. It would have been all right if my subconscious had emerged during the summer vacation, but this happened just before. At its worst, when I was teaching a science class I couldn't for the life of me remember if I'd already mixed the chemicals in the experiments or not. My sense of reality had vanished. My memory became hazy and I couldn't tell whether I'd actually done something or only dreamed it.

My consciousness had gone over to the other side and I couldn't get back. The Buddhist scriptures talk about it, how when you reach a certain point in your training this schizophrenic element appears. Inside me there was nothing certain I could rely on. Happily, I still had an awareness of where I was; if things had gotten any worse I might have become schizophrenic. I got more and more afraid. I had to cure that split personality at one stroke, but going to a psychiatrist wouldn't help. The solution lay in my training. So I became a renunciate. If there was nothing within me I could rely on, then the only thing to do was to give myself up to Aum. Besides, I'd always thought that someday I'd renounce the world.

I talked with the principal again and told him I wanted to leave after all. For a teacher to resign his post in the middle of a school year is a major problem. He was very understanding and he let me go on sick leave until the end of the holidays. But I ended up sort of forcing them to let me go. I didn't even say goodbye to any of my colleagues. I'm sure that caused some problems for the school. Most likely people thought I was totally irresponsible.

I became a renunciate on July 7. I contacted my parents and

---

*In English the word "astral" is an adjective, but in Japanese it often appears as a noun. It still refers to some kind of ethereal existence beyond the physical. [Tr.]

they came to see me while I was on sick leave. They were livid. I tried everything I could to persuade them but we got nowhere, no matter what I said. My parents didn't mind me being interested in Buddhism, but to them Aum Shinrikyo was beyond the pale. I explained that it might appear that way, but Aum was based on a firm foundation of Buddhist teaching. For someone on the outside, though, their reaction was only to be expected.

"Come back home right now," they said. "You have to choose between coming home or going over to 'them.'" I agonized over my decision. If I were to go home to Hokkaido I would just continue living the same old life I'd been living. Nothing would be solved. I thought that getting deeper into Buddhism was the only solution. So I became a renunciate. But I did agonize over it.

I had one good friend among my fellow teachers who'd come over just about every day with some beer. "You're not really going, are you?" he asked. He pleaded with me, tears in his eyes. But I was about to embark on something I'd been seeking since I was a child, so all I could tell him was, "I'm sorry. It's something I have to do."

After I took vows I went straightaway to Naminomura in Aso to do construction work. The roof of the Aum facility was just about finished. It was hard work, but engaging—different from anything I'd ever done before. It was invigorating, like using a different part of my brain. Afterward I went back to Mt. Fuji, where I did various jobs, and then went to work constructing Satyam No. 2 at Kamikuishiki-mura. They call the period just after you become a renunciate "Building up Spiritual Merit." It consists mainly of menial jobs with a bit of ascetic training. Compared with when I was teaching, I didn't have to worry about human relationships or responsibilities. Like when you're a new employee at a company, you just do what the people above tell you to do. Psychologically, it's a great relief.

Still, I was uneasy. "If this doesn't work out," I wondered, "then what?" I was over 30, after all. There was no turning back, so I had to train all the harder. Can't rely on anyone else. I'd chosen this life for myself, and if I couldn't gain something valuable from it, then leaving the world would only lead to misery.

The next year [1991] in September, I went back to Aso. This time I was part of the "Children's Group" and taught the children of renunciates. There were about eighty kids altogether. I was in charge of science. Other people taught Japanese, English, various subjects. Most of them were former teachers. We developed a curriculum and ran things pretty much like a real school.

MURAKAMI: *Did your teaching have a lot to do with religious education?*

Well, in Japanese classes they used Buddhist scriptures as their main text, but science doesn't have much to do with doctrine. I had trouble teaching science from an Aum viewpoint, and I asked the Founder [*Asahara*] for advice. "Since science and the lay world are one," he said, "you should do whatever you wish." "Are you sure it's all right?" I asked [*laughs*].

So it was easy for me. I'd tape programs from TV and use them as our text. It was fun. I taught the Founder's children, too, and sometimes he told me how much they were enjoying school. I only taught for about a year and then my ascetic training began.

As far as religious matters were concerned, the Master was—no doubt about it—a man of considerable power. I'm absolutely convinced of that. He was outstanding at adapting his sermon to his audience, and he had an enormous amount of energy. A long while after this I was transferred to what was called the Defense Ministry, where I worked installing and maintaining Cosmo cleaners, air filtration and cleaning equipment. Because of this I visited the Master's home twice a week. I was also in charge of maintaining the cleaner in the Master's own car. I had many chances to talk to him directly, and he said many thought-provoking things. I could feel he was trying as hard as he could to consider what was best for me, best for my development and growth. There's a huge gap between that image of him and the picture you get at his trial.

In court people say, "The Master's orders had to be obeyed absolutely." From my own personal experience, however, many times when I didn't agree with an order I'd suggest an alternative and he'd change his mind, saying, "All right. Let's do it that way, then." If you stated your opinion, he'd adjust things so you'd be satisfied. So at least for me, he didn't seem to be forcing people to do things.

MURAKAMI: *He might have acted differently depending on the type of order, and the type of people he was ordering about.*

I have no idea. It's a mystery. Each individual has his own image of the Master.

MURAKAMI: *What did the Master—Asahara—mean to you personally? You can call him a guru or mentor, but it seems to me each believer had a slightly different image of him.*

For me the Master was a spiritual leader. Not a prophet or anything, but the person who would provide the final answer to Buddhist teachings. The one who would interpret it for me. With Buddhism you can read the original scriptures all you want, but they're just words on paper. No matter how deeply you study scripture by yourself, well, I wouldn't exactly call it do-it-yourself Buddhism, but you do end up with your own skewed interpretation. What is critical is to progress, step by step, through proper training, to a correct understanding. After you've progressed one step, you stop and take stock and realize the progress you've made. It's a repetition of this. And you need a teacher who can guide your training in the right direction. It's the same as when you study math. In order to reach a certain level you have to trust what the teacher is telling you and do what he says. You learn one formula first, then another. Like that.

MURAKAMI: *But sometimes you reach a point where doubts arise in your mind about whether your teacher is correct. For instance, are you convinced about things like Armageddon or the Freemasons?*

I think part of what is said about the Freemasons is true, but I don't swallow it whole.

MURAKAMI: *At some point the character of Aum Shinrikyo began to change. Violent elements came to the surface. They manufactured guns, developed poison gas, tortured people. Did you have any inkling that this change was taking place?*

Not at all. It was only later I found out. When I was inside Aum I had no idea. Though I did start to feel that pressure from the outside was growing stronger. And there were more people who felt ill, or whose health started to decline. This might be a problem if I say this, but there were spies who infiltrated the organization.

MURAKAMI: *Did you know directly who the spies were?*

No. But we were under surveillance by plainclothes police, and I'm certain that several spies had infiltrated. Though I can't prove it.

Society is convinced that, from start to finish, the gas attack was the work of Aum—but I wonder. It's clear Aum was the principal agent in the crime, but it seems like other people, other groups, were involved in aspects of it. There would be major repercussions if this surfaced, though, so someone's keeping it under wraps. Of course, it would be difficult to prove anything.

MURAKAMI: *It would be difficult. But let's get back to life inside Aum. Was it entirely peaceful?*

No, there were problems. For instance, the first time I went to Aso, I couldn't believe how inefficient everything was. We'd construct a building only to have it torn down. The things we built weren't what was needed. It's just like a school festival. You work as hard as you can building a model, only to have it broken up as soon as the festival is over. So why do it? Because in the process of everyone working together you learn a lot: how to get along with others, various technical skills, all sorts of unseen elements. That's why you work as hard as you can, only to destroy it. In the midst of this communal labor you grow to understand your own mind better.

MURAKAMI: *Maybe the plans were just sloppy to begin with.*

That might well be [*laughs*]. But what can you do? You just have to accept it. Businesses in Japan are more or less the same, aren't they?

MURAKAMI: *But no business would build a dam only to turn around and destroy it.*

No, they probably wouldn't go that far.

MURAKAMI: *Did anybody complain about these inefficient ways?*

Some people spoke up, some didn't.

For a time I worked in the Science Group under Murai on the development of the Cosmo cleaner. A giant air-cleaning machine, in other words.

In connection with Cosmo cleaners, I was transferred to the newly formed Defense Ministry in 1994. Really something, isn't it? The name [*laughs*]. From construction to science to the Defense Ministry. I didn't take it all that seriously. I never thought we were trying to create our own state or anything.

I worked in Cosmo-cleaner maintenance. We made about sixty giant cleaners you attached to the sides of buildings. These developed into indoor Cosmo cleaners and activated Cosmo cleaners. We were in charge of maintaining them all. Truth be told, maintaining them was harder than building them. There were always problems—fluids leaking, faulty motors.

MURAKAMI: *Cosmo cleaners were used at Satyam No. 7, weren't they, where the sarin plant was located?*

I wasn't allowed in there. If I had been, I wouldn't be sitting here today. On the day of the gas attack, I was at Satyam No. 2 in Kamikuishiki, waiting for the police raid. At that point we already knew they would be forcing their way in to investigate. A few media people were there, too, I think. But by 9 A.M. the police still hadn't come, so I thought, "Today's not the day," and went back to work. I turned on the radio and heard about something out of the ordinary happening in the Tokyo subway. We weren't supposed to listen to the radio, but I did anyway [*laughs*]. I talked to the colleague next to me about it. "They'll be blaming Aum, too," we decided. The police raid burst into our place two days later.

MURAKAMI: *Mr. Inaba, do you admit now that one faction of Aum did indeed carry out the gas attack?*

I do. There are some parts I can't fully fathom, but since the people involved have confessed and are on trial, I believe that's what happened.

MURAKAMI: *What are your feelings about Asahara's level of responsibility?*

If he is responsible then he must be judged according to the law. But as I said before, there is such a huge gap between the Asahara I have in my mind and the Asahara I see on trial . . . As a guru, or religious figure, he had something very genuine. So I'm reserving judgment.

Inside me, also, are many wonderful things I received since entering Aum Shinrikyo. Putting those aside, though, what is bad must be clearly seen as such, and that's what I'm trying to do now. Inside me. And, honestly, I don't know how things will develop or what the future holds for me.

Generally people have the impression that Buddhism and

Aum are completely different. Some people just simply classify Aum as a kind of mind control, but that's far too simplistic. For me, it's something I staked my whole life on during my twenties and thirties.

MURAKAMI: *Esoteric Tibetan ascetic practice involves a one-to-one relationship between guru and disciple and aims at absolute devotion, doesn't it? But what about this, for instance: what started out as a wonderful discipline somehow begins to get strange along the way—in computer terms it would be like a virus infects the computer and its functions, which are then out of kilter. There's no third party to halt this process.*

I don't know about that.

MURAKAMI: *So there is a danger inherent in this, because it involves absolute devotion. This time you just happened not to be involved in the incident, but if we pursue the logic here, if your guru orders you to commit po-a, it means you must do it, right?*

But every religion gets implicated in that kind of thing. Even if, say, I was ordered to do that, I don't think I could have. Hmm . . . which means, maybe I wasn't devoted enough [*laughs*]. I hadn't given over my entire self. Or to turn it around, you could say I was still weak. And I'm the type of person who has to be convinced of things before I can move on. Too commonsensical, I suppose.

MURAKAMI: *So if you had been convinced, you might have carried it out? If they had said: "Mr. Inaba, you see, things are like this, and that's why we have to commit po-a." If they'd persuaded you, then what?*

Well, I don't know. It doesn't. Hmm . . . it's, well, hard to say.

MURAKAMI: *What I'm trying to understand is what place is given to the Self in Aum Shinrikyo doctrine. In your training, how much do you leave up to your guru, and how much do you decide for yourself? I'm still not clear on this, even after listening to you.*

In reality the Self can never be totally independent. There will always be some kind of intervention from outside. It's affected by environmental factors, experiences, patterns of thought. So it's not clear how far the pure Self extends. Buddhism begins with the realization that the Self that you believe is your Self is not the true Self. So Buddhism is perhaps the furthest you can get from mind control. It's closer to Socrates' idea that the wisest man knows he lacks wisdom.

MURAKAMI: *It's possible to view the Self as divided into surface and depth—an unconscious, something like a black box. Some people feel it's their mission to pry open that black box in search of the truth. This might be something close to the astral you discussed.*

Meditation is a method to reach the deepest part of your self. From a Buddhist perspective, deep within the subconscious lies each person's essential sort of distortion. And that's what it cures.

MURAKAMI: *I think human beings should both open that black box and accept it as it is, otherwise it may turn dangerous. When I hear the statements of those who were arrested, though, it seems they couldn't do this. They only analyzed things and left the intuitive part to someone else. Their way of looking at life became extremely static. So, when someone with great dynamism—an Asahara, for instance—tells them to do something, they can't refuse.*

I'm not exactly sure I can grasp what you're saying, but I think I know what you're getting at. It's essentially the difference between wisdom and knowledge.

But you have to understand that there are people who have nothing to do with this incident who are working as hard as they can for their personal growth, to reach salvation. Of course Aum did some terrible things, that's undeniable, but there are people being arrested for minor offenses and being intimidated who don't deserve that. For example, if I go out for a walk, the police will follow me. If I try to get a job, I'll be harrassed. People who've left Aum facilities can't even find places to live. The media just puts out its one-sided view. No wonder we find it harder and harder to trust the secular world.

They tell us if we abandon our beliefs they'll accept us, but people who have taken vows have pure motives, they are, in a sense, emotionally weak. If they could stay at home, work as usual, and train to improve themselves, no one would say anything. But they can't, and that's why they enter the temporary, isolated state called renunciation. People like that have a resistance to the obstacles of the worldly life, to those problems.

The structure of Aum has changed quite a lot, in very basic ways. It might look like nothing's changed, but there's been an internal transformation. There's a move to return to the way it was at the beginning, where it began at the level of yoga. Having made the Founder's child the new Leader, though, people might call that inexcusable and say we haven't learned a thing.

MURAKAMI: *I'm not saying that, but if you don't publicly reflect on what happened and show remorse, if you just continue as if nothing has happened, no one is going to believe you. I don't think it's as simple as saying: "That's something other people did. The basic teachings of Aum are correct. We're victims too." There are dangerous elements within the essence of Aum, within the structure of your doctrine. Aum has the duty to say all this in a public statement. Do that, and no one would mind if you continued your own style of religious activities.*

Ever so slowly, incompletely, we're trying to come up with a kind of interim report. It doesn't completely sum up everything, but the media will never publish it anyway. If we made mistakes, well, we want people to point these out. But the Buddhist establishment won't have anything to do with us, and remains silent.

MURAKAMI: *Isn't that because you always stick to your own vocabulary and way of phrasing things? You have to speak in ordinary terms, ordinary logic, like you're holding a normal conversation. If you make it sound like you're talking down to people, nobody's going to listen.*

Yes, it's very difficult. But what would happen if we did speak in an ordinary way? [*laughs*] Since the media has made these one-sided attacks on us, no one would believe us, or they would just react in disgust. No matter what we say, when it appears in the media it's always distorted. There's not a single media outlet that would transmit our true feelings. No one comes like you have to really listen to us.

If you boil it all down, though, you arrive at the question of how critical the Founder [*Asahara*] is to this, and his real motives haven't been revealed. As far as the gas attack goes, I think everything leads back to that. It's asking a lot for us to explain the whole affair in a way that everyone would understand.

I'm still a member of Aum, but the people who have left Aum don't think Aum is 100 percent bad, and those who remain don't think it's 100 percent correct. There are lots of people wavering. So it's not like the media reports it, that the remaining members are all dogmatic believers. Most of the really dogmatic devotees of Asahara have left.

Every member is deeply troubled. Some people who've left have come to me for advice, and we've talked about this. I think I've gained a little breathing space now, but there was a time when all I could think about was whether I'd be able to adjust to life outside.

At the moment I'm earning my living teaching children in their homes. The members here live as a community, helping each other out. The guys I live with are out working on construction sites. When they heard you were coming they wanted to meet you, but they couldn't very well skip work [*laughs*]. Everyone's just doing odd jobs. The guy next door, for instance, is a truck driver. He's been doing it for quite some time. Of course if his company heard he was an Aum member no one would hire him, so he keeps it a secret at work.

Other than rent I hardly spend anything. I don't watch TV. Meals are provided. No luxury items. Utilities take up a bit. We can get by on about 60,000 yen. College students use about 100,000 yen a month, don't you think? All of us are living like this, just scraping by.

The media says Aum is involved in all kinds of business deals, but that's not true. Of course the Aum-related company Aleph, Inc., is still in business, but since the police are interfering, it's not easy to keep it going. Some renunciates are old people who can only work from home, and some are ill. We have to take care of them. Everyone has to work to make sure they can be fed and housed. So there isn't a lot of room to maneuver as far as money is concerned.

MURAKAMI: *How are the Aum children you taught?*

They've all gone back to the secular world and attend normal schools. Since you can't raise children on a part-time job, their parents have all stopped being renunciates and are working full-time. I imagine it must have been hard for them to find work. I really don't know much about how the kids are doing. In many cases they were forcibly separated from their parents.

Our way of teaching doesn't involve hitting or any kind of violence. Our basic approach is to talk things through and use logic to persuade people. As renunciates, we have to follow our precepts strictly, or else what we say won't be very convincing. It's like telling someone not to smoke while you're sitting there puffing away. Who's going to believe you? Children watch how adults act very closely. Some of the Aum children were taken to juvenile homes, and I imagine the people there must have had their hands full [*laughs*].

# "This was like an experiment using human beings"

## Hajime Masutani (b. 1969)

*Mr. Masutani was born in 1969 in Kanagawa Prefecture. His family was "very ordinary," but he began to feel alienated from them, and they ended up barely speaking. He had no interest in sports or school, but loved drawing.*

*In college he studied architectural design. He didn't have much interest in religion until some new religions contacted him. Aum Shinrikyo was the most attractive, and he became a member.*

*Just before the gas attack, he criticized some of Aum's policies and was put in solitary confinement in Kamikuishiki. He felt in danger and ran away. For this Aum excommunicated him.*

*He likes to approach everything logically. Although critical of Aum teachings, he thinks highly of some of it. During his training he had several mystical experiences, but has little interest in "the supernatural," eschatology, or conspiracy theories about groups like the Freemasons. When still a member he disliked the fact that Aum was moving in these directions. Nevertheless, he found it difficult—until his life was threatened—to leave Aum.*

*He hides the fact that he was a former member and lives alone, working part-time. We talked for many hours and he truly opened up to me.*

* * *

I never felt any major frustration or difficulties in my life, really. It was more like something was missing. I was really into art, but the idea of spending my life painting pictures, making some money from them, had no appeal. In college, I happened to come across a book about Aum in a bookstore, and it really grabbed me. "Maybe instead of painting," I thought, "living a religious life will help me get closer to the reality inside me."

I was a freshman in college at the time, traveling alone in the Kansai region, when I heard there was an Aum dojo in Kyoto, and dropped by. It took place inside a rented building and was very spartan—even the altar was simple. It wasn't like some religions that spend money in a flashy way. It had integrity. The people wore simple clothes, too. Mr. Matsumoto was there and I was able to hear him preach.*

To be honest, I couldn't understand what he was getting at [laughs]. I was tired from the journey and kept dozing off. But I did feel a strong thread running through his sermon, and got the impression it was quite profound. I think I approached things with an artist's intuition, relying on emotions rather than logic.

After the sermon we were invited to stay if we wanted to talk. I was able to talk one-to-one with Hideo Murai, who was said to have reached salvation. He didn't have any holy atmosphere about him, and just struck me as an ordinary Aum follower. After we talked about the body and other things, he rather abruptly said: "Well, how about joining?" Later on, I realized that was one of Aum's standard tactics. Usually people who go to these kinds of places are lacking something or seeking something, but the dojo seemed pleasant enough, and being asked to join like that, out of the blue, I just went with the flow and filled out the application forms. It cost 30,000 yen to join, and I didn't have the money on me at the time, so I paid after I got back to Tokyo.

For a while I went to the Setagaya dojo, but spent most of my time distributing Aum leaflets. Instead of training, we had to build up merit. At the dojo they had maps dividing Tokyo into various sections and we'd be told what area to cover that day. We'd drive over there at night and they'd say, "You're covering this neighborhood," and off we'd go. We'd walk around, sticking leaflets in people's mailboxes. I took the job seriously. I had a sense of accomplishment whenever I finished, enjoying the physical activity involved. Also I believed that if we racked up spiritual merit, the guru [Asahara] would impart energy to us.

*Shoko Asahara's real name is Chizuo Matsumoto. [Tr.]

MURAKAMI: *So distributing leaflets was more fun for you than going to school?*

The direction of my life had changed. No matter how much I studied architectural design and found a good job, that's all there'd be. I came to think it was more meaningful to persist in spiritual training and to eventually reach enlightenment.

MURAKAMI: *So at this point you had already lost interest in ordinary life and had shifted to a more spiritual goal?*

That's right.

MURAKAMI: *People who agonize over fundamental issues usually go through a sort of set pattern: reading all sorts of books when they're young, discovering different philosophies and choosing from them a system of ideas. But you didn't do this. You let your mood carry you along and just went straight into Aum.*

I was young. Aum started to play a greater role in my life. For the most part I stopped attending classes, failed to pick up some credits I needed, and knew I'd be held back a year. It was just at this delicate stage that Mr. Matsumoto [*Asahara*] suddenly said: "You should become a renunciate." So I thought it was a good idea.

This was during what they call "Secret Yoga." Mr. Matsumoto [*Asahara*] would be sitting there, flanked by several of his senior disciples, and you'd sit facing them and get personal advice or make a confession or something. In those days ordinary believers could talk face-to-face with him. This was the period when Aum was trying to increase its members so it could expand, and I think he was just trying to boost the numbers rather than carefully considering my case. The staff also told me that "The reason you aren't able to cope in the secular world is because of the 'karma of renunciation.'" Soon afterward I became a renunciate. This was in 1990. I was among the first. At the time I was steeped in Aum and didn't hesitate. When the guru says "renounce the world" that's what the disciple's supposed to do. I believed Mr. Matsumoto [*Asahara*] was the person who could answer any question I had. I trusted him.

When I was a believer, before I became a renunciate, I participated halfheartedly in the election campaign. The guru wanted us to, so I did what I could, but I had no interest in the election. I questioned everything we did, like even then I wasn't in sync with what was going on [*laughs*]. For me enlightenment was uppermost, and anything else was wasted effort. Even if enlightened practitioners tell you something is correct, there might well be something in it you can't yet grasp. Aum followers tend to think that way. You don't understand something, but there's still some profound meaning in it.

My family was opposed to my taking vows but they've never mattered much to me. I left college, moved out of my apartment, threw out all my possessions, and went to live at the Aum headquarters at Mt. Fuji. We were limited to what we could bring with us—only two suitcases of clothes.

After that I was sent to Naminomura at Aso. Since I'd studied architectural design, I was transferred to the building site, though all I'd done in college was drafting. They selected me over some physically stronger people, so I thought there might be some mistake. "Are you sure that's right?" I asked. And they said, "Just go anyway," and that's what I did. In the end I was a laborer for just one day and told my superior Naropa [*Fumihiko Nagura*] that I couldn't continue. I just didn't have the physical stamina. So I was transferred to the Home Economics Division. I prepared meals and was in charge of collecting laundry. It took quite a while to get used to life there, but doing the tasks assigned to me by the guru was an act of devotion, so I did my best.

The work at Aso was so hard a lot of people left. I thought it was too late to return to society, so I stayed put. I must say, though, that I did have a sense of accomplishment working there. We followed the "Aum Diet" and every day consisted of very old rice and boiled vegetables. Live that way for a while and visions of the food you'd like to eat pop into your head, but I tried to create a Self that wouldn't be tempted by them. I was pretty much a vegetarian to begin with and the diet didn't bother me too much. I felt light and free from all the attachments in the world that can delude you.

Let's see . . . how long was I at Naminomura? We didn't have calendars so there was no sense of the days passing. I must have been there quite some time. We completed several buildings. If you live such a simple, unvarying life for so long, shut off from the outside, small irritations start to appear. A great conflict arose in me between those and my desire for salvation.

I was called back to Mt. Fuji to join the Animation Division. By then Aso was no longer the center of Aum activities and had become a kind of backwater, so I was happy to leave. In the Animation Division I drew pictures for cartoons. It was pretty crude stuff. We used animation to explain how Mr. Matsumoto [*Asahara*] had supernatural powers. Him hovering in the air and so on. A real film would have been convincing, but no one would be convinced by a cartoon. The final product was awful. Around this time I had more opportunities to be with Mr. Matsumoto [*Asahara*]. I found myself growing more mistrustful of him and of Aum.

After this I did all sorts of jobs and finally Shoko Asahara ordered me to concentrate on training. It involved study and meditation and was spiritually fulfilling in part, but very strenuous. Other than time out to eat and go to the toilet we had to sit there the entire day. We even had to sleep sitting up. We studied for a certain number of hours, and then took a test. This went on day after day.

I must have done that training for about half a year. My sense of time is vague, so I'm just guessing . . . Some people did it for years. You have no idea when you can leave. The guru decides. I was kept in training for a long time, then sent back to work, then back to train . . .

MURAKAMI: *Was Asahara the one who decided when you advanced to the next level? Like, "Tomorrow you'll move on to the next stage"?*

That's right, but I never advanced at all. I didn't even get a holy name.

MURAKAMI: *But you did it for a long time and worked hard at it. Why didn't you advance?*

Aum was very realistic about granting salvation to those who had contributed a lot to the organization. Of course people's spiritual levels were a factor, but how much you donated really made a difference. For men, their educational background was often the key. Tokyo University graduates were quickly raised to a higher level of salvation, or given a more important job, or made a leader. For women it depended on how attractive you were. No kidding. Not much different from the secular world (*laughs*).

I don't think I was of much use to Mr. Matsumoto [*Asahara*]. Up to a certain point I was sure my failure to advance was due to my lack of effort, but at the same time I thought that maybe everybody else felt the same way, namely that Tokyo University graduates seemed to enjoy special favor from the Master.

I often mentioned this to my friends, but they'd cut me off by saying, "You think that way because of your uncleanliness" or "That's karma," which means that whenever any doubts came to mind everything could be blamed on your own uncleanliness. Similarly, all good things were "Thanks to the guru."

MURAKAMI: *That's a pretty efficient system. Everything's recycled or brought to a conclusion within the system itself.*

I believed it was the path to follow in order to do away with the Self.

At first everyone who joined had very strong wills, but after living in Aum you'd lose that. No matter how dissatisfied you might be with Aum life it was preferable to life outside with its uncleanliness and attachments. Living with a group of like-minded people, it was psychologically easier to stay put.

MURAKAMI: *Around* 1993 *Aum became more violent. Did you sense this was happening?*

I did. Sermons increasingly focused on Vajrayana Tantra and more people seemed worked up about the idea that Vajrayana Tantra was about to take place. I couldn't follow the doctrine that the means didn't matter. I didn't feel comfortable with it. Our training started to include some bizarre elements: martial arts became a large part of our daily routine, and I could feel the atmosphere changing. I gave a lot of thought to whether I could continue being in Aum.

Not that it mattered much what I thought, since Mr. Matsumoto [*Asahara*] was convinced this was the shortest path to our goals. If that's the case, there's not much you can do. Either you stay or leave.

Our training started to include being hung upside down. Anyone breaking commandments had their legs tied up in chains and they were hung upside down. It doesn't sound like much if you just describe it, but it's torture, plain and simple. The blood drains from your legs and it feels like they're about to be torn off. By breaking commandments I mean anything from breaking the vow of chastity by having relations with a girl, or being suspected of being a spy, or having comic books in your possession . . . The room where I worked at the time was directly below the Fuji dojo and I could hear these loud screams from above, real shrieks, people yelling, "Kill me! Put me out of my misery!"—the kind of barely human voice wrung out of someone in excruciating pain. Pitiful screams, as if the space there itself was warped and twisted: "Master! Master! Help me!—I'll never do it again!" When I heard them I just shuddered.

I couldn't work out what possible point it could have. But what's weird is that many of the people who were hung upside down like that are still in Aum. They'd suffer, be taken to the edge of death, and then be kindly told "You did well." And they'd think, "I was able to overcome the trials given to me. Thank you, O Guru!"

Of course if they carried it too far, you'd die. They never told us, but that's how Naoki Ochi died. Finally they started drug initiation. Everyone thought it was LSD. You had visions and things, but I wasn't convinced it was a means of reaching salvation. There were rumors about someone dying during training, or someone planning to escape, being caught, and things done to him, but rumors in Aum always remained just that, and there was never any way to confirm them. Our ability to distinguish right from wrong was being eroded.

There were rumors, too, that spies had infiltrated Aum, and they used lie detectors to try to root them out. They called this an initiation, too, and everyone in Aum had to take a lie-detector test. I thought it was strange, because wouldn't the guru, who was supposed to know everything, be able to tell at a glance who the spies were? Aside from this I was once questioned about my best friend, who'd been placed in solitary confinement. I was given a polygraph test and asked all sorts of questions, including some unpleasant ones I couldn't accept. Afterward I asked the higher-ups, "Why do you have to ask such things? They're pointless." They were obscene questions that dealt with personal, private matters. Learning the answers wasn't going to get them anywhere. But I must have annoyed the higher-ups. Right afterward Tomomitsu Niimi told me: "You're being transferred. Pack your things now." I was put in solitary confinement. I asked him why, but he didn't answer. That's when I began to wonder what was going on. Training was supposed to be all about reaching salvation, but now it had become a form of punishment.

The solitary-confinement cell was the size of one tatami mat. The door was locked. It was summer, hot all the time, but they had a heater going. I was forced to drink gallons of a special Aum drink in a plastic bottle and sweat it out in the heat. Like they were trying to rid me of something bad. Of course I couldn't take a bath and the grime dripped off me. No toilet, just a chamber pot inside my cell. My head zoned out and I couldn't think straight.

MURAKAMI: *It's amazing you didn't die.*

It would have been easier if I had, and frankly at the time I think I really wanted to. But you know, when people are put in situations like that they prove remarkably resilient. Most of the people in solitary were wavering in their faith or were no longer useful to Aum. We had no idea when they would let us out. So I told myself, "Okay, I'll use this to my advantage to do some serious training." Keep on complaining and you'll never get out. The only thing to do was think positively, put up with it, then move on.

Part of our daily training consisted of an initiation called Bardo Leading. They'd take you to another room, blindfold you, handcuff your hands behind you, and make you sit up straight. Then they'd bang on a drum, ring a brass bell, and scream in a loud, crazed voice something like "Train! Train! There's no turning back, so we have to do our best!"

One day, though, when they took me over, I was suddenly pinned down by Siha [*Takashi Tomita*] and Satoru Hashimoto, and Niimi plugged up my nose and mouth. I couldn't breathe. "You think your superiors are fools, don't you?" they asked me. They were trying to kill me, but I used all my strength and was able to break free. "I've been doing my damnedest," I shouted, "so why are you doing this to me?" Things settled down after that and I was able to go back to my cell, but I felt I was finished with Aum. How could they treat me like this, I thought, when I was doing my best?

Later I underwent what they called "Christ Initiation" a number of times. This was like an experiment using human beings. Whenever Niimi gave me drugs to take he looked at me like I was a guinea pig. "Drink it!" he said, his voice cold and detached. I saw Jivaka [*Seiichi Endo*] and Vajira Tissa [*Tomomasa Nakagawa*] come by to check out the solitary cells. My mind was messed up because of the drugs, but I recall that quite clearly. They came to see our reaction to the drugs. I realized that the people in solitary were being used in drug experiments. We weren't worth much to them alive, so they must have thought that using us in human experiments was the only way we'd build up spiritual merit. That made me ponder long and hard where fate had led me.

"Can I just die like this?" I wondered. "A guinea pig in a human experiment? If that's my fate then the only way out is to return to the secular world. This is too inhuman, too terrible . . ." I was shocked, wondering where Aum had gone wrong.

After the drug initiation everyone was dead tired, so the door was left open for a time. I wasn't too zonked out by then so I prepared a change of clothes and after making sure the coast was clear, dressed and crept out of the building. There were guards, but I managed to give them the slip.

[*Mr. Masutani borrowed the bus fare from someone he bumped into on the street and returned to his parents' home in Tokyo. A few months after his escape he learned that he had been excommunicated. The reasons given for this, he says, are groundless.*]

So that's how I went back to living in the secular world—not because I wanted to live an ordinary life, but because I couldn't follow Aum any longer. The truth is I had nowhere else to go, so I went back to living with my parents. My family was so happy and said, "Thank goodness you're back!" but since I'd lived five years already with no emotional attachments to them it just didn't feel like a family anymore. I could never be satisfied with ordinary life; my parents couldn't understand this, however, so it all fell apart. We began to fight and I moved out.

MURAKAMI: *Before that, in March 1995, there was the gas attack. What are your feelings about that?*

At first I didn't think Aum had done it. They preached about Vajrayana Tantra, of course, and the atmosphere within Aum had taken a bizarre turn, but I couldn't imagine they'd go so far as to use sarin. We're talking about a group that wouldn't even kill a cockroach. When I was still in Aum I often heard from the staff how the Ministry of Science and Technology had made some comical blunder, so I couldn't imagine them carrying out something this complex.

The media reported it as definitely the work of Aum, but Aum and Fumihiro Joyu denied any connection with it. At first I was inclined to believe them. As the investigation continued, though, some facts emerged that contradicted Aum's claims, and I had my doubts. I reread my diary and it seems that it was around August of that year [1995] that I began to feel alienated from Aum. After that I was convinced that Aum carried out the attack.

Although I ran away from Aum because I could no longer agree with it or carry out its wishes, I couldn't readjust to secular life. Aum's stance of trying to overcome worldly attachments still struck me as more laudable than ordinary society. I began to reconsider what Aum—which I had devoted myself to—was all about. Trying to establish what was good about it, and what was wrong.

After leaving home I worked in a convenience store and did part-time jobs to get by. I stay in touch with my friends from Aum days, and we get together. Some of them still fully support Aum, and some admit that the gas attack was wrong, but think Aum doctrine is still sound. As many viewpoints as there are people. Even so, there are very few who have severed all ties to Aum and are living according to secular values.

I have no more interest in Aum, and am leaning now toward primitive Buddhism. All the people who've left Aum have incorporated some religious aspect into their lives.

MURAKAMI: *Of course, the individual is free to try to overcome desires and attachments and so on, but from an objective point of view it seems extremely dangerous to allow another, a guru, to take control of your own ego. Are there still many believers or ex-believers who don't recognize this?*

I don't think many have thought about it properly. Gautama Buddha said, "The Self is the true master of the Self" and "Keep the Self an island, approaching nothing." In other words, Buddhist disciples practice asceticism in order to find the true Self. They find impurities and attachments, and attempt to extinguish these. But what Mr. Matsumoto [*Asahara*] did was equate "Self" and "attachments." He said that in order to get rid of the ego, the Self must be disposed of as well. Humans love the "Self," so they suffer, and if the "Self" can be discarded then a shining true Self will emerge. But this is a complete reversal of Buddhist teachings. The Self is what should be *discovered*, not discarded. Terrorist crimes like the gas attack result from this process of easily giving up on the Self. If the Self is lost, then people will become completely insensitive to murder and terrorism.

In the final analysis, Aum created people who had discarded their Selves and just followed orders. Therefore enlightened practitioners in Aum, those most steeped in Aum doctrine, are not truly enlightened people who have mastered the truth. It's a perversion for believers who supposedly have renounced the world to run around collecting donations in the name of "salvation."

I don't believe that Mr. Matsumoto [*Asahara*] gradually turned strange. He had those ideas in mind from the start. What he did was push them forward in stages.

MURAKAMI: *So from the beginning he had the plan to go in the direction of Vajrayana Tantra? It wasn't that somewhere along the way he became deluded and the direction of Aum changed?*

There's some truth in both. One element was there from the start, and as he surrounded himself with yes-men his sense of reality faded and delusions took over.

However, I think that, in his own way, Asahara was seriously considering the question of salvation. Otherwise, no one would have renounced the world to follow him. To some extent there *was* something mystical about it all. The same thing holds true for me—yoga and ascetic practice led to some mystical experiences.

MURAKAMI: *Now Aum is attempting to continue with the same doctrines—minus Shoko Asahara and the Vajrayana Tantra. How do you feel about that?*

Since nothing about Aum has changed, there's a distinct danger that new crimes will occur—maybe not soon, but eventually. Also, people who remain in Aum have accepted the gas attack on a subconscious level, so they're not aware of the dangers of carrying on the same teachings. All they think about are the good points of Aum and the benefits they've received.

When I think about the victims of the gas attack and those colleagues of mine who were directly involved in carrying out the crime, I want to grab the people who still believe in Aum and shout at them:

"What the hell do you think you're doing?"—but they'd probably just withdraw deeper into their shells. All we can do is slowly show them the truth and make them aware of it.

How I can come to terms with the secular world is a difficult question. I've had enough of belonging to organizations—I just want to try to make it on my own. A part of me wants to extinguish the desires within me, but all I can do now is take one step at a time under my own steam.

MURAKAMI: *Since you were a freshman in college you spent at least seven years in Aum. Do you feel like that time was lost to you?*

No, I don't. A mistake is a mistake, but something of value comes from overcoming that. It can be a turning point in your life.

Some former Aum members have completely discarded the Aum experience and don't read the papers or watch any reports on it. They close their eyes to it, but that doesn't help you learn anything from your mistakes. It's like when you do badly in a test and you really examine where you went wrong. If you don't, the next time you'll make the very same mistake.

# "In my previous life I was a man"

## Miyuki Kanda (b. 1973)

*Ms. Kanda was drawn to mystical things as a little girl. When she was 16 she read a book by Shoko Asahara and was so moved that she and her two elder brothers all joined Aum together. To concentrate on her ascetic training she left high school and took vows.*

*Talking to her, I could understand how Aum Shinrikyo was a kind of ideal place. She clearly found ascetic life far more fulfilling than living in ordinary society, where she could find nothing of any spiritual value. Aum was a kind of paradise.*

*Of course one could view a case like hers—a 16-year-old girl raised in Aum—as a kind of abduction or brainwashing, but I tend to feel, more and more, that having people like her in the world isn't such a bad thing after all. Not everybody has to line up with everybody else, jostling shoulder to shoulder, struggling to make a go of it in "this world," do they? Why shouldn't a few people be able to think deeply about things that aren't directly relevant to society? The problem lies in the fact that Aum Shinrikyo was one of the few havens for such people, and in the end it turned out to be corrupt. Paradise was an illusion.*

*As we said goodbye I asked her if talking with someone from "this world" for so long would cause some uncleanliness to rub off on her. Perplexed for a moment, she replied, "Logically, that's true." She's a very serious person. She offered me homemade bread, which was light and delicious.*

● ● ●

Ever since I was little I've had mystical experiences. For instance, when I dreamed it was no different from reality. I'd call them stories rather than dreams—they were long and distinct, and after I woke up I could remember every detail. In my dreams I visited all sorts of worlds, had astral-projection-type experiences. I had them over and over, almost every day. In astral projection your body is fixed, your breathing stops, and you can fly. This happened most when I was very tired.

It was different from what you usually call dreams. Everything was extremely realistic. It would have been easier if you could make a clear-cut distinction, and say, "Okay, this is a dream and isn't the same as reality," but things very much like those in reality appeared in my dreams and confused me. "Is this reality? Or isn't it?" Gradually I couldn't distinguish between the two, or maybe I should say that my dreams became more real than reality. This bothered me. "So what is reality?" I asked myself. "Where is my true consciousness?"

These experiences influenced me a lot. I talked to my parents about them, but they couldn't understand what I was trying to say. I was a bit on the introverted side, but I had friends and went to school like everyone else. I wasn't particularly fond of school, though I worked hard at subjects I enjoyed. I loved to read, too, especially science fiction and fantasy. I read a lot of comics and watched cartoons. Math I was terrible at, and I didn't like sports very much.

My mother often told me: "Study! If you study you'll get into a good school and find a good job." The usual things parents say. To tell the truth, I just wasn't that concerned with school. I couldn't see the point. My dreams continued. I had all sorts of experiences, and passed through different worlds. It was fun for a time, but it never lasted. It always ended up falling apart. I experienced wars, where lots of people were killed. I felt how fearful death is, and a deep sadness that those around me had died. I realized that this world is impermanent, nothing lasts forever, and suffering is the result of this impermanence.

MURAKAMI: *In other words you experienced "another life," and you arrived at this conclusion after these emotionally charged experiences in a parallel world?*

That's right. I'd never experienced the actual death of anybody close to me, but when I saw people on TV who were sick and dying I realized, "Oh, the real world is impermanent, as well. The same kind of suffering is here, too." That's how my dreams and the real world were connected.

I went to a public high school in Kanagawa. Everyone talked about boys, love, fashion, where the best karaoke boxes were, and so on. I couldn't see any value in this, so I was always left out.

I spent most of my time alone, reading. I wrote things too. Since my dreams were narratives, I felt as if I only had to write them down and they'd become a book. Don't some writers do that—get an idea from their dreams and write their fiction based on it?

I didn't really want a boyfriend. When girls around me found boyfriends, I never felt envious. I couldn't see the point.

When I was 16 my brother lent me some Aum books, saying they were pretty good. I think the first ones were *Beyond Life and Death*, *Initiation*, and *Mahayana Sutra*. When I read them I thought, "This is exactly what I've been looking for!" I couldn't wait to join.

The books explained how the path to true happiness lay in being liberated. Once liberated, you will gain eternal happiness. For instance, even if in my life I feel happy, it won't last—but how wonderful it would be if happiness could last forever. Not just for me, but for everybody. In that sense I was quite taken with the word "liberation."

MURAKAMI: *What exactly do you mean by the word "happiness"?*

For instance, the happy feelings you have when you're chatting about all kinds of things with your friends or talking with your family. For me, conversation is very important.

If you ask what liberation, or enlightenment, means to me, I'd have to say that first there is suffering, and liberation is simply the end of suffering. When you reach liberation you are freed from the sufferings of this impermanent world. The books described some practical ascetic training you could do to help you reach liberation, so before I joined Aum I tried this for myself. I'd read the books at home and do *asana* [yoga] and breathing exercises every day.

My two brothers were attracted to Aum and said they wanted to join. The three of us had similar ways of thinking. My oldest brother experienced almost the same sorts of dreams, though his weren't as intense.

So the three of us set off for the Setagaya dojo and asked the person at the reception desk for membership applications. We planned from the start to join so we started to fill in our names and addresses, but they said they'd like to talk to us first and led us inside, where we talked with the Master of the dojo. When he asked our motives for joining, all of us said, "Enlightenment and liberation," which really surprised him. Apparently most people say they want to join to improve their situation in the world or gain supernatural powers and stuff like that.

The Master talked with us about many things, but what I felt most was a great—how shall I put it?—sense of calm, as if the air itself exuded peace. All three of us joined that day. The entrance fee, which included six months of fees, came to 30,000 yen each. I didn't have enough with me, so I borrowed some from my brothers.

MURAKAMI: *Didn't your parents have something to say about all three of you joining Aum Shinrikyo at once?*

They did. At that time there wasn't a big stir about Aum, so we just told them it was like a yoga study center. There were some problems later, though, when there were all sorts of rumors about Aum.

After joining we spent time folding fliers about Aum, sticking them in mailboxes, or handing them out on the street. It was a lot of fun. I always felt a sense of achievement afterward. I don't know why, but I felt more cheerful. These service activities built up merit. The more merit you accumulated, the stronger the energy you'd have to rise up to a higher level. In Aum we were always told that.

I made some friends, too. One of my friends from junior high joined and we distributed fliers together. I didn't go out of my way to make her join, I just told her about the group.

I continued my ascetic practice after joining, and soon I experienced what they call *dhartri siddhi*. That's the stage before being able to levitate, when your body starts to bounce up and down in the air. It suddenly happened at home when I was practicing breathing exercises. After that I was pretty much able to do it at will. At first, you don't even realize you're bouncing up and down in the air, but after a while you're able to control it to a certain degree.

In the beginning it's a real problem. You jump up! [*laughs*] You don't know what's going on. My family was a bit taken aback watching me. I was told that I'd reached this stage fairly quickly. I think that since I was small I've been pretty advanced, spiritually.

For a while after joining I continued going to high school as usual while I participated in Aum activities, but as time went on I found my school life pointless—actually, I hated it. What I was doing was the exact opposite of everyone else. To give you an example, my classmates would speak ill of the teachers, but Aum taught us never to say anything bad about others. I felt a strong contradiction there. All high school students can seem to talk about is how to have a good time, but Aum puts into practice the notion that "One should not pursue pleasure." It's the exact opposite.

In order to attain liberation, it's quicker to renounce the world and pursue your practice full-time rather than remaining at home. So I'd had the idea for a long time that I should become a renunciate.

MURAKAMI: *Renunciation means abandoning all attachments; were there any attachments you found particularly difficult to discard?*

I did feel a lot of confusion and conflict. Up until then I lived with my family, but now I wouldn't be able to see them. That was the hardest thing for me. And also food—after you become a renunciate you can only eat certain specified things.

My oldest brother had already left college to become a renunciate. My parents tried to persuade him to wait until he'd graduated, but he was adamant. My second brother stayed at home, with no apparent desire to become a renunciate.

My parents cried when I became a renunciate. They tried their hardest to hold me back. But I was sure that if I stayed I wouldn't be able to be any kind of positive force in their lives. What I sought was not ordinary "love," but love in a much broader sense. If I really could change myself, then that would be a positive influence for my parents. Naturally, it was hard to say goodbye, but I took the plunge and renounced the world.

After taking vows I was sent for training to the Seiryu-Shoja in Yamanashi Prefecture, then to the Setagaya dojo in Tokyo, where I was assigned to branch activities. I took care of lay followers, those who still lived at home. I was also involved in printing handbills and taking them to followers' homes, after which they would distribute them. I did feel a bit lonely in this new life, but I didn't regret my decision. I made some new friends in Aum. A lot of girls the same age as me became renunciates and we had a good time together at the Setagaya dojo. We had lots of things in common. After all, they'd also joined Aum because the world outside seemed without value. I was at the Setagaya dojo for a year, then was transferred to the Mt. Fuji headquarters, where I did office work. I was there a year and a half, then went to Satyam No. 6 at Kamikuishiki-mura, where I prepared "offerings." This involved cooking food that was then offered to the gods. After it had been offered up, the *samana* [renunciates] ate it in a service.

MURAKAMI: *Meals, in other words. What sorts of food did you eat?*

Bread, cookies, things like that—hamburger-type food at one point, rice, *kombu*, deep-fried dishes. The menu changed a little over time; at one point we cooked ramen noodles. As a rule, it was vegetarian. Soybean burgers.

The number of people preparing the food also changed over time. At the end there were just three of us, all women, all specially selected to work there because these were considered holy offerings.

MURAKAMI: *So they decided you had the qualifications to do that kind of work?*

Yes, I suppose so. It was really physically demanding work. We cooked from morning to night, and sometimes got so exhausted we collapsed. During one period when the number of *samana* was particularly high we had to cook even more. It was just work, work, work without a break.

So, for a hundred *samana* you'd make a hundred portions and offer these in front of the altar. We didn't just cook them, but had to carry them to the room where the altar was, and line them up neatly, then later distribute them to the *samana*.

Our superiors decided the menu. I think they based it on the average nutritional requirements for Japanese today. How did it taste? We sometimes served people from the outside, and they all said it was a bit plain. If it tastes too good there's the danger of attachments increasing, but this wasn't like a strict rule or anything. Meals that don't stimulate the taste buds would be a good description. Our goal was to provide the nutrition people needed in their activities, not to make anything especially delicious.

We didn't really have any special training to be cooks or any-thing. The Founder [*Asahara*] often reminded us to "Put your heart into your work." After we finished the meals we had to wash the machines, and he told us to "Clean them as if you are polishing your own hearts." I tried to put my heart and soul into the work. Before I took vows, when I still lived at home, I wasn't much interested in cooking, but the four years I was at Kamikuishiki, I cooked every day in Satyam No. 6.

MURAKAMI: *Wasn't Shoko Asahara living at Satyam No. 6?*

Yes. He had several homes, but that was his main residence, though he lived apart from us. Occasionally I saw him. Sometimes he ate the meals we prepared, but that was pretty rare. Someone else prepared his meals.

Along with working, I continued my ascetic practice, and I found myself growing in knowledge. I could clearly understand the state of my attachments, my energy level. And I could adjust my practice to correspond to these discoveries. It took me four years to reach liberation.

MURAKAMI: *When you say you reached liberation, was this some-thing the Master decided—like he said, "Okay, you've reached it."*

Yes, in the final analysis that's what happened. There were many conditions you had to fulfill to reach liberation, then the Master would finally determine whether you'd attained it. As a rule, most people attained liberation when they were in the midst of intense, concentrated training. There was a kind of extreme practice whose purpose was reaching liberation. When you were doing this lots of mystical experiences would occur, and when enough of these took place, plus a little something extra, and your mind became clear—that's when you reached liberation.

Only then were you given a holy name.

MURAKAMI: *In your case, ever since you were small you experienced dreams and astral projection and the like, but what happened to these after you became a renunciate and entered Aum?*

My spirituality rose even more, and I experienced even more unusual things. And I was able to control them much better. And I could remember my past lives, and was able to see what worlds the people around me would be reborn in next. It came to me in a flash: "This is my past life!"

To tell the truth, in my previous life I was a man. When I remembered things that happened when I was little, pieces of the puzzle fit together. When I was little I was always mistaken for a boy, and I thought it was strange, but if I were a boy in my previous life it made sense.

MURAKAMI: *Apart from your gender, how about other things? For example, a crime you committed in a previous life that's affecting you now?*

In my case my experiences when I was little were pleasant, but there were also painful ones. I believe these were because of evil things I had to atone for.

MURAKAMI: *I don't mean to be overly critical here, but aren't most people like that to some degree? Apart from spirituality or rebirth or anything, most people have something unpleasant happen to them.*

I suppose so. Hmm. But I think having those kinds of experiences when you're still little—when it's too early for your environment to be a major factor—there's got to be something from a previous existence that's having an effect.

MURAKAMI: *Even when you have no experience of reality you can still have unhappy experiences, right? You're hungry but no one feeds you, you want your mother to hold you, but she won't. Nothing to do with previous lives or anything. There are differences depending on the age you're at, but I think it's a question of the "pain" people experience as they struggle to come to terms with reality.*

But it's only in certain circumstances that you become aware of it.

When the gas attack occurred I was, as always, preparing offerings at Satyam No. 6. I heard about it from other Aum members. "Something's happened," they told me, "and apparently they're blaming Aum." I couldn't believe Aum was involved.

Before this, people said that sarin had been released inside the Kamikuishiki facilities and that we were under some kind of poison gas attack. Actually I thought it might be true, the reason being that a lot of people around me fell ill, including me. Blood came out of my lungs and mouth. I felt so bad there were times I was sick in bed. Later bloody phlegm came out, I had a headache, nausea, and I got tired easily. So I was convinced poison gas had been released. Otherwise so many people wouldn't get sick at the same time. It had never happened before.

I was shocked when the police raided us. We hadn't done anything wrong—it was too one-sided to label us as evil. They raided Satyam No. 6 as well. The places where we prepared the offerings were all searched, and they put a halt to our cooking, so we couldn't distribute meals to the *samana*. Everyone was forced to fast for a while. The police were frightening. I saw people being beaten up. They were sent flying and got concussion.

MURAKAMI: *You were in Satyam No. 6 around the time of the incident. Didn't you notice anything out of the ordinary going on?*

No. I spent every waking moment preparing offerings. I didn't see or hear anything unusual. Work kept us busy, and we didn't get out much, so we didn't know what was going on elsewhere. The friends I talked to most were the girls I worked with.

MURAKAMI: *Those who carried out the attack have been arrested and have begun to confess. It is obvious now that Aum was involved. What are your feelings about that?*

I heard almost nothing about it. I was living in a remote mountain village. No TV or newspapers, so I had little idea what was going on.

If you wanted to hear the news that much you could get hold of it. I just wasn't interested. I didn't think Aum had anything to do with it.

The next year, though, I began to have doubts, when they started to talk about enforcing the Anti–Subversive Activities Law. If that law was enforced all my colleagues would be scattered, I wouldn't be able to concentrate on my training, and it would mean the end of the sheltered environment I'd been living in. I'd have to go out and support myself. That frightened me.

MURAKAMI: *But a year and a half after the incident you still had no idea Aum had done it?*

That's right. I had no suspicions, and neither did anyone else I knew. Almost everybody in Satyam No. 6 was cut off from the outside world. There was no data coming in.

In the end the number of *samana* had declined greatly. One by one, people left. Even so, if you left all of a sudden and didn't have some means of support, you couldn't live. You have to have something—a part-time job, even—otherwise how can you pay your rent? *Samana* only receive a small amount of money they're given each month. People left one after the other. I was just about the last one, like a comb with some of the teeth missing. It got lonely. On November 1, 1996, we were ordered to vacate the Kamikuishiki facilities.

I moved to Saitama, where about ten Aum members were living. Our landlord was open-minded and said he didn't mind renting to Aum people. Admittedly the place we rented—a kind of office building—was only half finished and no one else would rent it. Everyone worked at part-time jobs so we would have enough to live on and could support the children and old people.

I thought I'd put my experience preparing offerings at Satyam No. 6 to good use and open a bakery on the first floor of our building. My parents offered to put up the capital.

MURAKAMI: *Pretty understanding parents.*

Yes. They are understanding [*laughs*]. And that's how I came to run a bakery. At first we gave it a cute name—"The Flying Bakers"—but the media found out about it. When we registered the business, newspaper and magazine reporters suddenly burst on the scene. The city hall must have leaked the information to the media. Anyway the name of our store came out and was shown on TV. Thanks to which our main customers refused to do business with us anymore. "It's a store run by Aum followers," they said.

Ordinary customers wouldn't buy from us either. We tried to sell over the Internet, but since the name was already known the orders were all canceled. We tried doing business under a new name, but things didn't go smoothly. Our business customers would transport our goods for us, only to be stopped by the police. "What are you doing there?" the police would ask them. "Don't you realize that store's run by Aum members?" We thought about trying to sell our goods elsewhere, but we knew the police would follow us and interfere, so there was no way we could make a living doing that.

Now we sell bread to *samana* and other followers. We bake it twice a week and deliver it ourselves. Somehow we're able to make ends meet. We don't sell to outsiders at all.

The police still hang around outside our store. If people are about to go in, they stop them and check their ID, then warn them that the shop is run by Aum. I suppose they have to make a show of actually doing something. Sometimes the police ask for bread and we give them some. When they ask for more we tell them to pay for it.

Sometimes we take cakes we've baked to people in the neighborhood and chat. They say things like, "We were afraid you people were up to no good, but it seems like you really are baking bread and cookies." The media's influence at work.

MURAKAMI: *After you left the satyam and started living in society, what were your thoughts on the gas attack, the incident with the lawyer, Mr. Sakamoto, and so on? The majority of people are convinced Aum Shinrikyo was involved.*

Well, it's pretty difficult for me to put my thoughts in order since there's such a huge gap between the Aum I experienced and the picture of Aum outsiders have. I've begun to think that maybe what people are saying about these incidents is true, but the testimonies at the trials seem to change all the time. I'm still confused about what's true and what isn't.

MURAKAMI: *Details in testimonies—like who said what to whom and when—have changed, but the fact remains that those five Aum leaders released sarin on the subway in order to indiscriminately kill commuters. What I'm after is your opinion about the attack itself. I'm not criticizing you as an individual, I merely want to know what you think.*

Well—I just can't believe it, or comprehend it. When I was living as a renunciate I never once killed anything—not a single cockroach or mosquito. I've practiced that always, and so has everyone else I know. So it's hard for me to believe this could happen.

I learned about Vajrayana Tantra in sermons, but I never thought it had anything to do with reality. I didn't base my actions on it or anything.

For me my guru was someone who would help me when I had problems during my training. That's how I understood it—and in that sense a guru was an important person for me.

MURAKAMI: *Was he an absolute presence for you, someone you were absolutely devoted to?*

Absolute? . . . Hmm . . . Of course the Founder has asked me at times, "Are you able to do this?" but in those cases I used my own judgment and sometimes replied that it would be a little difficult for me to do. I didn't just say "Yes" to everything, and the same holds true of others I knew. So my impression isn't that of some absolute presence. Though that's the image the media has latched on to.

Everyone's different. I'm sure there were yes-men who did everything they were told, but there were lots of people who had their own ideas and acted accordingly.

MURAKAMI: *What if you were in that situation—you saw the Master as an absolute guru, believed he was the only one capable of leading you, and he told you: "Do it"?*

Even the people who carried out the gas attack—and I've seen this with my own eyes—are people with a strong sense of Self. They are people who have their own opinions and are not slow to speak up in front of others. So I have trouble with your assumptions here. When I think about the way those people were when I knew them, I just can't imagine them doing it. If I actually saw them carrying out the attack, then maybe I'd believe it, but since I've seen and heard so much that contradicts what people say, I can't shake the doubts I have that they really carried out these attacks.

When I watch the Founder's trial, there are too many gray areas as far as I'm concerned, so I'm taking a wait-and-see attitude. At this stage I feel I can't judge anything until the Founder clarifies things. As his lawyer has put it, it's still not been proved that he actually ordered this to be done.

MURAKAMI: *So you'll reserve judgment until it's all over?*

I'm not saying there's no way he did it, but at this stage it's too early to decide. I won't be convinced until all the facts are on the table.

MURAKAMI: *You said your parents put up the money for your bakery. Do you still get along with them?*

Once I attained liberation I visited my home, and I would call a few times. There was never any talk of disowning me or anything. They told me to come back whenever I could. It's impossible for me to return to the secular world. If there was something wonderful there, something uplifting, things might change, but right now there isn't. I could only find that in Aum Shinrikyo.

My mind did waver at times during the seven or eight years I lived in Aum. When I underwent training, it was like the impurities inside me were welling up to the surface. As you train, you go deeper inside yourself and come face-to-face with your sins, your passions, as they rise up. In ordinary society most people keep these in check by drinking or having a good time, but that's impossible for those of us in training. We have to confront these things and prevail. It's very trying. Your heart does waver at times, but as the hesitation subsides you reach a point where you can reaffirm that, "Hey, I *can* continue my training." Not once did I seriously consider going back to the secular world.

The junior high friend of mine who entered at the same time is still in Aum and continuing her training. My eldest brother, who also became a renunciate, went back home just before the gas attack. He decided to start training at home again. Hmm—maybe he lost the battle to the impurities that come out, as I said, when you're training. If you don't triumph over these, you'll never reach liberation.

**Shin'ichi Hosoi** (*b.* 1965)

*Mr. Hosoi was born in Sapporo. He came to Tokyo to study at art school, hoping to become a cartoonist, but left after six months. While doing odd jobs, he came across Aum Shinrikyo and became a member. He worked in the Aum printing factory, then transferred to the Animation Division, where he could put his cartooning skills to work. Finally he ended up as a welder in the Science and Technology Division. In 1994 he was promoted to Master and was involved in the construction of Satyam No. 7, which housed a chemical plant. He just worked and had very little opportunity to do much training. Even so, he was able to accumulate a lot of practical experience.*

*After Aum was raided, he heard a warrant had been issued for his arrest so he turned himself in. After twenty-three days in detention the charges were dropped and he was released. While in detention that June, he posted his official resignation to Aum. He went back to Sapporo for a while but now lives in Tokyo again. During the interview he showed me several illustrations of life in the satyam.*

*Now he's a member of the Canary Association, a group formed by people who have left Aum, and he's critical of both Aum and Shoko Asahara.*

* * *

I didn't like elementary school. The reason was my older brother was handicapped—autistic—and he attended a special school; kids at my elementary school teased me about this and I had a lot of bad experiences.

Since I can remember, my mother spent all her time taking care of my brother and hardly paid any attention to me, so I played alone most of the time. I have a vivid memory of the age when I wanted attention and wasn't able to get any. "Think of your poor brother," is all I was told. This may have led me to hate my brother.

I was a pretty gloomy child, I suppose. What really decided this, I think, was when my brother died of hepatitis B. It was a huge shock to me. I was 14. Deep inside I'd always hoped that one day he'd be happy, that in the end he'd be saved. It was a kind of religious image. But reality wasn't at all like I'd imagined—that the weak would someday be saved.

Around this time the book *The Nostradamus Prophecies* was popular. You know—the idea that the human race would vanish in the year 1999. This was happy news to me because I hated the world. It was unfair, and the weak would never be saved. When I thought about the limits of society, the limits of people, it made me even more depressed.

I wanted to talk to somebody about my feelings, but everyone was too busy studying, or else all they wanted to talk about was cars or baseball. I became a big fan of Katsuhiro Otomo's [*manga*] comics, when he still wasn't that well known. They were so real, so alive to me; the stories themselves were dark, but made me think, "You know, these kinds of things might really come true." I often copied his work— *Sayonara Nippon, Short Peace, Boogie Woogie Waltz*, and others.

I wanted to leave home and go to Tokyo, so after graduating from high school I entered a school called the Chiyoda Industrial Arts School. They offered a major in cartooning. But I left after six months. There always seemed to be a wall separating me from the rest of the world, and coming to Tokyo the wall got higher. People treated me all right, and I got to know quite a few girls. I'd think, "This girl and I will get along okay," only to find I'd built a wall between us. Classes were fine; my problem was more with people. I just couldn't get along well with anyone. I went out partying, but drinking and all that didn't do a thing for me. All the while my dislike of the world grew more intense.

Now that I look back on it I wonder, "What was all *that* about?" I finally get the chance to meet a lot of people and what do I do? Drive them away. But I couldn't help it. So I left and made a living doing part-time jobs. I continued to study cartooning. My parents sent me a small allowance, but being all alone studying when you're

18 or 19 is hard on you. You're in a closed-off space and it affects you emotionally. I started to have a phobia about being with people.

They frightened me. I was convinced they were out to trick me or hurt me. Whenever I saw a happy couple walking down the street, or a family enjoying themselves, all I could think about was that they should all be smashed to smithereens—at the same time I hated myself for having such thoughts.

I'd left home to escape the depressing atmosphere after my brother died, but couldn't find any peace no matter where I went. Everywhere was the same, and I grew to loathe the outside world. Leaving my apartment was like entering hell. Finally I ended up with a hygiene fetish. I had to wash my hands as soon as I got home. I'd stand in front of the sink washing my hands for thirty minutes—even an hour—without stopping. I knew I was ill, but I couldn't stop myself. This went on for two or three years.

MURAKAMI: *I'm surprised you could live that way for so long. It couldn't have been easy.*

Yeah. I barely spoke to a soul those couple of years. I talked to my family occasionally, or to people at my job, that's it. I started to sleep longer, over fifteen hours a day. Otherwise I'd feel awful. My stomach bothered me, too. It would hurt all of a sudden. I'd go pale, break out in a sweat, and breathing was difficult. I was scared that if things kept on like this I might die.

I thought I'd try a dietary cure and yoga to see if they helped. That way I'd be able to get control of my life again. I went to a bookstore and came across Shoko Asahara's book *Beyond Life and Death*, which I stood reading for a while. It claimed that kundalini awakening could be attained in three months. I was amazed. "Is that really possible?" I wondered. I'd already read *Outline of Theosophy* and had some basic knowledge of yoga so I went back to my room and tried it out. Along with the dietary cure I did the training outlined in the book for three months. I'm the type of person who totally concentrates on something and I never missed a day. Four hours a day or so.

I was less interested in awakening kundalini than in just getting healthy. About two months into it the base of my spine started to vibrate, which is something you experience before kundalini awakening. But I still had my doubts. I felt a strong warmth like boiling water was coiling up my spine to my brain, as if it was wreaking havoc with the insides of my brain, writhing like a living thing. I was dumbfounded. Here was something beyond my control, something incredible happening inside my body. I actually fainted.

In three months I had reached kundalini awakening, just as Shoko Asahara's manual had said. So he was absolutely right. That's when I started to become really interested in Aum. The Aum magazine *Mahayana* had just published its fifth issue, and I bought it and all the back numbers and devoured them. They had photos and personal testimonies from some very appealing, remarkable individuals. If these kinds of people were devoted to him, then the "Revered Master" must be a pretty amazing man.

What I liked most about the Aum books was that they clearly stated that the world is evil. I was happy when I read that. I'd always thought that the world was unfair and might as well be destroyed, and here it was all laid out in black and white. Instead of simply destroying the world, though, Shoko Asahara said: "If one trains and is liberated, then one can change the world." I was fired up reading this. "I want to be this man's disciple and devote myself to him," I decided. If I could do that, I wouldn't mind abandoning all the dreams, desires, and hopes of this world.

MURAKAMI: *You say the world is unfair, but in what way?*

Well, things like inborn talent, family background. No matter what the situation, bright people are bright, people who can run fast can run fast. And people who are weak never see the light of day. There's an element of fate that I thought was too unfair. But in Asahara's books this is explained as the workings of karma. If in a previous life a person did evil things that's why he's suffering now, likewise if a person did good in a previous life that's why he now lives in such a good environment and is able to make full use of his abilities. I read this and was convinced. It was time for me to avoid evil and start accumulating merit.

Originally I just planned to use dietary cure and yoga to regain my health and after I got back on my feet I'd return to normal life, but at Aum I found myself developing a Buddhist mind-set completely new to me. One thing I can say is that Aum books helped me get back on my feet when I was in an awful state.

I think it was December 1988 when I went to the Setagaya dojo, became a member, and was able to talk to one of the enlightened practitioners. He gave me all sorts of advice. He told me I should participate in what they called the "Mad Intensive Training" seminar that took place once a year at the Mt. Fuji headquarters. It's a pretty radical name, isn't it? [*laughs*] You go through this for ten days, they told me, and your training makes tremendous progress, so by all means you should go; the problem was, though, it required a 100,000-yen donation and I didn't have that kind of money. Also, I wondered whether such rigorous training so soon after joining might not be counterproductive. The head of the training, Tomomitsu Niimi, insisted that I go, and eventually I gave in and went.

Aum was a small group at one time, with maybe two hundred renunciates. Since it was so small, you were able to meet Shoko Asahara soon after you joined. He was different then, kind of wiry and muscular. Back then he walked with heavy, vigorous strides. You felt something amazing, something awesome in his presence. You could feel this sort of terrifying ability he had to see through everything at a glance. People said, "He's so gentle," but when I first met him he scared me.

I had a chance to do "Secret Yoga" with him, one-on-one, and he told me, "You're in a serious state of *makyo*." That's the state you reach as your training progresses and spiritual impediments arise. I told him, "In order to progress in my training I'd like to become a renunciate as soon as possible." "Wait for a while," he said. "You can't escape *makyo*. You need to work at your training in order to free yourself from it."

The next time I saw Asahara, he had slipped into the dojo, all smiles, to observe the *bhakti* [*a service held by followers*]. When I saw him, I thought: "Wow, this is a man of a thousand faces." Now he wasn't frightening at all, he was beaming, and just being near him, watching him, made me ecstatic.

Three months after joining I was given permission to become a renunciate. When I did "Secret Yoga" with Asahara he said: "You can become a renunciate, but on one condition: leave your part-time job and get a job at a bookbinder's." I was pretty surprised. Why a bookbinder's? "Aum is planning to open a printing factory," he said, "so I want you to study bookbinding techniques." "Okay. I understand," I replied, and straightaway I found a job at a bookbinder's that included room and board.

I discovered that there are a lot of different machines in a bookbinding plant: folders, binders, cutting machines . . . I had no idea where to begin or how much I should learn. He'd simply said, "Study bookbinding." Anyway, I did my best to absorb everything I could. On Sundays, when the factory was deserted, I studied how the machines were constructed. I don't have much of a technical background, but I soon worked out which buttons to push and how certain parts fit together. I wasn't allowed to operate the machines, but I picked up a lot just by keeping my eyes open. After working there for three months I was instructed to become a renunciate. I packed my bags and left the factory for good.

Once you take vows, you can't eat the things you like—ice cream and so on. That was a bit tough for me. Food, rather than sex, was hardest for me to overcome. The night before I became a renunciate I ate and drank everything I could lay my hands on, because it was my last chance.

My parents were dead set against it, but I truly believed that my becoming a renunciate would, in the final analysis, be a blessing to them, so I didn't worry much about what they said. Originally in order to be a certified *samana* [renunciate] you have to donate 1.2 million yen and finish six hundred hours of standing worship, but as they were rushing to get the bookbinding plant up and running, they made an exception for me.

About an hour's drive from the Mt. Fuji headquarters was a place called Kariyado. The printing plant was a small prefab building. I was astounded to learn that I was the only one who had any background in bookbinding. I'd expected just to be a staff member of a team, but here I was a brand-new renunciate in charge of bookbinding. I couldn't believe it. There were anywhere from ten to twenty people assigned to bookbinding, ten to printing, and about twenty to photoengraving. It was a fairly large-scale operation.

The machines they'd purchased, however, were pieces of junk that had been sitting in a warehouse somewhere for decades. Everyone complained about it. All the machines were like antiques on their last legs. Just to get them up and running was a major task. I wasn't all that up to speed on these machines to begin with, so it took three months from the time we got them to the time they were operational. Even after that some of them didn't run well. I think we did a good job, considering.

The first thing we printed and bound was the twenty-third issue of *Mahayana*. Until then all Aum's publications had been contracted out to other printers, but now we could just about print them ourselves.

One thing that really surprised me was that after I became a renunciate there was no time set aside for us to do our ascetic training. I asked one of my superiors why and according to him you can't make progress until you accumulate merit, and I was at the stage where I should just work and build up merit. So I worked for a whole year in the bookbinding plant. Every day was tough. We'd snatch just four hours of sleep a night, especially during the elections—that was draining. I was in charge of the folding machine. We kept the machines running even when we went to the toilet. Every second counted.

After the election there were fewer print jobs. We had a lot of time on our hands. Things were in an uproar at Naminomura, but for those of us at the printing plant, the days were peaceful.

When we didn't have work to do we were free to train. During this period our leader was off somewhere else and we had a pretty laid-back attitude toward things.

In the beginning if I wasn't around the machines ground to a halt; after a time, though, everyone was able to operate them, so I asked the higher-ups for a transfer. You weren't supposed to ask for a transfer, but since I had training as a cartoonist I used some leftover paper and created a twenty-page comic-book version of the Jataka sutra. I completed three of these books and showed them to my superiors. I attached a letter saying, "I have this training as a cartoonist, and if it can be put to use for liberation purposes, I would like to be transferred."

I didn't expect anything to come of it. No one else acted this self-centeredly and I was sure they'd just ignore it, but I was surprised to get a phone call from the General Affairs office telling me to report the next day to the Design Division. There was a Cartooning Section there, but with only one person assigned to it; before long, however, there was a plan to create an Aum-produced operetta that would include animation, so they hurriedly assembled followers who could draw to help out. There were about twenty to thirty people, and later I was appointed head of the Animation Division.

We had some really talented people in our group, but the biggest help was that one of the *samana* had worked as an assistant camera-man at an animation studio. We formed teams and produced quite a lot of cartoons. I worked there for three years altogether. Looking back on it, those years were a very peaceful time for me.

I say things were calm, but actually human relations within the group were fragmented. Usually a leader of a division holds the rank of Master but I was just a *swami*, a lower rank. I felt pressure from above, at the same time as my subordinates tried to win me over to their viewpoints, so it wasn't easy. For example, in order to study the techniques we had to watch ordinary cartoons, but our leaders said we couldn't. But I had to watch some of them. People would confront me, saying: "The Master forbade this, so why are you watching it?" In other words, our Animation Division was split into two factions: one gave priority to improving the quality of our work, the other gave priority to our training. It got harder and harder to get things done.

Relations between the sexes weren't easy, either. There were many cases of men and women getting too close and running off with each other, so Asahara warned in his sermons: "Female *samana* are not to approach men. Don't just keep your distance, but detest them." I was often singled out for criticism. At any rate it was a pretty brutal atmosphere.

MURAKAMI: *It certainly doesn't look like you were heading for liberation, does it?*

I couldn't stand it anymore. There was a time when I was thinking of leaving. I did my best in spite of everything, since I was serious about achieving liberation, but it wore me out.

Twice I sent resignation letters to my superiors: "I can't be in Aum anymore." This was in '92, I think. My superior passed these along to Murai and others. They talked me out of it, so I just let things slide.

MURAKAMI: *If you had left Aum, do you think you would have made a successful transition to life in the secular world?*

I wonder. Certainly my attitude toward the world had changed since I became a renunciate. The world I had entered as a renunciate was a kind of hodgepodge. There were all sorts of people there I'd never met before. Everyone from gung-ho elite types to athletes, artists. In this jumbled-up place I discovered that all these diverse people had the same human weaknesses I had. I lost the prejudices I'd had. "Everyone's the same," I realized. Guys who got good grades suffered just like I did. It was a very valuable lesson for me.

The *samana*, too, had a fundamental loathing of the outside world. "The unenlightened"—that was their term for people who lived normal lives. Since these people were heading straight for hell, the *samana* had some choice words for them. For example, they didn't worry about it if they banged into a car belonging to someone from the outside. It was like they were the ones practicing the truth, looking down on everyone else. They were too busy striving for liberation, so even if they put a dent in someone's car, so what? I thought this was a bit much. No matter what they felt about the people outside, there was no need to make fun of them, or hate them that much. I'm sure I had my own list of things in the outside world I hated, but when I saw this, I just thought, "Enough." I no longer hated the things I use to hate.

MURAKAMI: *That's interesting. Usually when people join cults you expect those tendencies to get even worse, but in your case you managed to lay them aside.*

Maybe my tough experiences in middle management had something to do with it [*laughs*]. The Animation Division was closed in 1994. Most of the workers were called into a conference room and told to report to the Science Division. The name later changed to the Ministry of Science and Technology. They needed some welders and just assumed that people in the Animation Division must be good with their hands. I was speechless. How can you possibly compare animation to welding?

Before joining the Science Division we were all investigated to see if we were spies. I remember thinking: "If Shoko Asahara has supernatural powers, why can't he use them to weed out the spies?"

The majority of the Animation Division members were transferred to the Welding Division, and sent to Kamikuishiki. At Satyam No. 9 they were making storage tanks and stirrer machines. We didn't know the first thing about welding, so we were assigned as assistants. The order had gone out to speed up production, so we did our best, but it actually slowed down. Asahara gave the order to finish everything by May 1994. These were giant tanks, huge two-ton monsters. We'd bend these metal plates, shape them into a cylinder, weld the joints, fit premade panels over this and weld them.

The work was hard, up to sixteen hours a day. We were wiped out, and sometimes didn't get enough offerings [*food*]. We didn't eat for two days once. Everybody complained. Some people just downed tools. I wasn't used to this kind of work myself, and got injured, burned, my face blackened, my glasses were falling apart. But no one ran away. "This is all for the sake of enlightenment," I kept telling myself.

In time I was appointed a Master. Probably they recognized my leadership in the Animation Division and how hard I'd worked at welding. When you get promoted to Master they give you a wristband and say: "Give it your best!" That's it. I'll admit being a Master does change your outlook on the world. Friends of mine started to address me very formally, which brought home to me again the huge gap between Masters and those below.

After I became a Master I was one of a select few allowed free access to Satyam No. 7. The Security Group kept strict guard on it. Inside were all the storage tanks we'd assembled in Satyam No. 9. It looked like some chemical plant and had a weird feeling to it I can't explain, an oppressive atmosphere. I had no idea what they were going to manufacture there. The ceiling was as tall as a three-story building, with these huge tanks all in a row. And the smell was indescribable, like all sorts of industrial-strength detergents mixed together. And there was this weird light. The metal was all rusty, and the floor was wet. There was this strange, whitish mist hanging in the air. Everyone who worked there got ill. They all staggered around, and at first I thought they were just sleepy. Actually it was affecting their bodies.

I wasn't sure what was going on, but I saw that Aum was sinking a large amount of cash into this and whatever it was represented the cutting edge. I wondered if it would push enlightenment forward in one fell swoop. Only a limited number of people were allowed to see this, and I felt a sense of privilege at being one of the chosen. Still, I wondered what it was all about. It didn't look like weapons.

In autumn 1994, if memory serves, there was an accident. I was on the third floor of Satyam No. 7 taking a rest when this whitish smoke—like dry ice—came up behind us. The guy next to me said we'd better run for it. Just breathing a bit of it blinded me and gave me a piercing pain in my throat. It had an acrid, acidic smell. "If I stay here," I thought, "I'm going to die." Satyam No. 7 was a dangerous place.

On January 1, 1995, the order came to hide the inner recesses of Satyam No. 7. "Make all the equipment look like the face of the god Shiva," we were told, in order to conceal it. I was put in charge of the artwork. Huge slabs of Styrofoam were delivered in the middle of the night, and we glued them over those parts of the plant we didn't want people to see.

MURAKAMI: *But with so many huge tanks you weren't able to cover them all, were you?*

First we built a wall with boards on the facade of the factory, then put Styrofoam pictures of Shiva on top. The rest of the places we wanted to hide we made into makeshift altars. We used partition boards to hide the second-floor area, made it like a maze, you know, like photo exhibitions. Anyway, our superiors told us to do whatever it took to fool people. The CBI [*Construction Division*], led by Kiyohide Hayakawa, did most of the work. I designed the faces. The finished product was awful. Pure amateur junk.

"This won't fool anyone," I thought. Hiromi Shimada came over to see the finished product and declared it a religious facility, but the overall appearance was wrong. "This won't work," I thought, but everyone was scared of Hayakawa and kept their mouths shut.

On the day of the gas attack I was away from the Welding Division. I was assisting the number two man at the Ministry of Science and Technology, Kazumi Watanabe, at Seiryu Shoja. I heard that the Tokyo subway had been gassed with sarin, but I never imagined it was the work of Aum. From what I'd gathered up to then, I believed

Aum might take up weapons to fight in case of an attack by Freemasons or the U.S. or whatever, but I never thought Aum would be involved in indiscriminate killing. I mean, that would be outright terrorism.

Two days later, though, the police stormed Kamikuishiki. When I heard there were more than two thousand police outside, I realized this was no joke. Seiryu was left untouched in the first police raid for some reason. We gathered up plans at Seiryu that might be incriminating and burned them. We went to Murai's room, too, and burned all the books about weaponry. We found bulletproof vests, too, and cut them up. The police raid on Seiryu took place, I'm certain, after the sniper attack on Secretary Kunimatsu.*

I began to think that Aum actually did it after I saw with my own eyes what was supposed to be a vehicle for spraying sarin. That was in April, I think. I'm not sure if it was before or after the police raid.

MURAKAMI: *Where was that?*

In Seiryu. I can tell you I was pretty shocked when I saw this huge sprayer truck with a chimney attached. "We'd be in deep trouble if they found this," I thought. Right away we got orders from above and ten of us dismantled it.

After the police raid the people in Seiryu weren't able to work anymore, so all of them returned to Tokyo to distribute handbills. I went to Satyam No. 5, where I helped with bookbinding and drew comic books under the supervision of Michiko Muraoka. They were a parody of the police arresting Aum members on unrelated charges. Around that time Murai was stabbed to death.†

Naturally I was shocked when I heard this, but at the same time I felt a sense of peace. It's hard to describe my emotions at the time. How should I put it? I thought it was the end of Aum—a sort of indescribable feeling. I think I was paralyzed, unable to act. Although I didn't realize it at the time, I really wanted to get out. But I didn't

---

*Eleven days after the gas attack, the Tokyo police chief Takaji Kunimatsu was shot dead outside his apartment by an unidentified assailant who escaped on a bicycle. [Tr.]

†A few days after Takaji Kunimatsu was murdered, the Aum science minister Hideo Murai was stabbed to death. He may have been assassinated by Aum members because he knew too much. [Tr.]

have the strength to do it, so I just tried to blend in with the background. And there was my position to consider. Pride made it hard for Masters to get out. I'd lost a lot of respect for Shoko Asahara. He'd blown one thing after another. None of his predictions came true. The ones he made on Ishigaki Island were way off, the ones about Comet Austin were all wrong, and some of the *samana* were openly starting to say: "The Leader's predictions don't seem to come true, do they?"

Even Murai just did what he was told to do from above, no matter how absurd. For him it was just "Yes" this and "Yes" that. I began to have major doubts about everything. The people below me started to grumble. I got sick and tired of the whole selfish atmosphere. Still, I didn't have the willpower to quit, but when Murai was killed I felt I was able finally to go back to the real world.

Murai had been an important person to me. After Asahara he was the one person who most symbolized Aum. Everywhere I went Murai was somehow involved in what I was doing—at the printing plant, the Animation Division. Still, I didn't feel sad when he died. My strongest feeling was: "Aha! Now I can get out!" I know it's wrong to say this.

But before I could leave I was arrested. Someone told me: "Ikuo Hayashi and Masami Tsuchiya and others have confessed, and it seems like a lot of the Science and Technology people are being rounded up." "Suppose I'll be next," I joked, but a warrant for my arrest had actually been issued. My name was in the newspaper. "Wanted for murder and attempted murder," it said. I think that was on May 20, 1995. Of course I never murdered anyone, but either charge could bring the death penalty or a life sentence. I was stunned.

I couldn't very well go into hiding, so I followed advice from my superiors and turned myself in to the Yamanashi Prefecture police. At first I kept silent. "I refuse to answer," I said, and didn't for three days. But I couldn't keep that up forever. Aum threatened me, saying that if I talked I'd be cast into eternal damnation, but I no longer believed that. If I'm going to go to hell, well, let it happen, and I told the police everything I knew.

The investigation was harsh. The detective in charge tried to

329

force me to sign a statement saying that I knew sarin was being produced in Satyam No. 7. "If I didn't know, I didn't know," I said. Finally I felt cornered and wrote a false confession admitting that I knew about the sarin. Later on, I explained it all to a prosecutor.

In the end they dropped the charges and released me. Their decision to prosecute or not apparently rested on whether I had participated in a meeting at Satyam No. 2 concerning the making of sarin. Thankfully I hadn't. At first the police were pretty mean, accusing me of being one of the people who released the sarin. It was terrible. They shoved me around a bit. Going through that day after day affected my heart. They interrogated me three times a day and each session was really long. I was worn out. They held me for twenty-three days.

After I was released I went back to Sapporo. I began to have mental problems and stayed in the hospital for about a month. I had trouble breathing and my senses steadily dimmed. I felt as though I were floating. Something was terribly wrong with me. I underwent a lot of tests and in the end they said it was probably psychological.

MURAKAMI: *If Murai had ordered you to release the sarin, what do you think would have happened?*

I'm sure I would have hesitated. My way of thinking is a bit different from people like Toru Toyoda and others. Even if Asahara himself had ordered me to do it, if I wasn't convinced it was the right thing, I wouldn't have cooperated. I didn't do everything I was told. Of course the atmosphere around me was a big influence. I think even the people who did it were confused. If we'd been under attack from the police or the Self-Defense Forces or something, I might have done it, but this was different—killing complete strangers.

Anyway, the chances of me being selected to commit the crime were pretty slim. I wasn't one of the elite. The Ministry of Science and Technology was divided into the "Brain Trust" and the "Subcontractors," which included the kind of welding work I did: on-site labor. In contrast, Toyoda and the others were part of Asahara's handpicked elite "Brain Trust." There were about thirty masters in the ministry and I belonged to the lowest group.

Still, when I heard some of the names of people involved, it surprised me. Asahara must have selected the ones he thought would go along with it, no questions asked. These elite people did everything they were told. It was the same with Murai: not a word of criticism, no running away. They're impressive when you think about it. Most people couldn't handle it for as long as they did—three or four years.

Only Yasuo Hayashi was different. He belonged to the Subcontractors group. He wasn't a part of the elite, but had been promoted from the Construction Division. The people around him were superelite—guys doing research on superconductors, subatomic particles, and the like, and there he was, basically an electrician.

Hayashi started out as an all-right guy, but steadily his personality changed. We were at the same stage once and could have friendly talks together, but when he became a Master he started getting overbearing, arrogant. At first he was good-natured, but in the end he lashed out at people. He was the type who wouldn't blink an eye at stepping all over his subordinates if that's what it took. I think he just snapped.

From the beginning the Ministry of Science and Technology was given preferential treatment by Asahara. It had so much money. Even in the Ministry there was a big difference between the Brains and the Subcontractors. As someone once put it: "To be a success in the world of Aum you had to be either a graduate of Tokyo University or a beautiful woman." [laughs]

MURAKAMI: You were in Aum Shinrikyo for about six years. Do you ever feel you wasted that time?

No, I don't think it was a waste. I met a lot of people, shared some tough times. It's a good memory for me. I was able to confront human weaknesses, and I think I matured. It might sound odd to speak of it as fulfilling, but there was a sense of adventure: we didn't know what the next day would bring. When I was given some huge task to do, I felt uplifted because I could focus my energy on it and complete it.

I feel psychologically more at ease now. Of course I have the kinds of troubles ordinary people have, like being disappointed in love. So there are parts that aren't so easy. But hey—that's life. I feel I'm living like ordinary, everyday people now.

It took me a long time to reach this emotional equilibrium; about two years. After I left Aum I was completely lethargic. When I was there I had the strength that came from knowing I was a "practitioner of the truth," which gave me the strength to test myself to the limits. Now I have to use my own powers if I want to do anything. This hit me quite strongly after I left Aum and led to my depression. It wasn't an easy transition.

But what's different is that now I have confidence in myself. When I was in Aum I gained a lot of practical experience, and felt certain that even if things weren't working out there I'd be able to make it on my own. That was a major step for me.

I live in Tokyo now. What gets me through each day are my ex-Aum friends. We think alike, and it helps me know I'm not alone in this hard world.

# "Asahara tried to force me to have sex with him"

## Harumi Iwakura (b. 1965)

*Ms. Iwakura was born in Kanagawa Prefecture. Fair, slim, and attractive, it's perhaps easier to picture her if I say she is one of the "Aum beauties" we hear so much about. She smiled throughout the interview, was very attentive to her guest, and though not particularly eloquent, was quick to answer all the questions I put to her. She tends to dwell on small details, and gives the impression that deep down she's a strong person.*

*After graduating from junior college she worked in an office, and spent most of her time and money having a good time. Gradually, though, she grew dissatisfied with playing around and found herself attracted to Aum Shinrikyo, which she happened to hear about. She resigned and became a renunciate.*

*For a long time she was one of Shoko Asahara's "special people," but something happened and she was given electroshock treatment and lost her memory. For a long time afterward she wandered in a state of almost complete oblivion, regaining her senses just before the Tokyo gas attack. For this reason her memories of Aum are fragmentary. Her recollections of her pre- and post-Aum life are clear, but she finds it impossible to fully account for herself during the two years she was in Aum.*

*She has no aftereffects, she tells me, but she's determined never to have anything to do with Aum again. It's "over and done with." She doesn't particularly want to recall this lost period, either. Originally when she read several of my interviews with other Aum followers in* Bungei Shunju *she thought, "Count me out."*

*Now she works as a beautician and hopes to get more training, put aside some money, and open her own business. She lives simply, in an apartment that costs 30,000 yen a month.* "Sweltering in the summer, freezing in the winter," *is how she describes it.* "Thanks to Aum, though," *she says with a smile,* "a simple life doesn't bother me."

• • •

I started working in 1985, when the economy was still pretty good. You could go on company trips to hot springs and stuff like that, which I enjoyed. All I cared about was having a good time. I liked going out and though I wasn't much of a drinker, I often went out drinking with friends. It'd get late and I'd ask my girlfriends to put me up for the night. On any given week I'd be sleeping over at someone else's half the time.

On holidays I went looking for fun—Tokyo Disneyland, Toshimaen Park, the usual places. Sometimes with other girls, sometimes with boyfriends. I went overseas, too, Paris and other places. I had a few boyfriends, but never once contemplated marriage. I just couldn't handle it.

MURAKAMI: *To other people it must have looked like you were enjoying life.*

I suppose so, but I kept mulling over all kinds of things. Like, "I don't have any special skills, nothing that makes me stand out from the crowd. I don't even feel like I want to get married . . ."

When I reached my mid-twenties, more and more of my friends started to get married, leave the company, and move away. I wasn't as young as I had been. My lifestyle seemed increasingly pointless.

MURAKAMI: *And it was about this time that you got attracted to Aum Shinrikyo? What was it exactly that made you join?*

One day I wanted to get my hair cut. Usually I'd go to a place a friend ran, but that day I didn't have enough time so I went to a beauty shop in the neighborhood. The price for a haircut was really cheap, so I went there a few more times after this, and one day a man who worked there happened to show me an Aum Shinrikyo pamphlet. "I'm thinking of becoming a member," he told me, but my only thought was: "Whoa!—looks fishy to me."

He taught me some purification techniques. Like, for instance, you drink water and then vomit, or you empty your stomach and then run a string inside your nose. I'd always been a little weak. I often get eczema. See? (*shows her arm*) I've got some right now. When I told him this he said, "Well, why don't you give it a try?" So I did, and my eczema cleared up just like that. I tried it once and the next day— *poof!*—it was gone.

Also, I'd never had much of an appetite and could only manage half a child-size bowl of rice, but after trying these techniques I could down a huge bowl—which amazed my mother. My headaches disappeared, too, and my overall health improved.

"Wow—this is really something!" I thought. The man at the beauty shop said, "Why don't you join when I do?" but I hesitated for a long time. He persisted and I started to think maybe it wasn't such a bad idea after all.

MURAKAMI: *At that time did you know Aum Shinrikyo was a religion and not just a yoga training group?*

Yes, I knew that. This was when the election took place and they were wearing those elephant hats. But I wasn't interested in doctrine, or whatever, or Shoko Asahara. All I felt was that since my health had improved it was probably worth taking the time and effort to check it out. I'm sure curiosity played a big part in it.

At first I went to a nearby dojo and talked to the enlightened practitioners there. I don't remember what we talked about. It didn't leave much of an impression. I wasn't going there with any great expectations or anything. We just talked, and I filled it in.

MURAKAMI: *And you just listened to their explanation of doctrine and things?*

[*Laughs*] That's right.

MURAKAMI: *When you say you "filled it in" you mean you made an application there on the spot to be a member? So you just halfheartedly listened to what they said, and became a member without really under-*

*standing their doctrine? The other people I've interviewed up to now all became members after struggling with lots of Big Questions, but in your case it seems as though you just dived in.*

Hmm . . . It was pretty fast. When I joined they told me the entrance fee was 30,000 yen, with half a year's membership fee 18,000 yen, for a total of 48,000 yen. I said, "Gosh—I don't have that kind of money," and the man who originally asked me to join said he'd put up half. Not like he was my boyfriend or anything. Yes, he was very kind. But I think he might have thought he'd earn merit for himself by getting me to join. I thought if I only had to pay half, then okay.

After I joined we had duties to perform: go to the dojo and complete a set list of chores. At first I didn't feel like doing that. They'd ask you to come, but people who didn't want to didn't. But the man who originally invited me asked me over and over to go, and it was nearby, so I thought why not?

When I went to the dojo I saw renunciates in sweatshirts, all very calm, serene even, and I was taken with this way of spending time. It was a world light-years away from the noise and clamor of the company and commuting. I felt relaxed there. I'd sit there quietly, folding leaflets. I felt at ease doing that. It wasn't hard at all. Everyone was kind, and the whole atmosphere was so peaceful. On my days off I'd go to the dojo, sometimes going straight from work, fold handbills, then go home. This went on for a while. Aum's a twenty-four-hour operation, so I could go whenever I wanted.

At work a lot of people were having affairs with other people in the company. My father had had an affair and I couldn't stand it. Going to the dojo after the office was like day after night. It was so calm there. I could be at peace, my mind a blank, and just fold handbills. I loved that feeling.

I became a renunciate after the Ishigaki Island seminar in April 1990, so it was just two months from the time I joined to the time I took vows.

At Ishigaki they talked a lot about Armageddon. This was taught to people who'd been in Aum a long time, but people like me, lay members who still lived at home, weren't told the first thing about it. For lay followers who lived at home, what you were taught depended on the amount of money you donated. In my case, they just asked me to attend the seminar without explaining much. It cost hundreds of thousands of yen. I withdrew my savings to pay for it. By this time I'd begun to wonder if I could go on living as I had been. To attend the seminar I had to ask for time off out of the blue. I made up some story. People were pretty annoyed.

When I got to Ishigaki at first I wondered what was going on, but after a while I thought the way they did things made life easier—they'd give the order and you just did what they said. No need to think for yourself, or worry about every little detail, just do what you're told. We did things like group breathing exercises out on the beach.

There was a kind of unspoken understanding that everyone should become a renunciate, and most of the people who attended did just that, myself included. When you take vows you have to leave home, leave your job, and donate all your money. If I'd been 20 I don't think I would have gone through with it, but at 25 I thought, well, enough's enough.

MURAKAMI: *Did being in special surroundings like Ishigaki have any influence on your decision?*

Hmm . . . That wasn't the only reason; I think it was just a matter of time before I took vows. Even if that hadn't happened then I was already leaning in that direction. Not having to think for myself or make any decisions was a big factor. Just leave it up to them, and since the order comes from Mr. Asahara, who's enlightened, you know everything's been well thought out.

I didn't have much interest in doctrine itself, I mean I never reacted like, "Wow! This is fantastic!" or anything. I just thought it was great if all kinds of attachments could be eliminated. Do away with these and life would be easy, I thought. Attachments meaning things like your emotional attachment to your parents, a desire to be fashionable, hatred of others.

But once I entered Aum I found it was no different from ordinary society. Like someone would say, "So-and-so has a lot of hate inside him," well—that's no different from the backstabbing that

337

goes on outside, is it? Only the vocabulary has changed. "Nothing here's any different," I thought.

Anyway, I left my job. I forced my company to accept my resignation. I made up some excuse—I wanted to study abroad or something. They tried hard to talk me out of it, but I thought, "Please don't stop me," and it wasn't easy. I couldn't tell them the truth, but I was determined to leave.

My mother never watches TV talk shows and had no idea about Aum. When I told her that becoming a renunciate meant we couldn't see each other again, she cried a little. She had no idea. Though she'd thought it strange how my health and appetite had improved. "I suppose it's time for me to cut the apron strings," she said.

MURAKAMI: *It sounds like she still didn't really understand* [laughs]. *So how was life as a renunciate?*

Some people wanted to see their parents or go home, but that didn't bother me. I didn't think, "This is great!" or anything, just that life in Aum wasn't so bad.

I went to Naminomura at Aso and worked in the Home Economics Division. I cooked, did laundry. That was the first time I met Mr. Asahara. All of a sudden he said, "Come on over." "Huh?" I thought, and went, and we talked, just the two of us, for about twenty minutes inside a prefab building there.

The feeling I got was amazing. He'd say something about me and he'd be right on target. I don't know, it was just . . . What did he say? Like, "In the secular world you were doing this," or "In the secular world you played around too much and used up your merit." Later he said, "You've been out with many men." That kind of thing. People told me it was special to be able to talk directly with him that way, but I just thought, "Really?"

MURAKAMI: *Of course, if he looked into your background beforehand he could know quite a bit about you. What you did in the world outside, and so on.*

I know that, but he was the Final Liberated One, and in that special atmosphere, with him very deliberately saying these things, I just had to think, "Wow. That's something!" It really was. At first I was a bit scared, though. "You could never fool this man,"

I thought. Life at Aso was hard. It was really cold, and the people around me seemed like oddballs, they were so self-centered. They had no common sense, and thought only of themselves. There were some people originally from the same branch as me who were relatively normal, and those were the ones I hung out with. Once I even told Mr. Asahara how I felt. "Don't you think a lot of the people here are weird?" I asked. "That's not true," he replied.

In contrast, the people at the upper levels, the leaders, weren't strange at all. They were great. I was really able to talk freely, in private, with Masters I was friends with. People might not like me to say this, but Eriko Iida, Tomomitsu Niimi, and Hideo Murai were, for me, good people. The people below were weird, though, by and large. We just didn't hit it off.

I left Aso for Tokyo, and was doing clerical work at the Aum headquarters there when Mr. Asahara started phoning me almost every day. "How are you getting along?" he'd ask, and he'd give me advice on training to do in between work. That sort of thing. Nothing of any consequence. But it did make me happy to have him say those things. It wasn't like he'd call just anybody. People told me it was because of merit I'd accrued in the past world, but sometimes the phone calls would totally stop and I'd think: "Why isn't he calling?" That hurt. It seems strange to me now, but that's how I felt at the time.

Once Mr. Asahara tried to force me to have sex with him. This was at Fuji when I was in the Dubbing Division. That's where we'd use a machine to measure off so many meters of recording tape and make copies of sermons. Office work at the Tokyo headquarters was so superbusy I was lucky to snatch three hours' sleep at night, and I wanted a more laid-back job, so I asked Mr. Asahara to let me change. I wanted a relaxed life—train half the day and then spend the rest of the time making copies of tapes.

I was able to get by without sleeping with him. I'm glad it turned out like that. Mr. Asahara had asked me to his room. Before then a couple of times he'd said some suggestive things to me. Like he'd call me and ask, "When was your last period?" "What the—?" I thought, then wondered, "Gosh—when was it, anyway?" "You'll be undergoing a special initiation soon," he said. I asked one of the veteran Masters about this. "Well, actually . . ." he said, and told me it meant having sex with Mr. Asahara.

Mr. Asahara used to go after me, but I'd get really uptight. Like this. (*Hunches shoulders, stiffens her body.*) He can't see well, but he's very intuitive. So he must have known I was pretty jumpy about it. If he touched me I'd get like this. He finally gave up. "Whew—what a relief!" I thought. For most followers, though, having a sexual relationship with him was something to be happy about, grateful even.

MURAKAMI: *But you weren't?*

No. I hated the idea. Don't get me wrong—I respected him as a guru. Depending on the circumstances he could change the way he talked 180 degrees—a lot of people were attracted by that. And he was very sensitive to language. But his role as a guru and the question of sex were two different issues, and I hated the idea. I could believe that those types of initiations took place, but the idea that Mr. Asahara was involved gave me the creeps. I don't know how to put it exactly . . . It wasn't the image I had of him.

MURAKAMI: *Higher-ups in Aum must have known about Asahara's sexual relationships with female* samana, *right?*

One veteran Master told me that Ms. Iida and Ms. [Hisako] Ishii had both slept with him, and that she had as well. I didn't think about whether that was good or bad, I was just impressed by how profound Tantra was.

MURAKAMI: *Was there any kind of reaction because you refused to have a physical relationship with Asahara?*

I don't know. I lost my memory after that. I underwent electroshock. I still have the scars from the electricity right here. (*Raises her hair to show her neck, where a line of white scars remains.*) I remember things up to the time I entered the Dubbing Division, but after that it's a blank. I have no idea at what point, and for what reason my memory was erased. I asked people around me but no one would tell me. All they'd say was, "It seems you and a certain somebody were getting to a dangerous point." I couldn't recall anything like that, so I'd press them to tell me more. "It's been erased so we can't talk about it," they'd reply.

MURAKAMI: *But there wasn't anything in particular between you and the person they mentioned?*

I don't remember a thing. There was someone I liked very much who had been warned by Mr. Asahara, but the man people were mentioning was someone completely different, so I was confused. "Why *him*?" I thought.

Mr. Asahara was deadly serious about keeping up on all the gossip about relations between the sexes, and if couples were getting too close he'd try to break it up. He called me, too, saying, "Ms. Iwakura, haven't you been breaking commandments with Mr. So-and-so?" He sounded confident he knew what was going on, but I had absolutely nothing to do with that person. "What!" I replied. "I haven't done anything." And he'd go, "Oh, really? I understand," and hang up. It was pretty weird.

Anyway, my memory was erased, and when I came to myself it was already the beginning of the year of the gas attack [1995]. I'd gone into the Dubbing Division in 1993 and the two years after that are an absolute blank. Except I suddenly got a flashback of me working in an Aum-run supermarket in Kyoto. All of a sudden this scene came back to me. It's summer, I'm wearing a T-shirt, and I'm sticking price tags on packets of ramen. Detergent boxes are lined up on a shelf. It was frightening. Where I was and what I was doing during that time, I have no idea.

Suddenly I woke up and I was in a sealed room in Kamikuishiki. Sealed rooms were originally places for Masters to use for training, but in my case it was more like a prison. The room was less than three feet by six feet, without even a peephole in the door. Good thing it was winter because in summer it would have been unbearable. The room was locked from the outside, and I was only allowed out to use the toilet or take a shower.

A person who'd become a renunciate after me was in charge of me and I asked her, "What's going on here? I don't understand what's happening," but she couldn't tell me a thing. I saw a Master I knew and asked, "Why am I in here?" "It's the karma of ignorance," came the reply. "Animalistic karma has surfaced." But I thought that was an absolute lie. That couldn't be the reason they were treating me this way.

My suitcase was on the stairs and when I was getting some things I needed from it Mr. Murai happened to pass by. "You hanging in there?" he asked me, and I said: "I have no idea what's going on." He told me his room number and said, "I'll have them leave your door unlocked tonight. Come over and we'll talk." But the person in charge of me said: "We can't allow meetings."

I decided I'd run off while in the rest room and somehow find Mr. Murai, but the guard caught me, we struggled, and my T-shirt got ripped. It was terrible. If they take me back I'm finished, I thought, and I screamed at the top of my lungs. Everybody rushed out, including Mr. Murai, who told me to come to his room. And that's what I did.

In the past Mr. Murai was a very nice person, but now he was changed. He was very cold. All he said to me was, "Stop acting like this . . . pull yourself together."

This was around the time the police raids were about to begin, and they couldn't very well keep people in locked cells. I was moved to Satyam No. 6, then sent to the Fuji office. Mr. Asahara was on the verge of being arrested, so there wasn't any real office work to do and I had it easy.

MURAKAMI: *The gas attack occurred around then, with all the subsequent uproar. Did you believe that Aum had done something wrong?*

No, I didn't. I just thought the police had cooked up the whole thing as an excuse to confiscate more data about followers. I'd had some awful experiences, but I hadn't lost faith in Aum. Of course I wondered what was going on, why Mr. Murai had become like a totally different person. I knew something was strange.

I left Kamikuishiki because all the enlightened Masters had been arrested, and the remaining Masters just started to give orders on a whim. When I saw this going on I thought, "That's it. I've had enough." With Mr. Asahara out of the picture, it was the end of the road. There wasn't any problem about me leaving. I decided it was time, and left.

MURAKAMI: *Were you afraid at all of returning to the outside world? Afraid that you might not be able to make it?*

No, I never thought that. I knew I could make it. I went back to my mother's house and stayed there for about a month. She was really concerned about me. "It was on TV every day," she said, "and I was worried sick." I saw the reports about the gas attack on TV and at first I just told everybody, "Don't believe what you hear," but after a while everybody who had left was giving the same testimony, and I began to think: "You know, it looks like Aum did do it."

About a month after this, I decided I had to get a job. I knew it was hard for my mother. I felt sorry for her. She gave me 100,000 yen to tide me over, and I left home, and got a job as a maid in a hot-springs hotel. I was wondering how I could live on my own with all the heavy down payments on apartments you need in Japan, and came up with the idea of a hot-springs resort. I could work there and live free of charge.

At the job interview, of course, I kept my Aum background to myself and they hired me, but before long an officer from Public Security showed up and it all came out. The head of house-keeping told me not to worry about it—she wouldn't let on, she promised—and I should just keep on working, but I felt awful. I worked there for seven months. The pay wasn't good—about 200,000 yen a month. But tips helped out a lot. I slaved away every day hoping to get more tips. Once I got tipped three times in one day by the same guest. Often I got tipped when the guest first came and when they left. I saved money, got a driver's license, and bought a car.

MURAKAMI: *It sounds like you're a very optimistic person, someone who takes action.*

I didn't have any choice. I did it because I had to. Looking back on it, I think I did a good job as a maid.

Now I'm working at a beauty salon. The police came here once, too. It made me so angry. I mean, my memory has been erased and I felt *I* was a victim. But after a while I started to think that I'm not a victim, but more on the culprits' side. So I stopped being so cross with the police and began to tell them all I knew.

I'm quite healthy now, only my memory just won't come back. I don't have any contact with Aum people anymore. I don't have any nostalgia for the time I was in Aum.

MURAKAMI: *You were pretty friendly with some of the enlightened Masters. Do you think it's possible they were involved in the gas attack?*

I think if they were ordered to do it they probably would. Mr. Niimi in particular would definitely have done it. Ken'ichi Hirose I talked to occasionally, he's a very simple person. How can I put it? I feel sympathy for them. It wasn't the kind of atmosphere where you could disobey an order. It was more the feeling of "I'll be happy to do it!"

MURAKAMI: *At the trial many of the defendants testified that they wanted to disobey orders but were afraid they'd be murdered if they did, so they went along unwillingly. But actually it wasn't like that?*

Hmm—I wonder . . . Under the circumstances I think if they were chosen they would have happily gone ahead and done it.

MURAKAMI: *You're back in the secular world, working. In the past you had doubts about your life, thinking you had nothing you excelled at. Now how do you feel?*

I just accept the fact that I don't have any special talent. Before I entered Aum I couldn't talk about my feelings, even to people I was close to. Now, though, I open up a lot more.

My relatives have tried to arrange meetings with young men for me so I could find someone to marry. "It's about time you got married," they tell me, but I think that people who were in Aum, which has committed such brutal crimes, shouldn't get married. Of course I never committed any crimes myself, I was just doing my own thing as best I could.

Sometimes that makes me sad, though. I dine out with friends or have a good time, but many days I don't do anything and just come back here by myself. When I saw the fireworks last summer—with crowds of people enjoying the show—and me all alone—it made me cry. I'm over that now, though.

There were a lot of very appealing people in Aum. Completely different from the people I've known in the outside world. Relationships in society are always so . . . superficial, but in Aum we all lived together in one place, almost like a family.

I love children. My younger sister's children are adorable, but for me to get married, have a family, children—it's difficult, having been a member of Aum. When I think about talking about my Aum background on a date, I don't think I could . . . A big factor has got to be the fact that my own family was so dysfunctional. People raised in happy families probably wouldn't join Aum.

# "No matter how grotesque a figure Asahara appears, I can't just dismiss him"

## Hidetoshi Takahashi (*b.* 1967)

*Mr. Takahashi was born in 1967 in Tachikawa City in the Tokyo area. He studied geology in the College of Science at Shinshu University, and went on to graduate school, majoring in geodetic astronomy. He has always loved observing the heavens through a telescope. The gas attack was a major shock to him and he left Aum. He has appeared on TV to criticize Aum, and has published a book—*Return from Aum*—in which he discusses at length how he came to join the cult and why he left it.*

*While he was a student Mr. Takahashi had a chance to speak to Shoko Asahara when he gave a lecture at Shinshu University. Afterward, Yoshihiro Inoue urged him to join and he did. But grad-school work took most of his time and he grew apart from Aum and eventually left. Still, he found himself unable to concentrate on his studies, so once again he joined Aum, this time as a renunciate. It was just before the Matsumoto incident in May 1994.*

*In Aum he was assigned to the Ministry of Science and Technology under Hideo Murai. He was ordered directly by Asahara to develop computer software for predicting earthquakes. The data from this software was able to predict the Kobe earthquake of 1995 and Asahara praised him for his efforts.*

*He speaks very clearly and logically—a characteristic shared by many followers and former members of Aum—and unless something is logical, he isn't convinced. Certainly if one looks at things this way, our world does appear to be an illogical place plagued by contradictions and confusion, a hard place to live in.*

*Now he works for a surveying company and lives an*

*entirely ordinary life. He vows to spend his whole life trying to answer the question "What was Aum?" So, even now, when time allows, he goes to court to observe the trials.*

• • •

At college I felt a deep alienation between my outer and my inner Self. I was a cheerful, enthusiastic person with lots of friends, but once I was alone in my room, I was engulfed by loneliness and there was nobody I could share that world with.

I've been that way since childhood. I remember always going inside the closet when I was a child. I didn't want to see my parents, and even in my own room I didn't feel like I had my own space. When you're a child it feels like your parents are always interfering. For me the only place to escape to and find peace was the closet. Granted it's a strange habit, but alone there in the darkness I could feel my consciousness grow razor sharp. It's just you alone, face-to-face with yourself in the dark. In a sense, then, I was drawn to something like the Aum retreats since I was little.

In junior high I liked to listen to progressive rock. Pink Floyd's *The Wall*, for example. Definitely not the sort of music I'd recommend unless you want something to bring you down [*laughs*]. I found out about Gurdjieff through King Crimson. Their guitarist Robert Fripp was a follower of Gurdjieff. After he got into that his music changed drastically. I think much of my outlook on life was influenced by that kind of music.

At high school I was into sports, basketball and badminton, but after entering college I felt I had to draw a line between myself and society. I was what we call a "Moratorium Person": someone who doesn't want to grow up. Our generation grew up after Japan had become a wealthy country and we viewed society through this lens of affluence. I just couldn't adjust to the "adult society" I saw outside. It seemed warped to me somehow. Wasn't there some other way to live your life, some other way of viewing the world? During my college days I had a lot of free time, and was preoccupied with these questions.

When you're young you have all kinds of idealistic notions in your head, but coming face-to-face with the realities of your own life makes you see how immature you are. I felt very frustrated.

To free myself, to make a fresh start, I poked my nose into all sorts of things, hoping to find the energy I needed to live. Life is full of suffering, and the contradictions in the real world irked me. To escape these, I imagined my own sort of utopian society, which made it easier for me to be taken in by a religious group that espoused a similar vision.

When the Aum question comes up, people always start talking about relations between parents and children going sour, and family discord, but it can't be reduced to something so simplistic. Certainly one of the attractions of Aum lay in people's frustrations with reality and unrest in the family, but a much more important factor lies in apocalyptic feelings of "the end of the world," feelings all of us have about the future. If you pay attention to the universal feeling of all of us, all Japanese—all humankind, even—then you can't explain Aum's appeal to so many people by saying it's all based on discord in the family.

MURAKAMI: *Hold on a second. You really think all Japanese have a vision of the end of the world?*

It might be hard to generalize and say that all of them do, but I think inside all Japanese there is an apocalyptic viewpoint: an invisible, unconscious sense of fear. When I say that all Japanese have this fear I mean some people have already pulled aside the veil, while others have yet to do so. If this veil were suddenly drawn back everyone would feel a sense of terror about the near future, the direction our world's heading in. Society is the foundation stone for people's lives, and they don't know what's going to happen to it in the future. This feeling grows stronger the more affluent a country becomes. It's like a dark shadow looming larger and larger.

MURAKAMI: *Somehow the words "decline" or "collapse" seem to hit the mark more than "the end."*

Maybe so, but remember that when I was at school Nostradamus's *Prophecies* became famous, and that sense that "The End Is Nigh" wedged itself deep into my consciousness through the mass media. And I wasn't the only one to feel like that. I don't want this to deteriorate into some simplistic theory about "my generation," but I feel very strongly that all Japanese at that time had the idea drilled into them of 1999 being the end of the world. Aum renunciates have already accepted, inside themselves, the end of the world, because when they become a renunciate, they discard themselves totally, thereby abandoning the world. In other words, Aum is a collection of people who have accepted the end. People who continue to hold out hope for the near future still have an attachment to the world. If you have attachments, you won't discard your Self, but for renunciates it's as if they've leaped right off a cliff. And taking a giant leap like that feels good. They lose something—but gain something in return.

Therefore the idea of "the End" is one of the axes around which Aum Shinrikyo revolved. "Armageddon's coming, so become a renunciate," they urged, "donate all your money to Aum"—and of course that became their source of income.

MURAKAMI: *But there are lots of other religious groups that have used an apocalyptic vision as their selling point. Jehovah's Witnesses, for instance, the Branch Davidians at Waco. What makes Aum different?*

Robert Jay Lifton has said that there are many cults that have an apocalyptic creed, but Aum is the only one that marched straight toward it as part of their program.* That makes sense to me.

Even now there's an element about Aum, its driving force and direction, that I can't fully understand. It had such tremendous energy, and pulled in so many people—including me, of course. But how did it do this?

When I was at college many new religions tried to convert me, but in terms of grappling with the direction the world had taken, seriously formulating a religious worldview, searching earnestly for a lifestyle that fit this view, and then rigorously putting it into practice, Aum stood out head and shoulders above the rest. Aum was the most amazing group of all. I really admired them for the way they practiced what they preached. Compared to them, other religions were resigned, cozy, comfortable, passive. Aum training was very, very tough. Their religious view—that you must transform your own

---

*Robert Jay Lifton is the author of *Destroying the World to Save It: Aum Shinrikyo, Apocalyptic Violence, and the New Global Terrorism* (Metropolitan Books, 1999). [Tr.]

body before you can transform the world—had a hard-hitting realism. If there's any chance for salvation, I thought, it has to begin like this.

To give you an example, with the shortage of food in the world, if only everyone, bit by bit, reduced their consumption the way the Aum diet does, then this food problem would be solved. Not by increasing the supply, but by changing the body, because Aum people eat only a tiny amount of food. If mankind is going to live in harmony with the earth, we've reached the age when we have to start thinking in this way.

MURAKAMI: *That reminds me of Kurt Vonnegut's novel* Slapstick, *in which the Chinese shrink themselves to half their usual size in order to solve the world's food shortage.*

That's kind of funny. Actually I joined Aum twice. The second time I could already sense the violence that overshadowed Aum. The very first day back I thought: "Uh-oh. I've made a big mistake." Aum wore a cheerful mask at the branch offices, since the people there were all still living ordinary lives. But go to Kamikuishiki where it was just renunciates, people who have discarded everything, and you could already feel this urgent sense of desperation.

When I joined I was put to work straightaway making Cosmo cleaners. Aum was already claiming that it was being attacked from the outside with sarin gas, and Cosmo cleaners were designed to reduce the toxicity. Just prior to my taking vows the Leader gave a sermon. "I've been hit with poison gas," he told us, coughing and coughing. He was as limp as a rag doll, and his face was all dark. It seemed tremendously real. "I can only last another month," he said, "and at this rate Aum will be destroyed. Before this happens, I want those who believe in me to gather around me. All of you will serve as my shield." It was a powerful sermon. It forced lay followers to question their faith: here is the Leader in such dire straits and you're just sitting around? How can you call this faith? All at once about three hundred people took vows, and I was one of them, caught up in this wave. Things started to look strange to me when I was forced to undergo what they called "Christ Initiation." All the followers were made to take drugs. Any way you look at it, the whole thing was carelessly done. Using drugs in the name of religion, in order to enter some elevated state, is suspect in itself, but even supposing you accept it as a legitimate means, at the very least you've got to do it in an organized fashion. What they gave us was something close to LSD, I suspect, and for almost everyone it was their first such experience. Some people went crazy and were just left to their own devices. That really troubled me. Even if the Leader had planned this as a method of elevating our spiritual state, the way it was handled left a lot to be desired.

I felt a great deal of resistance to this whole "Christ Initiation," and after I went through it I struggled with whether or not I should leave Aum. It was such a shock it drove me to tears. "What the hell do they think they're doing?" I wondered. It wasn't just me—even a few of the leadership wavered over this initiation, some of the enlightened practitioners who hung on Asahara's every word. It felt like Aum was starting to fall apart.

I think I joined Aum as a kind of adventure. You have to be a bit forgiving of a system organized to open up an entirely unknown world for you—when in Rome, and all that—so I did accept that system. On the one hand I wanted to adjust to the Aum lifestyle and plunge ahead, while a part of me took a step back and watched it all with a sober eye.

So anyway, after this "Christ Initiation" I had too many doubts about Aum and I couldn't do the work I was assigned. I couldn't easily swallow the doctrine of Vajrayana. There weren't any other followers I could express my doubts to, and the Leader was too high up for me to talk to him directly. Even if I did say to someone I thought Aum was into some questionable things, I'd just get a stereotypical response: "Mr. Takahashi, all we can do is follow Aum." I decided I had to talk to one of the leaders if I wanted to get anywhere.

While all this was going on Mr. Niimi, Eriko Iida, and Naropa [*Fumihiko Nagura*] asked me to see them, and as another kind of initiation they tied me up and yelled all kinds of things at me: "Why can't you follow the life we lead in Aum?" "You're neglecting your training, aren't you?" "You're not devoted to the Guru!"

Thinking this was a good opportunity, I decided to bring up some of the doubts I'd been having. "Hold on just a second here," I said. "I have a lot of problems with what's going on in our church, and that's why I can't put everything I've got into our activities." I explained what I'd been feeling and Iida said: "We all feel the same way, but the only path for us is to follow the Guru."

I took it a step further: "You don't know all that much about the Guru, so how is it you can follow him? I believe in the Guru, too, but without really knowing who he is, I can't just follow him blindly." No matter how much I pressed them, the answer was always the same: "All we can do is believe him, and follow him."

I can't tell you how disappointed I was. Someone like her [*Eriko Iida*]—a Mahamudra enlightened practitioner whom everyone respected—and that's all she could say? "And you call yourself an enlightened practitioner?" I asked her. If this was all I was going to hear, then questions were a waste of time. I decided to ask my superior at the Ministry of Science and Technology, Hideo Murai, but he didn't respond at all. Total silence. My last resort would have been to ask the Leader himself. I decided to give it up and quietly devote myself to my training.

Yoshihiro Inoue was the only person I felt spiritually close to in Aum, and I wanted to question him about all this, but he was off on some secret work and I couldn't contact him. The upshot was I spent several months in turmoil.

A year after I joined Aum, Murai ordered me to collect seismology data, but with all the uncertainty about the direction Aum was taking and the general confusion, I knew I wouldn't be able to concentrate on work. I had no idea where Aum was going, so I just asked Murai point-blank: "There seems to be a hidden side to Aum. What's your take on it?" At the time I was involved in some astrology work which put me closer to the Leader and I was able to see the daily comings and goings of the higher-ups. It was like—how should I put it?—as if their activities were all hidden behind a veil or something. The person who held the key to this hidden region was Mr. Murai, so I came right out and asked him. I couldn't say it face-to-face, so I asked him over the phone. He was silent for a while, then he said: "I'm disappointed in you." At that instant I knew that my life in Aum was over.

I don't consider Aum's crimes simply reckless behavior. Of course part of it was reckless, but there was a religious viewpoint pervading those actions. That's what I want most to learn about.

Probably only Asahara and Murai can explain it fully. The other followers were mere pawns, but not these two—they gave the orders, and decided things with a clear vision of their goals. The opponent I was really struggling against, standing up alone to, was the very motives of those two people.

Most of the people arrested in the gas attack were absolutely devoted followers of the Leader who wouldn't let any doubts they might have about Aum stop them doing exactly as they were told. Compared to them, Toru Toyoda could still think for himself. Whenever I voiced doubts about Aum, he'd actually give it some thought. Then he'd say, "Okay, but Hidetoshi, the world is already in Armageddon, so it's a little too late for that."

I knew Toyoda quite well, as we entered Aum around the same time; after he took vows he was promoted to the leadership overnight. He rose up that fast. That's how Aum used him. "I really don't understand all that's going on in Aum myself," he told me, "but since I'm in the leadership now, I'd better behave like a leader." When I heard this I thought: "Wow, he has it tough, too. Even worse than I do." This was still before the gas attack. I was his driver for a while.

MURAKAMI: *If Murai had told you to release the sarin, would you have disobeyed?*

I think so, but there's a trick to doing it. The people who carried out the crime were put in a position where they were caught off guard by the orders and couldn't escape. They'd gather in Murai's room and suddenly the leaders would broach the topic, telling them: "This is an order from the top." *An order from the top*—that was like a mantra in Aum. The people who carried out the crime were chosen from among the strongest believers. "You've been specially chosen," they were told. The leaders appealed to their sense of duty. Faith in Aum meant total devotion.

That's why I wasn't chosen to commit the crimes. I was still at the bottom of the heap and hadn't yet reached enlightenment. In other words Aum didn't trust me enough.

MURAKAMI: *There's one thing I don't understand. When I did my interviews with victims of the gas attack, several of them told me that, based on their experience working for companies, if they had been in*

*Aum and been ordered to release the sarin they might well have done it. But you were actually in Aum, yet say you'd have run away from it. Why is that?*

Saying I'd run away might be less than honest. If I really search my heart I can say that if Murai had told me to do it, most likely I would have run away. However, if Yoshihiro Inoue had said to me, "Hidetoshi, this is part of salvation," and passed me the bag with the sarin in it, I would have been very perplexed. If he'd told me to come with him, I might have done so. In other words, it comes down to a question of ties between individuals.

Murai was my boss, but he was cold and too far above me. If he'd told me to do it I would have asked him why, and if he'd insisted and said, "It's a dirty job but it's for the sake of Aum and I really want you to do it," I like to think that I would have hidden my true feelings, said okay, and then, at the last minute, found a way to get out of it. Like [*Ken'ichi*] Hirose, who wavered and got off the train, I think I would have struggled over what I should do, but in the end would have found a way out.

But something about Inoue captivated me. He felt a strong sense of religious duty. If I'd seen him agonizing over the situation, I think I would have done anything to help out. He was a great influence on me. So if he'd pushed me, saying this was a mission only we could carry out, I might very well have gone along. I would have been operating on a different plane. What I mean is, in the final analysis, logic doesn't play a strong role in people's motivations. I doubt if the ones who did it were even capable of thinking logically when they were given the order to release the sarin. They didn't have the presence of mind, got caught up in events, panicked, and did what they were told. No one who had the strength to think logically about it would have carried it out. In extreme cases of guru-ism individuals' value systems are completely wiped out. In situations like that people just don't have the mental stamina to connect their actions with the deaths of many people.

No matter how much you resist and try to put a stop to things, the fact is that in a group like Aum your sense of Self steadily deteriorates. Things are forced on you from above and you're continually attacked for not accepting the status quo, not being devoted enough, and inevitably your spirit is broken. I was somehow able to hold out, but a lot of people who entered at the same time ended up broken.

MURAKAMI: *All right, but what if Shoko Asahara himself ordered you—"Takahashi, I want you to do it"—what would you have done?*

I think I would have stood up to him. If he'd been able to give me a reasonable explanation, I would have listened. But if he couldn't, I would have kept asking questions until I was convinced. That alone would have excluded me from the job. I'd spoken my mind in front of him before, and he told me I'm a very straight-forward type of person. I don't think either Shoko Asahara or Hideo Murai would have been able to move me because they never opened up to me.

MURAKAMI: *Hold on. A moment ago you used the expression "in extreme cases of guru-ism," so this implies that you yourself were out-side this system, right? If the essence of faith in Aum Shinrikyo is guru-ism, isn't that a logical contradiction?*

As I mentioned before, when we went through the "Christ Initi-ation" I started to have serious doubts about Aum's methods. I was completely disillusioned at the gulf between believers and the Leader.

MURAKAMI: *Then what kept you in Aum? There was Shoko Asa-hara, doctrine, and your fellow believers. Which of the three was it?*

I had almost nothing left. I placed all my faith in Inoue. I was lonely in Aum, isolated. They made me do research on astrology in the Ministry of Science and Technology, something I wasn't inter-ested in at all. There was no way I wanted to see scientific data about the movements of the stars used for some dubious enterprise like fortune-telling. One constant theme in Aum was the desire for supernatural power, but I can't understand the mentality of people who are into that. To me, it's a complete waste of time.

To get back to your question, why did I stay? I'd already aban-doned everything else. When I entered Aum I burned every photo album I owned. I burned my diaries. I broke up with my girlfriend. I threw everything away.

MURAKAMI: *But you were barely 20 years old. You could have started again. Don't take offense, but at that age there wasn't all that much to abandon, was there?*

Well, I'm sure it wouldn't seem like much . . . [*laughs*] But you know, I think I'm a pretty stubborn person, a trait all Aum followers share. This stubborn insistence on things that don't really matter to anyone else as we press on with our mission. Also, focusing like that you get a sense of fulfillment. And Aum was able to take full advantage of this. That's why they made you train so hard. The harder the training, the greater the sense of fulfillment.

When I joined Aum and took vows, I was drunk on the sense of having discarded the world, though I question whether it was actually my own will that led me to take vows. Maybe I just wanted to believe that. The gas attack brought me to my senses and I left Aum. Things I'd thought were mystical became illusions that vanished without a trace. It's like you're sleeping soundly and someone yells "Fire!" and suddenly you find yourself out on the street. That was the way it felt. I'll be grappling with these Aum incidents for the rest of my life. I don't want them to fade into the background.

MURAKAMI: *I'd like to ask you once more about the idea of the end of the world. Is the Apocalypse that Aum talks about the same as that of Judaism and Christianity? The idea of the millennium is a Western concept, after all, and Nostradamus has nothing to do with Buddhism.*

No matter what special spin Aum might put on its idea of Armageddon, I don't think it can compete with the Christian idea of the Apocalypse. It's absorbed into the Christian idea. That's why you can't really explain these Aum-related incidents by looking only at the core of what makes up Aum—namely, Buddhism and Tibetan esoteric religion.

Earlier I said that I don't think that an apocalyptic vision is confined to myself as an individual; what I meant was that, whether you're Christian or not, we all inevitably bear the same apocalyptic fate.

MURAKAMI: *To tell the truth, I don't really understand what you've been calling an apocalyptic vision. But I have the feeling that, if that vision is to have any kind of meaning at all, it has to lie in how you internally deconstruct it.*

You're absolutely right. Apocalypse is not some set idea, but more of a process. After an apocalyptic vision there's always a purging or purifying process that takes place. In this sense I think the gas attack was a kind of catharsis, a psychological release of everything that had built up in Japan—the malice, the distorted consciousness we have. Not that the Aum incident got rid of everything. There's still this suppressed, viruslike apocalyptic vision that's invading society and hasn't been erased or digested.

Even if you could get rid of it at an individual level, the virus would remain on a social level.

MURAKAMI: *You talk about society as a whole, but in the so-called secular world, ordinary people—by which I mean people who maintain a relative balance in their lives—deconstruct that kind of viruslike apocalyptic vision, as you put it, in their own way, and naturally substitute something else for it. Don't you think so?*

Yes, it does come down to a process of deconstruction. Something like that has absolutely got to take place. Shoko Asahara couldn't deconstruct it, and lost out to apocalyptic ideas. And that's why he had to create a crisis on his own. The apocalyptic vision of Shoko Asahara—as a religious figure—was defeated by an even greater vision.

I've been trying hard to come to terms with these Aum-related incidents. I go to the trial as often as I can. But when I see and hear Asahara at the trial I feel as though he's making an idiot out of me. I get nauseated, and actually vomited once. It's a sad and dreary feeling. Sometimes I think it's not worth watching, but I still can't take my eyes off him. No matter how grotesque a figure Asahara appears, I can't just dismiss him. We should never forget that, if even for a short time, this person named Shoko Asahara functioned in the world and brought about these tragic events. Unless I overcome the "Aum Shinrikyo Incident" inside me, I'll never be able to move on.

# *Afterword* *

•  •  •

As I worked on this book I attended several of the trials of the defendants in the Tokyo gas attack. I wanted to see and hear these people with my own eyes and ears, in order to come to some understanding of who they were. I also wanted to know what they were thinking now. What I found there was a dismal, gloomy, hopeless scene. The court was like a room with no exit. There must have been a way out in the beginning, but now it had become a nightmarish chamber from which there was no escape.

Most of the defendants have lost all faith in Shoko Asahara as their guru.† The leader they revered turned out to be nothing more than a false prophet, and they understand now how they were manipulated by his insane desires. The fact that following his orders led to them committing terrible crimes against humanity has made them do some real soul-searching, and they deeply regret their actions. Most of them refer now to their former leader simply as Asahara, dropping any honorific title. There's even a hint of insult mixed in at times. I can't believe that these people sought to become involved in such a horrific, senseless act at the beginning. On the

*This essay is based on a review of Ikuo Hayashi's book *Aum and I*, published in the October 1998 issue of the magazine *Hon no hanashi*.

†At the time of going to press Shoko Asahara was still on trial. In January 2000, Aum issued a statement deposing him as leader, changing its name to Aleph, and vowing to introduce reforms, including a promise to obey the law. [Tr.]

other hand, at a certain point in their lives they abandoned the world and sought a spiritual utopia in Aum Shinrikyo, something they do not repent or regret.

This is apparent when they are asked in court to clarify details of Aum doctrine and they quite often say something like, "Well, this may be difficult for ordinary people to comprehend, but . . ." They still believe they are at a higher spiritual level than "ordinary people" and have a sense of being specially chosen. Though they don't quite say as much, what I detect is a message along the lines of: "We are extremely sorry for the crimes we committed. We made a mistake. But the one who should be blamed is Shoko Asahara, who fooled us into following these orders. If only he hadn't gone over the edge we would have been able to pursue our religious goals peacefully and correctly, without bothering anyone." In other words: "The results were bad, and we regret them. However, the basic aims of Aum Shinrikyo are not flawed, and we don't feel there's any need to reject them outright."

This unwavering conviction in the "correctness of aims" is something I found not only in the Aum followers I interviewed, but even among those who have left and are now openly critical of the Aum organization. To all of them I posed the same question, that is, whether they regretted having joined Aum. Almost everyone answered: "No, I have no regrets. I don't think those years were wasted." Why is that? The answer is simple—because in Aum they found a purity of purpose they could not find in ordinary society. Even if in the end it became something monstrous, the radiant, warm memory of the peace they originally found remains inside them, and nothing else can easily replace it.

In that sense, then, the Aum path is still open to them. I don't mean that former members are likely to return to the fold. They are aware now that it is a very flawed and dangerous system, and agree that the years they passed in Aum were filled with contradictions and defects. At the same time I got the impression that, to a greater or lesser degree, there is still within them an Aum ideal—a utopian vision, a memory of light, imprinted deep inside them. If one day something that contains a similar light passes before their eyes (it needn't be a religion) what is inside them now will be pulled in that direction. In this sense what is most dangerous for our society at the moment is not Aum Shinrikyo itself, but other "Aum-like" entities.

After the Tokyo gas attack, society's attention was drawn exclusively to Aum Shinrikyo. The question was asked over and over again: "How could such elite, highly educated people believe in such a ridiculous, dangerous new religion?" Certainly it's true that the Aum leadership was composed of elite people with distinguished academic credentials, so it's little wonder that everyone was shocked to discover this. The fact that such upwardly mobile people easily rejected the positions in society that were promised them and ran off to join a new religion is a serious indication, many have said, that there is a fatal defect in the Japanese education system.

However, as I went though the process of interviewing these Aum members and former members, one thing I felt quite strongly was that it wasn't *in spite of* being part of the elite that they went in that direction, but precisely *because* they were part of the elite.

Perhaps the entity called Aum Shinrikyo resembles pre–World War II Manchuria. Japan established the puppet state of Manchuria in 1932, and in the same way, the best and brightest—the cutting-edge technocrats, technicians, and scholars—gave up the lives promised them in Japan and went off to the continent they saw as so full of possibilities. For the most part they were young, extremely talented, and well educated, their heads full of newly minted, ambitious visions. As long as they stayed in the Japanese state, with its coercive structure, they believed it was impossible to find an effective outlet for all their energy. And that's exactly why they sought out this more accommodating, experimental land, even if it meant jumping off the normal track. In that sense alone they had pure motives, and were idealistic, filled with a sense of purpose. As far as they were concerned, they were proceeding down the "proper path."

The problem is that something very vital was lacking. Now we can look back and see what was missing was a properly three-dimensional historical sense, or, on a more concrete level, an identity between language and actions. Such glib, prettified slogans as "The Five Races Living in Harmony" and "The Whole World Under One Roof" began to take on an independent existence, while in the background the inevitable moral vacuum that resulted was buried in the bloody realities of the time. In the end these ambitious technocrats were swallowed up in the terrible whirlwind of history.

Since the whole Aum Shinrikyo affair took place so recently, it is still too early to pin down exactly what was lacking in this case. However, in a broad sense what I've said about this "Manchuria-like" situation can be applied to Aum: the lack of a broad world vision, and the alienation between language and actions that results from this.

I'm sure each member of the Science and Technology elite had his own personal reasons for renouncing the world and joining Aum. What they all had in common, though, was a desire to put the technical skill and knowledge they'd acquired in the service of a more meaningful goal. They couldn't help having grave doubts about the inhumane, utilitarian gristmill of capitalism and the social system in which their own essence and efforts—even their own reasons for being—would be fruitlessly ground down.

Ikuo Hayashi, who released sarin gas in the Chiyoda Line of the subway, leading to the deaths of two subway workers, is clearly one of these types of people. He had a reputation for being an outstanding surgeon, devoted to his patients. Most likely it was precisely because he was such a good doctor that he began to mistrust the present-day medical system, shot through as it is with contradictions and defects. As a result, he was drawn to the active spiritual world that Aum provided with its vision of an intense, perfect utopia.

In his own book, *Aum and I*, he writes the following about the image he had at the time of Aum:

In his sermon Asahara spoke about the Shambhala Plan, which involved the construction of a Lotus Village. There would be an Astral Hospital there, and a Shinri School that would provide a thoroughgoing education [. . .] Medical care would be so-called Astral Medicine, which would be based on Asahara's visions of another [*astral*] dimension and memories of past lives he would see during meditation. Astral medicine would examine the patients' karma and energy level, and take into consideration death and transmigration [. . .] I'd had a dream of a green, natural spot with buildings dotting the landscape, where truly caring medical care and education were carried out. My vision and the Lotus Village were one and the same.

Hayashi thus had a dream of devoting himself to a utopia, undergoing strenuous training unsullied by the secular world, putting into practice a kind of medical care he could give all his heart to, and making as many patients happy as he possibly could. These motives are indeed pure, and the vision outlined here has its own beauty and splendor. Take a step back, however, and it's clear how completely these innocent remarks are cut off from reality. In our eyes this is like some strange landscape painting that lacks all sense of perspective. Still, if any one of us had been a friend of Dr. Hayashi's at the time he was considering becoming an Aum renunciate and we tried to give him some convincing proof that his ideas were alienated from reality, it would have been very difficult.

But what we should say to Dr. Hayashi is really quite simple, and it goes like this: "Reality is created out of confusion and contradiction, and if you exclude those elements, you're no longer talking about reality. You might think that—by following language and a logic that appears consistent—you're able to exclude that aspect of reality, but it will always be lying in wait for you, ready to take its revenge."

I doubt Dr. Hayashi would be convinced by this line of argument. Using technical terminology and a kind of static logic he would strenuously counterargue, outlining how proper and beautiful the path is down which he plans to travel. So at a certain point we could do nothing but fall silent.

The sad fact is that language and logic cut off from reality have a far greater power than the language and logic of reality—with all that extraneous matter weighing down like a rock on any actions we take. In the end, unable to comprehend each other's words, we'd part, each going our separate ways.

Reading Ikuo Hayashi's notes, we are often forced to stop and think, and ask ourselves such simple questions as: "Why did he have to end up where he did?" At the same time, we're seized by a sense of impotence, knowing that there was nothing we could have done to stop him. You feel strangely sad. What makes you feel emptiest of all is the knowledge that it is those who should be most critical of our "utilitarian society" who use the "utility of logic" as a weapon and end up slaughtering masses of people.

But at the same time who would ever think, "I'm an unimportant little person, and if I end up just a cog in society's system, gradually worn down until I die, hey—that's okay"? More or less all of us want answers to the reasons why we're living on this earth, and why we die and disappear. We shouldn't criticize a sincere attempt to find answers. Still, this is precisely the point where a kind of fatal mistake can be made. The layers of reality begin to be distorted. The place that was promised, you suddenly realize, has changed into something different from what you're looking for. As Mark Strand puts it in his poem: "The mountains are not mountains anymore; the sun is not the sun."

In order that a second, and a third Ikuo Hayashi don't crop up, it is critical for our society to stop and consider, in all their ramifications, the questions brought to the surface so tragically by the Tokyo gas attack. Most people have put this incident behind them. "That's over and done with," they say. "It was a major incident, but with the culprits all arrested it's wrapped up and doesn't have anything more to do with us." However, we need to realize that most of the people who join cults are not abnormal; they're not disadvantaged; they're not eccentrics. They are the people who live average lives (and maybe from the outside, more than average lives), who live in my neighborhood. And in yours.

Maybe they think about things a little too seriously. Perhaps there's some pain they're carrying around inside. They're not good at making their feelings known to others and are somewhat troubled. They can't find a suitable means to express themselves, and bounce back and forth between feelings of pride and inadequacy. That might very well be me. It might be you.

# APPENDIX
## Results of Trials of Aum Shinrikyo Members
### (as of August 4, 2000)

*Those tried in connection with the sarin gas attack
on the Tokyo subway:*

- Ringleader     First trial still in session, with
  Chizuo Matsumoto    the prosecution presenting
  (Shoko Asahara)    evidence

- Those who released the sarin gas

  | | |
  |---|---|
  | Ikuo Hayashi | Sentenced to life imprisonment; now serving the term |
  | Masato Yokoyama | Sentenced to death; appealing the sentence |
  | Yasuo Hayashi | Sentenced to death; appealing the sentence |
  | Toru Toyoda | Sentenced to death (July 17, 2000) |
  | Ken'ichi Hirose | Sentenced to death (July 17, 2000) |

- Drivers who transported those who released the sarin

  | | |
  |---|---|
  | Koichi Kitamura | Sentenced to life imprisonment; appealing the sentence |
  | Kiyotaka Tonozaki | Sentenced to life imprisonment; appealing the sentence |
  | Shigeo Sugimoto | Sentenced to life imprisonment (July 17, 2000) |
  | Tomomitsu Niimi | First trial still in session; defense is presenting evidence |
  | Katsuya Takahashi | Fugitive at large; subject of special police investigation |

- Person in charge of communications

Yoshihiro Inoue      Sentenced to life imprisonment;
prosecution is appealing the sentence

## *Other members of the leadership:*

| | |
|---|---|
| *Kazuaki Okazaki* | Sentenced to death; appealing the sentence |
| *Kiyohide Hayakawa* | Sentenced to death (July 28, 2000) |
| *Satoru Hashimoto* | Sentenced to death (July 25, 2000) |
| *Tomoko Matsumoto* | (Asahara's wife) Sentenced to six years in prison; on final appeal |
| *Hisako Ishii* | Sentenced to 3 years, 8 months in prison; now serving the term |
| *Fumihiro Joyu* | Sentenced to 3 years in prison; released on December 29, 1999 |
| *Yoshinobu Aoyama* | Sentenced to 12 years in prison; now appealing |
| *Tomomasa Nakagawa* | First trial still in session |
| *Seiichi Endo* | First trial still in session |
| *Masami Tsuchiya* | First trial still in session |

The year is 1984 and the city is Tokyo. A young woman named Aomame follows a taxi driver's enigmatic suggestion and begins to notice puzzling discrepancies in the world around her. She has entered, she realizes, a parallel existence, which she calls 1Q84 — "Q is for 'question mark.' A world that bears a question." Meanwhile, an aspiring writer named Tengo takes on a suspect ghostwriting project. He becomes so wrapped up with the work and its unusual author that, soon, his previously placid life begins to come unraveled. As Aomame's and Tengo's narratives converge over the course of this single year, we learn of the profound and tangled connections that bind them ever closer. *1Q84* is a tremendous feat of imagination from one of our most revered contemporary writers.

Fiction

## THE WIND-UP BIRD CHRONICLE

This heroically imaginative novel is at once a detective story, an account of a disintegrating marriage, and an excavation of the buried secrets of World War II. In a Tokyo suburb a young man named Toru Okada searches for his wife's missing cat. Soon he finds himself looking for his wife as well in a netherworld that lies beneath the placid surface of Tokyo. As these searches intersect, Okada encounters a bizarre group of allies and antagonists: a psychic prostitute, a malevolent yet mediagenic politician, a cheerfully morbid sixteen-year-old girl, and an aging war veteran who has been permanently changed by the hideous things he witnessed during Japan's forgotten campaign in Manchuria. *The Wind-Up Bird Chronicle* is a tour de force equal in scope to the masterpieces of Mishima and Pynchon.

Fiction

## COLORLESS TSUKURU TAZAKI
## AND HIS YEARS OF PILGRIMAGE

An instant number one *New York Times* bestseller, *Colorless Tsukuru Tazaki and His Years of Pilgrimage* is the remarkable story of a young man haunted by a great loss; of dreams and nightmares that have unintended consequences for the world around us; and of a journey into the past that is necessary to mend the present. Here Haruki Murakami—one of the most revered voices in literature today—gives us a story of love, friendship, and heartbreak for the ages.

Fiction

### ALSO AVAILABLE

*After Dark*
*After the Quake*
*Blind Willow, Sleeping Woman*
*Dance Dance Dance*
*The Elephant Vanishes*
*Hard-Boiled Wonderland and the End of the World*
*Kafka on the Shore*
*Norwegian Wood*
*South of the Border, West of the Sun*
*Sputnik Sweetheart*
*What I Talk About When I Talk About Running*
*A Wild Sheep Chase*
*Wind/Pinball*

## VINTAGE INTERNATIONAL
Available wherever books are sold.
www.vintagebooks.com